The American Revolution

Hugh F. Rankin

The American Revolution

Capricorn Books
New York

CAPRICORN BOOKS EDITION 1965
Copyright © 1964 by Hugh F. Rankin

FOR MARGE AND STEAMER

Contents

Maps

Maps drawn by J. Howell Peebles Jr.

Introduction

BETWEEN 1844 and 1850, the governor of the Chinese Province of Fuh-Kien was a sometime historian by the name of Sen-Ki-Yu. It was during this period that he wrote and published, in his native language, a work on universal geography. Included was a brief account of the United States. In 1850, when the Emperor Hein-Fung ascended the throne of China, Sen-Ki-Yu was dismissed from his post. Because of "his work and sacrifices for the truth of history," the United States legation at Peking used its influence to persuade the Chinese government to reinstate Sen-Ki-Yu as a member of the Foreign Office of the Emperor's government. His delightful account of the American Revolution, as translated by the United States legation at Peking, is excerpted from his brief history of the United States.

It was the English people who first discovered and took North America and drove out the aborigines. The fertile and eligible lands were settled by emigrants moved over there from the three [British] islands, who thus occupied them. These emigrants hastened over with a force like that of a torrent running down the gully. Poor people from France, Holland, Denmark and Sweden also sailed over to join them, and as they all daily opened up new clearings, the country continually grew rich in its cultivated lands. High English officers held it for their sovereign, and as cities and towns sprung up all along the coasts, their revenues were collected for his benefit. Commerce constantly increased in extent and amount, so that thus the inhabitants rapidly became rich and powerful.

During the reign of the Kemburg (A.D. 1736–1796) the English and French were at war for several years, during which the former exacted the duties throughout all their possessions, increasing the taxes more than previously. By the old tariff, for

13

instance, the duty on tea was levied when it was sold; but the English required that another tax should be paid by the buyer.

The people of America would not stand this, and in the year 1776 their gentry and leading men assembled together in order to consult with the [English] governor how to arrange the matter; but he drove them from his presence, dispersed the assembly, and demanded that the tax be collected all the more strictly. The people thereupon rose in their wrath, threw all the tea in the ships into the sea, and then consulted together how they could raise troops against the British.

There was at this time a man named Washington, a native of another colony, born in 1732, who had lost his father at the age of ten, but had been admirably trained by his mother. While a boy he showed a great spirit and aptitude for literary and martial pursuits, and his love for brave and adventurous deeds exceeded those of ordinary men. He had held a military commission under the English, and during the war with France, when the French leagued with the Indians, and made an irruption into the southern provinces, he led on a body of troops and drove them back; but the English general would not report this expeditious operation, so that his worthy deeds were not recorded [for his promotion].

The people of the land now wished to have him to be their leader, but he went home on plea of sickness and shut himself up. When they had actually raised the standard of rebellion, however, they compelled him to become their general.

Though neither arms nor depots, neither arms nor ammunition, stores nor forage, existed at this time, Washington so inspired everybody by his own patriotism, and urged them on by his own energy, that the proper boards and departments were soon arranged, and he was thereby enabled to . . . invest the capital. The British general had entrenched some marines outside the city, when a storm suddenly dispersed his ships. Washington improved the conjuncture by vigorously attacking the city, and succeeded in taking it.

The English then gathered a great army, and renewed the engagement. He lost the battle completely, and his men were so disheartened and terrified that they began to disperse. But his great heart maintained its composure, and he so rallied and reassured his army that they renewed the contest, and victory finally turned in their favor. Thus the bloody strife went on for eight years. Sometimes victorious and sometimes vanquished, Washington's determination and energy never quailed, while the English general began to grow old.

The King of France also sent a general across the sea to strengthen the tottering States. He joined his forces with those of Washington, and gave battle to the British army. The rulers of Spain and Holland likewise hampered their military operations, and advised them to conclude a peace. The English at last could no longer act freely, and ended the strife in the year 1783, by making a treaty with Washington. According to stipulations, the boundary line was so drawn that they had the desolate and cold region of the north, while the fertile and genial southern portions were confirmed to him.

Washington, having thus established the States, gave up his military command for the purpose of returning to his farm, but the people would not permit him thus to retire, and obliged him to become their ruler. He, however, proposed a plan to them as follows: "It is very selfish for him who gets the power in the State to hand it down to his posterity. In filling the post of shepherd of the people, it will be most suitable to select a virtuous man."

When Washington made peace with the British he dismissed all the troops, and directed the attention of the country entirely to agriculture and commerce. He also issued a mandate saying: "If hereafter a President should covetously plot how he can seize the forts and lands of another kingdom, or harass and extort the people's wealth, or raise troops to gratify his personal quarrels, let all the people put him to death." He accordingly retained only twenty national war vessels, and limited the army to 10,000 men. . . .

It appears from the above that Washington was a very remarkable man. . . . In ruling the State he honored and fostered good usages, and did not exalt military merit, a principle totally unlike what is found in other kingdoms. I have seen his portrait. His mien and countenance are grand and impressive in the highest degree. Oh, who is there that does not call him a hero?

Intriguing as was Sen-Ki-Yu's interpretation of the American Revolution, this internecine conflict was more than a one-man rebellion with Washington figuratively slaying the red-coated Philistines with the jawbone of an ass. The Revolution, when thrust into the common concept of warfare, becomes a most interesting contest. Not a struggle in which great bodies of troops were maneuvered as puppets on a string, it became, because of the relatively small number of troops engaged, almost a personal war. Personalities even from amongst the rank and file, seem to rise up to dominate certain actions.

The tyranny of word limitation was the one great consideration in the compilation of these accounts, and in a work of this nature, decisions are so often influenced by personal fancies. How, then, should a project of this kind be organized? To include all the facets of the American Revolution—military, naval, political, economic, philosophical, diplomatic and social—would require a multiple-volume effort. Then, too, there is already one excellent two-volume set of this nature, *The Spirit of 'Seventy-Six* (New York: Bobbs-Merrill, 1958), edited by Henry Steele Commager and Richard B. Morris.

One basic consideration that should be explained has possibly been best stated by W. Stull Holt in *American Scholarship in the Twentieth Century* (Cambridge: Harvard University Press, 1953), when he refers to "the reluctance of the liberally minded American scholar to admit that war can be regarded as a normal activity of civilized man." This, in turn, suggests that military history, particularly in those areas that feel the brunt of war, cannot be divorced from social history. This is especially true during the American Revolution. It has been decided, therefore, to use the military operations as the central theme and allow other facets to play about the periphery. True, this leaves an incomplete picture, but within the space allotted any other approach would leave the whole thin in every area.

Liberties have been taken with the eyewitness accounts included in this volume. The syntax and general expression have been left as they were, but the editorial pen has been applied to paragraphing, punctuation and spelling. Yet, in several instances, it has been felt best to reproduce the account just as the author put it down, the intent being to add a bit of the flavor of the eighteenth century.

To imply that this work is in any way definitive, or even gives an accurate account of any one battle, would indeed be drawing a long bow. Soldiers in battle, especially those of the lower echelon, are usually aware of only those happenings in their immediate vicinity, and even then the emotional mutation induced by the heat of combat often colors the remembrance of things past. But it must be stated in the defense of such unintentional inaccuracies, that these things are what the reporters thought happened.

There will be those who will disagree, perhaps justifiably, with the choice of accounts within the following pages. And quite often the choice has been made more difficult by an overabundance of material. There are, for instance, thirteen excellent journals of Arnold's trek through the wilderness in *March to Quebec* (New York: Doubleday & Company, 1938), edited by Kenneth Roberts, and at least ten would have served equally as well as that of Doctor Isaac Senter.

There are several people who should be mentioned for their aid. Charles Dwoskin waded through masses of x-ed-out lines in a great bundle of yellow paper while reading the first draft and came up with good advice. Mrs. Elizabeth H. Drew of New York City called my attention to a number of items. Then there are my colleagues, Professors William R. Hogan and Charles P. Roland, who listened (not always patiently) to my gripes over many a cup of black chicory coffee. Doctor Joseph E. Schenthal prescribed enough "piddling pills, powders, Bolus Linctus's—cordials" to slay the many vagrant viruses that so often assault this bend in the river. And then there is that jewel I married, the girl with the keen editorial eye and whose fingers fly so rapidly over the keyboard of the typewriter. Every historian should be so blessed.

HUGH F. RANKIN

Tulane University
New Orleans, Louisiana

Rebellion in Massachusetts

BUT America, an immense Territory, favour'd by Nature with all Advantages of Climate, Soil, great navigable Rivers and Lakes, &c. must become a great Country, populous and mighty; and will in a less time than is generally conceiv'd, be able to shake off any Shackles that may be impos'd on her, and perhaps place them on the Imposers. In the mean time every Act of Oppression will sour their Tempers, lessen greatly if not annihilate the Profits of your Commerce with them, and hasten their final Revolt; for the Seeds of Liberty are universally sown there, and nothing can eradicate them. . . .

Such had been the warning set forth by wise old Ben Franklin to Lord Kames in April, 1767. But Britain was in no mood to heed philosophical musings, and "oppressive" Parliamentary legislation against her recalcitrant colonists sent flames of resentment leaping high, only to fall back when British attention slackened.

Both factions found cause for discontent. The Americans grumbled, fumed, held congresses, submitted petitions and contrived retaliatory actions against such British measures as the Proclamation of 1763, the Sugar (or Molasses) and Currency Acts of 1764, the Stamp Act of 1765 and the Townshend Duties of 1767. A street brawl that left four colonists sprawled dead in Boston's dirty spring snow furnished fuel for such an able propagandist as Samuel Adams, who recast the scuffle as the Boston "Massacre."

Passive resistance through economic sanctions was but one of the methods employed by the colonists to indicate their resentment: they mobbed stamp masters, tarred and feathered those so foolish as to champion British measures, and even mustered the effrontery to capture and burn His Majesty's revenue cutter, the Gaspee.

But it was the Tea Act of 1773, designed to lift the East India Company out of its financial morass, that set the witches' brew of

19

rebellion to bubbling in the cauldron that was Massachusetts. This legislation, allowing the company to market its tea for less than the prices paid in the colonies for smuggled Dutch tea, raised a flurry of objections to the monopolistic advantages granted the East India group. On the night of December 16, 1773, there was quite an "Indian caper," termed by Governor Thomas Hutchinson as "the boldest stroke which has yet been struck in America." Stirred by the harangues of Sam Adams, a well-disciplined tribe of "Indians" rushed down to Griffin's Wharf and there canted some 342 chests of East India tea into the bay.

Britain accepted the challenge. Lord North, the King's first minister, and tractable servant of his royal master, reminded Parliament: "The Americans have tarred and feathered your servants, plundered your merchants, burnt your ships, denied all obedience to your laws and authority; yet so clement and so long forbearing has our own conduct been that it is incumbent on us now to take a different course. Whatever may be the consequences, we must do something, if we do not, all is over."

Punitive measures that became known as the Coercive (the Americans termed them "Intolerable") Acts came out of Parliamentary opinion "that the town of Boston ought to be knocked about their ears and destroyed." Among other restrictions in areas New Englanders considered their birthright, the port of Boston was closed, the government of Massachusetts was taken from its citizens and red-coated soldiers tramped the streets of Boston while maintaining an uneasy peace.

General Thomas Gage, faced with governing a sullen, resentful and practically unmanageable population, could only stand by in helpless rage as illegal provincial assemblies usurped his governmental authority and delegates rode off to attend a Continental Congress meeting in Philadelphia. Despite Lord Percy's characterization of the New Englanders as "a set of sly, artful, hypocritical rascalls, cruel & cowards; I must own I cannot but despise them completely," crackling tensions drove Gage onto the periphery of apprehension. To Lord Barrington, Secretary at War, he wrote: "If you think ten Thousand Men sufficient, send twenty, if one million is thought enough, give two; you will save both Blood and Treasure in the End. A large force will terrify, and engage many to join you, a middling one will encourage Resistance, and gain no friends. The crisis is indeed an alarming one, & Britain had never more need of Wisdom, Firmness, and Union than at this juncture. I sincerely wish a happy end to these broils."

The situation worsened as resolutions passed by upstart assemblies not only threw impudent insults into the face of Parliament, but, despite constant professions of loyalty to their King, gave offense to George III. Probing marches into the countryside and the confiscation of colonial powder supplies set the provincials to parading around New England while their politicians hurled angry threats. Something had to give—and soon.

On April 14, word came from London. Lord Dartmouth, Secretary of State for Colonies, urged Gage to do something—even if it was wrong: "It will surely be better that the conflict be brought on, upon such ground, than in a riper state of rebellion." Preparations were made for a march to Concord, the village where, it was said, the provincials were collecting arms. Paul Revere, Boston silversmith who sat well in a saddle, and who acted as post rider for the Massachusetts Provincial Congress, later (1798) wrote an account of his since famous "Midnight ride."

In the fall of 1774 and the winter of 1775, I was one of upwards of thirty, chiefly mechanics, who formed ourselves into a committee for the purpose of watching the movements of the British soldiers, and gaining every intelligence of the movements of the Tories. We held our meetings at the Green-Dragon tavern. We were so careful that our meetings should be kept secret, that every time we met, every person swore upon the Bible, that they would not discover any of our transactions, but to Messrs. [John] Hancock, [Samuel] Adams, Doctors [Joseph] Warren, [Benjamin] Church, and one or two more. . . .

In the winter, towards the spring, we frequently took turns, two and two, to watch the soldiers, by patrolling the streets all night. The Saturday night preceding the 19th of April, about 12 o'clock at night, the boats belonging to the transports were all launched, and carried under the sterns of the men-of-war. . . . We likewise found that the grenadiers and light infantry were all taken off duty.

From these movements, we expected something serious was to be transacted. On Tuesday evening, the 18th, it was observed that a number of soldiers were marching towards the bottom of the Common. About 10 o'clock, Dr. Warren sent in great haste for me, and begged that I would immediately set off for Lexington, where Messrs. Hancock and Adams were, and acquaint them of the movement, and that it was thought they were the objects.

When I got to Dr. Warren's house, I found he had sent an express by land to Lexington—a Mr. William Dawes. The Sunday before, by desire of Dr. Warren, I had been to Lexington, to Messrs. Hancock and Adams, who were at the Rev. Mr. Clark's. I returned at night through Charlestown; there I agreed with a Colonel Conant, and some other gentlemen, that if the British went out by water, we would show two lanthorns in the North Church steeple; and if by land, one, as a signal; for we were apprehensive it would be difficult to cross Charles River, or get over Boston neck. I left Dr. Warren, called upon a friend, and desired him to make the signals.

I then went home, took my boots and surtout, went to the north part of town, where I had kept a boat; two friends rowed me across Charles River, a little to the eastward where the *Somerset* man-of-war lay. It was then young flood, the ship was winding, and the moon was rising. They landed me on the Charlestown side. . . . I got a horse of Deacon Larkin. While the horse was preparing, Richard Devens, Esq., who was one of the Committee of Safety, came to me, and told me that he came down the road from Lexington after sundown that evening; that he met ten British officers, all well mounted and armed, going up the road.

I set off upon a very good horse; it was then about eleven o'clock, and very pleasant. After I had passed Charlestown neck . . . I saw two men on horseback, under a tree. When I got near them, I discovered they were British officers. One tried to get ahead of me, and the other to take me. I turned my horse very quick, and galloped towards Charlestown neck, and then pushed for the Medford road. The one who chased me, endeavouring to cut me off, got into a clay pond. . . . I got clear of him, and went through Medford, over the bridge, and up to Menotomy. In Medford, I awakened the captain of the minute men; and after that, I alarmed almost every house, till I got to Lexington. I found Messrs. Hancock and Adams at the Rev. Mr. Clark's; I told them my errand, and enquired for Mr. Dawes. They said he had not been there. I related the story of the two officers, and supposed that he must have been stopped, as he ought to have been there before me.

After I had been there about half an hour, Mr. Dawes came. We refreshed ourselves, and set off for Concord to secure the stores, &c. there. We were overtaken by a young Dr. Prescott, whom we found to be a high son of liberty. I told them of the ten officers that Mr. Devens met, and that it was probable we might be stopped before

Major inquired of me how far it was to Cambridge, and if there
any other road. After some consultation, the Major rode up to
ergeant and asked if his horse was tired. He answered him, he
-he was a Sergeant of Grenadiers and had a small horse.
n," said he, "take that man's horse." I dismounted, and the
ant mounted my horse, when they all rode towards Lexington
ing-house.

vent across the burying-ground and some pastures and came
e Rev. Mr. Clark's house, where I found Messrs. Hancock and
ns. I told them of my treatment, and they concluded to go from
nouse towards Woburn. I went with them and a Mr. Lowell, who
a clerk to Mr. Hancock.

*t, lethargic Lieutenant Colonel Francis Smith had been appointed
ommand the march to Concord. Young Lieutenant William
erland, of the 38th Regiment, chafed by the inactivity in Boston,
along as a volunteer. He later wrote a report, which he admitted
ained "Much Egotism," for Gage.*

n the evening of the 18th, about 9 o'clock, I learned there was
ge detachment going from this garrison, on which I immediately
ved to go with them. And meeting a few men in the street fully
utred, I followed them and embarked at the Magazine Guard
landed near Cambridge where I joined Major Pitcairn, who I
erstood was to command next to Colonel Smith.

ere we remained for two hours, partly waiting for the rest of
detachment and for provisions. About half an hour after two in
norning of the 19th we marched, Major Pitcairn commanding in
t the light infantry. . . .

little after we were joined by Lieutenant Grant of the Royal
llery who told us the country, he was afraid, was alarmed, of
ch we had little reason to doubt, as we heard several shots, it
g then between three and four in the morning—a very unusual
for firing. We were joined by Major Mitchel, Captain Cochrane,
tain Lumm and several other gentlemen, who told us the whole
ntry was alarmed and they had galloped for their lives, or words
nat purpose; that they had taken Paul Rivierre, but was obliged
t him go after having cut his girth and stirrups. A little after a
w came out of a cross road galloping. Mr. Adair and I called
im to stop, but he galloped off as hard as he could, upon which

we got to Concord. . . . I likewise mentioned, that we
alarm all the inhabitants till we got to Concord; the yo
much approv'd of it and said he would stop with either o
people between that and Concord knew him and wou
more credit to what we said.

We had got nearly half way. Mr. Dawes and the Docto
alarm the people of a house. I was about one hundred
when I saw two men, in nearly the same situation as th
were near Charlestown. I called for the Doctor and Mr
come up; in an instant I was surrounded by four. They
themselves in a straight road that inclined each way.
taken down a pair of bars on the north side of the roa
of them were under a tree in the pasture. The Doctor, bein
he came up and we tried to get past them; but they being
pistols and swords, they forced us into the pasture. T
jumped his horse over a low stone wall and got to Conc

I observed a wood at a small distance and made for t
I got there, out started six officers on horseback and ord
dismount. One of them, who appeared to have the
examined me, where I came from and what my name was?
He asked me if I was an express. I answered in the affir
demanded what time I left Boston. I told him, and added
troops had catched aground in passing the river, and
would be five hundred Americans there in a short time,
alarmed the country all the way up. He immediately rod
those who had stopped us, when all five of them came do
full gallop. One of them, whom I afterwards found to b
Mitchel of the 5th Regiment, clapped his pistol to my he
me by name and told me that he was going to ask me some
and if I did not give him true answers, he would blow my b
He then asked me similar questions to those above. He the
me to mount my horse, after searching me for arms. He the
them to advance and to lead me in front. When we got to
they turned towards Lexington. When we had got about
the Major rode up to the officer that was leading me, and
to give me to the Sergeant. As soon as he took me, t
ordered him, if I attempted to run, or anybody insulted
blow my brains out.

We rode till we got near Lexington meeting-house, when t
fired a volley of guns, which appeared to alarm them ve

Mr. Simms, Surgeon's Mate of the 43rd Regiment, who was on horseback, pursued him and took him a great way in front. A little after I met a very genteel man riding in a carriage they call a sulky, who assured me there were 600 men assembled at Lexington with a view of opposing us. . . . I waited with him until Major Pitcairn came up with the division, to whom he repeated much the same as he did to me. Then going on in front again, I met, coming out of a cross road, another fellow galloping; however, hearing him sometime before, I placed myself so that I got hold of the bridle of his horse and dismounted him. Our guide seemed to think that this was a very material fellow and said something as if he had been a member of the Provincial Congress.

A little while after this I mounted a horse I had, and Mr. Adair went in a chaise. It began now to be daylight, and we met some men with a wagon of wood who told us there were odds of 1,000 men at Lexington and added that they would fight us. Here we waited for some time, but seeing nothing of the division, I rode to the left about half a mile to see if I could fall in with them, but could see nothing of them. However, I saw a vast number of the country militia going over the hill with their arms to Lexington and met one of them whom I obliged to give up his firelock and bayonet, which I believe he would not done so easily but from Mr. Adair coming up.

On this, we turned back the road we came, and found the division who was halted in consequence of the intelligence the man in the sulky gave them, in order to make a disposition by advancing men in front and on the flanks to prevent a surprise. I went on with the front party which consisted of a sergeant and six or eight men. I shall observe here that the road before you go into Lexington is level for about 1,000 yards. Here we saw shots fired to the right and left of us, but as we heard no whissing of balls, I conclude they were to alarm the body that was there of our approach.

On coming within gun shot of the village of Lexington, a fellow from the corner of the road on the right hand, cocked his piece at me, but burnt priming. I immediately called to Mr. Adair and the party to observe this circumstance which they did and I acquainted Major Pitcairn of it immediately. We still went on further when three shot more were fired at us, which we did not return, and this is the sacred truth as I hope for mercy. These three shot were fired from a corner of a large house to the right of the church. When we came up to the main body, which appeared to me to exceed 400 in and about the village, who were drawn up in a plain opposite to the Church, several officers called out, "Throw down your arms, and you shall come to no harm," or words to that effect.

They refusing to act instantaneously, the gentlemen who were on horseback rode in amongst them of which I was one, at which instant, I heard Major Pitcairn's voice call out, "Soldiers, don't fire, keep your ranks, form and surround them." Instantly some of the villains who got over the hedge fired at us which our men for the first time returned, which set my horse a-going who galloped with me down a road above 600 yards, among the middle of them before I turned him. In returning, a vast number who were in a wood at the right of the Grenadiers fired at me, but the distance was so great that I only heard the Whistling of the Balls, but saw a great number of people in the wood. In consequence of their discovering themselves, our Grenadiers gave them a smart fire. I shall take the liberty of observing here that it is very unlikely that our men should have fired for some time, otherwise they must have hurt their own officers who galloped in amongst this arm'd mob. Our men kept up their fire, and on my coming up Colonel Smith turned to me and asked, "Do you know where a drum is," which I found, who immediately beat to arms, when the men ceased firing. . . .

We marched quietly from this to Concord, only seeing some horsemen on the tops of the heights with no other view, I suppose, than to know our number and make the cowardly disposition (which they did afterwards) with a view to murder us all.

There were far less than the 400 militia claimed by Lieutenant Sutherland assembled on Lexington Green. Forty-nine years later, the events of that bloody day were still vivid in the mind of Sylvanus Wood of Woburn:

I heard the Lexington bell ring, and fearing there was some difficulty there, I immediately arose, took my gun, and, with Robert Douglass, went in haste to Lexington, which was about three miles distant. When I arrived there, I inquired of Captain [John] Parker, the commander of the Lexington company, what was the news. Parker told me he did not know what to believe, for a man had come up about half an hour before, and informed him that the British troops were not on the road. But while we were talking, a messenger came up and told the captain that the British troops were within half a mile. Parker immediately turned to his drummer, William Diman, and ordered him to beat to arms, which was done. . . .

By this time many of the company had gathered around the captain at the hearing of the drum, where we stood, which was about half way between the meeting-house and Buckman's tavern. Parker says to his men, "Every man of you, who is equipped, follow me; and those of you who are not equipped, go into the meeting-house and furnish yourselves from the magazine, and immediately join the company." Parker led those of us who were equipped to the north end of Lexington Common, near the Bedford road, and formed us in single file. I was stationed about in the center of the company. While we are standing, I left my place, and went from one end of the company to the other, and counted every man who was paraded, and the whole number was thirty-eight, and no more.

Just as I had finished, and got back to my place, I perceived the British troops had arrived on the spot between the meeting-house and Buckman's, near where Captain Parker stood when he first led off his men. The British immediately wheeled so as to cut off those who had gone into the meeting-house. The British troops approached us rapidly in platoons, with a general officer on horseback at their head. The officer came up to within about two rods of the center of the company where I stood, the first platoon being about three rods distant. They there halted. The officer then swung his sword, and said, "Lay down your arms, you damned rebels, or you are all dead men—Fire!" Some guns were fired by the British at us from the first platoon, but no person was killed or hurt, being probably charged only with powder.

Just at this time, Captain Parker ordered every man to take care of himself. The company immediately dispersed; and while the company was dispersing and leaping over the wall, the second platoon of the British fired, and killed some of our men. There was not a gun fired by any of Captain Parker's company, within my knowledge. I was so situated that I must have known it, had anything of the kind taken place before a total dispersion of our company. I have been intimately acquainted with the inhabitants of Lexington, and particularly with those of Captain Parker's Company, and, on one occasion, and, with one exception, I have never heard any of them say or pretend that there was any firing at the British from Parker's Company, or any individual in it, until within a year or two. One member of the Company told me, many years since, that, after Parker's company had dispersed, and he was at some distance, he gave them "the guts of his gun."

At Concord, men were waiting. Among them was a twenty-three-year-old corporal, Amos Barrett:

We at Concord heard they was a-coming. The Bell rung at 3 o'clock for an alarm. As I was then a Minuteman, I was soon in town and found my captain and the rest of my company at the post. It wan't long before there was other minute companies. One company, I believe, of minute men was raised in almost every town to stand at a minute's warning. Before sunrise there was, I believe, 150 of us and more of all that was there.

We thought we would go and meet the British. We marched down towards Lexington about a mile and a half, and we see them a-coming. We halted and stayed there until we got within about 100 rods, then we was ordered to the about face and marched before them with our drums and fifes a-going and also the British. We had grand music.

We marched into town and then over the North Bridge a little more than half a mile, and then on a hill not far from the bridge where we could see and hear what was a-going on.

What the British came out after, was to destroy our stores that we had got laid up for our army. There was in the Town House a number of entrenching tools which they carried out and burnt them. At last they said it was better to burn the house, and set fire to them in the house—but our people begged of them not to burn the house, and put it out. It wan't long before it was set fire again, but finally it wasn't burnt. There was about 100 barrels of flour in Mr. Hubbard's malt house; they rolled that out and knocked them to pieces and rolled some in the mill pond, which was saved after they was gone.

When we was on the hill by the bridge, there was about eighty or ninety British came to the bridge and there made a halt. After a while they begun to tear up the plank of the bridge. Major Buttrick said if we were all of his mind, he would drive them away from the bridge; they should not tear that up. We all said we would go. We then wan't loaded; we were all ordered to load—and had strict orders not to fire till they fired first, then to fire as fast as we could.

We then marched on. Captain Davis's minute company marched

first, then Captain Allen's minute company, the one I was in next; we marched two deep. It was a long causeway, being round by the river. Captain Davis had got, I believe, within fifteen rods of the British, when they fired three guns one after the other. I see the balls strike in the river on the right of me. As soon as they fired them, they fired on us—their balls whistled well. We then was all ordered to fire that could fire and not kill our own men. It is strange that there warn't no more killed, but they fired too high. Captain Davis was killed, and Mr. Hosmer and a number wounded. We soon drove them from the bridge. When I got over there was two lay dead and another almost dead. We did not follow them. There was eight or ten that was wounded, and a-running and hobbling about, looking back to see if we was after them.

We then saw the whole body a-coming out of town. We then was ordered to lay behind a wall that run over a hill, and when they got nigh enough, Major Buttrick said he would give the word "fire," but they did not come quite so near as he expected before they halted. The Commanding officer ordered the whole battalion to halt and officers to the front march. The officers then marched to the front. There we lay behind the wall, about 200 of us with our guns cocked, expecting every minute to have the word, "fire." Our orders was, if we fired, to fire two or three times and then retreat. If we had fired, I believe that we could have killed almost every officer there was in the front, but we had no orders to fire and there wan't a gun fired.

They stayed about ten minutes and then marched back, and we after them. After a while we found them a-marching back towards Boston. We was soon after them. When they got about a mile and a half to a road that comes from Bedford and Billerica, they was waylaid and a great many killed. When I got there, a great many lay dead and the road was bloody.

From the outskirts of Concord until they reached Boston, the red-coated soldiers of the King experienced a hell on earth. A relief column under Lord Percy was waiting at Lexington. Lieutenant John Barker of the King's Own Regiment was among the bitter soldiers who made the march from Concord:

We set out upon our return. Before the whole had quitted the town we were fired on from houses and behind trees, and before we had gone one-half mile we were fired on from all sides, but mostly from the rear, where people had hid themselves in houses till we had passed and then fired. The country was an amazing strong one, full of hills, woods, stone walls, &c., which the rebels did not fail to take advantage of, for they were all lined with people who kept up an incessant fire upon us, as we did too upon them but not with the same advantage, for they were so concealed there was hardly any seeing them. In this way we marched between nine and ten miles, their numbers increasing from all parts, while ours was reducing by deaths, wounds and fatigue, and we were totally surrounded with such an incessant fire as it's impossible to conceive; our ammunition was likewise near expended.

In this critical situation we perceived the 1st Brigade coming to our assistance: it consisted of the 4th, 23rd, and 47th regiments, and the battalion of marines, with two field pieces, 6-pounders. . . .

As soon as the rebels saw this reinforcement, and tasted the field pieces, they retired, and we formed on a rising ground and rested ourselves a little while, which was extremely necessary for our men who were almost exhausted with fatigue. In about half an hour we marched again, and some of the Brigade taking the flanking parties, we marched pretty quiet for about two miles; they then began to pepper us again from the same sort of places, but at rather a greater distance. We were now obliged to force almost every house in the road, for the Rebels had taken possession of them and galled us exceedingly, but they suffered for their temerity, for all that was found in the houses were put to death.

When we got to Menotomy, there was a very heavy fire. After that we took the short cut into the Charlestown road, very luckily for us too, for the Rebels, thinking we should endeavour to return by Cambridge, had broken down the bridge and had a great number of men to line the road and receive us there—however, we threw them and went on to Charlestown without any great interruption. We got there between 7 and 8 o'clock at night, took possession of the hill above the town and waited for the boats to carry us over which came some time after. The Rebels did not choose to follow us to the hill, as they must have fought us on open ground, and that they did not like. The picquets of the army were sent over to Charlestown, and 200 of the 64th to keep that ground. They threw up works to secure themselves, and we embarked and got home very late at night.

In the report and depositions dispatched to London by the provincials, the cruelty of the British troops was emphasized. Yet, there were those who felt that "Never had the British army so ungenerous an enemy to oppose." Captain W. G. Evelyn scoffed at the boldness of the rustics, with "Though they are the most absolute cowards on the face of the earth, yet they are just now worked up to such a degree of enthusiasm and madness, that they are easily persuaded the Lord is to assist them in whatever they undertake, and that they must be invincible." Lieutenant Frederick Mackenzie was not too disturbed by the ruthlessness of the British troops:

During the whole of the march from Lexington, the Rebels kept an incessant irregular fire from all points at the column, which was more galling as our flanking parties, which at first were placed at sufficient distances to cover the march of it, were at last, from the different obstructions they occasionally met with, obliged to keep almost close to it. Our men had very few opportunities of getting good shots at the Rebels, as they hardly ever fired but under cover of some stone wall, from behind a tree, or out of a house; and the moment they had fired they lay down out of sight until they had loaded again, or the column had passed. In the road indeed in our rear, they were most numerous, and came on pretty close, frequently calling out, *"King Hancock forever."*

Many of them were killed in the houses on the road side from whence they fired; in some, seven or eight men were destroyed. Some houses were forced open in which no person could be discovered, but when the column had passed, numbers sallied forth from some place in which they had lain concealed, fired at the rear guard, and augmented the numbers which followed us. If we had had time to set fire to those houses many rebels must have perished in them, but as night drew on, Lord Percy thought it best to continue the march. Many houses were plundered by the soldiers, notwithstanding the efforts of the officers to prevent it. I have no doubt that this inflamed the Rebels, and made many of them follow us farther than they otherwise would have done. By all accounts some soldiers who stayed too long in the houses, were killed in the very act of plundering by those who lay concealed in them.

That night a river of angry provincials flowed in to station themselves around Boston. They started digging, even as the British threw up additional fortifications. War had come to America. After reviewing the casualty figures of April 19, one lieutenant lost his optimism as to the ease with which the locals could be subdued:

The sword is drawn; when it will be sheathed, time must determine. I confess, I fear that much to be wished-for period is to be removed to a greater distance than people in general seem to imagine.

Boston

From all over New England the Yankees poured in to help pen the redcoats on the peninsula that was Boston. Burly old Artemas Ward of the Massachusetts militia assumed the command. A surgeon aboard one of His Majesty's ships sniffed with contempt at the efforts of these homespun soldiers:

There is a large body of them in arms near the town of Boston. Their camp and quarters are plentifully supplied with all sorts of provisions, and the roads are crowded with carts and carriages, bringing them rum, cider, &c. from the neighboring towns, for without New-England rum, a New-England army could not be kept together; they could neither fight nor say their prayers, one with another; they drink at least a bottle of it a man a day. . . . This army, which you will hear so much said, and see so much wrote about, is truly nothing but a drunken, canting, lying, praying, hypocritical rabble, without order, subjection, discipline, or cleanliness; and must fall to pieces of itself in the course of three months, notwithstanding every endeavour of their leaders, teachers, and preachers, though the last are the most canting, hypocritical, lying scoundrels that this, or any other country ever afforded.

You are mistaken if you think they are Presbyterian, they are Congregationalists, divided and subdivided into a variety of distinctions, the descendants of Oliver Cromwell's army, who truly inherit the spirit which was the occasion of so much bloodshed in your country from the year 1642, till the Restoration. But these people are happily placed at a distance from you, and though they may occasion a little expence of men and money before they are reduced to order, yet they cannot extend the calamities of war to your island. They have been hitherto unmolested since the affair at Lexington. Time has been given for their passions to subside, but I do not suppose that the General's patience will continue much longer. He is at present confined to the town of Boston, and all supplies from the country stopped, and both the navy and army live upon salt provisions of that sort; I am well informed, there are nine months provisions in the town.

But swift couriers had spread the news of what Gage termed "an affair that happened here on the 19th instant." From Philadelphia came word, "All ranks or men amongst us are in arms. Nothing is heard now in our streets but the trumpet and the drum; and the universal cry is 'Americans, to arms!'" Even the Quakers, it was said, were forming military units. Silas Deane, delegate to the Continental Congress from Connecticut, bore witness to the hustle and bustle:

The militia are constantly out, morning and evening, at exercise; and there are already thirty companies in this city in uniform, well armed, and have made a most surprising progress. The uniform is worth describing to you: it is dark brown (like our homespun) coat, faced with red, white, yellow, or buff, according to their different battalions; white vest and breeches, white stockings, half-boots, black knee-garters. Their coat is made short, falling but little below the waistband of the breeches, which shows the size of a man to very great advantage. Their hats small . . . with a red, or white, or black ribbon, according to their battalions, closing in on a rose, out of which rises a tuft of fur of deer, made to resemble a buck's tail as much as possible, of about six or eight inches high. Their cartouche boxes are large, with the word "Liberty" and the number of their battalion on the outside in large white letters. Thus equipped they make a most elegant appearance, as their cartouche boxes are hung with a broad white wash-leather strap or belt, and their bayonet, &c. on the other side, with one of the same, which two, crossing on the shoulders diamond-fashion, gives an agreeable appearance viewed in the rear.

The Light Infantry are in green, faced with buff; vests &c. as the others, except the cap, which is a hunter's cap, or jockey. These are, without exception, the genteelist companies I ever saw. They have besides a body of Irregulars, or Riflemen, whose dress it is hard to describe. They take a piece of Ticklenburgh, or tow cloth, that is stout, and put into a tan vat until it has the shade of a dry or fading leaf; then they make a kind of frock of it, reaching down below the knee, open before, with a large cape. They wrap it round them tight, on a march, and tie it with their belt, in which hangs their tomahawk. Their hats, as the others. They exercise in the neighboring groves, firing at marks and throwing their tomahawks; forming on a sudden

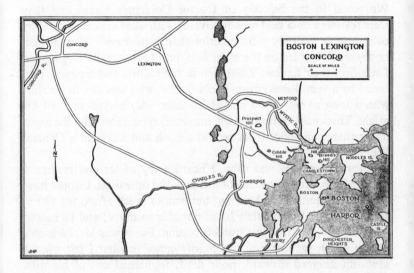

into one line, and then, at the word, break their order and take their posts, to hit their mark. . . .

A loyalist "Lady of Quality," Janet Schaw, appalled at the desertion of the loyalists by the home government, witnessed a gathering of the militia in Wilmington, North Carolina.

Good heavens! What a scene this town is! Surely you folks at home have adopted the old maxim of King Charles: "Make friends of your foes, leave friends to shift for themselves."

We came down in the morning in time for the review, which the heat made as terrible to the spectators as to the soldiers, or what you please to call them. They had certainly fainted under it, had not the constant draughts of grog supported them. Their exercise was that of bush-fighting, but it appeared so confused and so perfectly different from any thing I ever saw, I cannot say whether they performed it well or not; but this I know, that they were heated with rum till capable of committing the most shocking outrages. We stood in the balcony of Doctor Cobham's house and they were reviewed on a field mostly covered with what are called scrubby oaks, which are only a little better than brushwood. They at last, however, assembled on the plain field, and I must really laugh when I recollect their figures: 2,000 men in their shirts and trousers, preceded by a very ill-beat drum and a fiddler, who was also in his shirt with a long sword and a cue at his hair, who played with all his might. They made indeed a most unmartial appearance. But the worst figure there can shoot from behind a bush and kill even a General Wolfe.

Before the review was over, I heard a cry of tar and feather. I was ready to faint at the idea of this dreadful operation. I would have gladly have quitted the balcony, but was so much afraid the victim was one of my friends, that I was not able to move; and he indeed proved to be one, tho' in a humble station. For it was Mr. Neilson's poor English groom. You can hardly conceive what I felt when I saw him dragged forward, poor devil, frightened out of his wits. However at the request of some of the officers, who had been Neilson's friends, his punishment was changed into that of mounting on a table and begging pardon for having smiled at the regiment. He was then drummed and fiddled out of the town, with a strict prohibition of ever being seen in it again. . . .

Oh Britannia, what are you doing, while your true obedient sons are thus insulted by their unlawful brethren; are they also forgot by their natural parents?

Meanwhile, the bored besiegers of Boston were finding their fun where they could. John Trumbull, son of the Governor of Connecticut, and not yet known for his painting, was among those who flocked in to give the "lobsterbacks" a taste of American lead.

The entire army, if it deserved the name, was but an assemblage of brave, enthusiastic, undisciplined country lads; the officers, in general, quite as ignorant of military life as the troops, excepting a few elderly men, who had seen some irregular service among the provincials, under Lord Amherst. Our first occupation was to secure our positions, by constructing fieldworks for defense. . . .

Nothing of military importance occurred for some time; the enemy occasionally fired upon our working parties, whenever they approached too nigh to their works; and in order to familiarize our raw soldiers to this exposure, a small reward was offered in general orders, for every ball fired by the enemy, which should be picked up and brought to head-quarters. This soon produced the intended effect—a fearless emulation among the men; but it produced also a very unfortunate result; for when the soldiers saw a ball, after having struck and rebounded from the ground several times (*en ricochet*) roll sluggishly along, they would run and place a foot before it, to stop it, not aware that a heavy ball long retains sufficient impetus to overcome such an obstacle. The consequence was, that several brave lads lost their feet, which were crushed by weight of the rolling shot. The order was of course withdrawn, and they were cautioned against touching a ball, until it was entirely at rest.

More and more, one critical shortage was becoming evident—the lack of heavy artillery with which to carry on a siege. But a solution was being tossed around in the brain of a strutting little popinjay who had led the Governor's Foot Guards from New Haven into the lines around Boston. Years later, Benjamin Rush was to record his impression of Benedict Arnold:

His person was low but well made, and his face handsome. His conversation was uninteresting and sometimes indelicate. His language was ungrammatical and his pronunciation vulgar. I once heard him say "his courage was acquired, and that he was a coward till he was 15 years of age." His character in his native state, Connecticut, was never respectable, and hence its vote was withheld from him when he was created a general by the Congress of the United States.

Respectability was no consideration in the bold scheme brought forth by Arnold. Knowing that heavy cannon stood rusting on the crumbling and lightly garrisoned post at Ticonderoga, he persuaded the Massachusetts Committee of Safety to issue him a commission to capture that stronghold at the southern end of Lake Champlain. Unbeknown to him, Silas Deane and a group from Hartford had

interested the giant Ethan Allen and his "Green Mountain Boys"
in undertaking the same task. Arnold was still recruiting when he
heard of the rival expedition. Furious, he rode across country to
assume command of the assault. Frustrated by the Green Mountain
Boys, he still insisted on leading the attack alongside of Allen. In
1779, Ethan Allen wrote his Narrative, *couched in grandiloquent*
prose, and conspicuous in its scant mention of Benedict Arnold.

And while I was wishing for an opportunity to signalize myself . . .
directions were privately sent to me from . . . Connecticut, to raise
the Green Mountain Boys and, if possible, with them to surprise
and take the fortress, Ticonderoga. This enterprise I cheerfully
undertook and . . . made a forced march from Bennington, and
arrived at the lake opposite Ticonderoga on the evening of the ninth
day of May, 1775, with two hundred and thirty valiant Green Mountain Boys; and it was with the utmost difficulty that I procured
boats to cross the lake. However, I landed eighty-three men near the
garrison, and sent the boats back for the rear guard commanded
by Colonel Seth Warner. But the day began to dawn, and I found
myself under the necessity to attack the fort before the rear guard
could cross the lake; and, as it was viewed hazardous, I harangued
the officers and soldiers in the manner following:

"Friends and fellow soldiers. You have, for a number of years
past, been a scourge and terror to arbitrary power. Your valor has
been famed abroad and acknowledged, as appears by the advice and
orders to me from the General Assembly of Connecticut, to surprise
and take the garrison now before us. I now propose to advance
before you, and in person, conduct you through the wicket-gate;
for we must this morning either quit our pretensions to valor, or
possess ourselves of this fortress in a few minutes. And inasmuch
as it is a desperate attempt, which none but the bravest of men dare
undertake, I do not urge it on any contrary to his will. You that will
undertake voluntarily, poise your firelocks."

The men being at this time drawn up in three ranks, each poised
his firelock. I ordered them to face to the right, and at the head of
the centre-file, marched them immediately to the wicket-gate
aforesaid, where I found a sentry posted, who instantly snapped his
fusee at me. I ran immediately towards him, and he retreated through
the covered way into the parade within the garrison, gave a halloo,
and ran under a bomb-proof. My party, who followed me into the

fort, I formed on the parade in such a manner as to face the two barracks which faced each other. The garrison being asleep, except the sentries, we gave three huzzas, which greatly surprised them. One of the sentries made a pass at one of my officers with a charged bayonet and slightly wounded him. My first thought was to kill him with my sword; but in an instant, I altered the design and fury of the blow to a slight cut on the side of the head, upon which he dropped his gun and asked quarter, which I immediately granted him, and demanded of him the place where the commanding officer slept. He showed me a pair of steps in the front of a barrack on the west part of the garrison which led up to a second story in said barrack, to which I immediately repaired and ordered the commander, Captain De la Place, to come forth instantly, or I would sacrifice the whole garrison; at which the Captain came immediately to the door, with his breeches in his hand. When I ordered him to deliver to me the fort instantly, he asked me by what authority I demanded it. I answered him, "In the name of the great Jehovah, and the Continental Congress."

The authority of the Congress being very little known at that time, he began to speak again. But I interrupted him, and with my drawn sword over his head, again demanded an immediate surrender of the garrison; to which he then complied and ordered his men to be forthwith paraded without arms, as he had given up the garrison. In the mean time some of my officers had given orders, and in consequence thereof, sundry of the barrack doors were beaten down and about one-third of the garrison imprisoned, which consisted of the said commander, a Lieutenant Feltham, a conductor of artillery, a gunner, two sergeants, and forty-four rank and file; about one hundred pieces of cannon, one thirteen-inch mortar, and a number of swivels.

This surprise was carried into execution in the grey of the tenth day of May, 1775. The sun seemed to rise that morning with a superior lustre; and Ticonderoga and its dependencies smiled on its conquerors, who tossed about the flowing bowl, and wished success to Congress, and the liberty and freedom of America. . . .

That same day, Crown Point with its shadow of a garrison fell. A few days later, Arnold sailed to the head of the lake and subdued the post of St. John's on the Sorel River. The success of this operation meant that the rebels now had acquired artillery and had blocked an invasion route from Canada.

Back in Boston the siege droned on. The town itself was commanded by two promontories: Bunker Hill on Charlestown peninsula and Dorchester Heights on Dorchester Neck. Gage had unwisely abandoned Bunker Hill after Lexington and Concord. Now, with the advice of three newly arrived generals, William Howe, John Burgoyne and Henry Clinton, it was decided that these elevations should be secured and fortifications erected. The news leaked to the rebels. Peter Thacher reported subsequent events.

In consequence of undoubted information received from Boston by the commanders of the continental army at Cambridge, that General Gage with a party of his troops purposed the next day to take possession of Bunker's Hill, a promontory just at the entrance of the peninsula of Charlestown, they determined, with the advice of the Committee of Safety of Massachusetts Province, to send a party who might erect some fortifications upon the hill and prevent this design.

Accordingly on the 16th of June, orders were issued that a party of about one thousand men should that evening march to Charlestown and entrench upon the hill. About 9 o'clock in the evening the detachment marched upon this design to Breed's Hill situated on the further part of the peninsula next to Boston, for by a mistake of orders this hill was marked out for entrenchment instead of the other hill. As there were many things necessary to be done preparatory to the entrenchments being thrown up, which could not be done before lest the enemy should observe them, it was nearly 12 o'clock before the work was entered upon, for the clocks in Boston were heard to strike about 10 minutes after the men first took their tools in their hands. The work was carried on in every animation and success so that by the dawn of the day they had completed a small redoubt about eight rods square.

At this time an heavy fire began from three men-of-war, a number of floating batteries and from a fortification of the enemy's on Copp's Hill in Boston directly opposite the little redoubt. These kept up an incessant shower of shot and bombs, by which one man pretty soon fell. Not discouraged by the melancholy fate of their companion, the soldiers laboured indefatigably till they had thrown up a small breastwork extending from the north side of the redoubt . . . to the bottom of the hill, but were prevented by the intolerable fire of the enemy from completing the whole in such a manner as to make them defensible.

Between 12 and 1 o'clock a number of boats and barges filled with soldiers were observed approaching towards Charlestown. These landed their troops at a place called Morton's Point, situated a little to the eastward of our works. The brigade formed upon the landing tho' they were something galled by the fire of two small field pieces which were placed at the end of the entrenchment. They stood there thus formed till a second brigade arrived from Boston to join them.

Having sent out large flank guards in order to surround them, they began a very slow march towards our lines. At this instant flames and smoke were seen to arise in large clouds from the town of Charlestown which had been set on fire from some of the enemy's batteries with a design to favour their attack upon our lines by the smoke which they imagined would have been blown directly their way and covered them in their attack, but the wind changing at this instant, it was carried another way.

The provincials in the redoubt and the lines reserved their fire till the enemy had come within about ten or twelve yards and then discharged them at once upon them. The fire threw their body into very great confusion, and all of them after having kept a fire for some time retreated in very great disorder down to the point where they landed, and some of them even got into their boats.

At this time their officers were observed by spectators on the opposite shore to come down and then to use the most passionate gestures, and even to push forward the men with their swords. At length, by their exertions, the troops were again rallied and marched up to the entrenchments. The Americans reserved their fire and a second time put the regulars to flight, who once more retreated in precipitation to the boats.

The same or greater exertions were now again observed to be made by their officers which, notwithstanding the evident reluctance discovered by the soldiers, were successful, and having formed once more they brought some cannon to bear in such a manner as to rake the inside of the breastwork, and having drove the provincials there into the redoubt, they determined now, it appeared, to make a decisive effort. The fire from the ships and batteries, as well as from the cannon in the front of the army, was redoubled. Innumerable bombs were sent into the fort. The officers behind the army of the regulars were observed to goad forward the men in renewed exertion. The breastwork on the side of the redoubt was abandoned; the ammunition of the provincials was expended. The enemy advanced on three sides of the fort at once and scaled the walls. . . .

The retreat of this handful of brave men would have been effectually cut off had it not have happened that the flanking party which was to have surrounded the fort on the back side was kept back by a party of provincials who fought with the utmost bravery and kept them from advancing further than the beach. . . .

With very great signs of exultation, the British troops again took possession of the hill whither they had fled after their retreat from Concord, and it was expected that they would have prosecuted the advantage which they had gained by marching immediately to Cambridge, which was then indeed in an almost defenceless state. They did not, however, do this, but kept firing with the cannon from the hill and from the ships and batteries across the neck in order to prevent their attacking them. The wonder which was excited at the conduct of them soon ceased when a certain account arrived from Boston that of 3,000 who marched out on the expedition, no less than 1,500, among which were 92 commission officers, were killed and wounded. A more severe blow than the British troops had ever met with in proportion to the number who were engaged, and the time the engagement lasted from the first fire of the musketry to the last was exactly an hour and a half.

The British had won a hill, but at too great a cost. The Americans had lost Dr. Joseph Warren, perhaps their greatest political leader, who had died with a musket in his hands in the redoubt on Breed's Hill. Ann Hulton, genteel loyalist lady, was outraged "that gentlemen, brave British soldiers, should fall by the hands of such despicable wretches as compose the banditti of the country; amongst whom there is not one that has the least pretension to be called a gentleman. They are a most rude, depraved, degenerate race, and it is a mortification to us that they speak English and can trace themselves from that stock." But these rustics had gained the respect of Thomas Gage, who now sent a grim warning to England.

They are now spirited up by a rage and enthusiasm as great as ever people were possessed of, and you must proceed in earnest or give the business up. A small body acting in one spot will not avail. You must have large armies, making diversions on different sides to divide their force.

The loss we have sustained is greater than we can bear. Small armies can't afford such losses, especially when the advantage gained tends to little more than the gaining of a post—a material one indeed, as our own security depended on it. The troops were sent out too late, the Rebels were at least two months before-hand with us, and your Lordship would be astonished to see the tract of country they have entrenched and fortified; their number is great, so many hands have been employed.

We are here, to use a common expression, taking the bull by the horns, attacking the enemy in their strong parts. I wish this cursed place was burned. The only use is its harbour which may be said to be material, but in all other respects it is the worst place either to act offensively from, or defensively. I have before wrote to your Lordship my opinion that a large army must at length be employed to reduce these people, and mentioned the hiring of foreign troops. I fear it must come to that, or else to avoid a land war and make use only of your fleet. . . .

But Gage was seldom listened to in Whitehall. Soon he was to be replaced as Commander of the British forces in North America by William Howe, who had led the assault on Breed's Hill. And the rebels were soon to have a new general. In answer to the supplications of the Massachusetts Provincial Congress, the Continental Congress in Philadelphia not only assumed control of the army around Boston, but also nominated a new commanding general. John Adams, ever mindful of the need for unity, initiated action to win the support of Virginia.

Mr. Hancock himself had an ambition to be appointed commander-in-chief. Whether he thought an election a compliment due to him, and intended to have the honor of declining it, or whether he would have accepted, I know not. To the compliments he had some pretensions, for, at that time, his exertions, sacrifices, and general merits in the cause of his country had been incomparably greater than those of Colonel Washington. But the delicacy of his health, and his entire want of experience in actual service, though an excellent militia officer, were decisive objections to him in my mind. In canvassing the subject, out of doors, I found too that even among the delegates of Virginia there were difficulties. The apostolical reasonings among themselves which should be greatest, were not less energetic among the saints of the Old Dominion than they were among us of New England. In several conversations, I found more than one very cool about the appointment of Washington, and particularly Mr. Pendelton was very clear and full against it.

Full of anxieties concerning these confusions, and apprehending daily that we should hear very distressing news from Boston, I walked with Mr. Samuel Adams in the State Yard, for a little exercise and fresh air, before the hour of Congress, and there represented to him the various dangers that surrounded us. He agreed to them all, but said, "What shall we do?" I answered him that he knew I had taken great pains to get our colleagues to agree upon some plan, that we might be unanimous; but he knew that they would pledge themselves to nothing; but I was determined to take a step which should compel them and all the other members of Congress to declare themselves for or against something. "I am determined this morning to make a direct motion that Congress should adopt the army before Boston, and appoint Colonel Washington commander of it." Mr. Adams seemed to think very seriously of it, but said nothing.

Accordingly, when Congress had assembled, I rose in my place, and in as short a speech as the subject would admit, represented the state of the Colonies, the uncertainty in the minds of the people, their great expectation and anxiety, the distresses of the army, the danger of its dissolution, the difficulty of collecting another, and the probability that the British army would take advantage of our delays, march out of Boston, and spread desolation as far as they could go. I concluded with a motion, in form, that Congress would adopt the army at Cambridge, and appoint a General; that though this was not the proper time to nominate a General, yet as I had reason to believe this was a point of the greatest difficulty, I had no hesitation to declare that I had but one gentleman in my mind for that important command, and that was a gentleman from Virginia who was among us and very well known to all of us, a gentleman whose skill and experience as an officer, whose independent fortune, great talents, and excellent universal character would command the approbation of all America, and unite the cordial exertions of all the Colonies better than any other person in the Union.

Mr. Washington, who happened to sit near the door, as soon as he heard me allude to him, from his usual modesty darted into the library-room. Mr. Hancock—who was our President, which gave me an opportunity to observe his countenance while I was speaking on the state of the Colonies, the army at Cambridge, and the enemy—heard me with visible pleasure, but when I came to describe Washington for the commander, I never remarked a more sudden and striking change of countenance. Mortification and resentment were expressed as forcibly as his face could exhibit them. Mr. Samuel Adams seconded the motion, and that did not soften the President's physiognomy at all.

The subject came under debate, and several gentlemen declared themselves against the appointment of Mr. Washington, not on account of any personal objections against him, but because the army were all from New England, had a General of their own, appeared to be satisfied with him, and had proved themselves able to imprison the British army in Boston which was all they expected or desired at that time. Mr. Pendleton of Virginia, Mr. Sherman of Connecticut, were very explicit in declaring this opinion; Mr. Cushing and several others more faintly expressed their opposition, and their fears of discontents in the army and in New England. . . .

The subject was postponed to a future day. In the meantime, pains were taken out of doors to obtain a unanimity, and the voices were generally so clearly in favor of Washington that the dissentient members were persuaded to withdraw their opposition, and Mr. Washington was nominated, I believe by Mr. Thomas Johnson of Maryland, unanimously elected, and the army adopted.

On July 2, 1775, General George Washington rode into Cambridge. To say the least, he was not overly impressed with the army with which he was to fight a war.

The people of this Government have obtained a character which they by no means deserved—their officers, generally speaking, are the most indifferent people I ever saw. I have already broke one colonel and five captains for cowardice, and for drawing more pay and provisions than had men in their companies—there are two more colonels now under arrest, and to be tried for the same offences —in short, they are by no means such troops in any respect as you are led to believe of them, from the accounts which are published. But I need not make myself enemies among them by this declaration, although it is consistent with the truth. I dare say the men would fight very well (if properly officered), although they are exceedingly dirty and nasty people. Had they been properly conducted at Bunker's Hill . . . or those that were there properly supported, the regulars would have met with a shameful defeat, and a much more considerable loss than they did, which is now known to be exactly 1057, killed and wounded—it was [for] their behaviour on that occasion, that the above officers were broke, for I never spared one that was accused of cowardice, but brought 'em to immediate trial.

The British engaged in a number of coastal raids, not only to draw men away from Boston, but also to supplement an uninspired diet that had as its basic ingredient salt meat. Some ports, like Newport, merely experienced their moments of terror as British vessels threatened their homes, while Bristol, Rhode Island, after a bombardment, bought off the Rose *with forty sheep; but three-quarters of the buildings in Falmouth were lost. Not even the threat of British bombardment could discourage the rather fantastic patriotism of one bold lad in Newport whose exploit was reported in a number of newspapers:*

Early last Saturday morning one Coggeshall, being somewhat drunk or crazy, went on the long wharf and turned up his backside toward the bomb brig in this harbour, using some insulting words. Upon which the brig fired two four-pound shot at him; one of which went through the roof of Mr. Hammond's store on the said wharf and lodged in Mr. Samuel Johnston's distill house at the N.E. part of the cove, within the long wharf. The man was soon after taken up and sent out of town.

These coastal raids, coupled with the growing chill of winter, discouraged rebel re-enlistments. And until the ice on the rivers and lakes was thick enough to bear the weight of heavy cannon, artillery could not be brought down from Ticonderoga. Washington could only tighten the circle of earthworks around Boston through the constant employment of entrenching tools. Inside this cordon the British stirred restlessly from hunger and boredom. Lieutenant Martin Hunter had been stationed over on Bunker Hill.

About a month after the action I was taken ill, brought on by eating green apples, and obliged to go to Boston; and I am very certain I should not have recovered if it had not been for General Grant's good soup. He was so good as to send me a basin every day. Fresh meat was not then to be had for love or money.... The scarcity of meat at this time was so great that Lord Percy killed a foal, had it roasted, and invited a party to dinner, and Major Musgrave's fat mare was stolen, killed, and sold in the market for beef. . . .

Plays were acted every week by the officers and some of the Boston ladies. Miss Sally Fletcher acted the part of Zara. She was a very pretty girl and did it very well. A farce called "The Blockade of Boston," written, I believe, by General Burgoyne, was acted. The enemy knew the night it was to be performed and made an attack on the mill at Charlestown at the very hour that the farce began. I happened to be on duty in the redoubt at Charlestown that night. The enemy came along the mill-dam and surprised a sergeant's guard that was posted at the mill. Some shots were fired, and we all immediately turned out and manned the works. A shot was fired by one of our advanced sentries, and instantly the firing commenced in the redoubt, and it was a considerable time before it could be stopped. . . .

An orderly sergeant that was standing outside the playhouse door heard the firing and immediately ran into the playhouse, got upon the stage and cried, "Turn out! Turn out! They are hard at it, certain and tongs." The whole audience thought the sergeant was acting in the farce, and that he did it so well that there was a general clap, and such a noise that he could not be heard for a considerable time. When the clapping was over he again cried, "What the deuce are you all about? If you won't believe me, by Jasus, you need only go to the door, and there you will see and hear both!" If it was the intention of the enemy to put a stop to the farce for the night they certainly succeeded, as all the officers immediately left the playhouse and joined their regiments.

Others within the city were equally unhappy with the siege. There was John Leach, for instance, who was imprisoned for ninety-seven days, charged with "being a spy, and suspected of taking plans." His unhappy Puritan sensibilities were tormented by the wordly scenes around him.

From the 2d July to the 19th, a complicated scene of oaths, curses, debauchery and the most horrid blasphemy, committed by the

Provost Marshal, his deputy and his soldiers who were our guards, soldier prisoners, and the sundry soldier women for our neighbours; some placed over our heads, and some in rooms each side of us. They acted such scenes as was shocking to nature and language, horrible to hear, as if it came from the very suburbs of Hell. When our wives, children and friends came to see us (which was seldom they were permitted), we seemed to want them gone, notwithstanding we were so desirous of their company, as they were exposed to hear the most abandoned language, as was grating to the ears of all sober persons.

The feeling that the soldiers of the King were enemies of the Lord becomes evident in extracts from the diary of Private Aaron Wright. His military career began on June 29, 1775, at Northumberland, Pennsylvania.

We were sworn to be true and faithful soldiers in the Continental Army, under the direction of the Right Honourable Congress. After this we chose our officers, and lay there until the 7th of July, when we got orders to march next morning. When on parade, our 1st Lieut. came and told us he would be glad if we would excuse him from going, which we refused; but, on consideration, we concluded it was better to consent; after which he said he would go; but we said, "You shall not command us, for he whose mind can change in an hour, is not fit to command in the field where liberty is contended for." In the evening we chose a private in his place. The next morning we marched. . . .

Aug. 26. Crossed the Connecticut, near Hartford, and after marching ten miles, catched a Tory; took him two miles and tarred and feathered him for saying that he was sorry to see so many men going to fight the King, and that he had sent letters to Gage's camp. . . .

Aug. 31. Marched to . . . Cambridge, where a college was kept . . . thence to Prospect Hill.

Sept. 10. Great commotion on Prospect Hill among the riflemen, occasioned by the unreasonable confinement of a sergeant by an adjutant of Thompson's regiment; and before it was over, thirty-four men were confined, and two of them put in irons at headquarters in Cambridge; on the 12th they were tried by a court-martial, and one was whipped 17 lashes for stealing and drummed out of camp. . . .

Sept. 20. The Redcoats fired eight Bums and four cannon at our people on Ploughed Hill, which did us no other hurt than kill one steer that was in a pasture 300 yards from Ploughed Hill. . . .

Sept. 21. The red-coated Philistines fired thirty-one cannon and three bombs at the Sons of Liberty, who were building a parapet to secure themselves against the diabolical rage of the parliamentary tools on Bunker Hill. All they did was to wound two men, which happened by a stone which a bullet hit and drove it against a man's leg, but it did not break the bone. The other, a sod raised by the same ball, struck a man on the thigh and broke it. In the meantime our Sons of Freedom shot twice at the Philistines. . . .

Sept. 22. Being George Third's Coronation day, the Philistines fired many guns for joy; and two or three bombs at us, which did us no harm.

Oct. 5. The regulars below Roxbury fired eight-six cannon at our people and killed two cows and shot the arm of a musketman who stood behind an apple tree. The Philistines on Bunker Hill were peaceable. A corporal of the guard came to our picket guard last night and says that General Gage is to embark for England at one o'clock today. . . .

Oct. 7. Peace with our enemy, but disturbance enough with rum, for our men got money yesterday.

Oct. 15. Our clargymen preached with his hat on.

Oct. 17. Our floating batteries were launched and attacked the regulars' floating batteries below Roxbury, but to our sorrow, one of our cannons bursted, killing two of our men, and wounded the captain and six others very badly; but the residue, by the help of God, came home with the battery.

Dec. 1. John M'Murty, in Captain Chambers' company, killed John Penn by his rifle going off when, he says, he did not know it was loaded. He was cleaning the lock and put it on and primed it to see how she would "fier." It shot through a double partition of inch boards and through one board of a berth, and left its mark on the chimney. Penn put his hand on his breast and as he turned round, fell down dead and never spoke more.

Dec. 10. In the morning the drums in Colonel Little's regiment played and the men were all paraded to see who would enlist for a year, and about two-thirds of them followed the recruiting drum.

Jan. 9, 1776. Last night Major Knowlton was dispatched with 100 men to make an incursion into Charlestown. He crossed the mill dam that lies betwen Cobble Hill and Bunker Hill, and proceeded down the street toward the ferry. A part of the men, at the same time, under Captain Keys, were ordered to take part at the end of the street near Bunker Hill, to intercept any who should escape from the houses. Those who went down the street found six men and one woman in one house. One they killed because he would not be taken prisoner; the other six all submitted and were brought to headquarters. They burned ten houses, in one of which, according to the woman, there were seventeen men burnt. They also brought away six muskets; all of which was done without the loss of a man on our side.

March 3. Last night our people threw the first bombs into Boston, which set the regulars at the same work (which has not been for more than two months), but to our loss, two of our mortars were bursted. In the morning, before day of the 4th, the Parliamentary tools threw several near the fort on Lechmere Point and one into Prospect Hill fort (which they never did before), but it hurt no one, although there were above 1,000 men in it. Our men kept up a slow cannonading all day, and the enemy returned it slowly. In the evening the brass mortar "Congress" was brought to Cobble Hill, and as soon as it was dark they began to work with her; but at the third shot she bursted, after which the regulars saluted us with several bombs that did no harm, and Generals Greene and Putnam made their balls rattle in Boston, bravely.

On January 24, 1776, plump Henry Knox had lumbered into Cambridge, bringing with him 43 cannon and 16 mortars from Ticonderoga. Now Washington had the artillery to launch a bold stroke although there were some "crying out for powder—powder—ye Gods, give us powder!" In late February a council of war recommended the fortification of Dorchester Heights, which it was thought would "bring on a rumpus between us and the enemy." Reverend William Gordon, even now intent on writing a history of this rebellion, was among those who witnessed the preparations.

Our troops were busied in making fascines and in getting every other matter in readiness. A battle was expected and ardently wished for, whenever we should possess the hills. It was urged by some to go on so as that the engagement might happen on the 5th of March, the day on which the unarmed mob was fired upon at Boston by Captain Preston's men. It was accordingly concluded to enter upon the work the 4th at night.

In the mean time, to amuse the enemy, our bomb batteries being finished on Cambridge and Roxbury side, a few shells were thrown into the town Saturday night, March the third. . . . On the Lord's day night, more shells were thrown, besides firing a number of cannon into the town. The Monday night it was repeated and increased considerably, but not one of our friends in town was hurt; about half a dozen soldiers lost their limbs.

All things being ready, as soon as the evening admitted of it, the undertaking went forward. The covering party, consisting of 800 men, led the way; then the carts with the entrenching tools; after that the main working party under General Thomas, consisting of about 1,200. A train of more than 300 carts loaded with fascines, pressed hay, in bundles of seven or eight hundred, etc., closed the procession. Every one knew his place and business; the covering party, when upon the ground, divided, half went to the point next to Boston, the other to that next to the Castle. All possible silence was observed. The wind lay so as to carry what noise could not be avoided, by driving the stakes and picking against the frozen ground (for the frost was still more than a foot thick, about a foot and a half) to carry, I say, what noise could not be avoided into the harbour between the town and the castle, so as not to be heard and regarded by such as had no suspicion of what we were after, especially as there was a continued cannonade on both sides. Many of the carts made three trips, some four.

General Thomas told me that he pulled out his watch and found that, by ten o'clock at night, they had got two forts, one upon each hill, sufficient to defend them from small arms and grape shot. The men continued working with the utmost spirit, till relieved the Tuesday morning about three. The neighboring militia had been called in for three days to guard against accidents and were in by twelve at night, some before, in the evening. The night was remarkably mild, a finer for working could not have been taken out of the whole 365. It was hazy below so that our people could not be seen, tho' it was a bright moonlight above on the hills.

When the ministerialists saw in the morning early what we had been after, they were astonished upon seeing what we had done. General Howe was seen to scratch his head, and heard to say by those that were about him that he did not know what he should do, that the provincials (he likely called them by some other name) had done more work in one night than his whole army would have done in six months. In this strong manner did he express his surprise. He soon called a council of war and determined upon attempting to dislodge our people (the Admiral having informed him that if we possessed those heights he could not keep one of His Majesty's ships in the harbour).

Spectators in abundance, yours among the rest, were looking out upon the adjacent hills for a bloody battle. The wharf was thronged with soldiers, while numbers were going on board vessels; the provincials rejoiced at seeing it, clapped their hands and wished for the expected attack.

General Washington said to those that were at hand, "Remember, it is the fifth of March, and avenge the death of your brethren!" It was immediately asked what the General said by those that were not near enough to hear, and was as soon answered; and so from one another thro' all the troops, which added fresh fuel to the martial fire before kindled. . . .

The tide was turned, and the day too far spent to admit of the regulars coming out and attacking on the fifth of March. They would have been under great disadvantages had they landed after high water, at the point next to the town. General Howe proposed attacking therefore the next morning very early. . . .

I came home early, finding nothing could be done that evening; and being fatigued with riding forward and backward, and the exercise of body and mind natural to such a peculiar state of things, and designing to be up by daybreak and down in view of what might be going on, I went to bed about eight. I expected that the men-of-war would get as near Dorchester hills as possible, that the next morning at day break a most heavy cannonade would begin; and I thought it probable that the regulars would land under cover of it and proceed to attack the provincials. But when I heard in the night how amazingly strong the wind blew (for it was such a storm as scarce anyone remembered to have heard) and how it rained towards morning, I concluded that the ships could not stir, and pleased myself with the reflection that the Lord might be working deliverance for us and preventing the effusion of human blood.

The event proved that it was so. The storm hindered the attack; and it was so given out afterwards in general orders by General Howe as appears from one of the orderly books that fell into our hands. Immediately orders were given for embarking the troops, that the town might be speedily evacuated. The Tories were thunder-struck, and terribly dejected. All was hurry and confusion; the soldiers working like horses night and day, getting on board what they could as fast as possible. On the 17th of March, in the morning, they evacuated the town.

It was indeed an auspicious beginning for the first year of an insurrection. If success continued to mark the efforts of the provincials, their rebellion might yet be termed a revolution.

Canada

CANADA loomed as a prize for the rebels; this wilderness province held promise of becoming the fourteenth colony. Many advocated taking Quebec, the stronghold of the north, but Congress was dilatory. Finally, in the fall of 1775, a two-pronged attack was launched. The first arm, under the leadership of the lithe, young, Irish-born Brigadier General Richard Montgomery, was to strike north from Lake Champlain, take Montreal, then swing eastward to Quebec. The other, under Benedict Arnold, was to march northward along the Kennebec and Chaudière rivers and converge on the same objective. In early September, Montgomery laid siege to the fortress of St. John's guarding the Sorel River, the exit from Champlain and the water route to the St. Lawrence. Ethan Allen, no longer in command of the Green Mountain Boys, and apparently deserted by his ally, "the great Jehovah," was sent on a recruiting and scouting expedition in the vicinity of Montreal. With the glory of Ticonderoga still green in his memory, this quixotic fellow planned to freshen his laurels by capturing Montreal. But a motley army composed of British regulars and Canadian militia marched out to meet him. The majority of Allen's Canadian recruits, mindful of the penalty for treason, immediately deserted. Allen recounted his rendezvous with fate in his Narrative:

At this time I had but about forty men with me; some of whom were wounded. The enemy kept closing around me, nor was it in my power to prevent it; by which means, my situation, which was advantageous from the first part of the attack, ceased to be so in the last. And being almost surrounded with such vast unequal numbers, I ordered a retreat, but found that those of the enemy who were of the country, and their Indians, could run as fast as my men, though the regulars could not.

Thus I retreated near a mile and some of the enemy, with the savages, kept flanking me and the others crowded hard in the rear. ... One of the enemy's officers, boldly pressing in the rear, discharged his fusee at me. The ball whistled near me as did many others that day. I returned the salute and missed him as running had put us both out of breath, for I conclude we were not frightened. I then saluted him with my tongue in a harsh manner and told him, that inasmuch as his numbers were so far superior to mine, I would surrender provided I could be treated with honor and be assured of good quarter for myself and the men who were with me, and he answered that I should. Another officer coming up directly after, confirmed the treaty, upon which I agreed to surrender with my party which then consisted of thirty-one effective men and seven wounded. I ordered them to ground their arms, which they did.

The officer I capitulated with then directed me and my party to advance towards him, which was done. I handed him my sword and in half a minute after a savage, part of whose head was shaved, being almost naked and painted, with feathers intermixed with the hair on the other side of his head, came running towards me with incredible swiftness. He seemed to advance with more than mortal speed. As he approached near me, his hellish visage was beyond all description —snakes' eyes appear innocent in comparison with his—his features extorted, malice, death, murder, and the wrath of devils and damned spirits are the emblems of his countenance, and in less than twelve feet of me presented his firelock. At the instant of his present, I twitched the officer to whom I gave my sword between me and the savage. But he flew round with great fury, trying to single me out to shoot me without killing the officer. But by this time I was near as nimble as he, keeping the officer in such a position that his danger was my defence, but in less than half a minute I was attacked by just such another imp of Hell. Then I made the officer fly around with incredible velocity for a few seconds of time, when I perceived a Canadian, who had lost one eye, as he appeared afterwards, taking my part against the savages. And in an instant an Irishman came to my assistance with a fixed bayonet, swearing by Jasus he would kill them. This tragic scene composed my mind. The escaping from so awful a death, made even imprisonment happy, the more so as my conquerors on the field treated me with great civility and politeness.

The regular officers said they were very happy to see Colonel Allen. I answered them, that I should choose rather to have seen them at

General Montgomery's camp and no abuse was offered me 'till I came to the barrack yard at Montreal where I met General Prescott. He then asked me whether I was that Colonel Allen who took Ticonderoga. I told him I was the very man. Then he shook his cane over my head, calling many hard names, among which he frequently used the word "rebel," and put himself in a great rage. I told him that he would do well not to cane me, for I was not accustomed to it, and shook my fist at him, telling him that was the beetle of mortality for him if he offered to strike. Upon which Captain M'Cloud of the British pulled him by the skirt and whispered to him, as he afterwards told me, to this import, that it was inconsistent with his honor to strike a prisoner. . . .

The General stood a minute, when he made the following reply, "I will not execute you now; but you shall grace a halter at Tyburn, God damn you."

The siege at St. John's, meanwhile, dragged on for fifty-five days, forecasting a winter campaign in Canada. Benedict Arnold's expedition had marched out of Cambridge near the middle of September. The troops were transported by water as far as Fort Western on the Kennebec. From there they were to travel by batteaux and overland. Extracts from the diary of twenty-two-year-old Dr. Isaac Senter record the trials and heartbreaks of a desperate trek through a wilderness seldom before traveled by white men.

Saturday, Sept. 23rd. Arrived at Fort Western at 10 o'clock in the morning. We were now come to a rapid in the river beyond which our transports could not pass, nor could they all get up as far as this. Most of them were left at Garden's Town, where the batteaux were built, and the troops disembarked from them into the batteaux, except those who were obliged to take land carriage. The batteaux were made of green pine boards, which rendered them somewhat heavy. . . .

Sunday, 24th. Early this morning was called to attend a wounded soldier who was shot through the body last night by a malicious drunken fellow belonging to the army. . . .

Monday, 25th. This morning search being made for the fellow who was imagined to be the murderer—found and condemned by a court-martial to hang. This evening Captain Morgan marched up the river with a division of the riflemen. The rest of the army got very nigh in readiness to march. To each of them a select number of batteaux men were ordered, in general about five per boat. In these the provisions were put, tents, and camp equipage, &c. all excepting what was necessary for that party who went by land. This number (as nigh as I could guess) amounted to about 600. . . .

Friday, 29th. During all this time the batteaux were coming up and going over the falls . . . called Tacunnick. The rapid water is the distance of about half a mile, past which all our batteaux, camp equipage, &c. was carried by hand. By this time several of our batteaux began to leak profusely, made of green pine and that in the most slight manner. Water being shoal and rocks plenty, with a very swift current most of the way, soon ground out many of the bottoms. . . .

Sunday, Oct. 1st. I was now seven miles above Fort Halifax and for the first time encamped upon the ground. . . . Boats were now continually passing up by us when I impatiently awaited the coming of the last division. My boat's crew consisted of three Englishmen, sailors, one old Swiss, and a young Scotchman, a deserter from the British army at Boston; as indeed all the rest were deserters from them at different places. This day I spent in marching up and down the river to see the progress of the army passing the rapids. The river for about two miles was exceeding swift, water shoal, &c. Every batteaux crew were obliged to take to the water, some to the painter and others heaving at the stern. In these rapids the water was in general waistband high. With their united efforts, the stream was so violent as many times to drive them back after ten or twelve fruitless attempts in pulling and heaving with the whole boat's crew. . . .

Thursday, 5th. . . . I left the charge of the batteaux to my lads and proceeded up the river by land, till within half a mile, where I contracted with a couple of savages who followed the army to take charge of the boat, in consequence of the water growing exceeding rapid. They conducted her safe to the foot of Norridgewalk fall, where they were (that is the batteaux) all haul'd up. We now had a number of teams employed in conveying the batteaux, provisions, camp equipage, &c., over this carrying place. By this time, many of our batteaux were nothing but wrecks, some stove to pieces, &c. The carpenters were employed in repairing them, while the rest of the army were busy in carrying over the provisions, &c. A quantity of dry cod fish by this time was received, as likewise a number of barrels of dry bread. The fish lying loose in the batteaux, and being continually washed with the fresh water running into the batteaux. The bread casks not being water-proof, admitted the water in plenty, swelled the bread, burst the casks, as well as soured the bread. The same fate attended a number of fine casks of peas. These with the others were condemned. . . . Our fare was now reduced to salt pork and flour. Beef we had once and now and then we could purchase a fat creature, but that was seldom. A few barrels of salt beef remained on hand, but of so indifferent quality as scarce to be eaten, being killed in the heat of summer, took much damage after salting, that rendered it not only very unwholesome, but very unpalatable. . . .

Sunday, 15th. This day I got over all my affairs to the second portage, where I was obliged to tarry till the rear of the army came up. Many of us were now in a sad plight with the diarrhea. Our water was of the worst quality. The lake was low, surrounded with mountains, situate in a low morass. Water was quite yellow. With this we were obliged not only to do all our cooking, but use it as our constant drink. Nor would a little of it suffice, as we were obliged to eat our meals exceeding salt. This, with our constant fatigue, called for large quantities of drink. No sooner had it got down that it was puked up by many of the poor fellows. . . .

Friday, 20th. My lads with the remainder of the baggage arrived early this morning. I crawled out from under my topsy-turned boat, ordered her launched and boarded, proceeding down our water labyrinth into the Dead River, which was distant from this about three-quarters of a mile. Still continued to rain exceeding hard. I had almost forgot to mention the sufferings of a poor ox who had continued to march with us through all our difficulty to this day. He was drove by two men whose business it was to get him along as fast as the army marched. That whenever we came to a pond or lake he was drove round it. Rivers and small streams he swam and forded without any difficulty. Being in the front of the army, he was ordered to fall a victim two miles up the Dead River, and each man to receive a pound as they passed. This was a very agreeable repast, as we had been principally upon salt [pork] for twelve days, and that was scanty. . . .

Sunday, 22nd. We were in motion this morning by light. Several of our batteaux were now under water almost out of sight, in consequence of the rivers rising. From a Dead river it had now become live enough. The rise of the water in this storm was computed at 10 feet. This sudden alteration in the river not only impeded our water carriage, but rendered the marching of the party by land of the utmost difficulty, as the river was no longer confined to her banks, but extended in many low flat places, a mile or more each way upon the upland. Added to this, all the small rivulets (and they were not a few) were swelled up to an enormous size, as obliged the land party to trace them up for many miles till a narrow part offered, and then could only cross by felling large trees over them. . . .

Tuesday, 24th. Approaching necessity now obliged us to double our diligence. Three miles only had we proceeded ere we came to a troublesome water-fall in the river, distant half a mile. Not more than the last mentioned distance before we were brought up by another, distance the same. As the number of falls increased, the water consequently became more rapid. The heights of land upon each side of the river which had hitherto been inconsiderable, now became prodigiously mountainous, closing as it were up the river with an aspect of immense height. The river was now become very narrow, and such a horrid current as rendered it impossible to proceed in any other method than by hauling the batteaux up by the bushes, painters, &c. Here we met with several boats returning loaded with invalids, and lamentable stories of the inaccessibleness of the river, and the impracticability of any further progress into the country. Among which was Mr. Jackson, . . . complaining of the gout most severely, joined to all the terrors of the approaching famine. I was now exhorted in the most pathetic terms to return, on pain of famishing upon contrary conduct, and the army were all returning except a few who were many miles forward with Colonel Arnold. However his elocution did not prevail; I therefore bid him adieu and proceeded. Not far had I proceeded before I discovered several wrecks of batteaux belonging to the front division of riflemen, &c., with an increased velocity of the water. A direful, howling wilderness not describable. With much labour and difficulty I arrived with the principal part of my baggage (leaving the batteaux made fast) to the encampment. Two miles from thence I met . . . Colonel Green's division, &c., waiting for the remainder of the army to come up, that they might get some provisions ere they advanced any further. Upon enquiry, I found them almost destitute of any eatable whatever, except a few *candles*, which were used for supper, breakfast the next morning, by boiling them in water gruel, &c.

Wednesday, 25th. Every prospect of distress now came thundering on with two-fold rapidity. A storm of snow had covered the ground of nigh six inches deep, attended with very severe weather. We now waited in anxious expectation for Colonel Enos' division to come up, in order that we might have a recruit of provisions ere we could start off the ground. . . . They accordingly came up before noon, when a council of war was ordered. Here sat a number of grimacers—melancholy aspects who had been preaching to their men the doctrine of impenetrability and non-perseverance. Colonel Enos in the chair. The matter was debated upon the expediency of proceeding on for Quebec. The party against going urged the impossibility, averring the whole provisions, when averaged, would not support the army five days. . . .

Expresses returned, but no word from Colonel Arnold as he was now in the advanced part of Morgan's division, equipped in the best manner to go in to the inhabitants as soon as possible. He carried no other stores except a small quantity of specie, attended with a good pilot in a British canoe, hands sufficient to carry everything over the various carrying places, and proceeded by water with great expedition. . . .

The officers who were for going forward, requested a division of the provisions, and it was necessary that they have a far greater quantity in proportion to the number of men, as the supposed distance that they had to go ere they arrived into the inhabitants was greater than what they had come after leaving the Kennebec inhabitants. To this the returning party (being predetermined) would not consent, alleging that they would either go back with what provisions they had, or if they must go forward they'd not impart any. Colonel Enos, though he voted for proceeding, yet he undoubtedly pre-engaged to the contrary, as every action demonstrated. To compel them to a just division, we were not in a situation, as being the weakest party. Expostulations and entreaties had hitherto been fruitless. Colonel Enos, who more immediately commanded the division of *returners*, was called upon to give positive orders for a small quantity, if no more. He replied that his men were out of his power, and that they had determined to keep their possessed quantity whether they went back or forward. They finally concluded to spare $2\frac{1}{2}$ barrels of flour, if determined to pursue our destination; adding that we never should be able to bring in any inhabitants. Thus circumstanced, we were left the alternative of accepting their small pittance and proceed, or return. The former was adopted, with a determined resolution to go through or die. Received it, put it on board of our boats, quit the few tents we were in possession of, with all other camp equipage, took each man to his duds on his back, bid them adieu, and away—passed the river, passed over falls and encamped. . . .

Monday, 30th. Cooking being very much out of fashion, we had little else to do than march as quick as light permitted. . . . We had not gone far before we came to a place about four feet deep, which we immediately forded, although much frozen on each side. This *Balneum Frigidium* served to exercise our motion in order to keep from freezing. . . . Nor were we possessed of any certainty that our course would bring us either to the lake or river, not knowing the point it lay from where we started. However we came to a resolution to continue it. In this state of uncertainty we wandered through hideous swamps and mountainous precipices, with the conjoint addition of cold, wet and hunger, not to mention our fatigue—with the terrible apprehension of famishing in this desert. The pretended pilot was not less frightened than many of the rest; added to that the severe execrations he received from the front of the army to the rear, made his office not a little disagreeable. Several of the men towards evening were ready to give up any thoughts of ever arriving at the desired haven. Hunger and fatigue had so much the ascendancy over many of the poor fellows, added to the despair of arrival, that some of them were left in the river, nor were heard of afterwards. . . .

Tuesday, 31st. The appearance of daylight roused us as usual, and we had advanced with all possible speed till about 11 o'clock, ere we saw the Chaudière river, which we last night imagined within a mile. Animated afresh with the sight of a stream . . . we proceeded with renewed vigour. . . . We now began to discover the wrecked batteaux of those who conducted the ammunition, &c. These were seven in number, who followed the seven mile stream into Chaudière lake, river, &c., and soon came to an encampment, where I found Captain Morgan and most of the boatmen who were wrecked upon a fall in the river, losing everything except their lives which they all saved by swimming, except one of Morgan's riflemen. This was the first man drowned in all the dangers we were exposed to, and the third [lost] by casualties, except some lost in the wilderness, the number unknown. . . .

Wednesday, Nov. 1st. Our greatest luxuries now consisted in a little water, stiffened with flour, in imitation of shoemaker's paste, which was christened with the name of Lillipu. Instead of the diarrhea, which tried our men most shockingly in the former part of our march, the reverse was now the complaint, which continued for many days. We had now arrived, as we thought, to almost the zenith of distress. Several had been entirely destitute of either meat or bread for many days. These chiefly consisted of those who devoured their provisions immediately, and a number who were in boats. The voracious disposition many of us had now arrived at, rendered almost anything admissable. Clean and unclean were forms now little in use. In company was a poor dog [who had] hitherto lived through all the tribulations, became a prey for the sustenance of the assassinators. This poor animal was instantly devoured without leaving any vestige of the sacrifice. Nor did the shaving soap, pomatum, and even lip salve, leather of their shoes, cartridge boxes, &c., share any better fate. . . .

Thursday, 2nd. Long ere this necessity had obliged us to dismiss all our camping equipage, excepting a small light tin kettle among a number; but nothing to cut our wood, &c. According to our strength and spirits, we were scattered up and down the river at the distance of perhaps twenty miles. Not more than eight miles had we marched, when a vision of horned cattle, four footed beasts, &c., rode and drove by animals resembling Plato's two footed featherless ones. Upon a nigher approach our vision proved real! Exclamations of joy. Echoes of gladness resounded from front to rear! with a *Te Deum*. Three horned cattle, two horses, eighteen Canadians and one American. A heifer was chosen as victim to our wants; slain and divided accordingly. Each man was restricted to one pound of beef. Soon arrived two more Canadians in canoes, ladened with a coarse kind of meal, mutton, tobacco, &c. Each man drew likewise a pint of this provender. The mutton was destined for the sick. They proceeded up the river in order to the rear's partaking of the same benediction. We sat down, eat our rations, blessed our stars, and thought it luxury. Upon a general computation we marched from 20 to 30 miles per day. Twenty miles only from this to the settlements. . . .

Friday, 3rd. Last night's lodging was nature's bed without any covering. Every moment expecting to bring the inhabitants in view. Forded a very considerable river, emptying itself into the Chaudière. . . . The politeness and civility with which the poor Canadian peasants received us, added to our joy when we were conducted to the place of rendezvous, and served out firkin butter and hot bread, which we attacked with great spirit. This place is called Sartigan, naturally excellent soil, beautifully situated. Inhabited with part Canadian French, the other natives. . . .

Sartigan, Saturday, 4th. The five miles march last evening brought us to the Colonel's quarters, and this morning the savages assembled in *statu quo*, and waited on the Colonel to know our reasons for coming among them in a hostile manner, pretending they were unacquainted with our intentions. . . . In the assembly the savages were prepared with an interpreter. They addressed the Colonel in great pomp, and one of their chiefs delivered an oration with all the air and gesture of an accomplished orator.

After this being explained or translated, the Colonel returned the following answer. "Friends and brethren:—I feel myself very happy in meeting with so many of my brethren from the different quarters of the great country, and more so as I find we meet as friends, and that we are equally concerned with this expedition. Brethren, we are the children of those people who have now taken up the hatchet against us. More than one hundred years ago, we were all as one family. We then differed in our religion, and came over to this great country by consent of our king. Our fathers bought lands of the savages, and have grown a great people. Even as the stars in the sky. We have planted the ground, and by our labour grown rich. Now a new king and his wicked great men want to take our lands and money without our consent. This we think unjust, and all our great men from the river St. Lawrence to the Mississippi, met together in Philadelphia, where they all talked together, and sent a prayer to the king, that they would be brothers and fight for him, but would not give up their lands and money. The king would not hear our prayer, but sent a great army to Boston and endeavoured to set our brethren against us in Canada. The king's army at Boston came into the fields and houses, killed a great many women and children while they were peaceably at work. The Bostonians sent to their brethren in the country, and they came in unto their relief, and in six days raised an army of fifty thousand and drove the king's troops on board their ships, killed and wounded fifteen hundred of their men. Since that they durst not come out of Boston. Now we hear the French and Indians have sent to us, that the king's troops oppress them and make them pay a great price for their rum, &c.; press them to take up arms against the Bostonians, their brethren, who have done them no hurt. By the desire of the French and Indians, our brothers, we have come to their assistance with an intent to drive out the king's soldiers; when drove off we will return to our own country, and leave this to the peaceable enjoyment of its proper inhabitants. Now if the Indians, our brethren, will join us, we will be very much obliged to them, and will give them one Portuguese ["Johannes"] per month, two dollars bounty, and find them their provisions, and they at liberty to *chuse* their own officers."

This declaration had the desired effect, about fifty of them embodied according to agreement, took their canoes and proceeded. From our last lodgings hired a peasant, and proceeded down the river in a canoe five miles to a victualling house or other place of rendezvous. This village, St. Joseph's, made a further agreement, and continued down the river about four miles further, as we found nothing agreeable since our arrival, except one quart of New England rum (if that was to be allowed so), for which I paid one hard dollar. We were making enquiry at every likely stage, for this purpose visited an old peasant's house, where was a merry old woman at her loom, and two or three fine young girls. They were exceedingly rejoiced with our company. Bought some eggs, rum, sugar, sweetmeats, &c., where we made ourselves very happy. Upon the old woman being acquainted from whence we came, immediately fell singing and dancing "Yankee Doodle" with the greatest air of good humour. After making the old woman satisfied for her kickshaws, saluted her for her civilities, &c., marched. . . .

Tuesday, 7th. Water carriage now failing, was either obliged to foot pad it, or hire a horse—chose the latter. Chaplain Spring hired another in the same village, for which we were to pay three hard dollars. . . . In lieu of a saddle, we had an old piece of cushion, across which was a rope, which served as stirrups. Arrived within four leagues of Quebec. Terrible road, mud and mire to the horse's belly.

Wednesday, 8th. Were within four leagues of Quebec this morning, all possible dispatch was used to arrive ere the enemy got any reinforcements of either men or provisions. Arrived at Point Levi 11 o'clock A.M. Snow over shoes. In open sight of the enemy nought but the river divided us. Few of the army arrived this day. Provisions buying up. Canadian mechanics at work making scaling ladders, lannuts, &c., as many of the men being destitute of shoes, as fast as the beefs were killed, the hides were made into savage shoes. Nothing of great moment while we lay there. We are daily preparing to cross the river St. Lawrence. The enemy had destroyed all the boats, canoes, &c., for many miles up and down the river, upon the side we were ere our arrival. The confusion in Quebec was very great. But if we had been in a situation to have crossed the river immediately upon our arrival, they would have fallen an easy prey. Our army daily coming up, our preparations for crossing, the enemy's for repelling us, were the chief occurrences for this four days past.

Fate was to deal these intrepid marchers a cruel blow. Squatting down before Quebec, they conducted a most ingenious siege, constructing fortifications of snow and ice. No less courageous was the defense conducted by General Guy Carleton. Montgomery joined forces with Arnold on December 27, and their force of around 800 men paraded and made threats, but did not dare attack the citadel of Quebec. But an assault must be made before the first of the year, for then expiring enlistments would thin the American force. The strategy was to wait until a heavy snow would blanket their movements. Snow fell on the last day of the year, and so began the abortive effort that cost Montgomery his life and Arnold a wounded leg. George Morison, of Captain William Hendrick's company of Pennsylvania riflemen, described the attack in elegant prose.

The scaling ladders that had been left at the other side of the river were brought over. Our arms were examined and put in the best order. . . .

On the 27th, in the evening, the whole army capable of bearing arms assembled according to orders and were on the point of marching to battle, but the order was countermanded. On the 30th, orders were issued to parade at 2 o'clock the next morning. Accordingly on the 31st we were under arms at the time appointed. The plan of attacks is as follows:—The General to attack by Cape Diamond at the south end of the town, at the head of 200 men. Colonel Arnold to attack through the suburbs of St. Roche at the head of 360 men, including the riflemen commanded by Captains Morgan, Hendricks and Smith, together with a piece of artillery. Colonel Livingston and Major Brown at the head of 160 Canadians and Massachusetts troops to make a false attack near St. John's gate. This was the central division, and were to let off the rockets as signals for the general attack.

All things being in readiness, each division moves on towards the town, impatient to commence the assault. The morning is very stormy, which hinders the enemy from seeing our movements. The snow is very deep, which increases momently by the snow that is falling. The piece of artillery on a sled cannot be got along and is left behind. All eyes are now directed to the place from whence the rockets are to ascend; they are let off precisely at 5 o'clock—instantly the enemy beat to arms, for when they saw the signals they conjectured that ill was intended them.

Our advance party, consisting of thirty men, impetuously rush on and attack a battery on a wharf. Captain Morgan, being in front, advances to their aid, followed by Captain Hendricks. We fire into the portholes with our rifles with such effect that the enemy cannot discharge a single cannon—save one on our approach that did no damage. Perhaps there is no similar instance in modern warfare of a battery being silenced by a few riflemen. Several discharges of musketry are now made upon us from the houses and other unexpected places. Colonel Arnold receives a bad wound in his leg, and is carried to the hospital. We now scale the battery with our ladders, led on by the intrepid Morgan and our brave captain. This bold act so confounds the guard that thirty of them instantly surrender and are immediately secured. This affair occupies us but about twenty minutes—one killed and six or seven wounded.

During this combat, the main body now commanded by Major Meigs approaches, being much interrupted by the deepness of the snow and an incessant fire of the enemy from walls and houses, which killed and wounded several without our people being able to annoy them in the least. They enter the town at our right, just as we had finished our task—we gave them a cheer and they returned it. We are reinforced with a small party, then push on through alleys to the next battery, rush close up to it unobserved, fire in at the portholes, wound some of the guards, and deter them from using their cannon. By keeping close to the battery, we not only stop the mouths of the artillery, but prevent the musketry from injuring us, a considerable body of whom we now perceive behind the battery ready to salute us as we mount the walls. Our officers deem it proper to suspend scaling the wall until the main body comes up, at whose delay we are astonished. In the mean time, we challenge the enemy to come out into the open space and fight us which, however, they do not choose to accept. Some cowards fire upon us from the windows of houses, which only serves to make us laugh. They point out the muzzles of their guns, screening themselves behind the window frames, and fire at random; the bullets seldom coming within perches of us—some of us amuse ourselves by emptying our rifles in at these windows.

We have heard for some time, heavy discharges of musketry and artillery in different parts of town:—we are elated with this music and shout—"Quebec is ours." We again invite the enemy to come out from behind their covert and try our rifles, which we offer to them for sale at a very low rate. They, however, decline the offer, observing that they shortly expect them for nothing. Our main body now appears, having taken a wrong route through narrow and crooked streets, exposed to a cowardly fire from houses. We heartily cheer each other, and now prepare to storm the battery. The ladders are laid to the wall. Our gallant officers are mounting, followed by several men, when a furious discharge of musketry is let loose upon us from behind houses. In an instant we are assailed from different quarters with a deadly fire. We now find it impossible to force the battery or guard the portholes any longer. We rush on to every part, rouse the enemy from their coverts, and force a body of them to an open fight; some of our riflemen take to the houses and do considerable execution. We are now attacked by thrice our number.

The battle becomes hot, and is much scattered; but we distinguish each other by hemlock sprigs previously placed in our hats. All our officers act most gallantly. Betwixt every peal the awful voice of Morgan is heard, whose gigantic stature and terrible appearance carries dismay among the foe wherever he comes. My brave captain is sublimated with the most exalted courage—he seems to be all soul, and moves as though he did not touch the earth. But whilst he is most heroically animating us with his voice and example, a ball flies into his breast and lays him dead upon the spot. We have no time to weep. We are now attacked in our rear. The enemy increases momently; they call out to us to surrender, but we surrender them our bullets and retreat to the first battery. Here we maintain ourselves until 10 o'clock when, surrounded on every side, many of our officers and men slain, and no hopes of escape, we are reluctantly compelled to surrender ourselves prisoners of war after having fought manfully for more than three hours.

The division under the General [Montgomery] was also unsuccessful. He, together with several officers and eleven men, were killed in the beginning of the attack, and the rest retreated. He was interred with military honors by order of General Carleton. It was in consequence of the failure of this division, that the enemy turned their whole force upon us. There were about 100 killed and wounded, and nearly 400 taken prisoners.

After we were taken prisoners, we were taken to an old French College, our officers were taken from amongst us. Some rum and a biscuit apiece was given us. We were kindly treated both by General Carleton and the people of the town until one Deway was placed over us, who sold the provisions allowed us for his own profit. But the Lord of Hosts soon delivered us out of his hands, for he was taken with the smallpox which swept him off the face of this earth. On the 31st of March, a plot was laid amongst us to free ourselves. The plan was as follows: we made officers of our sergeants, and formed ourselves into three divisions. The first division was to take the guard that stood over us. The second was to secure the guard at St. John's gate. The third, among whom was the artillery men, was to seize the cannon and turn them upon the town. Then we procured a person to go over to the army under Colonel Arnold now blockading [the] place and notify the Colonel of the plot and the signals to be used. But the scoundrel that knew of it informed the barrack master. The consequence was that the sergeants were all put in irons, seven to a bolt, and the privates handcuffed two and two together.

Here we lay wretched, ragged, and covered with vermin, until the 8th of May when Colonel Arnold retreated up the river. Then General Carleton ordered our irons to be knocked off, and on the 6th of June his Excellency came into the jail and observed to us, that if he could depend upon our word of honor to behave peaceably and not to take up arms in future against His Majesty, he would engage to send us home. He then presented a paper purporting his request, which we all signed. . . .

Benedict Arnold, hobbling about on his wounded leg, vowed that he would never leave Quebec "until first I enter it in triumph." But in the spring the ice in the St. Lawrence began to break up. On May 6, 1776, the first vessel of a relief force beat her way upstream. The rebels scampered back to Montreal. There were skirmishes, not to be dignified by the name of battles, that drove them back. First Montreal, then Chambly, St. John's, and finally their flight down Lake Champlain to refuge at Ticonderoga. Carleton, moving cautiously, stopped at St.

John's to assemble the prefabricated boats that had been sent from England. Arnold hammered together from green timber a ragged fleet of something resembling ships. Then, in the battle of Valcour Bay on Lake Champlain, the ragamuffin fleet of the Americans was destroyed. But Carleton, because of the season, turned back to Canada and the comfort of winter quarters. The first rebel attempt to draw Canada into the rebellion as a fourteenth colony had seen incomparable hardships and sufferings, bravery and heroism, fanfaronade and braggadocio, yet had ended in failure and the first setback for the Americans. For the first time the Lord seemed to have deserted them against the hosts of the English Pharaoh.

A Declaration of Independence

NEW YORK was a military prize. With its harbor, and the Hudson River stretching northward into the hinterland, the city posed a key point in both American and British considerations. Even before the British evacuation of Boston, Washington had started troops marching for New York. And shortly after the last British sail had dropped below the Boston horizon, the main American force had marched to that city. Strutting in their invincibility, the soldiers were reluctant to accept discipline and irritated by the restrictions of martial life. Rum, women, and the dreams of going home played about the inner reaches of their minds. Women were there in plenty—Solomon Nash noted that "Several limbs and heads of men were found at the holy ground which was supposed to be killed by the whores."

General Nathanael Greene, in command of the brigade stationed on Long Island near a village called Brooklyn, found it necessary upon several occasions to reprimand his soldiers in General Orders.

Complaint having been made by the inhabitants situated near the mill pond, that some of the soldiers come there to go into swimming in the open view of the women & that they come out of the water & run to the houses naked with a design to insult & wound the modesty of female decency. 'Tis with concern that the General finds himself under the disagreeable necessity of expressing his disapprobation of such a beastly conduct. Whoever has been so void of shame as to act an infamous part, let them veil their past disgrace by their future good behavior, for they may depend upon it, any new instances of such scandalous conduct will be punished with the utmost severity.

This is not meant to prohibit the troops from going into the water to bathe, but from going in, in improper places. Where is the modesty, virtue & sobriety of the New England people for which they have been remarkable? Is a good character as a soldier of no value when it is esteemed so great a blessing as a citizen? . . . The General flatters himself, notwithstanding the complaints that have been made, the offenders are but few, but he is determined those few shall not have it in their power to bring disgrace upon the whole brigade. . . .

Many complaints are made of the troops stealing the people's watermelons in & about the camp. Such practices, if continued, will be punished in the most exemplary manner. The General desires the officers to bring every offender to justice. . . .

Even the execution on June 28, 1776, of Thomas Hickey, a member of Washington's Life Guards, convicted of a plot to assassinate the General, was used to emphasize the advantages of a virtuous life.

The unhappy fate of Thomas Hickey, executed this day for mutiny, sedition and treachery, the General hopes will be a warning to every soldier in the army, to avoid those crimes and all others, so disgraceful to the conduct of a soldier and pernicious to his country whose pay he receives and bread he eats. And in order to avoid those crimes, the most certain method is to keep out of the temptation of them, and particularly to avoid lewd women, who by the dying confession of this poor criminal, first led him into practices which ended in an untimely and ignominious death.

Meanwhile, the politicians in the Continental Congress in Philadelphia were considering a more drastic measure—a complete break with the mother country. During the first year of the rebellion, "Independence" had been a word to be whispered, never shouted, in legislative halls. These were cautious men, many of whom realized the advantages to be gained by a continued tie with England. Even after George III, on August 23, 1775, had formally declared the colonies to be in a state of rebellion, the Pennsylvania Assembly had instructed its delegates to the Congress to "dissent and utterly reject any propositions, should such be made, that may cause or lead to a separation from our mother country." But there had been an undercurrent of sentiment carefully masked from the public eye. Thomas Gage had noted, "I am convinced that the Promoters of this Rebellion have no real Desire of Peace, unless they have a Carte Blanche." And Lord Dartmouth had been warned through intelligence channels that if the British employed foreign mercenary soldiers, the colonists would "get up an Independency." And German mercenaries had been hired. Early in January,

1776, Nathanael Greene, ex-Quaker turned soldier, and part-time philosopher, had written: "Permit me, then, to recommend from the sincerity of my heart, ready at all times to bleed in my country's cause a declaration of independence; and call upon the world, and the great God who governs it, to witness the necessity, propriety, and rectitude thereof. . . ."

Still no one dared shout the word. It took a disreputable, intemperate, and discontented son of a Quaker corset maker to light the torch of the independence movement. Tom Paine, who had arrived in the colonies from England in 1774, cut a wide swath through the timidity of the uncertain with his anonymous pamphlet, suggestively entitled Common Sense, which appeared in January, 1776. Marshaling disputations that appealed to the economic, political, and religious prejudices, Paine's facile pen, in cogent argument, subtly shifted the blame for oppression from Parliament to that "royal brute," George III. This 55-page pamphlet, its language that of the common man, quickly sold 120,000 copies.

They had been good words, words of fire, a tocsin of rebellion, calculated to stir up a lethargic people. Thomas Paine, despite his penchant for flaming rhetoric, could not be termed an original thinker; rather his forte lay in taking what others had said, tying their words into a neat bundle that could be easily handled and digested by the masses. Yet he had plowed new ground in his public disrespect for the King and in his flouting of the English constitution. To some, such as John Adams, Common Sense was little more than "a poor, ignorant, malicious, short-sighted, crapulous mass"; he often referred to Tom Paine as "that insolent blasphemer of things sacred, and transcendant libeller of all that is sacred." Still, before he knew the author of the pamphlet, he wrote:

You ask what is thought of *Common Sense*. Sensible men think there are some whims, some sophisms, some artful addresses to super-stitious notions, some keen attempts upon the passions in the pamphlet. But all agree, there is a great deal of good sense delivered in clear, simple, concise, and nervous style. His sentiments of the abilities of America, and of the difficulty of a reconciliation with Great Britain, are generally approved. But his notions and plans of continental government are not much applauded. Indeed, this writer has a better hand in pulling down than building. It has been very generally propagated through the continent that I wrote this pamphlet. But although I could not have written anything in so manly and striking a style, I flatter myself I should have made a more respectable figure as an architect, if I had undertaken such a work. This writer seems to have very inadequate ideas of what is proper and necessary to be done in order to form constitutions for single colonies, as well as a great model of union for the whole.

The spark had been fanned. On April 12, 1776, the Provincial Congress of North Carolina instructed its delegates to the Continental Congress "to concur with the Delegates of the other Colonies in declaring Independency...." And on May 15, the Virginia Convention instructed its representatives to "propose" independence. As a result, Richard Henry Lee, his hand swathed in a black handkerchief to conceal the scars of an injury, rose in the Congress in Philadelphia and set forth these words:

RESOLVED, That these United Colonies are, and of a right ought to be, free and independent States, that they are absolved from all allegiance to the British Crown, and that all political connection between them and the State of Great Britain is, and ought to be totally dissolved.

That it is expedient forthwith to take the most effectual measures for forming foreign Alliances.

That a plan of confederation be prepared and transmitted to the respective Colonies for their consideration and approbation.

It was a bold step, this brash resolution designed to strip the colonies from the mother country. Indecision marked the debates prior to naming a committee to draft a formal declaration of independence. Thomas Jefferson of Virginia, Benjamin Franklin of Pennsylvania, John Adams of Massachusetts, Robert Livingston of New York, and Roger Sherman of Connecticut were named. Adams explained why Jefferson was selected to draw up the Declaration of Independence.

You inquire why so young a man as Mr. Jefferson was placed at the head of the committee for preparing a Declaration of Independence? I answer: It was the Frankfort advice* to place Virginia at the head

* A meeting of the Massachusetts and Pennsylvania delegations at Frankfort at which the Pennsylvanians urged the Massachusetts delegates to remain in the background and allow Virginia to take the lead.

of everything. Mr. Richard Henry Lee might be gone to Virginia, to his sick family, for aught I know, but that was not the reason for Mr. Jefferson's appointment. There were three committees appointed at the same time, one for the Declaration of Independence, another for preparing the Articles of Confederation, and another for preparing a treaty to be proposed to France. Mr. Lee was chosen for the Committee of Confederation, and it was not thought convenient that the same person should be upon both. Mr. Jefferson came into Congress in June, 1775, and brought with him a reputation for literature, science, and a happy talent of composition. Writings of his were handed about, remarkable for the peculiar felicity of expression. Though a silent member in Congress, he was so prompt, frank, explicit and decisive upon committees and in conversation—not even Samuel Adams was more so—that he soon seized upon my heart; and upon this occasion I gave him my vote, and did all in my power to procure the votes of others. I think he had one more vote than any others and that placed him at the head of the committee. I had the next highest number, and that placed me the second. The committee met, discussed the subject, and then appointed Mr. Jefferson and me to make the draught, I suppose because we were the first two on the list.

The sub-committee met. Jefferson proposed to me to make the draught.

I said, "I will not."

"You should do it."

"Oh! No."

"Why will you not? You ought to do it."

"I will not."

"Why?"

"Reason enough."

"What can be your reasons?"

"Reason first—You are a Virginian, and a Virginian ought to appear at the head of this business. Reason second—I am obnoxious, suspected and unpopular. You are very much otherwise. Reason third—you can write ten times better than I can."

"Well," said Jefferson, "if you are decided, I will do as well as I can."

"Very well. When you have drawn it up we will have a meeting."

A meeting we accordingly had, and conned the paper over. I was delighted with its high tone and the flights of oratory with which it abounded, especially that concerning Negro slavery, which, though I knew his Southern brethren would never suffer to pass in Congress, I certainly never would oppose. There were other expressions which I would not have inserted, if I had drawn it up, particularly that which called the King tyrant. I thought this too personal; for I never believed George to be a tyrant in disposition and in nature; I always believed him to be deceived by his courtiers on both sides of the Atlantic, and, in his official capacity only, cruel. I thought the expression too passionate, and too much like scolding, for so grave and solemn a document; but as Franklin and Sherman were to inspect it afterwards, I thought it would not become me to strike it out. I consented to report it, and do not now remember that I made or suggested a single alteration.

We reported it to the committee of five. It was read, and I do not remember that Franklin or Sherman criticized any thing. We were all in haste. Congress was impatient, and the instrument was reported, as I believe, in Jefferson's handwriting, as he first drew it. Congress cut off about a quarter of it, as I expected they would; but they obliterated some of the best of it, and left all that was exceptionable, if anything in it was. I long wondered that the original draught has not been published. I suppose the reason is the vehement philippic against Negro slavery.

As you justly observe, there is not an idea in it but what had been hackneyed in Congress for two years before. The substance of it is contained in the declaration of rights and the violations of those rights, in the Journals of Congress, in 1774. . . .

Many found the document difficult to accept. Mr. Jefferson's declaration, its numerous "He has" clauses shifting the blame for the break onto the shoulders of George III, and the pronouncement that all men were endowed by their Creator with "Life, Liberty and the pursuit of Happiness" were neither apt nor suitable to the end in view. Sentence by sentence it was debated, with some of the more objectionable phraseology, including the polemics against slavery and the slave trade, stricken. There were other deletions, including any impression of "censure upon the English peoples." On July 2, a day that John Adams felt "will be the most memorable epocha in the history of America," the Continental Congress acted on Richard Henry Lee's "resolution respecting independency." Caesar Rodney, even then racked with the misery of a fatal malady, rode through the night "tho' detained by thunder and rain" to break the deadlock in the Delaware delegation, and *"give my voice in the matter of Independence."* On July 4, the Declaration was adopted, although as Thomas McKean was to explain to Rodney's nephew, it was not signed until much later.

On Monday, the 1st of July, the question was taken in the committee of the whole, when the State of Pennsylvania (represented by the seven gentlemen then present) voted against it. Delaware (having then only two representatives present) was divided; all the other states voted in favor of it. Whereupon, without delay, I sent an express (at my private expense) for your honored uncle, Caesar Rodney, Esq., the remaining member for Delaware, whom I met at the State House door, in his boots and spurs, as the members were assembling. After a friendly salutation (without a word on the business), we went into the Hall of Congress together, and found we were among the latest. Proceedings immediately commenced, and after a few minutes the great question was put. When the vote for Delaware was called, your uncle arose and said, "As I believe the voice of my constituents, and of all sensible and honest men is in favor of Independence, and my own judgment concurs with them, I vote for Independence," or in words to the same effect. The State of Pennsylvania . . . (there being only five members present, Messrs. Dickinson and Morris, who had been in the committee of the whole, voted against Independence, were absent), voted for it, three to two—Messrs. Willing and Humphrey in the negative. Unanimity in the thirteen states, an all-important point on so great an occasion, was thus obtained; the dissension of a single state might have produced very dangerous consequences.

Now, that I am on this subject, I will tell you some truths not generally known. In the printed public journal of Congress for 1776, vol. 2, it would appear that the Declaration of Independence was signed on the 4th of July by the members, whose names are there inserted, but the fact is not so, for no person signed it on that day, nor for many days after, and among the names subscribed, one was against it Mr. Read, and seven were not in Congress on that day, namely Messrs. Morris, Rush, Clymer, Smith, Taylor and Ross, of Pennsylvania, and Mr. Thornton of New Hampshire; nor were the six gentlemen last named at that time members; the five for Pennsylvania were appointed delegates by the convention of that state on the 20th of July, and Mr. Thornton entered Congress for the first time on the 4th of November following. The names of Henry Wisner of New York and Thomas McKean of Delaware are not printed as subscribers, though both were present and voted for Independence.

Here false colors are certainly hung out; there is culpability somewhere. What I can offer as an apology or explanation is, that on the 4th of July, 1776, the Declaration of Independence was ordered to be engrossed on parchment and then to be signed. And I have been told, that a resolve had passed a few days after, and was entered in the *secret* journal, that no person should have a seat in Congress during that year, until he should have signed the Declaration, in order (as I have been given to understand) to prevent traitors or spies from worming themselves against us. . . .

The public announcement of the Declaration of Independence was greeted with demonstrations of joy. Bells tolled all the day long, and salutes wasted badly needed gunpowder. In New York, the soldiers let off steam in a fashion calculated to ease boisterous spirits. On Broadway, near the Battery, was a gilded equestrian statue of George III. Isaac Bangs was one of those who thought of it as a beautiful and shining target.

Last night the statue in the Bowling Green representing George Ghwelps, alias George Rex, was pulled down by the populace. In it were 4,000 pounds of lead, and a man undertook to take 10 ozs. of gold from the superfices, as both man & horse were covered with gold leaf. The lead, we hear, is to be run up into musket balls for the use of the Yankies, when it is hoped that the emanations from the leaden George will make as deep impressions in the bodies of some of his redcoated and Tory subjects, and that they will do the same execution in poisoning and destroying them as the superabundant emanations of the folly and pretended goodness of the real George, have made upon their minds, which have, effectually poisoned and destroyed their souls, that they are not worthy to be ranked with any beings who have any pretensions to the principles of virtue & justice, but would to God that the unhappy contest might be ended, without putting us to the disagreeable necessity of sending them to dwell with those beings, for the company of whom alone their tempers and dispositions are now suitable.

But even with the gallons of rum and Madeira consumed in countless toasts that ranged from sublime and patriotic expressions to the ridiculous "Perpetual itching without the benefit of scratching to the Enemies of America," there were those who reflected that perhaps independence was not the most expedient step to be taken at this time. Among them was Lieutenant Alexander Graydon.

The Declaration is variously relished here, some approving, others condemning it. For my own part, I have not the least objection did I know my rulers and the form of government. Innovations are always dangerous, particularly here, where the populace have so great an ascendancy, and popular governments I could never approve of. However, I acquiesce in the measure as it becomes daily more necessary, altho' I am of opinion that delaying it awhile longer would have had no bad tendency. On the contrary, it would still keep the door open for reconciliation, convince the world of our reluctance to embrace it, and increase our friends on t'other side of the water. But the greatest danger is that subtle, designing knaves, or weak, insignificant block heads may take the lead in public affairs. This they have already done, and much I fear, that such will be our rulers. But perhaps you will tell me that "of the evils, we must chuse the least," either submit to Britain or declare Independency—Granted! But there is no reason that we should not have put it off as long as possible. However, the matter is now settled and our salvation depends upon supporting measures.

The British were even then dropping anchor in New York harbor. Ambrose Serle, civilian secretary to Admiral Lord Richard Howe, sniffed with contempt at the puffings of these rustics in their pompous documents.

The Congress have, at length, thought it convenient to throw off the mask. Their Declaration of the 4th of July, while it avows their right to Independence, is founded upon such reasons only, as proves that Independence has been their object from the beginning. A more impudent, false and atrocious proclamation was never fabricated by the hands of man. Hitherto, they have thrown all the blame and insult upon the Parliament and ministry: now they have the audacity to calumniate the King and the people of Great Britain. 'Tis impossible to read this paper, without horror at the daring hypocrisy of these men, who call GOD to witness the uprightness of their proceedings, nor without indignation at the low and scurrilous pretenses by which they attempt to justify themselves. Surely, Providence will honor its own truth and justice upon this occasion and, as they have made an appeal to it for success, reward them after their own deservings.

In England, the Declaration became a point of argument in the continuing struggle between the Whigs and the Parliamentary friends of George III. John Wilkes, long a symbol of liberty for the Americans, defended the separation on the floor of the House of Commons, and swore that the King's ministers had "drove the Americans into their present state of Independency." And when one of the King's friends spoke disparagingly of Jefferson's rhetoric, Wilkes' elegant retort was published in American newspapers.

An honorable gentleman near me attacks the American declaration of independency, in a very peculiar manner, as a wretched composition, very ill written, drawn up with a view to captivate the people. That, sir, is the very reason why I approve it most as a composition, as well as a wise political measure, for the people are to decide this great controversy. If they are captivated by it, the end is obtained The polished periods, the harmonious, happy expressions, with all the grace, ease and elegance of a beautiful diction, which we chiefly admire, captivate the people of America very little. But manly sense they relish, even in the most awkward and uncouth dress of language. Whatever composition produces the effect you intend in the most forcible manner, is, in my opinion, the best, and that mode should always be pursued. It has the most merit, as well as success, on the great theatre of the world, no less than on the stage, whether you mean to inspire, pity, terror, or any other passion.

Edward Gibbon, well versed in the fall of empires, noted that the Americans "have now crossed the Rubicon. . . ." The door to reconciliation had been insolently slammed shut in Britain's face.

New York

*E**VEN as the American soldiers celebrated the Declaration of Independence in riotous fashion, British warships and transports were plowing their way past Sandy Hook and heaving to off Staten Island. By the middle of July the largest fleet ever seen in American waters had assembled, and was beginning to land soldiers on Staten Island. And when the* Phoenix *and the* Rose *beat their way up the Hudson past American shore batteries, Washington discovered that his army was still a stranger to discipline. He voiced his displeasure in General Orders on July 13.*

The General was sorry to observe yesterday that many of the officers and a number of the men instead of attending to their duty at the beat of the drum, continued along the banks of the North River, gazing at the ships; such unsoldierly conduct must grieve every good officer, and give the enemy a *mean* opinion of the army, as nothing shows the brave and good soldier more than in the case of alarms, coolly and calmly repairing to his post and there waiting his orders, whereas a weak curiosity at such a time makes a man look mean and contemptible.

Washington was soon to feel slighted by the British refusal to recognize his position. General William Howe and his brother, Admiral Lord Richard Howe, had been appointed peace commissioners to the rebels. Henry Knox witnessed the first exchange on July 15.

Lord Howe sent a flag of truce up to the city. They came within about four miles of the city, and were met by some of Colonel Tupper's people, who detained them until his Excellency's pleasure should be known. Accordingly, Colonel [Joseph] Reed and myself went down in the barge to receive the message. When we came to

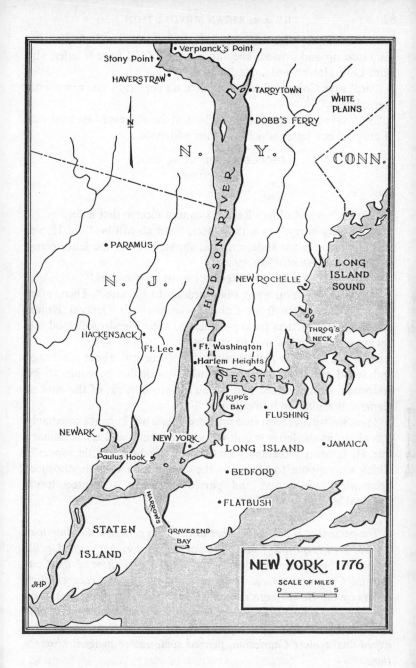

NEW YORK 1776

SCALE OF MILES
0   5

them, the officer, who was, I believe, captain of the *Eagle* man-of-war, rose up and bowed, keeping his hat off: "I have a letter, sir, from Lord Howe to Mr. Washington."

"Sir," says Colonel Reed, "we have no person in our army with that address."

"Sir," says the officer, "will you look at the address?" He took out of his pocket a letter which was thus addressed:

GEORGE WASHINGTON, ESQ.,

NEW YORK

HOWE

"No sir," says Colonel Reed, "I cannot receive that letter."

"I am very sorry," says the officer, "and so will be Lord Howe, that any error in the superscription should prevent the letter being received by *General Washington*."

"Why, sir," says Colonel Reed, "I must obey orders."

"Oh, yes, sir. You must obey orders, to be sure." Then, after giving him a letter from Colonel Campbell to General Howe, and some other letters from prisoners to their friends, we stood off, having saluted and bowed to each other.

After we had got a little way, the officer put about his barge and stood for us and asked by what particular he chose to be addressed. Colonel Reed said, "You are sensible, sir, of the rank of General Washington in our army?"

"Yes, sir, we are. I am sure my Lord Howe will lament exceedingly this affair, as the letter is quite of a civil nature, and not a military one. He laments exceedingly that he was not here a little sooner"; which we suppose to allude to the Declaration of Independence; upon which we bowed and parted in the most genteel terms imaginable.

The persistent Howe made other attempts to persuade the American general to accept the "Mr. Washington" letter, but ruffled pride refused to be shaken. A later meeting with a committee of the Continental Congress was equally futile in so far as any reconciliation efforts by the Howes were concerned. In the meantime, the British on Staten Island amused themselves in the manner of soldiers since time immemorial. Young Lord Rawdon, just returned from an abortive expedition against Charleston, penned some rather pungent observations.

The fair nymphs of this isle are in wonderful tribulation, as the fresh meat our men have got here has made them as riotous as satyrs. A girl cannot step into the bushes to pluck a rose without running the most imminent risk of being ravished, and they are so little accustomed to these vigorous methods that they don't bear them with the proper resignation, and of consequence we have the most entertaining courts-martial every day.

To the southward they behave much better in these cases, if I may judge from a woman who having been forced by seven of our men, made a complaint to me, "not of their usage," she said, "No, thank God, she despised that," but one of them having taken an old prayer book for which she had a particular affection. . . .

All the English troops are encamped, or in cantonment, upon this island, as healthy and spirited a body of men as ever took the field. Several transports with Highlanders have been taken by the rebel privateers; the rest are all arrived, and are so enraged against the Yankees for some insults offered to their captive comrades that I think the first corps of psalm-singers who come in the way of their broad swords will be in a very awkward situation. . . .

On August 21, taking advantage of a confusion caused by a violent thunderstorm, Howe landed his troops on Long Island unopposed. A Hessian officer at Flatbush voiced his annoyance with rebel warfare.

The rebels approached twice, fired howitzers and used grape and ball, so that all our artillery had to come up. At noon I slept a little while, and was waked by two cannon-balls which covered me with earth. The rebels have some very good marksmen, but some of them have wretched guns, and most of them shoot crooked. But they are clever at hunter's wiles. They climb trees, they crawl forward on their bellies for one hundred and fifty paces, shoot, and go as quickly back again. They make themselves shelters of boughs, etc. But today they are much put out by our green coats, for we don't let our fellows fire unless they can get good aim at a man, so that they dare not undertake anything more against us.

Had the Americans continued to utilize their "hunter's wiles," they might have fared better. Howe, remembering the red-coated bodies strewn on the slopes of Bunker Hill, now surprised Washington by executing a flanking movement. The American general made his mistake by trying to fight the British in the European manner. And for the British, the myth of the prowess of the American riflemen began to lose some of its former glamour. One Hessian colonel noted that "The greater part of the riflemen were pierced with the bayonet to the trees. These dreadful people ought rather to be pitied than feared; they always require a quarter of an hour's time to load a rifle, and in the meantime they feel the effects of our balls and bayonets." Washington's mistakes were soon brought home to him in a most graphic manner. One of his anonymous riflemen recorded his impressions that day.

Last Monday we were sent over to Long Island, and about midnight were alarmed by some of our scouting parties, who advised us that the enemy were coming up the Island with several field pieces. Upon which near 3,000 men were ordered out, chiefly of Marylanders and Pennsylvanians, to attack them on their march. About sunrise we came up with a large body of them. The Delaware and Maryland battalions made one part. Colonel Atlee with his battalion a little before us, had taken post in an orchard and behind a barn, and on the approach of the enemy, he gave them a very severe fire for a considerable time, till they were near surrounding him, when he retreated to the woods. The enemy then advanced to us, when Lord Stirling who commanded [us], immediately drew up in a line, and offered them battle in the true English taste. The British then advanced within about 300 yards of us, but when they perceived we stood their fire so coolly and resolutely, they declined coming any nearer, though treble our number.

In this situation we stood from sunrise till 12 o'clock, the enemy firing on us the chief part of the time, when the main body of the British, by a route we never dreamed of, had surrounded us, and driven within the lines, or scattered in the woods, all our men except the Delaware and Maryland battalions, who were standing at bay with double their number. Thus situated, we were ordered to attempt a retreat by fighting our way through the enemy, who posted themselves and nearly filled every road and field between us and our lines. We had not retreated a quarter of a mile, before we were fired on by an advanced party of the enemy, and those in the rear playing their artillery upon us.

Our men fought with more than Roman valor. We forced the advanced party which first attacked us to give way, through which opening we got a passage down to the wide of a marsh, seldom before waded over, which we passed, and then swam a narrow river, all the while exposed to the enemy's fire. Captains Ramsay's and Scott's companies were in front and sustained the first fire of the enemy, when hardly a man fell. The whole right wing of our battalion, thinking it impossible to march through the marsh, attempted to force their way through the woods where they, almost to a man, were killed or taken. The Maryland battalion has lost 259 men, amongst whom are twelve officers. . . . Who killed and who prisoners is yet uncertain. . . . 1,000 men missing in all. We took a few prisoners. Many of our officers lost their swords and guns.

Most of our generals on a high hill in the lines, viewed it with glasses as we were retreating, and saw the enemy we had to pass through, thought we could not. Many thought we would surrender in a body without firing. When we began to attack, General Washington wrung his hands and cried out, "Good God! what brave fellows I must this day lose!" Major Gist commanded the Maryland battalion. . . . The Major, Captain Ramsay and Lieutenant Plunkett were foremost and within 100 yards of the enemy's muzzles, when they were fired upon by the enemy, who were chiefly under cover of an orchard, save a few that showed themselves and pretended to give up, clubbing their firelocks till we came within forty yards, when they immediately blazed in our faces. They entirely overshot us, and killed some men away behind in the rear. I had the satisfaction of dropping one the first fire. I was so near I could not miss. I discharged my rifle seven times that day.

Although not actually enaged in the fighting, a fifteen-year-old private, Joseph Plumb Martin, steeled himself "to snuff a little gunpowder" when his Connecticut regiment was ordered across to Long Island in reserve.

The officers of the new levies wore cockades of different colors to distinguish them from the standing forces, as they were called; the field officers wore red, the captains white, and the subaltern officers green. While we were resting here our lieutenant colonel and major (our colonel not being with us) took their cockades from their hats; being asked the reason, the lieutenant colonel replied that he was willing to risk his life in the cause of his country, but unwilling to stand a particular mark for the enemy to fire at. He was a fine officer and a brave soldier.

We were soon called upon to fall in and proceed. We had not gone far, about half a mile, when I heard one of the rear ask another where his musket was. I looked round and saw one of the soldiers stemming off without his gun, having left it where we last halted; he was inspecting his side as if undetermined whether he had it or not, he then fell out of the ranks to go in search of it. One of the company, who had brought it on (wishing to see how far he would go before he missed it) gave it to him. . . .

We overtook a small party of artillery here, dragging a heavy twelve-pounder upon a field carriage, sinking halfway to the naves in the sandy soil. They plead hard for some of us to assist them to get off their piece; our officers, however, paid no attention to their entreaties, but pressed forward towards a creek, where a large body of Americans and British were engaged. By the time we arrived, the enemy had driven our men into the creek, or rather millpond (the tide being up), where such as could swim got across; those that could not swim, and could not procure anything to buoy them up, sunk. The British, having several fieldpieces stationed by a brick house, were pouring the canister and grape upon the Americans like a shower of hail. They would have doubtless have done more damage than they did, but for the twelve-pounder mentioned above; the men, having gotten it within sufficient distance to reach them, and opening a fire upon them, soon obliged them to shift their quarters. There was in this action a regiment of Maryland troops (volunteers), all young gentlemen. When they came out of the water and mud to us, looking like water rats, it was truly pitiful sight. Many of them were killed in the pond, and more were drowned. Some of us went into the water after the fall of the tide, and took out a number of corpses and a great many arms that were sunk in the pond and creek.

Because of Howe's reluctance to charge the last breastworks of the Americans, and because of a northeaster that blew in to dampen operations, Washington was able to pull his bedraggled troops back across the East River into New York.

While attempting to instill at least an element of discipline into an army that Henry Knox termed "only a receptacle for ragamuffins," Washington accepted the advice of his officers and began preparations to evacuate the city. The presence of the British fleet constituted a threat to which he could muster little defense. A young Yale graduate, David Bushnell, offered an expedient—only a straw—but it was grasped. Sergeant Ezra Lee, of the Connecticut Line, left an account of how he became the crew of Bushnell's American Turtle, *America's first submarine.*

Its shape was most like a round clam, but larger, and set up on its square side. It was high enough to stand in or sit as you had occasion, with a composition head [metal door plate] hanging on hinges. It had six glasses inserted in the head and made water tight, each the size of a half dollar piece, to admit light. In a clear day a person might see to read in three fathoms of water. The machine was steered by a rudder having a crooked tiller, which led in by your side through a water joint; then sitting on the seat, the navigator rows with one hand and steers with the other. It had two oars of about twelve inches in length, and four or five in width, shaped like the arms of a windmill which led also inside the water joints, in front of the person steering, and was worked by means of a wench (or crank), and with hand labour, the machine might be impelled at the rate of three knots an hour for a short time.

Seven hundred pounds of lead were fixed on the bottom for ballast, and two hundred weight of it was so contrived as to let it go in case the pumps choked, so that you could rise at the surface of the water. It was sunk by letting in water by a spring near the bottom, by placing your foot against which the water would rush in, and when sinking, take off your foot and it would cease to come in and you would sink no further; but if you had sunk too far, pump out water until you got the necessary depth. These pumps forced the water out of the bottom, one being on each side of you as you rowed. A pocket compass was fixed on the side, with a piece of bright wood on the north side, thus—and another on the east side, thus—to steer by while under water. Three round doors were cut in the head (each three inches diameter) to let in fresh air until you wished to sink, and then they were shut down and fastened. There was also a glass tube twelve inches long and one inch diameter, with a cork in it, with a piece of light wood fixed to it, and another piece at the bottom of the tube to tell the depth of descent; one inch rise in the cork in the tube gave about one fathom of water.

It had a screw that pierced through the top of the machine with a water joint which was so very sharp that it would enter wood with very little force, and this was turned with a wench or crank, and when entered fast in the bottom of the ship, the screw is then left, and the machine is disengaged by unscrewing another one inside that held the other. From the screw now fixed on the bottom of the ship a line led to and fastened to the magazine to prevent its escape either side of the ship. The magazine [of powder] was directly behind you on the outside, and was freed from you by unscrewing a screw inside. Inside the magazine was a clock machinery, which immediately sets a-going after it is disengaged, and a gun lock is fixed to strike fire to the powder at the set time after the clock should run down. The clock might be set to go longer or shorter; twenty or thirty minutes was the usual time to let the navigator escape. This magazine was shaped like an egg and made of oak dug out in two pieces, bound together with bands of iron, corked and paid over with tar so as to be perfectly light, and the clock was formed so as not to run until the magazine was unscrewed.

I will now endeavor to give you a short account of my voyage in this machine. The first night after we got down to New York with it that was favorable (for the time for a trial must be when it is slack water and calm, as it is unmanageable in a swell or strong tide) the British fleet lay a little above Staten Island. We set off from the city; the whale boats towed me as nigh the ships as they dared to go and then cast me off. I soon found that it was too early in the tide, as it carried me down by the ships. I, however, hove about and rowed for five glasses by the ships' bells before the tide slacked, so that I could get alongside of the man-of-war [the *Asia*] which lay above the transports. The moon was about two hours high, and the daylight about one. When I rowed under the stern of the ship I could see the men on deck and hear them talk. I then shut down all the doors, sunk down and came under the bottom of the ship. Up with the screw against the bottom, but found it would not enter [the copper-sheathed hull]. I pulled along to try another place, but deviated a little one side and immediately rose with great velocity and come above surface two or three feet between the ship and the daylight, then sunk again like a porpoise. I hove about to try again, but on further thought I gave out, knowing that as soon as it was light the ship's boats would be rowing in all directions, and I thought the best generalship was to retreat as fast as I could, as I had four miles to go before passing Governor's Island. So I jogg'd as fast as I could, and my compass being then of no use to me, I was obliged to rise up every few minutes to see that I sailed in the right direction, and for this purpose keeping the machine on the surface of the water and the doors open. I was much afraid of getting aground on the island, as the tide of the flood set on the north point.

While on my passage up to the city, my course, owing to the above circumstances, was very crooked and zigzag, and the enemy's attention was drawn down towards me from Governor's Island. When I was abreast of the fort on the island, 3 or 400 men got upon the parapet to observe me; at length a number came down to the shore, shoved off a 12-oared barge with five or six sitters and pulled for me. I eyed them, and when they had got within fifty or sixty yards of me, I let loose the magazine in hopes that if they should take me they would likewise pick up the magazine, and then we should all be blown up together. But as kind Providence would have it, they took fright and returned to the island, to my infinite joy. I then weathered the island and our people, seeing me, came off with a whale boat and towed me in. The magazine, after getting a little past the island, went off with a tremendous explosion, throwing up large bodies of water to an immense height.

Before we had another opportunity to try an experiment, our army evacuated New York and we retreated up the North River as far as Fort Lee. A frigate came up and anchored off Bloomingdale. I now made another attempt upon a new plan. My intention was to have gone under the ship's stern and screw on the magazine close to the water's edge. But I was discovered by the watch and obliged to abandon this scheme; then shutting my doors I dove under her, but my cork in the tube (by which I ascertained my depth) got obstructed and deceived me, and I descended too deep and did not touch the ship. I then left her. . . .

Howe foresaw Washington's decision to evacuate New York. Another flanking action seemed to be in order: while men-of-war bombarded the rebel position, a detachment under General Clinton was to cross the East River, force the defenses at Kipp's Bay and turn the American left flank. Francis, Lord Rawdon described for his uncle this action of September 15, 1776,.

This landing must, I suppose, have been the most striking spectacle to our Hessian allies of any they had ever met with in their lives. Four frigates having passed the town with little loss on the 14th, anchored within musket shot of the shore at Kipp's Bay, from one end to the other of which the rebels had thrown up a breastwork.

On the 15th, General Clinton embarked early in the morning (in some flat-bottomed boats which had been brought past the town in the night) with the light infantry, the British, and the Hessian grenadiers, making between them four thousand men. . . .

We embarked in Newtown Creek and, as soon as we got into the East River, formed the line, and pushed directly for Kipp's Bay. As we approached we saw the breastworks filled with men, and two or three large columns marching down in great parade to support them. The Hessians, who were not used to this water business and who conceived that it must be exceedingly uncomfortable to be shot at whilst they were quite defenceless and jammed so close together, began to sing hymns immediately. Our men expressed their feelings as strongly, though in a different manner, by damning themselves and the enemy indiscriminately with wonderful fervency.

The ships had not as yet fired a shot, but upon a signal from us, they began the most tremendous peal I ever heard. The breastwork was blown to pieces in a few minutes, and those who were to have defended it were happy to escape as quick as possible through the neighboring ravines. The columns broke instantly, and betook themselves to the nearest woods for shelter. We pressed to shore, landed, and formed without losing a single man. As we were now without artillery, upon an island where the enemy might attack us with five times our number, and as many cannon as he thought proper, it was necessary to attain some post where we might maintain ourselves till we were reinforced, which we knew could not be done quickly. We accordingly attacked and forced a party of the rebels from the Inchenberg, a very commanding height, taking from them a new brass howitzer, some waggons of ammunition, and the tents of three or four battalions who were encamped on it.

General Vaughan was the only man of the British hurt. He was wounded in the thigh, but not badly. Two Hessians were killed and fifteen wounded. The rebels lost about a hundred men. We are now between New York and the main body of the rebels, whom we saw drawn up at about two miles distance; and we could perceive that the garrison of the town was getting past us through some woods in our front. We were not in a situation to interrupt them, and indeed their retreat ensured the town to us without further trouble. As soon as we were reinforced, we advanced towards the body we had seen drawn up, but they retreated immediately, and we moved forward till we got possession of the heights above Harlem, a pass which secures the island to us. New York, in the meantime, being summoned, immediately surrendered. The rebels had fortified it very strongly, and we found great quantities of stores of all kinds and a number of cannon. The immense heaps of shot and shells really surprised me.

Washington was reported so furious at the precipitous flight of his troops that he rushed among them, trying to force a stand by beating them with the flat of his sword. Howe, on the other hand, was to fall under heavy criticism for not pursuing and crushing the rebels in their retreat. Despite the delightful story that he tarried too long over the cakes and wine of Mrs. Robert Murray, the delay seems to have been the result of the tardiness of the landing boats in bringing up reinforcements. The following day the Americans redeemed themselves in the skirmish at Harlem Heights. For Joseph Hodgkinson, a lieutenant in the 12th Massachusetts Regiment, it was but a continuation of the landing at Kipp's Bay.

Now you must think they were in high spirits and thought all was their own: so on Monday morning they thought they would attack us with about six thousand men and drive us all over Kingsbridge. But they were much mistaken. But, however, as soon as we heard that they were advancing towards us, the General sent out 200 Rangers under command of Colonel Knowlton, who soon met the enemy and fired on them and sent them on the retreat, till they got pretty near us. Then the enemy halted back of a hill, blowed a French horn which was for a reinforcement, and as soon as they got it, they formed in two columns. But our brigade was posted in the edge of a thick wood and by some climbing up a tree could see the enemy's motion. While they was a-forming, the General sent a party to attack them which answered the end for which they were sent: for our people made the attack and retreated towards us where we wanted them to come, and then the enemy rushed down the hill with all speed to a plain spot of ground. Then our brigade marched out of the woods, then a very hot fire on both sides and lasted for upwards of an hour. Then the enemy retreated up the hill, and our people followed them and fought them near an hour longer till they got under cover of their ships, which was in North River. Then our people left them.

The loss on our side is about 40 killed and 60 or 70 wounded. There was more killed in our regiment and about 20 wounded. One of our corporals was badly wounded through the knees, but I hope he will do well. The loss on the enemy's side is not sartin, but according to the best accounts that we had, they had near 500 killed and near as many wounded. . . . This was the first time we had any chance to fight them and I doubt not if we should have another opportunity but we should give them another dressing.

The journal of Ambrose Serle described the flames that swept through the city on September 21, 1776.

This morning, about 1 o'clock, we were alarmed with the appearance of a fire in the town; and presently after it burst out, at several places into a most tremendous blaze. The wind was rather strong, which increased the rapidity of the flames, and these extended in a line for almost the length of a mile, consuming onward from the East River, for several hours together, to the North River up to St. Paul's Church, which wonderfully escaped, while Trinity Church (called the Old English Church, being the oldest fabric upon the Establishment in town) was utterly destroyed. Many houses were consumed in and about Whitehall near the fort.

Some rebels, who lurked about the town, set it on fire, and some of them were caught with matches and fire-balls about them. One man, detected in the act, was knocked down by a grenadier and thrown into the flames for his reward. Another who was found cutting off the handles of the water buckets to prevent their use, was first hung up by the neck till he was dead and afterwards by the heels upon a sign post by the sailors. Many others were seized, on account of combustibles found upon them, and secured, and, but for the officers, most of them would have been killed by the enraged populace and soldiery. The New England people are maintained to be at the bottom of this plot, which they have long since threatened to put into execution.

I walked on shore about noon, surveyed the devastation, which has taken in, 'tis supposed, about one-fifth of the city. . . .

Possibly it was because of this conflagration that a captured spy, a young man named Nathan Hale, received such summary justice. Hale's friend, Stephen Hempstead, tells how the Americans gained a martyr.

I was attached to Captain Hale's company in Colonel Webb's regiment of Continental troops, and in his confidence. After the retreat of our army from Long Island, he informed me that he was sent for to headquarters, and was solicited to go over to Long Island to discover the disposition of the enemy's camp, &c., expecting them to attack New York, but that he was too unwell to go, not having recovered from a recent illness; that upon a second application he had consented to go, and said I must go with him as far as I could with safety and wait for his return.

Accordingly we left the camp at Harlem Heights, with the intention of crossing over the first opportunity, but none offered until we arrived at Norwalk, fifty miles from New York. In that harbor was an armed sloop and two row galleys. Captain Hale had a general order to all armed vessels to take him to any place he should designate. He was set across the Sound in the sloop at Huntingdon, Long Island, by Captain Pond, who commanded the vessel.

Captain Hale had changed his uniform for a plain suit of citizen's brown clothes, with a round broad broad-brimmed hat; assuming the character of a Dutch schoolmaster, leaving all his other clothes, commission, public and private papers with me, and also his silver shoe buckles, saying they would not comport with his character of schoolmaster, and retaining nothing but his college diploma, as an introduction to his assumed calling. Thus equipped, we parted for the last time in life.

He went on his mission and I returned back to Norwalk, with orders to stop there until he should return, or I heard from him, as he expected to return back again to cross the Sound if he succeeded in his object. The British army had, in the mean time, got possession of New York, whither he also passed, and had nearly executed his mission, and was passing through the British picket guard between the lines of the two armies, within a mile and a half of his own quarters, when he was stopped at a tavern at a place called the "Cedars." Here there was no suspicion of his character being other than he pretended, until most unfortunately he was met in the crowd by a fellow countryman and an own relation [Samuel Hale of Portsmouth, New Hampshire] (but a Tory and a renegade), who had received the hospitality of his board and the attention of a brother from Captain Hale at his quarters at Winter Hill in Cambridge the winter before.

He recognized him and most inhumanly and infamously betrayed him, divulging his true character, situation in the army, &c., and having him searched, his diploma corroborated his relative's statement. Then without any formality of trial or delay, they hung him instantaneously, and sent a flag over to our army, stating that "they had caught such a man within their lines this morning, and hung him as a spy." Thus suddenly and unfeelingly did they rush this young and worthy man into eternity, not allowing him an hour's preparation nor the privilege of writing to his friends, nor even to receive the last consolation of his religion, refusing to let the chaplain pray with him as was his request. . . .

Howe, procrastinating, possibly missed his great opportunity to eliminate the American Army with one crushing blow. Washington was troubled by expiring enlistments and undisciplined soldiers. The observations of young Lewis Morris, Jr., present a rather sad commentary on patriotism.

As for the militia of Connecticut, Brigadier Wolcott and his whole brigade have got the cannon fever and very prudently sculked home. Such people are only a nuisance and had better be in the chimney corner than in the field of Mars. We have men enough without them who will fight and whose glory is the defence of their country.

Colonel Hand's regiment plunder everybody in Westchester County indiscriminately, even yourself have not escaped. Montressor's Island they plundered and committed the most unwarrantable destruction upon it; fifty dozen of bottles were broke in the cellar, the paper tore from the rooms and every pane of glass broke to pieces. His furniture and cloathes were brought over to Morrisiana and sold at publick auction. Jimmy Delancey, Oliver and John, after giving their parole, are gone off to the enemy and their house is plundered. . . . Such brimstones will certainly meet with their deserts.

Not until October 12 did Howe move. He first attempted to land at Throg's Neck. Frustrated by a small detachment of riflemen, he re-embarked his troops and landed them at Pell's Point. Washington moved back to White Plains as a valiant delaying action by John Glover's polyglot "brigade" slowed the British. Howe followed at a leisurely pace. Not until late October was there contact among the hills that seemed so incongruous about a village called White Plains. A newspaper reprinted a colorful description of the action.

Last Monday, the 28th, we received intelligence that the enemy, with their whole body, were advancing towards us. The army was immediately alarmed, and part of General Wadsworth's brigade, with some of the regiments under General Spencer (consisting in the whole of five or six hundred men), were sent out as an advanced party to skirmish with the enemy and harass them in their march. We marched on to a hill about one mile and a half from our lines, with an artillery company and two field pieces, and placed ourselves behind walls and fences in the best manner we could to give the enemy trouble.

About half after nine o'clock our advanced parties all came retreating in before the enemy, and the light parties of the enemy, with their advanced guard consisting of two or three thousand, came in sight, and marched briskly towards us, keeping the high grounds, and the light horse pranced on a little in the rear, making a very martial appearance. As our light parties came on to the hills and discovered where we were, the enemy began to cannonade us, and to fling shells from their howitzers and small mortars. Their light parties soon came on, and we fired upon them from the walls and fences, broke and scattered them at once. But they would run from our front and get round upon our wings to flank us, and as soon as our fire discovered where we were, the enemy's artillery would at once begin to play upon us in the most furious manner. We kept the walls until the enemy were just ready to surround us, and then we would retreat from one wall and hill to another, and maintain our ground there in the same manner, till numbers were just ready to surround us.

Once the Hessian grenadiers came up front of Colonel Douglass's regiment, and we fired a general volley upon them at about twenty rods distance, and scattered them like leaves in a whirlwind; and they ran off so far that some of the regiment ran out to the ground where they were when we fired upon them and brought off their arms and accoutrements and rum, that the men who fell had with them, which we had time to drink round with before they came on again.

They formed at a distance, and waited until their artillery and main body came on, and they advanced in solid columns upon us, and were gathering all around us, ten to our one. Colonel Douglass's and Silliman's regiments fired four or five times on them as they were advancing and then retreated, but not until the enemy began to fire on their flanks. Colonels Silliman, Douglass and Arnold behaved nobly, and the men gained much applause. . . . Our loss in the whole may be seventy or eighty killed or wounded. It is said by all the deserters and captives, who agree in their stories, that the enemy had about three hundred killed and wounded.

The scene was grand and solemn; all the adjacent hills smoked as though on fire, and bellowed and trembled with a perpetual cannonade and fire of field pieces, howitzers and mortars. The air groaned with streams of cannon and musket shot. The hills smoked and echoed terribly with the bursting of shells; the fences and walls were knocked down and torn to pieces, and men's legs, arms and bodies, mangled with cannon and grape shot all around us. I was in the action, and under as good advantage as any man, perhaps, to observe all that passed, and write these particulars of the action from my own observations. No general action was designed on our part, and I believe that one thousand men were never, at one time, engaged with the enemy. They came on the hills opposite our lines and halted, and after cannonading for a short time, they became very still and quiet.

On the 31st it was observed that they had near finished four or five batteries which they had erected against us and as our ground, near the center of the town of White Plains, was not good, being overlooked by the neighboring hills, the generals, last night, drew off most of the troops from the lines there, and this morning the guards and sentries burned the town and forage around it and came off about nine o'clock. We carried off all our stores, and planted our artillery on the hills about a mile and a half back of the center of the town. The enemy advanced this forenoon on to the ground we left, but as soon as they came over the hill we saluted them with our cannon and field pieces, and they advanced no further. Our sick and wounded are sent out eight or ten miles. Our men are in good spirits, and with much patience endure great hardships and fatigue. . . . All things seem to be quiet at Fort Washington.

Things were not destined to remain quiet at Fort Washington. On precipices on either side of the Hudson stood Fort Washington, on Manhattan Island, and Fort Constitution, now called Fort Lee, on the Jersey side. Inasmuch as three British vessels had already sailed past the forts with relative ease, Washington doubted the advisability of maintaining the position. Yet, in characteristic fashion, he listened to the pleas of Nathanael Greene, who was in command of the Hudson River forts. The General's advice to Greene was "that it would be best to evacuate the place; but, as the orders were discretionary, and

his opinion differed from mine, it unhappily was delayed. . . ." Robert
Auchmuty, a Boston loyalist exiled to London, received an unidentified
account of the fall of the river forts.

Fort Washington is certainly one of the strongest places that
can be conceived, as well from its peculiar advantageous situation
as from the endless lines, redoubts and other works that surround
it, in which the rebels have exerted all their art, and the most surprising labour, to guard every place where they could imagine it possible
to approach the fort. In short, it was rendered impregnable as far as
nature and art could contribute to make it so.

The honour of reducing the important place was solicited by
General Knyphausen, in which he was indulged by General Howe.
Everything therefore being prepared, agreeable to the most masterly
disposition, the attack was begun at daybreak on Saturday morning
the 15th instant. A detachment of Hessians with cannon marched
round from General Howe's army by Kingsbridge along the clear
road (which you will remember is a kind of causeway) through a
hollow way, commanded on both sides by very steep, craggy hills on
which the rebels had redoubts which enfiladed the whole length of the
valley. The Hessians, with great firmness, marched through this way
until they came to the north end of the steep mountain on Harlem
River, on the left side, which they began to clamber up, notwithstanding the heavy fire from the rebels on the top of the hills, and
after very great difficulties and labours gained the summit; which
as soon as the rebels saw, they ran away towards the fort with great
precipitation.

At the same time that this Hessian detachment marched around by
Kingsbridge, the 43rd and 71st, two Highland regiments, pushed
over Harlem or Kingsbridge River in flat-bottomed boats about two
miles and a half below Kingsbridge, and directly opposite to the most
rugged and steep part of the mountain, where the rebels had raised
no works, thinking it utterly impossible for any human being to
climb up a rocky precipice nearly perpendicular. There, however,
these brave North Britons landed, and with incredible labour,
scrambled up by means of small bushes growing out through the
cracks of the rocks on the side of the mountain, all the while sustaining a heavy fire from the rebels at the top; which, as soon as they had
reached, they began a very spirited attack upon the rebels, who were
in the bushes on top of the mountains, driving them from behind

trees and rocks; and by this means greatly facilitating the operation of the Hessians, who had very hard work, some to scramble over the rocks and fight all the way, in order to make way for others who was to drag their cannon along a very steep road commanded on all sides. All these difficulties were at last overcome by firmness, patience, and the most manly perseverance, and they had the pleasure of soon dispersing all the rebels they could find in their route, who ran towards the fort in the utmost panic.

These operations, you will observe, were on the north and east side of the rebels' works. But the success of them would, in all human probability, have been very precarious, had it not been for Lord Percy's attack on the very strong lines on the heights of the Harlem side in which the chief body of rebels had planted themselves. For at the same instant that the Hessians and Highlanders began their attack, his Lordship with the brigades under his command attacked the lines with singular bravery, rushing into them with the greatest fury, and driving the rebels from line to line, and from work to work, till he got them crammed up in the fort, before the Hessians and Highlanders could get to it with their cannon.

About one o'clock this was the situation of the wretches, who seeing themselves surrounded on all sides by the troops with fixed bayonets, and the cannon within two hundred paces, sent out a white flag, begging the general would not fire upon them, for that they were consulting about surrendering, which they were not long about. By 4 o'clock they had laid down their arms, delivered themselves up prisoners, and the troops took possession of the fort with everything in it. What number of them were killed I can't exactly learn, some say 600, others about half that number. But the prisoners amount to upwards of three thousand men, all of them from Pennsylvania, Maryland, and Virginia.

When Washington ran away from Kingsbridge they had, it seems, been 5,000 men, all southern people, which were the best troops in the rebels' army who, refusing to go into New England, had engaged to defend this strong place to the last extremity. . . .

This grand point being gained, by which York Island and a great part of the province was cleared from the rebels, General Howe, I think, on the morning of the 20th instant, landed 5,000 men under the command of Lord Cornwallis up the North River on the Jersey shore, a few miles above the other famous fortification, called Fort Constitution or Fort Lee. His Lordship immediately marched to

attack this place, and got to it by 1 o'clock the same day, but found
it had been evacuated by the rebels so precipitately that the pots
were left absolutely boiling on their fires, and the tables spread for
dinner of some of their officers. In the fort they found but twelve
men, who were all dead drunk. There were forty or fifty pieces of
cannon found loaded, with two large iron sea mortars and one brass
one, with a vast quantity of ammunition, provision and stores, with
all their tents standing.

"*I feel mad, vexed, sick, and sorry. Never did I need the consoling
voice of a friend more than now. Happy should I be to see you. This
is a most terrible event: its consequences are justly to be dreaded.
Pray what is said upon this occasion?*" So wrote a dejected Nathanael
Greene after the fall of the forts. There was only one course left open
to Washington—retreat and maneuver his little army away from direct
contact with the enemy. Despondent, it was reported that he once
passed his hand over his throat and remarked, "*My neck does not feel
as though it was made for a halter: we must retire to Augusta county in
Virginia, and if overpowered we must pass the Allegheny mountains.*"
Although a man given to moods, there was still a certain stubbornness
in him. He fell back and schemed. There had to be a way to stop the
juggernaut.

Campaign in the Jerseys

*D*URING *the first year of the war, the employment of militia had resulted in an army whose strength was fluid. Returns fluctuated daily as these citizen soldiers sought their chimney corners without the formality of a furlough. Enlistments in the Continental Line were for short periods of time, with terms of service expiring at critical moments. Washington had long urged the establishment of a more permanent army. Finally, on September 16, 1776, Congress had overcome its "jealousy of a standing army," and had passed resolutions to erect a more stable fighting force. Surgeon James Thacher commented on the nature of the new army.*

After the battle of Lexington, such was the enthusiasm for the cause of liberty, and so general and extensive the alarm, that thousands of our citizens, who were engaged in the cultivation of their farms, spontaneously rushed to the scene of action, and an army was assembled almost without the efforts of public authority. . . .

There is [an] evil of a very serious complexion which has manifested itself in our camp. Since the troops from the Southern states have been incorporated and associated in military duty with those from New England, a strong prejudice has assumed its unhappy influence, and drawn a line of distinction between them. Many of the officers from the South are gentlemen of education, and unaccustomed to that equality which prevails in New England, and, however desirable, it could scarcely be expected that people from distant colonies, differing in manners and prejudices, could at once harmonize in friendly intercourse. Hence we too frequently hear the burlesque epithet of *Yankee* from one part, and that of *Buck-skin*, by way of retort, from the other.

The troops which compose the Continental Army being enlisted for a few months only, their time of service will soon expire. Congress, being apprised of the absolute necessity of a permanent army, have lately resolved "to raise a standing army of about seventy-five thousand men, to serve for the term of three years, or during the war." These troops, when raised, are to be systematically arranged on the Continental establishment, and according to their apportionment, the quota for Massachusetts is fifteen battalions, or about twelve thousand men. To encourage enlistments, each soldier is to receive a bounty of twenty dollars, besides his wages and rations, and one hundred acres of land, if he serve during the war. The officers are to receive land in proportion to their respective ranks, from two hundred and five hundred acres. Their monthly pay is to be as follows:

Colonel, a month,	.	$75.00	Lieutenant,	. .	$27.00
Lieutenant-Colonel,	.	60.00	Ensign,	. .	20.00
Major,	. .	50.00	Sergeant-Major,	.	9.00
Chaplain,	. .	33.33	Quarter-Master Sergeant		9.00
Surgeon,	.	33.33	Drum-Major,	. .	8.00
Surgeon's-Mate,	.	18.00	Fife-Major,	. .	8.33
Adjutant,	. .	40.00	Sergeant,	. .	8.00
Quarter-Master,	.	27.50	Corporal,	. .	7.33
Regimental Pay-master,	26.67	Drummer and Fifer,		.	7.33
Captain,	. .	40.00	Privates,	. .	6.67

Each commissioned officer is allowed the privilege of taking a soldier from the ranks for a waiter, and he is exempted from camp and other duty, except in time of action. The officers are also allowed a number of rations in proportion to their rank. A surgeon draws three, and a mate two rations. One pound of beef or pork; one pound of bread or flour a day; a small quantity of vegetables, when to be had; one gill of rum or whiskey a day, a small quantity of vinegar, salt, soap and candles, a week, constitute a ration.

After the fall of the Hudson River forts, Washington had only one course—retreat southward through the Jerseys. He was like a mouse teasing a cat; one British officer complained, "As we go forward into the country, the rebels flee before us, & when we come back they always follow us, 'tis almost impossible to catch them. They will neither fight, nor totally run away, but they keep at such distance that we are always above a day's march from them. They seem to be playing at

Bo Peep." Washington explained his strategy, "for I shall continue to retreat before them so as to lull them into security." The British Army seemed to take out their frustration upon civilians. As Adam Stephen wrote Thomas Jefferson, "The Enemy, like locusts, sweep the Jerseys with the besom of destruction. They, to the disgrace of a civilized nation, ravish the fair sex from the age of ten to seventy." "An officer of distinction in the American army" described the situation so graphically that the Pennsylvania Council of Safety ordered his account published in the local press and distributed as a broadside.

I have had an opportunity of hearing a number of the horrid depredations committed by that part of the British army which was stationed near Pennytown, under the command of Lord Cornwallis. Besides the sixteen young women who had fled to the woods to avoid their brutality, and were there seized and carried off, one man had the mortification to have his wife and only daughter (a child of ten years of age) ravished; this he himself, almost choked with grief, uttered in lamentations to his friend, who told me of it, and also informed me that another girl of thirteen years of age was taken from her father's house, carried to a barn about a mile [away], there ravished, and afterwards made use of by five more of these brutes.

Numbers of instances of the same kind of behaviour I am assured of have happened, here their brutish lust were their stimulus, but wanton mischief was seen in every part of the country. Everything portable they plunder and carry off, neither age nor sex, Whig or Tory, is spared; an indiscriminate ruin attends every person they meet with, infants, children, old men and women, are left in their shirts without a blanket to cover them in this inclement season. Furniture of every kind destroyed or burnt, windows and doors broke to pieces; in short, the houses left uninhabitable, and the people left without provisions, for every horse, cow, ox, hogs and poultry carried off, a blind old gentleman near Pennytown plundered of everything, and on his door wrote, "Capt. Wills of the Royal Irish did this."

This was not all exaggeration. Charles Stedman, loyalist serving in the British Army, noted: "But no sooner had the army entered the Jerseys, than the business (we say business for it was a perfect trade) of plunder began. The friend and the foe, from the hand of rapine, shared alike." The American soldiers were more discriminating in their pillaging; they had only the Tories. Cellars were pillaged. At Brunswick, according to Lieutenant James McMichael, "Here our soldiers drank of spiritous liquors. They have chiefly got a disorder, which at camp is called the Barrel Fever, which differs in its effects from any other fever—its concomitants are black eyes and bloody noses." Even in retreat, the soldiers had their fun.

December 2—Yesterday, on the appearance of the enemy at Brunswick, General Washington ordered a retreat to Princeton, where we arrived early in the morning. We are in a terrible situation, with the enemy close upon us, and whole regiments of Marylanders and Jerseymen leaving us. Tomorrow we go to Trenton, where the General is determined to make a stand.

A Tory from Monmouth lower county, was brought in here today by a party of Pennsylvania boys. He mistook us for the regulars, and came quite into camp without perceiving his mistake. This afternoon, after taking off his breeches and giving him an absolution, by setting him on ice (to cool his loyalty), they set him to work bringing in fagots. He seems pleased with his new office, knowing that he got off easy. Notwithstanding General Stirling deprecates severity to the infernal Tories we catch, they get absolution often.

Not until the Delaware River flowed between his army and the enemy did Washington slow his retreat. Despite a dwindling army and sinking spirits, there was a persistent air of optimism in Samuel B. Webb.

You ask me our situation; it has been the Devil, but is to appearance better. About 2,000 of us have been obliged to run damn'd hard before about 10,000 of the enemy. Never was finer lads at a retreat than we are. 'Tis said the enemy are bound for New York via South Amboy; it wants confirmation. No fun for us that I can see; however, I cannot but think we shall drub the dogs. Those gone for New England will meet their deserts. I hope, sure I am, the lads of that country will not behave in the dam'd cowardly, rascally manner the people of this country have. Never mind, all will come right one of these days.

Disaster seemed to compound itself. General Charles Lee, whose actions would lead some to believe that he had originated eccentricity, had taken his time in answering Washington's pleas that he join his command with the main army. Lee, who spent the night of December 12 at a tavern away from his troops, was writing a letter to Horatio Gates in which he referred to Washington: "Entre nous, *a certain great man is most damnably deficient.*" *Captain James Wilkinson, an aide, chronicled the capture of Lee.*

General Lee wasted the morning in altercation with certain militia corps who were of his command, particularly the Connecticut light horse, several of whom appeared in large full-bottomed perukes, and were treated very irreverently. The call of the adjutant general for orders also occupied some of his time, and we did not sit down to breakfast before 10 o'clock. General Lee was engaged in answering Gates's letter, and I had risen from the table and was looking out an end window down a lane about one hundred yards in length, which led to the house from the main road, when I discovered a party of British dragoons turn a corner of the avenue at a full charge.

Startled by this unexpected spectacle, I exclaimed, "Here, Sir, are the British cavalry!"

"Where?" replied the general, who had signed his letter in the instant.

"Around the house," for they had opened files and encompassed the building.

General Lee appeared alarmed, yet collected, and his second observation marked his self-possession: "Where is the guard?— damn the guard, why don't they fire?" and after a momentary pause, turned to me and said, "Do, Sir, see what has become of the guard?"

The woman of the house at this moment entered the room and proposed to him to conceal himself in a bed, which he rejected with evident disgust. I caught up my pistols which lay on the table, thrust the letter he had been writing into my pocket, and passed into a room at the opposite end of the house, where I had seen the guard in the morning. Here I discovered their arms, but the men were absent. I stepped out of the door and perceived the dragoons chasing them in different directions, and receiving a very uncivil salutation, I returned into the house.

Too inexperienced immediately to penetrate the motives of this enterprise, I considered the *rencontre* accidental, and from the terrific tales spread over the country of the violence and barbarity of the enemy, I believed it to be a wanton murdering party, and determined not to die without company. I accordingly sought a position where I could not be approached by more than one person at a time, and with a pistol in each hand, I awaited the expected search, resolved to shoot the first and the second person who might appear, and then appeal to my sword. I did not remain long in this unpleasant situation, but was apprised of the object of the incursion by the very audible declaration, "If the General does not surrender in five minutes, I will set fire to the house"; which after a short pause was repeated with a solemn oath; and within two minutes I heard it proclaimed, "Here is the general. He has surrendered." A general shout ensued, the trumpet sounded the assembly, and the unfortunate Lee mounted on my horse, which stood ready at the door, was hurried off in triumph, bareheaded, in his slippers and blanket coat, his collar open, and his shirt very much soiled from several days' use.

Tom Paine was now marching with the army. His tart pen captured the misery of the day in the first of the series entitled The American Crisis.

These are the times that try men's souls. The summer soldier and the sunshine patriot will, in this crisis, shrink from the services of his country; but he that stands it now, deserves the love and thanks of man and woman. Tyranny, like Hell, is not easily conquered; yet we have this consolation with us, that the harder the conflict the more glorious the triumph. What we obtain too cheap, we esteem too lightly. 'Tis dearness only that gives everything its value. Heaven knows how to set a proper price upon its goods; and it would be strange indeed, if so celestial an article as FREEDOM should not be highly rated. Britain, with an army to enforce her tyranny, has declared that she has a right not only to tax, but "to bind us in all cases whatsoever," and if being bound in that manner is not slavery, then there is not such a thing as slavery upon earth. Even the expression is impious, for so unlimited a power can belong only to God. . . . Would that Heaven might inspire some Jersey maid to spirit up her countrymen, and save her fair fellow sufferers from ravage and ravishment.

But no Joan of Arc appeared, nor did Paine's eloquent appeal to patriotism persuade many that they should remain with the army after their enlistments expired on December 31. Howe, following

European custom, settled into winter quarters, his cantonments stretching across New Jersey as far south as Trenton. While his New York hours were made more pleasurable by the blond, attractive Mrs. Loring, loyalists in Philadelphia composed a derisive "Address" chiding him for his inactivity.

> Awake, arouse, Sir Billy,
> There's forage in the plain,
> Ah! leave your little Filly,
> And open the campaign.
> Heed not a woman's prattle,
> Which tickles in the ear,
> But give the word for battle,
> And grasp the warlike spear.
> Behold each soldier panting
> For glory, and renown,
> To them no spur is wanting,
> March, and the day's your own.

Washington kept the enemy off balance with irritating little dragonnades, but his plans included more than nuisance raids. Those troops who planned to return home by the first of the year were to be useful one more time. Some time later, one of Washington's aides, possibly Lieutenant Colonel John Fitzgerald, reconstructed, in diary form, the events of that Christmas season of 1776.

Dec. 22, 1776—I rode along the river yesterday morning and could see the Hessians in Trenton. It is a pretty village, containing about 130 houses and a Presbyterian meeting-house. A stone bridge spans the Assunpink creek on the road leading south to Bordentown. There are apple orchards and gardens. Rall has his own regiment and Knyphausen a few dragoons and fifty riflemen. The Hessians call them Yagers. He has six cannon. Knyphausen has two of them, two stand in front of Rall's headquarters, and two up by the Pennington road. A scout just in says that General Howe has issued a proclamation, offering a pardon to everyone in New Jersey who will lay down their arms and take the oath of allegiance. He says that Howe and Cornwallis are well satisfied with what they have accomplished. Cornwallis is going to England to tell the King that the rebellion is about over. Howe is going to have a good time in New York attending dinner parties. From what I can see, I am quite certain Washington intends to make some movement soon. He keeps his own counsel, but is very determined.

Dec. 23—Orders have been issued to cook rations for three days. Washington has just given the counter sign, "Victory or Death." He has written a letter to General Cadwallader at Bristol, which he entrusted to me to copy. He intends to cross the river, make a ten mile march to Trenton and attack Rall just before daybreak. . . .

Dec. 25—Christmas morning. They make a great deal of Christmas in Germany, and no doubt the Hessians will drink a great deal of beer and have a dance tonight. They will be sleepy tomorrow morning. Washington will set the tune for them about daybreak. The rations are cooked. New flints and ammunition have been distributed. Colonel Glover's fishermen from Marblehead, Massachusetts, are to manage the boats just as they did in the retreat from Long Island.

Christmas, 6 P.M.—The regiment have had their evening parade, but instead of returning to their quarters are marching towards the ferry. It is fearfully cold and raw and a snow storm setting in. The wind is northeast and beats in the faces of the men. It will be a terrible night for the soldiers who have no shoes. Some of them have tied old rags around their feet; others are barefoot, but I have not heard a man complain. They are ready to suffer any hardship and die rather than give up their liberty. I have just copied the order for marching. Both divisions are to go from the ferry to Bear Tavern, two miles. They will separate there; Washington will accompany Greene's division with a part of the artillery down the Pennington road; Sullivan and the rest of the artillery will take the river road.

Dec. 26, 3 A.M.—I am writing in the ferry house. The troops are all over, and the boats have gone back for the artillery. We are three hours behind the set time. Glover's men have had a hard time to force the boats through the floating ice with the snow drifting in their faces. I have never seen Washington so determined as he is now. He stands on the bank of the river, wrapped in his cloak, superintending the landing of his troops. He is calm and collected, but very determined. The storm is changing to sleet, and cuts like a knife. The last cannon is being landed, and we are ready to mount our horses.

Dec. 26, Noon—It was nearly 4 o'clock when we started. The two divisions divided at Bear Tavern.

At Birmingham, three and one half miles south of the tavern, a man came with a message from General Sullivan that the storm was wetting the muskets and rendering them unfit for service. "Tell General Sullivan," said Washington, "to use the bayonet. I am resolved to take Trenton."

It was broad daylight when we came to a house where a man was chopping wood. He was very much surprised when he saw us. "Can you tell us where the Hessian picket is?" Washington asked. The man hesitated, but I said, "You need not be frightened, it is General Washington who asks the question." His face brightened, and he pointed toward the house of Mr. Howell.

It was just 8 o'clock. Looking down the road I saw a Hessian running out from the house. He yelled in Dutch and swung his arms. Three or four others came out with their guns. Two of them fired at us, but the bullets whistled over our heads. Some of General Stephen's men rushed forward and captured two. The others took to their heels, running towards Mr. Calhoun's house, where the picket guard was stationed, about twenty men under Captain Altenbrockum. They came running out of the house. The Captain flourished his sword and tried to form his men. Some of them fired at us, others ran towards the village.

The next moment we heard drums beat and a bugle sound, and then from the west came the boom of cannon. General Washington's face lighted up instantly, for he knew it was one of Sullivan's guns. We could hear a great commotion down towards the meeting-house, men running here and there, officers swinging their swords, artillery-men harnessing their horses. Captain Forrest unlimbered his guns. Washington gave the order to advance, and we rushed on to the junction of King and Queen streets. Forrest wheeled six of his cannon into position to sweep both streets. The riflemen under Colonel Hand and Scott's and Lawson's battalions went upon the run through the fields to gain possession of the Princeton road. The Hessians were just ready to open fire with two of their cannon when Captain [William] Washington and Lieutenant [James] Monroe, with their men rushed forward and captured them. We saw Rall riding up the street from his headquarters, which were at Stacy Pott's house. We could hear him shouting in Dutch, "My brave soldiers, advance." His men were frightened and confused, for our men were firing upon them from fences and houses and they were falling fast. Instead of advancing they ran into an apple orchard. The officers tried to rally them, but our men kept advancing and picking off the officers.

It was not long before Rall tumbled from his horse and his soldiers threw down their guns and gave themselves up as prisoners.

While this was taking place on the Pennington road, Colonel John Stark, from New Hampshire, in the advance on the river road, was driving Knyphausen's men pell mell through the town. Sullivan sent a portion of his troops under St. Clair to seize the bridge and cut off the retreat of the Hessians toward Bordentown. Sullivan's men shot the artillery horses and captured two cannon attached to Knyphausen's regiment.

Dec. 26, 3 P.M.—I have been talking with Rall's adjutant, Lieutenant Piel. He says that Rall sat down to a grand dinner at the Trenton Tavern Christmas day, that he drank a great deal of wine and sat up nearly all night playing cards. He had been in bed but a short time when the battle began and was sound asleep. Piel shook him, but found it hard work to wake him up. Supposing that he was wide awake, Piel went out to help rally the men, but Rall not appearing, he went back and found him in his night shirt. "What's the matter?" Rall asked. Piel informed him that a battle was going on. That seemed to bring him to his senses. He dressed himself, rushed out and mounted his horse to be mortally wounded a few minutes later.

We have taken nearly 1,000 prisoners, six cannon, more than 1,000 muskets, twelve drums, and four colors. About forty Hessians were killed or wounded. Our losses only two killed and three wounded. Two of the latter are Captain Washington and Lieutenant Monroe, who rushed forward very bravely to seize the cannon.

I have just been with General Washington and Greene to see Rall. He will not live through the night. He asked that his men be kindly treated. Washington promised that he would see they were well cared for. . . .

It is a glorious victory. It will rejoice the hearts of our friends everywhere and give new life to hitherto waning fortunes. Washington has baffled the enemy in his retreat from New York. He has pounced on the Hessians like an eagle upon a hen and is safe once more on this side of the river. If he does nothing more, he will live in history as a great military commander.

Trenton had been a battle of individuals rather than a tactical operation. Even the dirty weather had played an important role; dampened powder had forced the Americans to become acquainted with the messy business of the bayonet, the sponton and the sword.

*Only the roaring cannon rose above the shouting voices as men struggled
for their lives in the spitting snow. It was street fighting that contained
all the dramatics of the assault upon Quebec.*

*Victory is the basic element of military morale and enterprise.
Even as a young private noted in his diary on December 28, "This
Day we have been washing our things," the General was planning to
recross the Delaware because "a fair opportunity is offered of driving
the enemy entirely from, or at least to the extremity of, the province of
New Jersey." A noncommissioned officer identified only as "Sergeant
R——" related the next episode.*

Three or four days after the victory at Trenton, the American
army recrossed the Delaware into New Jersey. At this time our troops
were in a destitute and deplorable condition. The horses attached
to our cannon were without shoes, and when passing over the ice
they would slide in every direction, and could advance only with
the assistance of our soldiers. Our men too, were without shoes or
other comfortable clothing; and as traces of our march towards
Princeton, the ground was literally marked with the blood of the
soldiers' feet. Though my own feet did not bleed, they were so sore
that their condition was little better.

While we were at Trenton, on the last of December, 1776, the
time for which I and most of my regiment had enlisted expired. At
this trying time General Washington, having now but a little handful
of men, and many of them new recruits in which he could place
little confidence, ordered our regiment to be paraded, and personally
addressed us, urging that we should stay a month longer. He alluded
to our recent victory at Trenton; told us that our services were
greatly needed, and that we could now do more for our country than
we ever could at any future period; and in the most affectionate
manner entreated us to stay. The drums beat for volunteers, but not
a man turned out. The soldiers worn down by fatigue and privations,
had their hearts fixed on home and the comforts of the domestic
circle, and it was hard to forego the anticipated pleasures of the
society of our dearest friends.

The General wheeled his horse about, rode in front of the regiment
and addressing us again said, "My brave fellows, you have done all I
asked you to do, and more than could reasonably be expected; but
your country is at stake, your wives, your houses, and all that you
hold dear. You have worn yourselves out with fatigues and hardships,

but we know not how to spare you. If you will consent to stay only one month longer, you will render that service to the cause of liberty, and to your country, which you probably never can do under any other circumstances. The present is emphatically the crisis, which is to decide our destiny." The drums beat a second time. The soldiers felt the force of the appeal. One said to another, "I will remain if you will." Others remarked, "We cannot go home under such circumstances." A few stepped forth, and their example was immediately followed by nearly all who were fit for duty in the regiment, amounting to about two hundred volunteers. An officer inquired of the General if these men should be enrolled. He replied, "No! men who will volunteer in such a case as this, need no enrollment to keep them to their duty."

When we were about commencing our march for Princeton, Lord Cornwallis left that place with the intention of attacking, and at one blow cutting off the rebel army. He appeared near Wood Creek, or the Assunpink river, where a skirmish took place at the bridge over the creek. The Hessians were placed in front of the British troops, and endeavored to force the bridge. They retired, and we were left undisturbed for the night.

Leaving our fires kindled to deceive the enemy, we decamped that night, and by a circuitous route took up our line of march for Princeton. General Mercer commanded the front guard of which the two hundred volunteers composed a part. About sunrise of the 3rd January 1777, reaching the summit of a hill near Princeton, we observed a light-horseman looking towards us, as we view an object when the sun shines directly in our faces. General Mercer observing him, gave orders to the riflemen who were posted on the right to pick him off. Several made ready, but at that instant he wheeled about, and was out of their reach. Soon after this as we were descending a hill through an orchard, a party of the enemy who were entrenched behind a bank and fence, rose and fired upon us. Their first shot passed over our heads, cutting the limbs of the trees under which we were marching. At this moment we were ordered to wheel. As the platoon which I commanded was obeying the order, the corporal who stood at my left shoulder, received a ball and fell dead on the spot. He seemed to bend forward to receive the ball, which otherwise might have ended my life. We formed, advanced, and fired upon the enemy. They retreated eight rods to their packs, which were laid in a line. I advanced to the fence on the opposite side of the ditch which the enemy had just left, fell on one knee and loaded my musket with ball and buckshot. Our fire was most destructive; their ranks grew thin and the victory seemed nearly complete, when the British were reinforced. Many of our brave men had fallen, and we were unable to stand such superior numbers of fresh troops.

I soon heard General Mercer in a tone of distress, "Retreat!" He was mortally wounded and died shortly after. I looked about for the main body of the army which I could not discover—discharged my musket at part of the enemy, and ran for a piece of wood, at a distance where I thought I might shelter. At this moment Washington appeared in front of the American army, riding towards those of us who were retreating, and exclaimed, "Parade with us, my brave fellows, there is but a handful of the enemy, and we will have them directly." I immediately joined the main body, and marched over the ground again. . . .

The British were unable to resist this attack, and retreated into the College, where they thought themselves safe. Our army was there in an instant, and cannon were planted before the door, and after two or three discharges, a white flag appeared at the window, and the British surrendered. They were a haughty, crabbed set of men, as they fully exhibited while prisoners, on their march to the country. In this battle, my pack, which was made fast by leather strings, was shot from my back, and with it went what little clothing I had. It was, however, soon replaced by one which belonged to a British officer, and was well furnished. It was not mine long, for it was stolen shortly afterwards. . . .

In this battle and that of Trenton, there were no ardent spirits in the army, and the excitement of rum had nothing to do in obtaining the victories. As I had tried powder and rum on Long Island to promote courage, and engaged here without it, I can say that I was none the less courageous here than there. The army retreated to Pluckemin mountains. The weather was extremely cold, and we suffered greatly from its severity. We stayed three or four days and then marched through New Jersey towards New York. The inhabitants manifested very different feelings towards us, from those exhibited a few weeks before, and were now ready to take arms against the British. At Morristown I was sick of the small pox and many of our little army died there of that disease.

*Washington, with what Henry Knox termed "another tussle," had
given hope to what had appeared a lost cause. At Morristown he went
into a belated winter quarters "where I shall watch the motions of the
Enemy and avail myself of every favourable circumstance." It was to be
a long, hard winter.*

War Without Battles

TRENTON and Princeton were a tonic for the sagging spirits of the country, reflected in Colonel Stephen Moylan's "America will, by God, it must be free. . . . How your heart went pit-a-pat when the news reached you, and what an agreeable feel you must have had when you heard of their facing to the right about. But that feel is very short of those which we all enjoyed. When pursuing the flying enemy it is unutterable, inexpressable. I know I never felt so much like Homer's Deitys before; we trod on air, it was a glorious day!"

British soldiers were restless, grumbling that General Howe "was diverting himself in New York, in feasting, gunning, banqueting, and in the arms of Mrs. Loring." Although there were no battles, rebel parties so harassed their enemy that every foraging party felt their sting. One disgruntled British officer held little brief for his superiors.

I believe General Howe to be an honest man; I am sure he is a brave man, but I am equally sure he is a very weak man and in every respect unqualified for a Commander-in-Chief, and he has got none but very silly fellows around him. Together with his own incapacity as Commander-in-Chief, he has the misfortune to have a great parcel of generals under him, most [of] them (even from age) improper for American service. How can it be otherwise when most of them are only superannuated lieutenant colonels made generals for this occasion. I could be very ludicrous on this occasion, but it is truly too serious a truth that brave men's lives should be sacrificed to be commanded by such a parcel of old women.

For excepting Earl Percy and Lord Cornwallis, both Lieutenant Generals, and Brigadier-Generals Leslie and Sir William Erskine, the rest are, upon my soul, a parcel of old women and unfit for service as any ladies their age. Lord Percy has hitherto escaped any reflections upon his military conduct, but he is greatly disgusted with

General Howe, and I believe justly. Lord Cornwallis, I believe is a very brave man, but he and our countrywoman, Mother James Grant, allowed themselves to be fairly out-generaled by Washington, the 4th of January last and missed a glorious opportunity. . . .

Washington, in the meantime, was attempting to alleviate the wretched condition of those Americans held as prisoners of war. To Admiral Lord Richard Howe, he suggested that steps be taken "that the unhappy Creatures, whose Lot is Captivity, may not in the future have the miseries of Cold, disease and Famine, added to their other misfortunes. You may call us Rebels, and say that we deserve no better treatment; But remember, my Lord, that supposing us Rebels, we still have feelings equally as keen and sensible as loyalists, and will, if forced to it, most assuredly retaliate upon those, upon [whom] we look, as the unjust invaders of our Rights, Liberties and properties."

But the accusation of cruel treatment of prisoners was a shoe that could fit either foot. Because of false rumors that Charles Lee was suffering close confinement in New York (that worthy even won a lottery while a prisoner of war), six Hessian officers captured at Trenton were thrown into jail. Lieutenant Colonel Archibald Campbell, captured at sea in June, 1776, suffered a similar fate. From the stinking little Concord jail he wrote an acrid, bitter description of his surroundings.

I am lodged in a dungeon of twelve or thirteen feet square, whose sides are black with the grease and litter of successive criminals. Two doors with double locks and bolt shut me up from the yard, with an express prohibition to enter it, either for my health, or the necessary calls of nature.

Two small windows, strongly grated with iron, introduce a gloomy light to the apartment and these are at this hour without a single pane of glass, although the season for frost and snow is actually in the extreme. In the corner of the cell, boxed up with a partition, stands a necessary house, which does not seem to have been emptied since its first appropriation to the convenience of malefactors. A loathsome black hole, decorated with a pair of fixed chains is granted me for my inner apartment, from where a felon was but a moment before removed to make way for your humble servant, and in which his litter and his very excrement to this very hour remains.

The attendance of a single servant on my person is also denied me, and every visit from a friend is positively refused. In short, sir, was a fire to take place in any chamber of the gaol, which is all of wood, the chimney stacks excepted, I might perish in the flames before the gaoler could go through the ceremony of unbolting the door although, to do him justice in his station, I really think him a man of attention & humanity. His house is so remote from the gaol, that any call from within, especially if the wind is high, might be long of reaching him effectually.

There was a dirty little war being fought among civilians; the "Whigs," as those espousing the rebel cause termed themselves, bestowed the epithet of "Tory" on those who remained loyal to George III. The Whigs had their own definition of a loyalist: "A Tory is a thing whose head is in England, and its body in America, and its neck ought to be stretched." When possible, the Tories repaid the compliment. One incident occurred in Westchester County, New York.

When the king's troops were in that part of the country, your old acquaintance, Mr. ——, was very active in giving them every assistance in his power. The rebels had information of his conduct. They had before taken his fat cattle, &c., to the number of about forty; and when the royal army retired, attempted to make him prisoner. But he escaped them, by half an hour, and got hither. They then stripped the house of everything worth carrying away, except the provisions laid up for the winter, "because he was a damned Tory, and had gone to the king's troops for protection."

The next day came the light dragoons, provided with bags, and carried off all the beef, pork and gammons, "because he was a damned rebel, and had run away for fear of the king's army." The poor gentleman is now in town with his family, with little, next to nothing, to subsist on. He cannot return, and if he could, he could not live unless he could eat stones.

There was a time, for instance, in South Carolina, when Tories had the upper hand over James Jenkins and his friends.

My brother Francis, being a bachelor, insisted on our moving down in the Neck and living with him, as he had room and land enough for us all; accordingly, we did so. We were now in the midst of a neighborhood of hot Whigs and warm friends of the country.

But there was a body of Tories over Little Pee Dee who were becoming very troublesome, constantly committing depredations on their neighbors. In consequence of this my cousin, John Jenkins, being the only Whig in that settlement, feeling his life to be constantly in jeopardy, took refuge in the Neck. By this time our family had become quite large—father, mother, four sons and one cousin. But it did not continue so long, for at the call of their beloved country, my brothers and cousin left us, and made the swamp their camp and the battlefield their home. They, and all the Neck company, were now called into the army, in which they continued, by intervals, until the close of the war.

Meanwhile, our troublesome neighbors, taking the advantage of our unprotected condition (for there were scarcely a half dozen men left on the Neck), came down on a plundering expedition, and scoured out the settlement like a swarm of hungry Egyptian locusts. When I saw them coming to our house, I took refuge in the top of a tree about eighty yards distant, whence I could see all their movements, undiscovered. In this situation I was when they took the last horse we had on the place, and although large enough to carry a gun, I durst not open my mouth, for they would have shot me down with the same indifference that they would a squirrel or a crow.

The neutrality of many of those who remained in Philadelphia disgusted John Adams.

This city is a dull place in comparison with what it was. . . . More than one half the inhabitants have removed into the country as it was their wisdom to do. The remainder are chiefly Quakers, as dull as beetles. From these neither good is to be expected nor evil to be apprehended. They are a kind of neutral tribe, or the race of insipids. Howe may possibly attempt this town, and a pack of sordid scoundrels, male and female, seem to have prepared their minds and bodies, houses and cellars, for his reception; but these are few, and more despicable in character than number.

America will lose nothing by Howe gaining this place. No such panic will be spread by it now as was spread by the expectation of it in December. However, if we can get together twenty thousand men by the first of April, Mr. Howe will scarcely cross Delaware River this year. . . .

And in Boston, it was not the Tories so much as the profiteers who disturbed the local citizens, Abigail Adams reported to John.

I have nothing new to entertain you with, unless it be an account of a new set of nobility, which has lately taken the lead in Boston. You must know that there is a great scarcity of sugar and coffee, articles which the female part of the state is very loath to give up, especially whilst they consider the scarcity occasioned by the merchants having secreted a large quantity. There had been much rout and noise in town for several weeks. Some stores had been opened by a number of people, and the coffee and sugar carried into the market and dealt out by pounds.

It is rumored that an eminent, wealthy, stingy merchant [Thomas Boylston], (also a bachelor) had a hogshead of coffee in his store, which he refused to sell to the committee under six shillings per pound. A number of females, some say a hundred, some say more, assembled with a cart and trucks, marched down to the warehouse and demanded the keys, which he refused to deliver. Upon which one of them seized him by his neck, and tossed him into the cart. Upon his finding no quarter, he delivered the keys, when they tipped up the cart and discharged him; then opened up the warehouse, hoisted out the coffee themselves, put it into the trucks and drove off.

At Morristown, Washington inoculated his soldiers against smallpox, and housed them as best he could against the winter. But with warmer weather, life seemed to hold a promise of hope, and there was time for the amenities. Martha Washington came to New Jersey and held court. The General would sometimes join the ladies after his morning's work. One Virginia coquette could scarce contain her excitement.

Now let me speak of our noble and agreeable commander (for he commands both sexes, one by his excellent skill in military matters, the other by his ability, politeness and attention). We visit them twice or three times a week by particular invitation—every day frequently from inclination. He is generally busy in the forenoon, but from dinner till night he is free for all company. His worthy lady seems to be in perfect felicity while she is at the side of her "Old Man," as she calls him.

We often make parties on horseback, the General, his Lady, Miss

Livingston, and his aides-de-camp . . . all polite, sensible gentlemen, who make the day pass with a great deal of satisfaction to the visitors. But I had forgot my subject, almost, this is our riding party, generally at which time General Washington throws off the hero and takes on the chatty, agreeable companion. He can be downright impudent sometimes—such impudence, Fanny, as you and I like, and really, I have wished for you often.

Newly raised Continentals were swelling Washington's army. But they were an undisciplined mass, and the General shuddered at their immoralities. Extracts from his General Orders imply disgust.

As few vices are attended with pernicious consequences, in civil life, so there are none more fatal in a military one, than that of GAMING, which so often brings disgrace and ruin upon officers, and injury and punishment upon the soldiery. And reports prevailing which, it is feared, are too well founded, that this destructive vice has spread its baneful influence in the army, and, in a peculiar manner, to the prejudice of the recruiting service. The Commander-in-Chief, in the most pointed and explicit terms, forbids ALL officers and soldiers playing at cards, dice or any games except those of EXERCISE for diversion; it being impossible, if the practice be allowed at all, to discriminate between innocent play for amusement and criminal gaming for pecuniary and sordid purposes. . . .

The British scoffed.

The American republicans, like the rebels of all ages, from their *justice*, *peaceloving*, and *mercy*, pretend to have the especial favors of God, and none of the devil's, on their side, and for this reason we rarely see a proclamation from the rebel camp, without a pious sentence bringing up the rear. The late orders given by the head rebel at Morristown, in the Jerseys, a copy of which is printed in all the rebel prints, is a greater illustration of this Yankee piety than any yet come out. In this Mr. Washington forbids card playing under the penalty of a courtmartial, ostensibly for the reason that it is wicked and brings a disgrace on the officers, but in reality to enlist the parsons and other old women stronger in the cause of rebellion . . . when the time comes, he'll find that he can't "fool the Lord" with pretended piety of Presbyterian general orders.

Yet the British gained respect for their adversary. Three times Howe tried to lure Washington into open battle, and three times the American general resisted the temptation. Nicholas Cresswell, British civilian and a visitor to Mount Vernon before the outbreak of hostilities, held Washington in greater veneration than he did the British Commander in Chief.

Washington is certainly a most surprising man, one of Nature's geniuses, a Heaven-born General, if there is any of that sort. That a Negro-driver should, with a ragged banditti of undisciplined people, the scum and refuse of all nations on earth, so long keep a British general at bay, nay, even oblige him, with as fine an army of veteran soldiers as ever England had on the American continent, to retreat— it is astonishing! It is too much! By Heavens, there must be double-dealing somewhere! General Howe, a man brought up to war from his youth, to be puzzled and plagued for two years together, with a Virginia tobacco planter. O! Britain, how thy laurels tarnish in the hands of such a lubber! . . .

He undoubtedly pants for military fame and, considering the little military knowledge and experience he had before he was made a general, he has performed wonders. He was generally unfortunate (indeed I may with propriety say always) in every action where he was immediately concerned until the affair at Trenton in the Jerseys. Since that unlucky period (for us) he has only been too successful. His education is not very great nor his parts shining, his disposition is rather heavy than volatile, much given to silence. In short, he is but a poor speaker and but shines in the epistolary way. His person is tall and genteel, age betwixt forty and fifty, his behaviour and deportment is easy, genteel, and obliging, with a certain something about him which pleases everyone who has anything to do with him. There cannot be a greater proof of his particular address and good conduct than his keeping such a number of refractory, headstrong people together in any tolerable degree of decorum. . . .

From my personal acquaintance with him, and from everything that I have been able to learn of him, I believe him to be a worthy honest man, guilty of no bad vice, except we reckon ambition amongst the number, and here we ought to reckon charitably. The temptation was very great to a mind naturally ambitious. Nature made him too weak to resist it.

As an officer he is quite popular, almost idolized by the southern provinces, but I think he is not so great a favorite with the northern ones. The ignorant and deluded part of the people look up to him as the Savior and Protector of their country, and have implicit confidence in everything he does. The artful and designing part of the people, that is, the Congress, and those at the head of affairs, look upon him as a necessary tool to compass their diabolical purposes.

He certainly deserves some merit as a general, that he with his banditti, can keep General Howe dancing from one town to another for two years together, with such an army as he has. Confound the great Chucklehead, he will not unmuzzle the mastiffs, or they would eat him and his ragged crew in a little time were they properly conducted with a man of resolution and spirit. Washington, my enemy as he is, I should be sorry if he should be brought to an ignominious death.

By now it was spring, and spring was the time for war. Howe was forced to put aside his indolent ways and take to the field. After several feints, hoping to entice the Americans into battle, Howe maneuvered his troops through New Jersey. When Washington refused the bait, the British suddenly marched to Amboy and ferried across to Staten Island. Washington concerned himself with just where the British general would make his next move: would it be Philadelphia, up the Hudson to make a junction with the force then advancing from Canada, or would it be to the southward? The perplexed general could only wait.

Invasion from the North

WHILE Washington fretted and Howe procrastinated, things were beginning to take shape to the north. General John Burgoyne, known as "Gentleman Johnny," raconteur, man about London, and a better than average playwright, was assembling an expedition that was expected to divide the former colonies and bring them to their senses. He had made a habit of returning to England after every campaign, there to ingratiate himself with Lord George Germain and forward his own martial career. He had proposed a three-pronged movement of troops calculated to split New England from the remaining colonies. The principal army, under Burgoyne, was to sweep majestically southward by way of Lake Champlain, Ticonderoga, and Saratoga. Howe was expected to send troops up the Hudson, while a smaller force under Lieutenant Colonel Barry St. Leger was to strike inland from Fort Oswego on Lake Ontario. The three groups were to converge on Albany.

Burgoyne had arrived in Canada on May 6, 1777. He hoped to supplement his 7,213 men (three brigades of British regulars and three of Hessians) with Canadian loyalists and Indians. Only about 250 Tories and 400 Indians joined the expedition. A massive artillery train of 138 guns was to be manhandled along forest trails. Large numbers of women and children also followed their men to war in the wilderness. On June 27, Burgoyne arrived at Crown Point. On June 30 he issued his orders for the attack on Ticonderoga: "During our progress occasions may occur, in which neither difficulty nor labor nor life are to be regarded. THIS ARMY MUST NOT RETREAT."

General Philip Schuyler, whose complaints had alienated many, was in command of the Northern Department. Washington thought well of this general, but Schuyler was thoroughly despised by New England, his nearest source of troops. On the other hand, soldiers from south of New York had little use for Yankees, as witness Persifor Frazer of Pennsylvania.

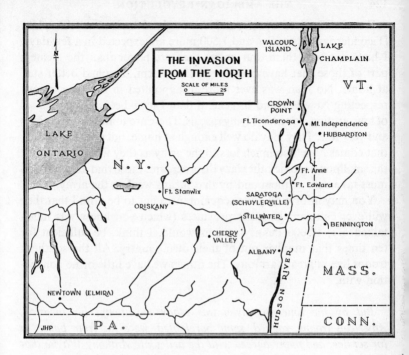

THE INVASION
FROM THE NORTH

SCALE OF MILES
0   25

LAKE
ONTARIO

N.Y.

VALCOUR
ISLAND

LAKE
CHAMPLAIN

VT.

CROWN
POINT

Ft. Ticonderoga   • Mt. Independence
                   • HUBBARDTON

Ft. Stanwix

ORISKANY

CHERRY
VALLEY

NEWTOWN (ELMIRA)

ALBANY

STILLWATER

SARATOGA
(SCHUYLERVILLE)

• Ft. Anne

Ft. Edward

• BENNINGTON

MASS.

HUDSON RIVER

PA.

CONN.

JHP

Five hundred troops from New England arrived at this place [Ticonderoga] yesterday, and 1,500 more are expected in a few days. I have not seen them, but unless they are better than the greatest part of those that have been here before them, they had better stay at home. No man was ever more disappointed in his expectations respecting New England in general than I have been. They are a set of low, griping, cowardly, lying rascals. There are some few exceptions and very few. They may do well enough at home, but every fresh man that comes here is so much loss to the army as they will get sick with the smallpox or some other lazy disorder, and those that are seasoned must take care of them and by that means weaken the army. . . .

You may inform all your acquaintances not to be afraid that they will ever conquer the other provinces (which you know was much talked of); 10,000 Pennsylvanians would, I think, be sufficient for ten times that number out of their own country. All the southern troops live in great harmony. The others we have little or no connection with.

But by the time Burgoyne was ready to attempt his invasion, American troops, ragged, some barefooted, were far from being fit for service, and many agreed with the articulate Anthony Wayne that Ticonderoga was "the last place in the world that God made . . . the ancient Golgotha or place of skulls."

On the first of July, the British army embarked and sailed for Ticonderoga: "The music and drums of the different regiments were continually playing and contributed to make the scene and passage extremely pleasant." Arthur St. Clair, commandant of Ticonderoga, apparently felt secure in his fortress, so much so that he had neglected to fortify Sugar Loaf Hill, or Mount Defiance, that overlooked the stronghold and was the key to the subsequent evacuation of Fort Ticonderoga. Lieutenant William Digby of Burgoyne's army explained why the fort became untenable.

July 4th. Before day light, we shifted our camp farther back a small way from the range of their shot, until our 12-pounders could come up to play on them in return. By their not throwing shells, we supposed they had none, which from our camp being on a rocky eminence, would have raked us much. As to their balls, we did not mind them, being at too great a distance to suffer from any point blank shot from their cannon.

About noon we took possession of Sugar Loaf hill, on which a battery was immediately ordered to be raised. It was a post of great consequence, as it commanded a great part of the works of Ticonderoga, all their vessels, and likewise afforded us the means of cutting off their communication with Fort Independent, a place also of great strength and the works very extensive. But here the commanding officer was reckoned guilty of a great oversight in lighting fires on that post, tho' I am informed it was done by the Indians, the smoke of which was soon perceived by the enemy in the fort; as he should have remained undiscovered till night, when he was to have got two 12-pounders up, tho' their getting there was almost a perpendicular ascent, and drawn up by most of the cattle belonging to the army.

They no sooner perceived us in possession of a post, which they thought quite impossible to bring cannon up to, than all their pretended boastings of holding out to the last, and choosing rather to die in their works than give them up, failed them, and on the night of the 5th, they set fire to several parts of the garrison, kept a constant fire of great guns the whole night, and under the protection of that fire and clouds of smoke, they evacuated the garrison, leaving all their cannon, ammunition and a great quantity of stores. They embarked what baggage they could during the night in their batteaux, and sent them up to Skenesborough under the protection of five schooners, which Captain Carter of the artillery, with our gun boats, followed and destroyed with all their baggage and provisions.

As I [happened] to be one of the lieutenants of the Grenadiers picket that night, when we perceived the great fire in the fort, the general was immediately made acquainted with it, and our suspicion of their abandoning the place, who with many other good officers, imagined it was all a feint in them to induce us to make an attack, and seemingly with a great deal of probability, tho' to me, who could be but a very poor judge, it seemed quite the contrary, as I never before saw such great fires. . . .

6th. At the first dawn of light, three deserters came in and informed that the enemy were retreating the other side of Mount Independent. The General was, without loss of time, made acquainted with it, and the pickets of the army were ordered to march and take possession of the garrison and hoist the King's colors.

Lieutenant Thomas Anburey was one of the first to enter the fort.

When we came to the bridge of communication, we were obliged to halt till it was sufficiently repaired for the troops to pass, as the enemy, in their abandoning the works, had destroyed it, and had left four men who were, upon the approach of our army, to have fired off the cannon of a large battery that defended it, and retire as quick as possible. No doubt this was their intention, as they left lighted matches close to the cannon.

Had these men obeyed their instructions they would, situated as our brigade was, have done great mischief. But, allured by the sweets of plunder and liquor, instead of obeying their orders, we found them dead drunk by a cask of Madeira. This battery, however, through the folly of an Indian, nearly [had] been productive of fatal consequences to the 9th regiment, for just at that time it was passing the bridge, as he was very curious in examining everything that came in his way, he took up a match that lay upon the ground, with some fire still remaining in it, when a spark dropping upon the priming of the cannon, it went off, loaded with all manner of combustibles, but it fortunately happened the gun was so elevated, no mischief ensued.

Howe, leaving all but fifty-two of his guns at Ticonderoga, began the pursuit. On July 7th, at Hubbardton, there was a clash. The Americans were driven off. Two days later, the 9th Regiment surged forward against the sagging strongpoint called Fort Anne. Among the attackers was Sergeant Roger Lamb.

Early next morning, 9th July, an American soldier came from the fort. He said that he had deserted, though it was afterwards discovered that he was a spy. He stated that there were one thousand men in the fort, and that they were in the greatest consternation, under an apprehension of the British attacking and storming them. Upon this intelligence, Colonel Hill dispatched a message to General Burgoyne, stating his situation and how far he had advanced, which was eight or ten miles from the main army.

Not many minutes after this message was sent off, the pretended deserter disappeared. He had viewed the situation and seen the strength of the British, which did not amount to above one hundred and ninety men including officers. It was soon found that he had made a faithful report to his friends, for in less than half an hour they came out of the fort with great fury. The British outline of sentries received them with the greatest bravery and steadiness, and obliged them to retreat. They then formed again, and came on with redoubled violence. The officers could be heard encouraging them on to the attack, though their numbers could not be seen, the woods being so thick, but it was soon found that they not only outflanked, but were endeavoring to surround the British. In order to prevent this, they were obliged to change their ground and retire up a high hill which was in their rear. In performing this maneuver, several of the men were killed and wounded. When the troops arrived at the summit of the hill, they formed in Indian file, and kept up a well directed fire till all the ammunition was expended. The enemy observing that the firing ceased, were encouraged to press forward with redoubled vigor and endeavored to surround them in order to cut them off. Just at this critical moment a war whoop was heard, which resounded through the woods. This sound, which was so obnoxious at that time to the Americans, threw them into the utmost consternation.

The war whoop was sounded by Captain Money, deputy quartermaster general. He had been detached by General Burgoyne early in the morning from Skenesborough, with a party of Indians, in order to join this detachment. When they came within four miles of Fort Anne, they heard the firing. Captain Money ordered them to advance as fast as possible to assist, but they refused to obey him, and either stood still or advanced very slow. Being anxious to join the party at all events, he ran forward by himself with all his might, and came to the bottom of the hill where, just as all the ammunition was expended, he gave the war whoop. . . .

After the Americans had retreated, we formed on the hill. It was a distressing sight to see the wounded men bleeding on the ground, and what made it more so, the rain came pouring down like a deluge upon us. And still to add to the distress of the sufferers, there was nothing left to dress their wounds. . . . The poor fellows earnestly entreated me to tie up their wounds. Immediately I took off my shirt, tore it up, and with the help of a soldier's wife (the only woman that was with us, and who kept close by her husband's side during the engagement), made some bandages, stopped the bleeding of their wounds, and conveyed them in blankets to a small hut about two miles in our rear. . . .

The rebels were retreating, but British pursuit slowed to a crawl. Schuyler was felling trees across the road, destroying bridges, and burning everything that might be of use to the enemy. Burgoyne's Indians, as one Hessian officer wrote, "behaved like hogs," and roamed the countryside. William Weeks, paymaster for the 3rd New Hampshire Regiment, hated the savages.

There is a very good crop in these parts, but soon comes a desolation; wherever we march we keep our horses in the fields among corn and oats, so that the enemy, if they gain the ground, may have poor fare for them and their horses. Tories are very troublesome here—many of them take up arms against us & lurk in the woods with the Indians waiting for a sculp. It is believed the Tories have sculp'd many of their countrymen, as there is a premium from Burgoyne for sculps. They are daily taken and brought in by our scouts & I believe some of them will swing very soon.

The Indians treat both sexes with the same barbarity, have kill'd and sculp'd whole families together, Men, women & children. At one place as our men were passing, they saw a man, his wife & children sculp'd (by those savages), gaping & expiring & the hogs rooting their bodies.

A few days ago I rode a little distance from camp where we had a few men stationed to guard the sick. I had just passed the place where a party of Indians happened to lay & stopped at the first house talking with an officer. As I sat upon my horse, out rushed those Indians & fired at some men swimming in the water and chased some as they were passing. I, seeing this, screamed to the guard to pursue them, and rode towards them. They discharged their pieces towards us, & fired one ball into the house not far from the door where I was. Immediately upon our pursuing them they ran into the woods & got off. We were in such haste they had not time to get a sculp. They killed two; one shot in the water, who got out & ran a considerable distance before he fell. Since then they have cut off more of our men—One hundred Indians in the woods do no more harm than 1000 British troops. They have been the death of many brave fellows—I hope they will meet with their reward for their cursed cruelty.

Although Indians could lose themselves among the trees, Tories were easier to round up. Patrols often brought them in.

We lay down in a thick spot of woods by the side of the road. It was not long before there came along two regulars driving a number of horses. We jumped up and seized them. The regulars were so very much frighted, that they made no resistance, neither could they speak plain. We found, by the noise, there were a number more behind driving cattle. One of our prisoners called to the sergeant for help; upon this, we thought it wise to make the best of our way into the woods. Our prisoners attempted to get away from us; we were therefore obliged to make them feel that our hatchets were heavy. I told them, "If you will behave like prisoners, we will use you well. But if you don't, we must kill you." After this they behaved well and did everything we bid them.

On our way to our encampment, we thought we would take in with us as many Tories as we could find, and in order to find them, we gave our prisoners their guns, taking out the flints. When we came near a house, we told our prisoners, "You must keep before us, and if you see any man, you must cock your guns and present them at them, and demand who they are for, the King, or country?" They did so. And the Tories answered, "They were for the King, or they should have moved off long ago." They seemed to be glad to see the regulars, and told them, "You are our brothers."

I knew one of the Tories as soon as I came in sight of him. I therefore put my hat over my face for fear the fellow should know me, till the redcoats had done their duty. After he had, in a most strong manner, declared "He was for the King," I asked him further, "Will you be true to the King, and fight for him till you die?"

"Oh Yes," said the Tory.

Upon this, he discovered his error, knew me, and immediately said, "What King do you mean? I mean King HANCOCK."

"Ah," said I, "we have found you out, we don't have kings in America yet; you must come along with us."

But it was the Indians who furnished the Americans with a choice bit of propaganda, even though the victim, one Jane McCrea, was herself of loyalist inclinations and engaged to David Jones, an officer in Burgoyne's Tory troops. When Burgoyne pardoned Wyandot Panther, supposedly the murderer of the young girl, for fear his other Indians would desert, it only added fuel to the flame. Lieutenant Anburey felt it to be a horrible, but unavoidable accident.

Some Indians, who were out on a scout, by chance met with her in the woods. They first treated her with every mark of civility they are capable of, and were conducting her into camp when, within a mile of it, a dispute arose between the two Indians, whose prisoner of war she was, and the words growing very high, one of them, who was fearful of losing the reward for bringing her safe into camp, most inhumanely struck his tomahawk into her skull and she instantly expired.

The situation of the General, whose humanity was much shocked at such an instance of barbarity, was very distressing and critical, for however inclined he might be to punish the offender, still it was hazarding the revenge of the savages, whose friendship he had to court, rather than seek their enmity.

The chief of the tribe to which the Indian belonged readily consented to his being delivered up to the General, to act with him as he thought proper, but at the same time said, it was the rules of their war, that if two of them at the same instant seized a prisoner, and seemed to have equal claim, in case any dispute arose between them, they soon decided the contest, for the unhappy cause was sure to become a victim to their contention.

Sam Adams, loyal to New England, catalogued some of the reasons why Horatio Gates, himself no friend to Schuyler, was chosen to replace the New Yorker as Commanding General in the Northern Department.

Schuyler has written a series of weak and contemptible things in a style of despondency which alone, I think, is sufficient for the removal of him from that command. For if his pen expresses the true feelings of his heart, it cannot be expected that the bravest veterans would fight under such a general, admitting they had no suspicions of treachery.

In a letter, dated the 4th instant at Stillwater, he writes in a tone of perfect despair. He seems to have no confidence in his troops, nor the states from whence reinforcements are to be drawn. A third of his Continental Troops, he tells us, consists "of Boys, Negroes and aged men not fit for the Field or any other Service," ... "a very great part of the Army naked, without Blanketts, ill armed and very deficient in Accoutrements, without a Prospect of Relief." "Many, too many of the Officers would be a Disgrace to the most contemptible Troops that ever was collected." The exertions of others of them of a different character "counteracted by the worthless." "Gen'l Burgoyne is bending his Course this Way, and unless we are well reenforced" (which he does not expect) "as much farther as he pleases to go."

Was ever a poor general more mortified? But he has by this time received his quietus. Gates takes the command there, agreeably to what you tell me is the wish of the people, and I trust our affairs in that quarter will soon wear a more promising aspect.

Despite such veiled threats as John Adams's "I think we shall never defend a post until we shoot a General," Horatio Gates seemed to be in no great hurry to assume his new command. By the time he arrived in Albany on August 19, the tide had begun to reverse itself. Even as Burgoyne was settling in at Fort Edward on the Hudson, Barry St. Leger's detachment had moved through the Mohawk Valley with relative ease until he hit old Fort Stanwix, now renamed Fort Schuyler, guarding the portage between Wood Creek and the Mohawk River. Second in command was Marinus Willet, whose account of the subsequent siege was printed in contemporary newspapers.

Saturday evening, August 2, five batteaux arrived with stores for the garrison. About the same time we discovered a number of fires a little better than a mile from the northwest corner of the fort. The stores were all got safe in, and the troops which were a guard to the batteaux marched up. The captain of the batteaux and a few of his men, delaying their time about the boats, were fired on by a party of Indians, which killed one man and wounded two; the captain himself was taken prisoner.

Next morning the enemy appeared in the edge of the woods, about a mile below the fort, where they took post in order to invest it on that quarter, and to cut off the communication from the country, from whence they sent in a flag, who told us of their great power, strength and determination in such a manner as gave us reason to suppose they were not possessed of strength sufficient to take the fort. Our answer was, a determination to support it. All day on Monday we were much annoyed by a sharp fire of musketry from the Indians and German riflemen, which, as our men were obliged to be exposed on the works, killed one and wounded seven. The day after, the firing was not quite so heavy and our men under better cover, all the damage was one man killed by a rifle ball.

This evening indicated something in contemplation by the enemy; the Indians were uncommonly noisy, the most horrid yellings a great part of the evening in the woods hardly a mile from the fort. A few cannon were fired among them.

Wednesday morning there was an unusual silence; we discovered some of the enemy marching along the edge of the woods downwards. About eleven o'clock, three men got into the fort, who brought a letter from General Herkimer of the Tryon County militia, advising us that he was at Oriskany (eight miles from the fort), with part of his militia, and proposed to fight his way to the fort for our relief—in order to render him what service we could in his march—it was agreed that I should make a sally from the fort with two hundred & fifty men . . . and one field piece (an iron three-pounder). The men were instantly paraded. . . .

Nothing could be more fortunate than this enterprise. We totally routed two of the enemy's encampments, destroyed all their provisions that was in them, brought off upwards of fifty brass kettles, and more than a hundred blankets (two articles which were much needed by us), with a number of muskets, tomahawks, spears, ammunition, clothing, deer skins, a variety of Indian affairs, and five colors which, on our return to the fort, were displayed on our flag staff under the Continental Flag.

Nicholas Herkimer, burly son of a German immigrant, and called "Old Honikol" by his men, had indeed been ambushed at Oriskany, an Indian name meaning "Field of Nettles." He had been wounded at the outset, but "did not leave the field till the action was over; he seated himself down on a log, with his sword drawn, animating his men."

Soon after Herkimer's defeat, Marinus Willet and a Lieutenant Stockwell had slipped over the walls to seek aid. Schuyler, however, had already dispatched Benedict Arnold with 950 volunteers to the relief of Fort Stanwix. Hon Yost Schuyler, nephew of Herkimer, and reputed something of a half-wit, had been brought into camp and condemned to death as one of those planning a Tory uprising in Tryon County. Realizing the veneration with which the Indians held the feeble-minded, Arnold resorted to stratagem. Timothy Dwight recorded the story some years later after hearing it from those who were there.

Arnold wisely determined to avail himself of this man's services. He proposed to him a scheme for alarming the enemy, particularly the savages, by announcing to them that a formidable army was in full march to destroy them, and assured him of his life and estate if he would enter heartily into the interests of his country and faithfully execute a mission of this nature. Schuyler, who was shrewd, resolute, versed in the language and manners of the Indians, acquainted with some of their chiefs, and therefore perfectly qualified for this business, readily engaged in the enterprise. His father and brother were in the mean time kept as hostages for his fidelity, and were both to be hung without mercy if he proved unfaithful. One of the Sachems of the Six Nations, a friend of the Americans, was let in on the secret, and cheerily embarked in the design. Having settled the whole plan of proceeding with this warrior, Schuyler made the best of his way to Fort Stanwix.

Colonel St. Leger had pushed the siege with considerable activity and advanced his works within one hundred and fifty yards of the fort. Upon Schuyler's arrival, he told the lamentable story of being taken by Arnold, his escape by hanging, and the danger which he had encountered in his flight. He showed them also, several holes made by shot in his coat, while he was attempting to escape, and declared at the same time that a formidable army of Americans were marching with full speed to attack the British. The Americans, he observed, had no hostility towards the Indians, and wished not to injure them, but added that, if the Indians continued with the British, they must unquestionably take their share of whatever calamities might befall their allies.

The Indians being thus thoroughly alarmed, the chief who was in the secret, arrived as if by mere accident, and in the mysterious manner of that people began to insinuate to his countrymen, that a bird had brought him intelligence of great moment. This hint set their curiosity afloat, and excited a number of anxious enquiries. To these he replied in hints and suggestions, concerning warriors in great numbers, marching with the utmost rapidity, and already far advanced. In the mean time he had dispatched two or three young warriors in the search of intelligence. These scouts, who had received their cue, returned, as they had been directed, at different times and confirmed, as if by accident also, all that had been said by Schuyler and the Sachem. The Indians, already disgusted with the service, which they found a mere contrast to the promises of the British commanders and their own expectations, and sore with the loss which they had sustained in the battle with General Herkimer, were now so completely alarmed that they determined upon an immediate retreat.

St. Leger, who had unwisely boasted, at first, of his own strength, and his future exploits against the Americans, and spoken contemptuously of their weakness and cowardice; who had predicted in magnificent terms the certainty of their flight, and the ease and safety with which the Indians would reach Albany, had disgusted these people thoroughly by failing altogether of the fulfillment of his promises. In vain, therefore, did he exert all his address when he saw them preparing to quit the ground, to dissuade them from their purpose. . . .

In a mixture of rage and despair he broke up his encampment with such haste, that he left his tents, cannon and stores to the besieged. The flight of this army (for it could not be called a retreat) was through a deep forest and spongey soil. . . . The Sachem, who had been partner to Schuyler in the plot, accompanied the flying army. Naturally a wag, and pleased to see the garrison rescued from their danger, he engaged several of the young men to repeat, at proper intervals, the cry, "They are coming!" This unwelcome sound . . . quickened the march of the fugitives whenever it was heard. The soldiers threw away their packs, and the commanders took care not to be in the rear. Mortified beyond measure by so disastrous an issue of an expedition, from which they had promised themselves no small reputation and profit, these gentlemen began to speedily accuse each other of folly and misconduct in their respective departments during the enterprise. Accusation begat accusation, and reproach, reproach, until they at length drew their swords upon each other. Several of the Sachems now interfered, and with that native good sense which is found everywhere, persuaded them to a reconciliation. . . .

One arm of Burgoyne's invasion had thus collapsed. Disaster was to become increasingly frequent. Before he learned of the dissipation of the Mohawk expedition, Burgoyne suffered another blow. To the east lay the Hampshire Grants which Burgoyne felt to be a country that "now abounds in the most active and rebellious race of the continent, and hangs like a gathering storm on my left." But it was a land as yet unravaged by foraging armies. To Lieutenant Colonel Friedrich Baume, Burgoyne gave a mixed command of Hessians, British regulars, provincials, loyalist militia and about eighty Indians. His instructions were to disrupt enemy operations, gather dragoon horses, recruit loyalists, and bring in supplies of cattle, horses and carriages.

Unbeknownst to Burgoyne, the man called John Stark had called out the people of the Grants. They gathered quickly, although as Captain Peter Clark noted, "We are almost all of something disordered with the quick step, occasioned by change of climate and diet. . . ." As Baume's troops approached Bennington, there were frequent skirmishes, and at Bennington Stark's men were waiting. Baume requested reinforcements. A Hessian, Lieutenant Glich, reported the development of a battle.

The 15th was a day of continued rain . . . an absolute torrent, to afford shelter against which human ingenuity has as yet devised no covering. Under this the men toiled on, the earth which they threw up being repeatedly washed down again, and the holes and ditches they dug filled in a moment, and so rendered worse than useless. But their patience equalled the difficulties which it was called upon to surmount. Each man felt, too, that he was laboring for his own personal safety, not less than for the benefit of the whole. . . .

The morning of the sixteenth rose beautifully serene. The storm of the preceding day having expended itself, not a cloud was left to darken the face of the heavens, whilst every leaf hung motionless, and the long grass waved not under the influence of a perfect calm. Every object around, too, appeared to peculiar advantage, for the fields looked green and refreshed, the river was swollen and tumultuous, and the branches were all loaded with dewdrops, which glittered in the early rays like so many diamonds. . . .

All was perfectly quiet at the outposts, not an enemy having been seen, nor an alarming sound heard, for several hours previous to sunrise. So peaceable, indeed, was the aspect which matters bore, that our leaders felt warmly disposed to resume the offensive without waiting for the additional corps for which they had applied, and orders were already issued for the men to eat their breakfasts, preparatory to more active operations. But the arms were scarcely piled and the haversacks unslung, when symptoms of a state of affairs different from that which had been anticipated, began to show themselves, and our people were recalled to their ranks in all haste, almost as soon as they had quitted them. From more than one quarter scouts came to report that columns of armed men were approaching, though whether with friendly or hostile intentions, neither their appearance nor actions enabled our informants to ascertain. . . .

During the last day's march, our little corps was joined by many of the country people, most of whom demanded and obtained arms as persons friendly to the royal cause. How Colonel Baume became so completely duped as to place reliance on these men, I know not; but having listened with complacency to their previous assurances that in Bennington a large majority of the populace were our friends, he was somehow or other persuaded to believe that the armed bands, of whose approach he was warned, were loyalists on their way to make tender of their services to the leader of the King's troops. Filled with this idea, he dispatched positive orders to the outposts that no molestations should be offered to the advancing columns, but that the pickets retiring before them should join the main body, where every disposition was made to receive friend or foe. Unfortunately for us, these orders were but too faithfully obeyed. About half past nine o'clock I, who was not in the secret, beheld to my utter amazement, our advanced parties withdraw, without firing a shot, from thickets which might have been maintained for hours against any superiority of numbers, and the same thickets occupied by men whose demeanor, as well as their dress and style of equipment, plainly and incontestably pointed them out as Americans. . . .

With the solitary exception of our leader, there was not a man among us who appeared otherwise than satisfied that those to whom he had listened were traitors. . . . Colonel Baume remained convinced of their fidelity. He saw no reason to doubt that the people whose approach caused so much apprehension, were the same of whose arrival he had been forewarned, and he was prevented from placing himself entirely in their power, only by the positive refusal of his followers to obey orders given to that effect, and the rash impetuosity of the enemy.

We might have stood about half an hour under arms, watching the proceedings of a column of four or five hundred men who, after dislodging the pickets, had halted just at the edge of the open country, when a sudden trampling of feet in the forest on our right, followed by the report of several muskets, attracted our attention. A patrol was instantly sent out in the direction of the sound, but before the party composing it had proceeded many yards from the line, a loud shout, followed by a rapid though straggling fire of musketry, warned us for a meeting the reverse of friendly. Instantly the Indians came pouring in, carrying dismay and confusion in their countenances and gestures. We were surrounded on all sides; columns were advancing everywhere against us, and those who we had hitherto trusted as friends, had only waited till the arrival of their support might justify them in advancing. . . .

The column in our front no sooner heard the shout, than they replied loudly and cordially to it. Then, firing a volley with deliberate and murderous aim, rushed furiously towards us. Now then, at length, our leader's dreams of security were dispelled. He found himself attacked in front and flanked by thrice his number, who pressed forward with the confidence which our late proceedings were calculated to produce, whilst the very persons in whom he had trusted, and to whom he had given arms, lost no time in turning them against him. These followers no sooner heard their comrades cry than they deliberately discharged their muskets among Riedesel's dragoons, and dispersing before any steps could be taken to seize them, escaped, excepting one or two, to their friends.

If Colonel Baume had permitted himself to be duped into a great error, it is no more than justice to confess that he exerted himself manfully to remedy the evil and avert its consequences. Our little band, which had hitherto remained in column, was instantly ordered to extend, and the troops lining the breastworks replied to the fire of the Americans with extreme celerity and considerable effect. So close and so destructive, indeed, was our first volley, that the assailants recoiled before it and would have retreated, in all probability, into the woods. But ere we could take advantage of the confusion produced, fresh attacks developed themselves, and we were warmly engaged on every side and from all quarters. It became evident that each of our detached posts was about to be assailed at the same instant. . . .

It was at this moment, when the heads of columns began to show themselves in rear of our right and left, that the Indians who had hitherto acted with spirit and something like order, lost all confidence and fled. Alarmed at the prospect of having their retreat cut off, they stole away, after their own fashion, in single files, in spite of the strenuous remonstrances of Baume and of their own officers, leaving us more than ever exposed by the abandonment of that angle of the entrenchments which they had been appointed to maintain. . . .

The solitary tumbril, which contained the whole of our spare ammunition, became ignited and blew up with a violence which shook the very ground under our feet, and caused a momentary cessation in firing, both on our side and that of the enemy. But the cessation was only for a moment. The American officers, guessing the extent of our calamity, cheered their men to fresh exertions. They rushed up the ascent with redoubled ardor, in spite of the heavy fire which we poured in to check them, and finding our guns silent, they sprang over the parapet and dashed within our works.

For a few seconds the scene which ensued defies all power of language to describe. The bayonet, the butt of the rifle, the sabre, the pike, were in full play; and men fell, as they rarely fall in modern war, under the direct blow of their enemies. . . . Outnumbered, broken, and somewhat disheartened by late events, our people wavered and fell back, or fought singly and unconnectedly, till they were either cut down at their posts, obstinately defending themselves, or compelled to surrender. Of Riedesel's dragoons, few survived to tell how nobly they behaved. Colonel Baume, shot through the body by a rifle ball, fell mortally wounded, and all order and discipline being lost, flight or submission was alone thought of.

It was about half past four that afternoon when the relief column under Lieutenant Colonel Heinrich von Breymann reached Van Schaick's Mill, about six miles from the battlefield. Breymann was not prepared to cope with the ambush laid by the rebels and was forced to beat a hasty retreat, leaving his artillery behind.

Captain Peter Clark expressed the general rebel sentiment that the victory had resulted from intervention of Divine Providence. The battle, he said, had been "equal to Bunker Hill excepting there was not so many cannon. . . . The Lord of Hosts sent them off in such haste they left their all and run."

Despite the unexpected setbacks at Fort Stanwix and Bennington, Burgoyne insisted upon plowing ahead to Albany. Yet, on August 20, he wrote Lord George Germain in tones so woeful and pessimistic that the Secretary of State for the Colonies was well aware that Burgoyne's expedition held little promise of success. Germain explained his reasoning.

I am sorry to find that Burgoyne's campaign is so totally ruined; the best wish I can form is that he may have returned to Ticonderoga without much loss. His private letter to me, dated the 20th of August, contains nothing material about the affair near Bennington but military reasoning about the propriety of that attack; but what alarms me most is that he thinks his orders to go to Albany to force a junction with Sir William Howe are so positive that he must attempt at all events the obeying them, tho' at the same time he acquaints me that Sir William Howe has sent him word that he has gone to Philadelphia, and indeed nothing that Sir William says could give him reason to hope that any effort could be made in his favor.

Even in the forests of upper New York, Burgoyne acted the dandy and man about town. The wife of General von Riedesel, the Hessian commander, reported that Gentleman Johnny "spent half the nights in singing and drinking, and amusing himself with the wife of a commissary, who was his mistress, and who, as well as he, loved champagne." But Horatio Gates, who assumed command of the American Army on August 19, noticed that the British general had been somewhat subdued. To the Continental Congress he wrote, "Your excellencies will perceive by the enclosed letters, that the glorious victory at Bennington has reduced the boasting stile of Gen. Burgoyne so much, that he begins in some degree to think and talk like other men."

That "old midwife," as Burgoyne termed Gates, was receiving reinforcements, although General William Heath had some doubts as to their effectiveness: "The greater part that I saw appeared able, but it is more probable that there were some advanc'd in life, and some lads, and a number of Negroes. (The latter were generally able bodies, but for my own part I must confess I am never pleased to see them mixed with white men.)" By this time Gates had realized that "It is evident that Gen. Burgoyne designs to risque all upon rash stroke."

So at a place called Bemis Heights (named for the man who kept a tavern in its shadow), Gates dug in, blocking a southward movement. Occupying an eminence to the north, with the design of executing a flanking action, Burgoyne sent two other columns, one of which he personally led, against the Americans on September 19, 1777. It soon was obvious that a most "obstinate" battle was developing. Almost at the first fire, Lieutenant Anburey became aware that Burgoyne's forces lost some of their manpower.

The Indians were running from wood to wood, and just as soon as our regiment had formed in the skirts of one, several of them came up, and by their signs were conversing about the severe fire on our right. Soon after the enemy attacked us, and at the very first fire the Indians run off through the woods.

As to the Canadians, little was to be depended upon their

adherence, being easily dispirited, with an inclination to quit as soon as there was an appearance of danger; nor was the fidelity of the Provincials to be relied on who had joined our army, as they withdrew on perceiving the resistance of the Americans would be more formidable than expected.

The desertion of the Indians, Canadians, and Provincials, at a time when their services were most required, was exceedingly mortifying.

The battle had been brought on by Daniel Morgan and his riflemen. After a skirmish with the vanguard of the British, the main force had sent them reeling back into their own lines. James Wilkinson, adjutant to Gates, was sent out to see what the trouble was.

I crossed an angle of the field, leaped a fence and just before me on a ridge saw Lieutenant Colonel Butler with three men, all treed. From him I learned they had caught a Scotch prize; that having forced the picket, they had closed with the British line, had been instantly routed and from the suddenness of the shock and the nature of the ground, were broken and scattered in all directions. Returning to the camp to report to the General, my ears were saluted with an uncommon noise, when I approached and perceived Colonel Morgan, attended by two men only, and who with a *turkey call* was collecting his dispersed troops.

Lieutenant William Digby of Burgoyne's army described the fury of the battle.

[Sept.] 19th. At day break intelligence was received that Colonel Morgan, with the advance party of the enemy, consisting of a corps of riflemen, were strong about three miles from us; their main body amounting to great numbers encamped on a very strong post about half a mile in their rear; and about 9 o'clock we began our march, every man prepared with sixty rounds of cartridges and ready for instant action. We moved in three columns, ours to the right on the heights and farthest from the river in thick woods. A little after 12 our advanced pickets came up with Colonel Morgan and engaged, but from the great superiority of fire received from him—his numbers being much greater—they were obliged to fall back, every officer being either killed or wounded except one, when the line came up to their support and obliged Morgan in his turn to retreat with loss.

About half past one, the fire seemed to slacken a little. But it was only to come on with double force, as between 2 & 3 the action became general on their side. From the situation of the ground, and their being imperfectly acquainted with it, the whole of our troops could not be brought to engage together, which was a very material disadvantage, though everything possible was tried to remedy that inconvenience, but to no effect. Such an explosion of fire I never had any idea of before, and the heavy artillery joining in concert like great peals of thunder, assisted by the echoes of the woods, almost deafened us with the noise. To an unconcerned spectator, it must have had the most awful and glorious appearance, the different battalions moving to relieve each other, some being pressed and almost broke by their superior numbers. This crash of cannon and musketry never ceased till darkness parted us, when they retired to their camp, leaving us masters of the field; but it was a dear bought victory, if I can give it that name, as we lost many brave men. The 62nd had scarce ten men a company left, and other regiments suffered much, and no very great advantage, honor excepted, was gained by the day.

On its turning dusk, we were near firing on a body of our Germans, mistaking their dark clothing for that of the enemy. General Burgoyne was everywhere and did everything that could be expected of a brave officer, & Brigadier General Fraser gained great honor by exposing himself to every danger. During the night we remained in our ranks, and tho' we heard the groans of the wounded and dying, yet could not assist them till morning, not knowing the position of the enemy, and expecting the action to be renewed at daybreak. . . .

For the Americans, Benedict Arnold, whom Gates disliked and had placed in a subordinate position, had rushed onto the field and fought "like a madman." It had been a stubborn but indecisive battle. One young Hessian mused, "The action today has caused the house of a poor farmer to become famous; for it has given to this day's engagement the name of the 'Battle of Freeman's House.' " The British busied themselves with burying their dead. Lieutenant Anburey was on the burial detail and was heartsick "on seeing fifteen, sixteen, and twenty buried in one hole."

I, however, observed a little more decency than some parties had done, who left heads, legs and arms above ground. No other distinction is paid to officer or private, than the officers are put in a hole by themselves. Our army abounded with young officers, in the subaltern line, and in the course of this unpleasant duty, three of the 20th Regiment were interred together, the age of the eldest not exceeding seventeen. This friendly office to the dead, though it greatly affects the feeling, was nothing to the scenes in bringing in the wounded; the one were past all pain, the other in the most excruciating torments, sending forth dreadful groans. They had remained out all night, and from the loss of blood and want of nourishment, were upon the point of expiring. Some of them begged they might lay and die, others again were insensible, some upon the least movement were put in the most horrid tortures, and all had near a mile to be conveyed to the hospitals; others at their last gasp, who for want of our timely assistance must have inevitably expired. These poor creatures, perishing with cold and weltering in their blood, displayed such a scene, it must be a heart of adamant that could not be affected by it, even to a degree of weakness.

In the course of the late action, Lieutenant Harvey of the 62nd, a youth of sixteen and a nephew of the Adjutant General of the same name, received several wounds and was repeatedly ordered off the field by Colonel Anstruther. But his heroic ardor would not allow him to quit the battle, while he could stand and see his brave lads fighting beside him. A ball striking one of his legs, his removal became absolutely necessary, and while they were conveying him away, another wounded him mortally. In this situation the Surgeon recommended him to take a powerful dose of opium, to avoid a seven or eight hours of most exquisite torture. This he immediately consented to, and when the Colonel entered the tent with Major Harnage, who were both wounded, they asked whether he had any affairs they could settle for him? His reply was, "That being a minor, everything was already adjusted." But he had one request, which he had just life enough to utter, "Tell my uncle I died like a soldier!"

Burgoyne's situation hourly grew more critical. Behind him, Ticon-deroga was attacked by the Americans, and "our front is therefore better protected than our rear." The only salvation lay in a relief force striking up the Hudson from New York. Sir Henry Clinton, left in command of that city when Howe moved southward, finally carried by assault Fort Clinton and Fort Montgomery in the Hudson highlands. These forts had been defended by militia since the Continental troops

stationed there had been called to support Gates. Surgeon Thacher
heard of the capture of Clinton's messenger to Burgoyne.

After the capture of Fort Montgomery, Sir Henry Clinton dispatched a messenger by the name of Daniel Taylor, to Burgoyne, with intelligence. Unfortunately he was taken on his way as a spy, and finding himself in danger, was seen to turn aside and take something from his pocket and swallow it. General George Clinton, into whose hands he had fallen, ordered a severe dose of emetic tartar to be administered. This produced the happiest effect as respects the prescriber, but it proved fatal to the patient. He discharged a small silver bullet, which after being unscrewed was found to enclose a letter from Sir Henry Clinton to Burgoyne. "Out of thine own mouth thou shalt be condemned." The spy was tried, convicted and executed. The following is an exact copy of the letter enclosed.

Fort Montgomery, October 8th, 1777

Nous voici—and nothing between us but Gates. I sincerely hope this little success of ours may facilitate your operations. In answer to your letters of the 28th of September by C. C. I shall only say, I cannot presume to order, or even advise, for reasons obvious. I heartily wish you success.

Faithfully yours,

H. CLINTON

But Clinton came with too little and too late. Even as one Hessian
lamented, "At no time did the Jews await the coming of the Messiah
with greater expectancy than we awaited the coming of General
Clinton," the general was preparing to turn back. Gates's army had
swelled to around 11,000; Burgoyne's was down to less than 5,000 fit
for duty. The British general seemed obsessed with the idea of flanking
the American Army and making a dash to Albany. Although his
generals protested such reckless action, and urged caution, Burgoyne
refused to listen until he had made a reconnaissance in force, probing
the American lines for a weak point. On October 7th Burgoyne
moved out with 1,500 men and ten artillery pieces. James Wilkinson
scouted the beginning of the battle of Bemis Heights, sometimes called
the battle of Stillwater.

On the afternoon of October 7th, the advanced guard of the center beat to arms; the alarm was repeated throughout the line, and the troops repaired to their alarm posts. I was at headquarters when this happened, and with the approbation of the General, mounted my horse to inquire the cause. But on reaching the guard where the beat commenced, I could obtain no other satisfaction, but that some person had reported the enemy to be advancing against our left. I proceeded, over open ground, and ascending a gentle acclivity in front of the guard, I perceived, about half a mile from the line of our encampment, several columns of the enemy, sixty or seventy rods from me, entering a wheat field which had not been cut, and was separated from me by a small rivulet, and without my glass I could distinctly mark their every movement. After entering the field they displayed, formed the line, and set down in double ranks with their arms between their legs. Foragers then proceeded to cut the wheat or standing straw, and I soon after observed several officers mounted on the top of a cabin, from whence they were endeavoring to reconnoitre our left, which was concealed from their view by intervening woods.

Having satisfied myself, after fifteen minutes attentive observation, that no attack was meditated, I returned and reported to the General, who asked me what appeared to be the intentions of the enemy.

"They are foraging, and endeavoring to reconnoitre your left, and I think, sir, they offer you battle."

"What is the nature of the ground, and what your opinion?"

"Their front is open, and their flanks rest on the woods, under cover of which they may be attacked; their right is skirted by a lofty height. I would indulge them."

"Well, then, order on Morgan to begin the game."

I waited on the Colonel, whose corps were formed in front of our centre, and delivered the order. He knew the ground and inquired the position of the enemy. They were formed across a newly cultivated field, their grenadiers with several field pieces on the left, bordering on a wood and a small ravine formed by the rivulet before alluded to; their light infantry on the right, covered by a worm fence at the foot of the hill before mentioned, thickly covered with wood; their centre composed of British and German battalions. Colonel Morgan, with his usual sagacity, proposed to make a circuit with his corps by our left, and under cover of the wood to gain the height on the right of the enemy, and from thence commence the attack, so soon as our fire should be opened against their left. . . .

This proposition was approved by the General, and it was concerted that time should be allowed the Colonel to make the proposed circuit and gain his station on the enemy's right before the attack should be made on their left. Poor's brigade was ordered for this service, and the attack was commenced in due season on the flank and front of the British grenadiers, by the New Hampshire and New York troops. True to his purpose, Morgan at this critical moment poured down like a torrent from the hill, and attacked the right of the enemy in front and flank. Dearborn, at the moment when the enemy's light infantry were attempting to change front, pressed forward with ardor and delivered a close fire; then leapt a fence, shouted, charged and gallantly forced them to retire in disorder. Yet, headed by that intrepid soldier, the Earl of Balcarras, they were immediately rallied and reformed behind a fence in rear of their first position. But being now attacked with great audacity in front and flanks by superior numbers, resistance became vain, and the whole line, commanded by Burgoyne in person, gave way and made a precipitate and disorderly retreat to his camp, leaving two twelve- and six six-pounders on the field with more than 400 officers and men killed, wounded and captured, and among them the flower of his officers. . . .

James Wilkinson, never above exaggerating his own importance, was busy throughout the afternoon.

I was peremptorily commanded to repair to the rear and order up Ten Broeck's brigade of York militia, 3,000 strong. I performed this service, and regained the field of battle at the moment the enemy had turned their backs, fifty-two minutes after the first shot was fired.

The ground which had been occupied by the British grenadiers presented a scene of complicated horror and exultation. In the square space of twelve or fifteen yards lay eighteen grenadiers in the agonies of death, and three officers propped up against stumps of trees, two of them mortally wounded, bleeding and almost speechless. What a spectacle for one whose bosom glowed with philanthropy, and see how vehement the impulse which excites men of sensibility to seek such scenes of barbarism!

I found the courageous Colonel Cilley astraddle a brass twelve-pounder, and exulting in its capture; whilst a surgeon, a man of great worth, who was dressing one of the officers, raising his blood-besmeared hands in a frenzy of patriotism, exclaimed, "Wilkinson, I have dipt my hands in British blood!" He received a sharp rebuke for his brutality, and with the troops I pursued the hard-pressed flying enemy, passing over killed and wounded until I heard one exclaim, "Protect me, Sir, against this boy."

Turning my eyes, it was my fortune to arrest the purpose of a lad, thirteen or fourteen years old, in the act of taking aim at the wounded officer who lay in an angle of a worm fence. Inquiring his rank, he answered, "I had the honor to command the grenadiers." Of course, I knew him to be Major Ackland, who had been brought from the field to this place on the back of Captain Shrimpton of his own corps, under a heavy fire, and was here deposited, to save the lives of both. I dismounted, took him by the hand, and expressed my hopes that he was not badly wounded.

"Not badly," replied this gallant officer and accomplished gentleman, "but very inconveniently. I am shot through both legs. Will you, Sir, have the goodness to have me conveyed to your own camp?" I directed my servant to alight, and we lifted Ackland into his seat, and ordered him to be conducted to headquarters.

I then proceeded to the scene of renewed action, which embraced Burgoyne's right flank defence and, extending to his left, crossed a hollow covered with wood, about 40 rods, to the entrenchment of the light infantry. The roar of cannon and small arms at this juncture was sublime, between the enemy behind their works, and our troops entirely exposed, or partially sheltered by trees, stumps, or hollows, at various distances, not exceeding 120 yards. The right flank defence of the enemy, occupied by the German corps of Breymann, consisted of a breastwork of rails piled horizontally between perpendicular pickets, driven into the earth, en potence to the rest of his line and extended about 250 yards across an open field, and was covered on the right by a battery of two guns. The interval from the left of the British light infantry was committed to the defence of the provincialists, who occupied a couple of log cabins. The Germans were encamped immediately behind the rail breastwork, and the ground in front of it declined in a very gentle slope for about 120 yards, when it sunk abruptly. Our troops formed in a line in this declivity, and covered breast high, were warmly engaged with the Germans.

From this position, about sunset, I perceived Brigadier General Learned advancing towards the enemy with his brigade in open column. . . . On saluting this brave old soldier, he enquired, "Where can I put in with the most advantage?" I had particularly examined the ground between the left of the Germans and the light infantry, occupied by the provincialists, from whence I had observed a slack fire. I therefore recommended to General Learned to incline to his right and attack at that point. He did so with great gallantry. The provincialists abandoned their position and fled. The German flank was by this means left uncovered. They were assaulted vigorously, overturned in five minutes, and retreated in disorder, leaving their gallant commander, Lieutenant Colonel Breymann, dead on the field.

Burgoyne, supported by the opinion of his surviving officers, decided to surrender. Refusing Gates's terms, Burgoyne submitted a "Convention" of his own, allowing the British the honors of war, and a free passage to Great Britain "on condition of not serving again in North America during the present condition." To the consternation of his officers (and astonishment of the British), Gates accepted Burgoyne's proposal with only minor changes. Perhaps Gates felt that this was the beginning of the end, for shortly afterwards he wrote his wife, "If old England is not by this lesson taught humility, then she is an obstinate old slut, bent upon her ruin." Lieutenant Digby termed October 17 "A day famous in the annals of America."

About 10 o'clock, we marched out, according to treaty, with drums beating & the honors of war, but the drums seemed to have lost their former inspiring sounds, and though we beat the Grenadiers march, which not long before was so animating, yet then it seemed by its last feeble effort as almost ashamed to be heard on such an occasion.

As to my own feelings, I cannot express them. Tears (though unmanly) forced their way and if alone, I could have burst to give myself vent. I never shall forget the appearance of their troops on our marching past them; a dead silence universally reigned through their numerous columns, and even then they seemed struck with our situation and dare scarce lift up their eyes to view British troops in such a situation. I must say their decent behavior during the time (to us so greatly fallen) merited the utmost approbation and praise.

The meeting between Burgoyne and Gates was well worth seeing. He paid Burgoyne almost as much respect as if he was the conqueror; indeed, his noble air, tho' prisoner, seemed to command respect from every person. A party of light dragoons were ordered as his guard, rather to protect his person from insults than any other cause.

Thus ended all our hopes of victory, honor, glory &c., &c., &c. Thus was Burgoyne's army sacrificed to either the absurd opinions of a blundering ministerial power, the stupid inaction of a general [Howe] who, from his lethargic disposition, neglected every step he might have taken to assist their operations, or lastly, perhaps, his own misconduct in penetrating so far, as to be unable to return, tho' I must own my partiality to him is great. . . .

Although the Continental Congress was to repudiate the Saratoga Convention, Burgoyne's army did march to Boston with the fullest intention of embarking for England. Not until later were they taken to Virginia and Pennsylvania prison camps. Hannah Winthrop wrote a graphic description of the defeated army as it marched into Boston in early November.

Last Thursday, which was a very stormy day, a large number of British troops came softly thro' the town via Watertown to Prospect Hill. On Friday we heard the Hessians were to make a procession in the same route; we thought we would have nothing to do with them, but view them as they passed.

To be sure, the sight was truly astonishing. I never had the least idea that the Creation produced such a sordid set of creatures in human figure—poor, dirty, emaciated men, great numbers of women who seemed to be the beasts of burden, having a bushel basket on their back, by which they were bent double, the contents seemed to be pots and kettles, various sorts of furniture, children peeping through gridirons and other utensils, some very young infants who were born on the road, the women bare feet, clothed in dirty rags. Such effluvia filled the air while they were passing, had not they been smoking all the time I should have been apprehensive of being contaminated by them.

After a noble looking advanced guard, General Johnny B[urgoyn]e headed this terrible group on horseback. The other G[enera]ls also, clothed in blue cloaks. Hessians, Anspachers, Brunswickers, etc., etc., followed on. The Hessian G[enera]ls gave us a polite bow as they passed. Not so the British, their baggage wagons drawn by poor, half starved horses. But to bring up the rear, another fine, noble looking guard of American brawny victorious yeomanry, who assisted in bringing these sons of slavery to terms. Some of our wagons drawn by fat oxen, driven by joyous looking Yankees closed the cavalcade.

But Saratoga was one of the most significant victories of the American Revolution. In New York, Tory Enos Stevens observed, "News that General Begoyn is taken & evry man is put on a long fase." A more meaningful observation was: "Rebellion, which a twelvemonth ago was really a contemptible pigmy, is now become a giant more dreadful to the minds of men than Polyphemus of old, or the Sons of Anak."

The Road to Philadelphia

*H*OWE *had long planned to take Philadelphia, seat of the Continental Congress and a commercial town of great import. Many loyalists were reported in that city. A quick and easy victory was expected. Ministerial approval had been given as early as March. Dispatches from Burgoyne around the first of July, 1777, indicated that his campaign was going well. Then, too, if Howe struck southward, Washington could be lured away from a position that allowed him to furnish quick support to those opposing Gentleman Johnny. And if the Americans did move northward after Philadelphia was taken, Howe could sally out and trap Mr. Washington between his army and that of Burgoyne coming down the Hudson.*

Washington, perplexed, watched Howe nervously. He weakened his own army somewhat by sending reinforcements to the Northern Department, especially after he heard of the incredible fall of Ticonderoga.

On a muggy July 8, Howe embarked his troops aboard 260 vessels, and then, according to disgusted Thomas Jones, "after spending a fortnight in dalliance with Mrs. Loring, while the troops were lying on board the transports together in the sultry heat of summer, he went on board his brother's ship, and orders were given for sailing."

Washington remained uncertain of Howe's destination. He shifted his army back and forth. Not until he heard that the British fleet was standing up Chesapeake Bay was he reasonably sure that the enemy's objective was Philadelphia. His army, including militia, now numbered around 16,000 and were becoming somewhat unmanageable. Steps were taken to curb plundering by soldiers, "Resembling Sheep Stealers & thieves more than honest men fighting and Struggling for the Liberties of America." In his orders of August 4, Washington attempted to increase the mobility of his army.

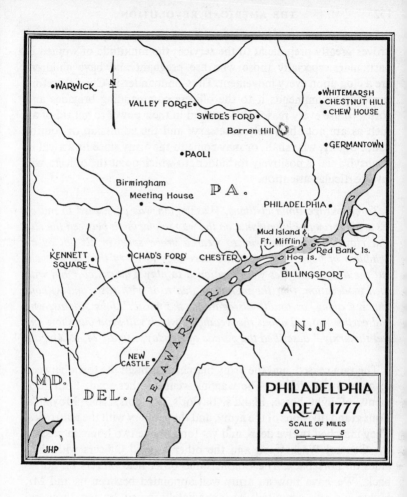

WARWICK

VALLEY FORGE

SWEDE'S FORD

Barren Hill

WHITEMARSH
CHESTNUT HILL
CHEW HOUSE

PAOLI

GERMANTOWN

PA.

Birmingham
Meeting House

PHILADELPHIA

Mud Island &
Ft. Mifflin

KENNETT
SQUARE

CHAD'S FORD

CHESTER

Red Bank Is.

Hog Is.

BILLINGSPORT

DELAWARE R.

N.J.

NEW
CASTLE

MD.

DEL.

PHILADELPHIA
AREA 1777

SCALE OF MILES
0   5

JHP

In the present marching state of the army, every encumbrance proves greatly prejudicial to the service; the multitude of women in particular, especially those who are pregnant and have children, are a clog upon every movement. The Commander-in-Chief therefore earnestly recommends it to the officers commanding brigades and corps, to use every reasonable method in their power to get rid of all such as are not absolutely necessary; and the admission or continuance of any, who shall, or may come to the army since its arrival in Pennsylvania, is positively forbidden, to which point the officers will give particular attention.

To encourage timid civilians, Washington was persuaded to march his army through Philadelphia on the way to placing it between the city and Howe. Every man was to wear a green sprig in his hat as an "emblem of hope," and not only were they to carry their arms well, but the drums and fifes were cautioned to play a quickstep, "but with such moderation, that the men may step to it with ease, and without dancing along, or totally disregarding the music." John Adams, who had earlier worried about the weather, "which will spoil our show and wet the army," described the parade of Sunday, August 24, to Abigail.

The rain ceased, and the army marched through the town between seven and ten o'clock. The wagons went another road. Four regiments of light horse, Bland's, Baylor's, Sheldon's, and Moylan's. Four grand divisions of the army, and the artillery with the matrosses. They marched twelve deep, and yet took above two hours in passing by. General Washington and the other general Officers with their aides on horseback. The Colonels and other field officers on horseback. We have now an army well appointed between us and Mr. Howe and this army will be immediately joined by ten thousand militia, so that I feel as secure as if I were at Braintree, but not so happy. My happiness is nowhere to be found but there.

After viewing this fine spectacle and firm defense, I went to Mr. Duffield's meeting to hear him pray, as he did most fervently, and I believe he was most sincerely joined by all present for its success.

The army, upon an accurate inspection of it, I find to be extremely well armed, pretty well clothed, and tolerably disciplined. . . . There is such a mixture of the sublime and the beautiful together with the useful in military discipline, that I wonder every officer we have is not charmed with it. Much remains to be done. Our soldiers have not quite the air of soldiers. They don't step exactly in time. They don't hold up their heads quite erect, nor turn out their toes so exactly as they ought. They don't all of them cock their hats, and such as do, don't all wear them the same way.

Howe had landed at Head of Elk, Maryland, before him a 55-mile march overland to Philadelphia. Skirmishing developed between the two armies as Washington fell back to the Brandywine and began fortifying the heights above Chad's Ford, the most likely stream crossing for an army on the march for Philadelphia. Other fords were guarded.

The British general planned to use the same strategy that had proved so successful at Long Island—a flanking action. At sunrise on September 11, 1777, before the fog lifted, they marched out of their encampment at Kennett Square. The Hessian General von Knyphausen was to feint toward Chad's Ford, while the flanking unit under the command of Lord Cornwallis marched to the forks of the Brandywine, turned the flanks and surrounded the rebel army. Washington ordered Brigadier General William Maxwell, who was after the battle termed "a damned bitch of a general," across the Brandywine "to bring on the action." Stephen Jarvis, native American but loyalist, serving in the Queen's Rangers, was in the initial action at Chad's Ford.

We came in sight of the enemy at sunrise. The first discharge of the enemy killed the horse of Major Grymes, who was leading the column, and wounded two men in the division directly in my front, and in a few moments the Regiment became warmly engaged and several of our officers were badly wounded. None but the Rangers and [Patrick] Ferguson's Riflemen were as yet engaged. The enemy retired, and there was a cessation for a short time, to reconnoiter the enemy, who had taken up their position in a wood which skirted the road that led down to the river.

The Rangers were ordered to advance and drive the enemy from that position. We marched from the right of companies, by files, entered the wood, and drove the enemy from it, into a large open field where there was a large body of the enemy formed. Major Wemyss, who commanded the Rangers, ordered the Regiment to halt and cover themselves behind the trees, but the right of the Regiment was hotly engaged with the enemy, and Captain Dunlap came to Major Wemyss and requested him to let the Regiment charge or the two companies would be cut off. The Major then ordered the adjutant, who was very glad of the opportunity, to desire the troops in our rear to support him, and ordered the Regiment to charge. At this instant my pantaloons received a wound, and I don't hesitate to say that I should have been very well pleased to have seen a little blood also.

The enemy stood until we came near to bayonet points, then gave us a volley and retired across the Brandywine. Captain Williams and Captain Murden were killed, and many of the officers were wounded in this conflict. The Brandywine, on each side, was skirted with wood, in which the Rangers took shelter, whilst our artillery were playing upon a half moon battery on the other side of the river, which guarded the only fording place where our army could cross. In this position we remained waiting for General Howe to commence his attack on the right flank of General Washington's main army.

Washington received conflicting reports as to the movements of the enemy. Patrols said there was no sign of the enemy on the flanks. But between three and four o'clock in the afternoon there was intelligence that the enemy were pouring across Jones Ford, some four miles up the Brandywine above Chad's Ford.

General Washington's headquarters were at Benjamin Ring's Tavern, about three-quarters of a mile east of Chad's Ford. He was there, and thereabout, all the fore part of the day of the battle. When he ascertained that the main body of the enemy were at Birmingham Meeting House and engaged with our troops, he was anxious to proceed thither by the shortest and speediest route. He found a resident of the neighborhood, named Joseph Brown, and asked him to go as guide. Brown was an elderly man, and extremely loath to undertake that duty. He made many excuses, but the occasion was too urgent for ceremony. One of Washington's suite dismounted from a fine charger, and told Brown that if he did not instantly get on his horse and conduct the General by the nearest and best route to the place of action, he would run him through on the spot.

Brown thereupon mounted, and steered his course direct towards Birmingham Meeting House with all speed—the General and his attendants being close on his heels. He said the horses leapt all the fences without difficulty, and was followed in a like manner by the others. The head of General Washington's horse, he said, was constantly at the flank of the one on which he was mounted, and the General was constantly repeating to him, "*Push along, old man—Push along, old man.*" When they reached the road, about half a mile west of Dilworthtown, Brown said that the bullets were flying so thick that he felt very uncomfortable, and as Washington no longer required, nor paid attention to his guide, the latter embraced the first opportunity to dismount and make his escape.

Surgeon Ebenezer Elmer of the New Jersey Continentals was with the troops at Birmingham Meeting House.

We marched on some distance till we came in sight of the enemy who had crossed the river and were coming down upon us. We formed about four o'clock on an eminence, the right being in the woods.

Presently a large column came in front, playing the Grenadiers March, and now the battle began which proved excessive severe. The enemy came on with fury. Our men stood firing on them most amazingly, killing almost all before them for near an hour till they got within six rods of each other, when a column of the enemy came upon our right flank which caused them to give way, which soon extended all along the line. We retreated and formed on the first ground, and gave them another fire, and so continued on all the way, but unfortunately for want of a proper retreat, three or four of our pieces were left on the first ground.

The division under Nathanael Greene covered the retreat from Jones' Ford and allowed Washington's army to remain intact. The finale at Chad's Ford was an anticlimax. When the booming of the artillery was heard upstream, Stephen Jarvis was among those who crossed.

The Fourth Regiment led the column, and the Queen's Rangers followed, the battery playing upon us with grape shot, which did much execution. The water took us up to our breasts, and was much stained with blood before the battery was carried and the guns turned upon the enemy.

Immediately after our regiment had crossed, two companies . . . was ordered to move to the left and take possession of a hill which the enemy was retiring from, and wait until further orders. From the eminence we had an extensive view of the American Army, and we saw our brave comrades butting them up in great style. The battle lasted until dark, when the enemy retreated and left us masters of the field. We were then ordered to leave our position and join our regiment. We did so and took up our night's lodgings on the field of battle, which was strewed with dead bodies of the enemy. . . .

To Private Elisha Stevens it had been a frightful experience.

The Battel was at Brandy wine it Began in the morning and Held til knight with out much seasation of arms Cannon Roaring muskets Cracking Drums Beating Bombs flying all round; men a dying wounded's Horred Grones which would Greave the Heardest of Hearts to See Such a Sorriful Sight as this to see our Fellow Creators Slain in Such a manner as this.

Washington maneuvered his army, and at one time prepared for battle, but a torrential rain thwarted martial ambition. Anthony Wayne had been ordered to circle around to get in the rear of the British forces to harass them. It was impossible to keep secret the presence of between 1,500 and 2,000 men. A manuscript found on the field after the Battle of Germantown described the experiences of a British officer on the night of September 22, 1777.

I was relieved from picket at sunset (the preceding sunset I mounted [guard]), and was waked at nine at night to go on the bloody business. The men were ordered to unload—on no account to fire. We took a circuit in dead silence. About one in the morning fell in with a rebel vidette (a vidette is a horse sentinel) who challenged three times and fired. He was pursued but escaped. Soon after two foot sentries challenged and fired—who escaped also. We then marched in briskly, still silent. Our company was advanced immediately preceding a company of riflemen who always are in front; a picket fired upon us at the distance of fifteen yards, miraculously without effect. This unfortunate guard was instantly dispatched by the riflemen's swords. We rushed on through a thick wood and received a smart fire from another unfortunate picket, as the first instantly massacred.

We then saw their wigwams, or huts, partly by almost extinguished light of their fires and partly by the light of a few stars, & the frightened wretched rebels endeavoring to form. We then charged. For two miles we drove them, now and then firing scatteringly from behind trees, fences, &c. The flashes of the pieces had a fine effect in the night—then followed a dreadful scene of havoc. The light dragoons came on, sword in hand. The shrieks, groans, shouting, imprecations, deprecations, the clashing of swords and bayonets, &c., &c., (no firing from us & little from them except now and then a few as I said before, scattering shots) was more expressive of horror than are the thunder of artillery, &c., on the day of action.

They threaten retaliation, vow they will give no quarter to any of our battalions. We are always on the advanced post of the army— our present one is unpleasant—our left too open and unguarded. We expect reinforcements.

Howe had given Washington another lesson in flanking movements at Brandywine, and at the "Paoli Massacre" Major General "No Flint" Grey had given Anthony Wayne a lesson in the use of the bayonet. The Continental Congress fled the city before the British Army's triumphant entry into Philadelphia. Patrols were often in sight of each other. Lieutenant James McMichael of the Pennsylvania Line liked to pen bits of doggerel in his diary.

Just when we came into our camp, an army did appear,
They were on an adjacent hill, which was to us quite near,
They travers'd all the hill about, as tho' we were their foes,
And seem'd uneasy the secret to disclose.
But we with mirth and jollity did seat ourselves to rest
Upon the hill right opposite, tho' they seem'd quite distress'd.
Then taking Carnaghan's canteen, which had in it some rum,
We took to us a little draught, my rhyme to end did come.

Although Cornwallis had entered Philadelphia with a conqueror's promenade, Howe maintained the greater portion of his army at Germantown, five miles northwest of the city, a mobile force to protect the supply routes until the forts on the Delaware could be taken. He had not fortified the long narrow town for fear that such a course might be interpreted by the rebels as an admission of weakness.

Four columns, under Greene, Sullivan, Smallwood, and Armstrong, were to hit the enemy from the front, the left, the right and the rear simultaneously. It was too intricate a maneuver for poorly trained troops. All four attacks were to be launched at 5 A.M.; the men were to wear identifying white paper in their hats and to open the attack with the bayonet. Greene's division arrived late; other units failed to carry through their orders. The division of Sullivan and Wayne launched the attack. British Lieutenant Martin Hunter was on outpost duty at Biggentown.

The first that General Howe knew of Washington marching against us, was by his attacking us at daybreak. General Wayne commanded the advance, and expected to be fully revenged for the surprise that we had given him. When the first shots were fired at our pickets, so much had we all Wayne's affair in remembrance, that the battalion was out and under arms in a minute. At this time the day was just broke; but it was a very foggy morning, and so dark that we could not see a hundred yards before us. Just as the battalion had formed, the pickets came in and said that the enemy were advancing in force.

They had hardly joined the battalion when we heard a loud cry of "Have at the bloodhounds; revenge Wayne's affair!" and they immediately fired a volley. We gave them one in return, cheered, and charged. As it was near the end of the campaign, it was very weak. It did not consist of more than three hundred men, and we had no support nearer than Germantown, a mile in our rear. On our charging they gave way on all sides, but again and again renewed the attack with fresh troops and greater force. We charged them twice, till the battalion was so reduced by killed and wounded, that the bugle was sounded to retreat; indeed, had we not retreated at the very time we did, we should have all been taken or killed, as nearly two columns of the enemy had nearly got around our flank. But this was the first time we had retreated before the Americans, and it was with great difficulty we could get our men to obey our orders.

The enemy were kept so long in check that the two brigades had advanced to the entrance of Biggenstown, when they met our battalion retreating. By this time General Howe had come up, and seeing the battalion retreating, all broken, he got into a passion and exclaimed: "For shame, light infantry! I never saw you retreat before. Form! Form! It's only a scouting party." However, he was soon convinced it was more than a scouting party, as the heads of the enemy columns soon appeared. One coming through Biggenstown, with three pieces of cannon in their front, immediately fired at the crowd that was standing with General Howe under a large chestnut tree. I think I never saw people enjoy a discharge of grape before, but we really all felt pleased to see the enemy make such an appearance, and to hear the grape rattle about the Commander-in-Chief's ears, after he had accused the battalion of having run away from a scouting party. He rode off immediately full speed, and we joined the two brigades that were now formed a little way in our rear; but it was not possible for them to make any stand against Washington's whole army, and they all retreated to Germantown, except Colonel Musgrave, who, with the 40th Regiment, nobly defended Chew's house till we were reinforced from Philadelphia.

The house of Pennsylvania Chief Justice Benjamin Chew was of sturdy stone construction. This was the house that Musgrave made into the fortress described by a British officer.

The light infantry defended themselves for some time with great spirit, but the fog was so thick that they could not distinguish what was opposed to them. The 40th Regiment came to their support, and they together, by well timed and heavy discharges, contrived to advance a great way upon the enemy who retired, not being aware of the small party that attacked them. However, no reinforcement appearing, and the light infantry ammunition being almost expended, Colonel Musgrave, who commanded the 40th Regiment and had been sparing of his ammunition, told the light infantry that he would cover their retreat, which he did in a most masterly manner, till he arrived at his old encampment.

The light infantry were by this time secure, but the rebels were in the encampment of the 40th Regiment, and Colonel Musgrave found himself entirely surrounded, and all means of retreating cut off. Without being embarrassed, he immediately ordered his regiment to get into a large stone house (which had been his quarters) with the greatest expedition possible, but the rebels pressed so close upon their heels, that they must have inevitably have entered the house at the same time, if he had not faced the regiment about and given them a fire which checked them enough for him to have time to get his regiment into the house and shut the door.

Musgrave ordered all the window shutters of the ground floor to be shut, as the enemy's fire would otherwise have been too heavy upon there. He placed, however, a certain number of men at each window, and at the hall doors, with orders to bayonet everyone who should attempt to come in. He disposed of the rest in the two upper stories, and instructed them to cover themselves, and direct their fire out of the window. He then told them "That their only safety was in the defence of that house; that if they let the enemy get into it, they would undoubtedly every man be put to death; that it would be an absurdity for any one to think of giving himself up, with hopes of quarters; that their situation was nevertheless by no means a bad one, as there had been instances of only a few men defending a house against numbers; that he had no doubt of their being supported and delivered by our army; but that at all events they must sell themselves as dear as possible to the enemy."

By this time the rebels had brought up four pieces of cannon (three-pounders) against the house, and with the first shot they burst open both the hall doors, and wounded some men with the pieces of stone that flew from the wall. Captain Hains, a brave intelligent officer, who commanded on the ground floor, reported to Colonel Musgrave what had happened, and that he had thrown chairs, tables, and any little impediments he could before the door, and that he would endeavor to keep the enemy out as long as he had a single man left. He was very soon put to the test, for the rebels directed their cannon (sometimes loaded with round, sometimes with grape shot) entirely against the upper stories, and sent some of the most daring fellows from the best troops they had, to force their way into the house under cover of their artillery. To do them justice, they attacked with great intrepidity, but were received with no less firmness. The fire from the upper windows was well directed and continued. The rebels, nevertheless, advanced, and several of them were killed with bayonets getting in at the windows and upon the steps, attempting to force their way in at the door.

Timothy Pickering, Washington's adjutant, was with the General when the fortress in their midst was discovered.

In the march of the army, General Washington, following Sullivan's column, kept in the road leading to and through German-town to Philadelphia. When we had entered the northern part of the village, we heard in advance of us (I was riding by the General's side) a very heavy fire of musketry. General Sullivan's divisions, it was evident, were warmly engaged with the enemy, but neither was in sight. This fire, brisk and heavy, continuing, General Washington said to me: "I am afraid General Sullivan is throwing away his ammunition. Ride forward and tell him to preserve it.". . .

At this time I had never heard of Chew's house, and had no idea that an enemy was in my rear. The first notice I received of it was from the whizzing of musket balls across the road, before, behind and above me as I was returning after delivering the orders to Sullivan. Instantly turning my eyes to the right, I saw the blaze of the muskets, whose shot were still aimed at me, from the windows of a large stone house, standing back about a hundred yards from the road. This was Chew's house. Passing on, I came to some of our artillery who were firing very obliquely on the front of the house. I remarked to them, that in that position their fire would be unavailing, and that the only chance of their shot making any impression on the house would be by moving down and firing directly on its front.

Then immediately passing on, I rejoined General Washington who, with General Knox and other officers, was in front of a stone house (nearly all the houses in Germantown were of stone), next northward of the open field in which Chew's house stood. I found they were discussing, in Washington's presence, this question: whether the whole of our troops then behind should immediately advance, regardless of the enemy in Chew's house, or first summon them to surrender. General Knox strenuously urged the sending of a summons. Among other things he said, "It would be unmilitary to leave a castle in our rear." I answered, "Doubtless that is a correct general maxim, but it does not apply in this case. We know the extent of this castle (Chew's house), and to guard against the danger from the enemy sallying and falling on the rear of our troops, a small regiment may be posted there to watch them, and if they sally, such a regiment will take care of them. But," I added, "to summon them to surrender will be useless. We are now in the midst of battle, and its issue is unknown. In this state of uncertainty, and so well secured as the enemy find themselves, they will not regard a summons—they will fire on your flag." However, a flag was sent with a summons. Lieutenant Smith of Virginia, my assistant in the office of adjutant general, volunteered his service to carry it. As he was advancing, a shot from the house gave him a wound of which he died. . . . When poor Smith was brought off wounded, Major Gibbs, who was in the General's family, said to me, "While you were absent, I offered to carry the flag; and bless my stars that it was not accepted."

Mistakes on the field including American troops firing on other American troops through the mist, and the need of reinforcements and ammunition were all seeds of retreat. Washington's withdrawal from Germantown was orderly, although there were some who complained that the General was too hasty.

There was one final phase before Howe could return to the arms of Mrs. Loring. The Delaware forts had to be reduced to allow supply ships to use that river. The rebels abandoned their half-finished fort at Billingsport. The Hessians attacked Fort Mercer and were thrown back with heavy losses; the dead included their commander, Colonel von Donop. Then Howe turned his attention to Fort Mifflin on Fort Island in the Delaware, "a burlesque upon the art of fortification," located on a "mud flat." John Laurens described the gallant resistance of its defenders.

At break of day on the fifteenth [November], the enemy's batteries began a heavy cannonade upon Fort Mifflin, and their fleet set sail to come up the river with the tide. One of their ships, an old East Indiaman, cut down for a floating battery and armed with eighteen twenty-four pounders, and two sloops, advanced between Hog Island and the northern point of Tinicum, at a distance of about one thousand yards from our grand battery. Six other vessels and a galley carrying a thirty-six pounder, approached the chevaux-de-frise, about six hundred yards from the fort. The garrison saluted them with red hot bullets. At eight o'clock the fire of the six vessels and galley commenced and was seconded by that of the land batteries. A quarter of an hour after, the sloops with eight pieces, thirty-two and twenty-four pounders, brought their guns to bear on the right of the battery, and after many successive broadsides, laid the parapet in ruins and dismounted one of the two pieces which was on that side, there being only two embrasures on the right, from whence the fire of the sloops was returned.

The musketry from the tops drove the cannoneers from the platform, and the land batteries, making a cross fire with that of the vessels, rendered the right of the battery untenable. Major Fleury, who commanded a number of men appointed to answer the fire of the enemy's tops, and Captain Lee, of the artillery, remained in this dangerous part of the battery till all their men were either killed or wounded, and the cannon battered to pieces. . . .

At one o'clock the ammunition of the fort was exhausted. Only two cannon remained fit for use—the rest were dismounted or broke to pieces. The parapet was destroyed; one of the sloops which had moved towards the middle of the fort had demolished the bank, and was knocking down the palisades. A body of troops appeared on the opposite shore ready to embark, and our garrison was small. The commandant called a council at two o'clock, the result of which was, that the garrison must either have ammunition and a reinforcement, or boats.

The enemy's fire raged; ours languished. The blockhouse flew about in splinters; a piece of timber detached from one of them knocked down a lieutenant and Major Fleury; the former was killed by the blow, and the latter lay senseless. Major Talbot, who ran to their assistance, was wounded in the leg and arm with two grape shot. Night came on, and the transport boats arriving instead of reinforcements, the garrison evacuated their post and embarked at half after eleven, at the very moment when the sound of oars announced the approach of troops to storm our levelled palisades.

With Fort Mifflin abandoned, Washington gave up the defense of the Delaware. Howe could now settle in for the winter in Philadelphia. A French officer, serving with the Americans, summed up the campaign and the lessons learned.

If General Howe does not take care, he may find himself made very uneasy, even in his camp at Germantown, by the Americans; and if one of their divisions . . . gone astray in the woods . . . had not been two hours late, the English would have been repulsed as far as Philadelphia and perhaps farther. There was a very thick mist, and still these folks are so little warlike! But they are beginning to get used to fire. Without all these obstacles, Howe would have been cut to pieces. He has beaten these folks in two spirited battles since he landed in Chesapeake Bay. Let him look out for a third battle! He buys them by dint of men, and it is not so easy for him to recruit his army as it is for these folks who have plenty of militia and resources.

But the principal advantage of General Howe's army over General Washington's in the two battles fought by them, must be ascribed to their being more trained to the use of the bayonet. The American army know their superior dexterity in firing well, and rely entirely upon it. The British Army know it likewise, and dread it. Hence in all engagements the British soldiers rush on with the bayonet after one fire, and seldom fail of throwing the Americans into confusion. Habit, which forms men to do anything, I am persuaded would soon render these brave people as firm at the approaches of a bayonet, as the whistling of a musket ball. General [Charles] Lee, I am told, took great pains to eradicate the universal prejudice he found among the Americans, in favor of terminating the war with fire arms alone. "We must learn to face our enemies," said he, "man to man in the open field, or we shall never beat them." The late General Montgomery, who served his apprenticeship in the British Army, knew so well that nothing but the bayonet would ever rout troops that had been trained to it, that he once proposed in the Convention of New York, of which he was a member, that directions should be given, both in Europe and in this country, to make all muskets intended for the American soldiers two inches longer than the muskets now in use in the British Army, in order that they may have an advantage of their enemy, in a charge with bayonets, for, he said, "Britain will never yield but to the push of the bayonet."

"Lord—Lord—Lord"—Valley Forge

FOLLOWING the fall of the Delaware forts, Washington appeared to be marching aimlessly. He led a discontented army. It was growing cold, and his soldiers longed for fireside warmth. Officers groused because of the partiality that had been shown Frenchmen who came over as officers in the American Army. Perhaps they were envious—these Frenchmen seemed to have a way with American women. One compared them with those of France.

The women in this country attach very little importance to a thousand petty things which in France our women make us pass as the greatest favors, which we regard as so much more decisive from the fact that they rarely fail of being crowned with success.

Here a woman will kiss you all day, will do a thousand foolish things with you; crush your foot, make your arm black and blue by dint of pinching you while walking with you, and give you a couple of slaps. In short, she will give you in a single day the same provocations which one of our women could not do, without being thought too free, after a month's acquaintance. You are often no further advanced for all of that. It all vanishes like a dream, and they are laughing at you; at least that is what has happened to me. I only perceived afterwards that it was nothing but curiosity, and that she wanted to see how the French go about it when making love. . . . I am neither amorous or jealous. I take what presents itself on my way. She lets herself when she is in a good humor, and when she isn't, I withdraw. I talk English like a demon, and that is what I want. Perhaps the Devil will serve me, but not love. It is chimerical being in a country still somewhat wild.

The Chevalier de Pontgibaud, a French volunteer serving as aide-de-camp to the Marquis de Lafayette, enjoyed one experience.

I was astonished, on my return, to find what peculiar ideas our hosts, the Americans of New England, had of the French. One day I dismounted from my horse at the house of a farmer upon whom I had been billeted. I had hardly entered the good man's house when he said to me,

"I am very glad to have a Frenchman in the house."

I politely enquired the reason for this preference.

"Well," he said, "you see the barber lives a long way off, so you will be able to shave me."

"But I cannot even shave myself," I replied. "My servant shaves me, and he will shave you also if you like."

"That's very odd," said he. "I was told that all Frenchmen were barbers and fiddlers."

I think I never laughed so heartily. A few minutes later my rations arrived, and my host seeing a large piece of beef amongst them said,

"You are lucky to be able to come over to America and get some beef to eat."

I assured him that we had beef in France, and excellent beef too.

"That is impossible," he replied, "or you wouldn't be so thin."

Such was—when liberty was dawning over the land—the ignorance shown by the inhabitants of the United States Republic in regard to the French.

Beef was to become a rarity in the ragged little army that Washington maneuvered until he reached the spot known as Valley Forge. Excerpts from the diary of Surgeon Albigence Waldo reveal the philosophical misery that raged in the surgeon's soul.

Dec. 11th—I am prodigious sick & cannot get anything comfortable—what in the name of Providence can I do with a fit of sickness in this place where nothing appears pleasing to the sicken'd eye & nauseating stomach. But I doubt not Providence will find a way out for my relief—But I cannot eat beef if I starve—for my stomach positively refuses such company, & how can I help that?

Dec. 12th—A bridge of wagons made across the Schuylkill last night, consisting of 36 wagons, with a bridge of rails between each. Some skirmishing down the river. Militia and dragoons brought into camp several prisoners. Sun set—We are ordered to march over the river—it snows—I'm sick—eat nothing—no whiskey—no baggage—Lord—Lord—Lord. The army were till sunrise crossing the river—

some at the wagon bridge, & some at the raft bridge below. Cold & uncomfortable. . . .

Dec. 14th—Prisoners & deserters are continually coming in. The Army, who have been surprisingly healthy hitherto, now begin to grow very sickly from the continued fatigues they have suffered this campaign. Yet they still show spirit of alacrity & contentment not to be expected from so young troops. I am sick—discontented—and out of humor. Poor food—hard lodging—cold weather—fatigue—nasty clothes—nasty cookery—vomit half my time—smoked out of my senses—the Devil's in it—I can't endure it—why are we sent here to starve and freeze—what sweet felicities have I left at home—a charming wife—pretty children—good food—good cookery—all agreeable—all harmonious. Here, all confusion—smoke & cold—hunger & filthiness—a pox on my bad luck. Here comes a bowl of beef soup—full of burnt leaves and dirt, sickish enough to make a Hector spew—away with it Boys—I'll live like the chameleon upon air.

Poh! Poh! cries Patience within me—you talk like a fool. Your being sick covers your mind with a melancholic gloom, which makes everything about you appear gloomy. See the poor soldier when in health—with what cheerfulness he meets his foes and encounters every hardship—if barefoot—he labors thro' the mud & cold with a song in his mouth extolling War & Washington—if his food be bad—he eats it notwithstanding with seeming content—blesses God for a good stomach—and whistles it into digestion.

But harkee, Patience, a moment. There comes a soldier—his bare feet are seen thro' his worn out shoes—his legs nearly naked from the tatt'red remains of an only pair of stockings—his breeches not sufficient to cover his nakedness—his shirt hanging in strings—his hair dishevell'd—his face meagre—his whole appearance pictures a person forsaken & discouraged. He comes and cries with an air of wretchedness & despair—I am sick—my feet lame—my legs are sore—my body cover'd with this tormenting itch—my clothes worn out—my constitution is broken—my former activity is exhausted by fatigue—hunger & cold—I fail fast, I shall soon be no more! And all the reward I shall get will be—"Poor Will is dead."

Dec. 15th—Quiet. Eat persimmons, found myself better for their lenient operation. . . .

Dec. 21st—[Valley Forge] Preparations made for huts. Provisions scarce. Mr. Ellis went homeward—sent a letter to my wife. Heartily wish myself at home—my skin & eyes are almost spoil'd with continual smoke.

A general cry thro' the camp this evening among the soldiers—"No meat! No meat!"—the distant vales echo'd back the melancholy sound—"No meat! No meat!" Imitating the noise of crows & owls also, made a part of the confused music.

What have you for dinner, boys? "Nothing but fire cake & water, Sir." At night—"Gentlemen, the supper is ready." What is your supper, lads? "Fire cake & water, Sir."

Dec. 22nd—Lay excessive cold & uncomfortable last night—my eyes are started out of their orbits like a rabbit's eyes, occasion'd by a great cold—and smoke.

What have you got for breakfast, lads? "Fire cake and water, Sir." The Lord send that our Commissary of Purchases may live on fire cake and water, till their glutted guts are turned to pasteboard....

I am ashamed to say it, but I am tempted to steal fowls if I could find them—or even a whole hog—for I feel as if I could eat one. But the impoverish'd country about us affords but little matter to employ a thief—or keep a clever fellow in good humor—But why do I talk of hunger & hard usage when so many in the world have not even fire cake & water to eat. . . .

At 12 of the clock at night, Providence sent us a little mutton—with which we immediately had some broth made & a fine stomach for same. Ye who eat pumpkin pie and roast turkies—and yet curse fortune for using you ill—curse her no more—least she reduce your allowance of her favors to a bit of fire cake & a draught of cold water, & in cold weather, too.

23rd— . . . This evening an excellent player on the violin in that soft kind of music, which is so finely adapted to stir up the tender passions, while he was playing in the next tent to mine, these kind of soft airs—it immediately called up remembrances—all the endearing expressions—the tender sentiments—the sympathetic friendship that has given so much satisfaction and sensible pleasure to me from the first time I gained the heart & affections of the tenderest of the fair. A thousand little incidents which have occur'd since our happy connection—and which would have pass'd totally unnoticed by such who are strangers to the soft & sincere passion of love, were now recall'd to my mind, and filled me with these tender emotions, and agreeable reflections, which cannot be described—and which, in spite of my philosophy, forced out the sympathetic tear—I wish'd to have the music cease—and yet dreaded its ceasing—least I lose sight of those dear ideas—which gave me pain and pleasure at the same instant. Ah, Heaven, why is it that our fate so often deprives us of the enjoyment of what we most wish to enjoy this side of thy brighter realms. There is something in this strong passion of love far more agreeable than what we can derive from any of the other passions—and which duller souls & cheerless minds are insensible of, & laugh at—let such fools laugh at me. . . .

Dec. 25th, Christmas—We are still in tents—when we ought to be in huts—the poor sick, suffer much in tents this cold weather— But we now treat them differently from what they used to be at home, under the inspection of old women & Doctor Bolus Linctus. We give them mutton & grog—and a capital medicine once in a while—to start the disease from its foundations at once. We avoid— piddling pills, powders, Bolus's Linctus's—cordials—and all such insignificant matters whose powers are only render'd important by causing the patient to vomit up his money instead of his disease. But very few of the sick men die. . . .

Dec. 28th—Yesterday, upwards of fifty officers in General Greene's Division resigned their commissions—six or seven of our regiment are doing the like today. All this is occasion'd by officers' families being so much neglected at home on account of provisions. Their wages will not by considerable purchase a few trifling comfortables here in camp, & maintain their families at home, while such extravagant prices are demanded for the common necessaries of life. . . . When the officer has been fatiguing through the wet & cold and returns to his tent where he finds a letter directed to him from his wife, fill'd with the most heart-aching, tender complaints a woman is capable of writing, acquainting him with the incredible difficulty with which she procures a little bread for herself & children, and finally concluding with expressions bordering on despair of procuring a sufficiency of food to keep soul & body together through the winter— that the money is of little consequence to her—that she begs him to consider that charity begins at home, and not suffer his family to perish with want, in the midst of plenty. . . .

Dec. 31st—We got some spirits and finish'd the year with a good drink & thankful hearts in our new hut, which stands on an eminence that overlooks the Brigade, & in sight of the front line. . . .

1778, January 1st—New Year. I am alive. I am well. . . .

Jan. 3rd—Our hut, or rather our hermit's cell, goes on briskly—

having a short allowance of bread this morning, we divided it with great precision—eat our breakfast with thankful hearts for the little we had—took care of the sick, according to our daily practice—and went to work on our little humble cottage. Now, ye poets, give me my wife & children, with your daisies, your roses, your tulips, and your other insignificant poetical materials, & I believe I should be pretty contented in this humble cottage which the muses have so often described. . . .

Fresh beef and flour make me perfectly sick—especially as we have no spirits to drink with it—but others stand it, so must I. . . .

Sunday, Jan. 4th— . . . I was called to relieve a soldier tho't to be dying—he expir'd before I reach'd the hut. He was an Indian—an excellent soldier—and an obedient good natur'd fellow. He engaged for money doubtless as others do—but he has serv'd his country faithfully—he has fought for those very people who disinherited his forefathers—having finished his pilgrimage, he was discharged from the War of Life & Death. His memory ought to be respected, more than those rich ones who supply the world with nothing better than money and vice. There the poor fellow lies, not superior to a clod of earth—his mouth wide open—his eyes staring. Was he affrighted at the scene of death—or the consequences of it?—doubtless both—but he has doubtless acted agreeable to the dictates of Nature in the course of his whole life—why should he then be afraid of the consequences of death? Where, then, is his immaterial part taken its flight—undoubtedly the scene changes, and admits him into another state—and there fixes him forever. But what is that state—is it happy or miserable? He has been an honest fellow—has done his duty to his Maker and his fellow creatures as far as his inclinations and abilities would permit of—therefore we'll suppose him happier now than ever.

What a frail, dying creature is man. We are certainly not made for this world—daily evidences demonstrate the contrary. . . .

Jany. 5th—Apply'd for a furlough. Surgeon General not at home—come back mumping & sulky.

Jany. 6th—Apply'd again—was deny'd by reason of inoculations being set on foot—& because the Boston surgeons had too many of them gone home—one of whom is to be broke for his lying & deceiving in order to get a furlough—and I wish his curs'd tongue was pull'd out, for thus giving an example of scandal to the New England surgeons, tho' the Connecticut ones are well enough respected at present. Came home sulky and cross—storm'd at the boys—and swore round like a piper and a fool till most night—when I bought me a Bear skin—dress'd with the hair on. This will answer me to lie on . . . it serves to keep off those melancholy ideas which often attend such a person, and who loves his family and wishes to be with them. If I should happen to lose this little journal, any fool may laugh that finds it, since I know that there is nothing in it but the natural flowings & reflections of my own heart, which is human as well as other peoples—and if there is a great deal of folly in it, there is no intended ill nature, and am sure there is much sincerity, especially when I mention my family, whom I cannot help saying, and am not asham'd to say, that I love. . . .

8th—Unexpectedly got a furlough. Set out for home. The very worst of riding—mud & mire.

Yet in that slough of despondency called Valley Forge, there were moments of merriment. David Bushnell, designer of the unsuccessful submarine, now came up with an idea for a torpedo. Nearly all newspapers carried an account of the result.

This city [Philadelphia] has recently been entertained with a most astonishing instance of the activity, bravery, and military skill of the Royal Navy of Great Britain. The affair is somewhat particular and deserves your notice. Some time last week, two boys observed a keg of singular construction floating in the river opposite to the city. They got into a small boat and, attempting to take up the keg, it burst with a great explosion and blew up the unfortunate boys.

On Monday last, several kegs of like construction made their appearance. An alarm was immediately spread thro' the city. Various reports prevailed, filling the city and the royal troops with unspeakable consternation. Some reported that the kegs were filled with armed rebels, who were to issue forth in the dead of night, as the Grecians did of old from their wooden horse at the siege of Troy, and take the city by surprise, asserting that they had seen the points of their bayonets through the bung holes of the kegs. Others said they were charged with the most inveterate combustibles, to be kindled by secret machinery, and setting the whole Delaware in flames, were to consume all the shipping in the harbor, whilst others asserted that they were constructed by art magic, and would of themselves ascend the wharfs in the night time and roll, all flaming, through the streets of the city destroying every thing in their way.

Be this as it may—certain it is that the shipping in the harbor, and all the wharfs in the city, were fully manned. The battle begun, and it was surprising to behold the incessant fire that was kept up against the enemy—the kegs. Both officers and men exhibited the most unparalleled skill and bravery on the occasion; whilst other citizens stood gazing as solemn witnesses of their prowess. From the *Roebuck* and other ships of war, whole broadsides were poured into the Delaware. In short, not a wandering chip, stick, or drift-log but felt the vigor of British arms.

The action began about sunrise, and would have been completed with great success by noon, had not an old market-woman, coming down the river with provisions, unfortunately let a small keg of butter fall overboard, which (as it was then ebb) floated down to the scene of action. At the sight of this unexpected reinforcement of the enemy, the battle was renewed with great fury; the firing was incessant till the evening closed the affair. The kegs were either totally demolished or obliged to fly, as none of them have shown their *heads* since.

Francis Hopkinson, formerly a member of the Continental Congress from New Jersey, composed a ballad, some verses of which cast little credit upon Sir William Howe.

> Sir William he, snug as a flea,
> Lay all this time a snoring
> Nor dream'd of harm as he lay warm
> In bed with Mrs. Loring.
>
> Now in a fright, he starts upright,
> Awak'd by such a clatter;
> He rubs both eyes, and boldly cries,
> For God's sake, what's the matter?
>
> At his bed-side he then espied,
> Sir Erskine at command, sir,
> Upon one foot, he had one boot,
> And th' other in his hand, sir.
>
> "Arise, arise," Sir Erskine cries,
> "The rebels—more's the pity,
> Without a boat are all afloat,
> And rang'd before the city.

> "The motley crew, in vessels new,
> With Satan for their guide, sir,
> Pack'd up in bags, or wooden kegs,
> Come driving down the tide, sir.

> "Therefore prepare for bloody war,
> These kegs must all be routed,
> Or surely we despised shall be,
> And British courage doubted."

The silence of bitterness, however, often drowns out laughter. Although it has never been established that there was a "cabal" planning to supplant Washington with Horatio Gates, the officers of the Army thought there was, as did Washington. Certainly, there were members of Congress, including a number from New England, who were openly critical of the General's conduct of the war. Some said Richard Henry Lee was involved. At the time it was felt that Thomas Mifflin, recently resigned Quartermaster General, was the responsible party. The supposed plot had come to light when James Wilkinson, while in his cups, revealed a phrase in a letter from Thomas Conway: "Heaven has been determined to save our country, or a weak General and bad counsellors would have ruined it." Conway, an Irishman, formerly of the French Army, and now holding a brigadier general's post in the American forces, had made himself unpopular by his arrogance. Tench Tilghman, Washington's aide, revealed current thought in a letter to General John Cadwalader.

This damned faction, founded solely upon the ambition of one man, for Gates is but a puppet, is so fraught with every mischief that every honest man ought on the first discovery to give the alarm, as he would the discovery of a fire which, if suffered to get head, would destroy one of our most valuable arsenals. Many of our best officers have already taken the alarm and will speak in very plain terms if matters require it. I cannot say that I am in the least uneasy. I am so conscious that every action of the General's will bear the light (from the commencement of the war to this day) that I wish they may be called to view. I am certain that their splendor will confound all those who, like Moses, work in the dark, and would wish to undermine the men they dare not attack by day. . . .

If matters are pushed much farther, a scene will open that few people know anything about. Arnold will speak and show who oblig'd Burgoyne to strike. I will give you a part of the secret history. Upon the 7th October, Arnold, seeing an advantage, sent to Morgan to begin the engagement and pawned his honor to support him. Morgan attacked accordingly, and Arnold advanced his way. Gates sent Arnold word to halt. He returned for an answer; he had promised Morgan to support him, and support him he would, by God. Victory crowned the work, and the surrender was the consequence of it. There are other matters of a like nature, which would never have been known had not one man attempted to have robbed all the rest of their share of the glory.

Before it was all over, Conway had fought a duel with Cadwalader and had been wounded in a most appropriate place—his mouth. Conway, thinking himself dying, wrote a most abject letter of apology to Washington. But he survived. He had likewise submitted to Congress a letter of resignation, and seemed surprised when it was accepted. Although there had been certain members of Congress who had openly voiced their distrust of Washington, this was a Congress in exile at York, Pennsylvania, of whom it was said, "All but a few of the men of superior minds, had disappeared from it. Their measures were feeble, and vacillating; and their party feuds seemed to forbode some impending calamity." Whether or not there was a plot, Washington weathered it and came out of it stronger than the Congress. Nathanael Greene expressed current army thinking with, "The poor and shallow politicians unmasked their batteries before they were ready to attempt any execution."

Sighing spring winds were now melting the snows at Valley Forge, and there was an army to be trained for the field. In February, a most fabulous character rode into camp, Frederick William Augustus Henry Ferdinand, Baron von Steuben. Claiming to have been a lieutenant general on the staff of Frederick the Great (he had never been more than a captain), this colorful impostor took over Washington's mob and made soldiers of them. His method was described by Major William Fleury.

At six o'clock in the morning the division is ordered to general parade, and the soldiers in the squads of always eight, are drilled in ordinary marching. A non-commissioned officer marches at their right, a little in advance, to give the time and the step, and he drills them in marching with and without music or drums. This drill lasts two hours. At nine o'clock is the parade; the soldiers are then taught the few movements in which they are to be instructed after the use of arms. At noon, particular instruction is given to the non-commissioned officers. At three o'clock, drilling in divisions as in the morning; at six o'clock P.M., meeting of the adjutants in my quarters for instructions in theoretic maneuvering and the emphasis to be used in giving the word of command.

One more thing was needed to make this army a fighting machine capable of defeating the British Army—the military genius and experience of Charles Lee. Washington ordered Elias Boudinot, American Commissary of Prisoners, to arrange an exchange. Lee was exchanged for General Prescott, who had been captured in Rhode Island. Boudinot was a disgusted witness to the banner welcome arranged for the return of the prodigal.

When the day arrived, the greatest preparations were made for his reception. All the principal officers of the army were drawn up in two lines, advanced of the camp about two miles towards the enemy. Then the troops with their inferior officers formed a line quite to headquarters. All the music of the army attended.

The General, with a great number of the principal officers and their suites, rode about four miles on the road towards Philadelphia and waited until General Lee appeared. General Washington dismounted and received General Lee as if he had been his brother. He passed through the lines of officers and the army, who all paid him the highest military honors, to headquarters, where Mrs. Washington was, and there he was entertained with an elegant dinner, and the music playing the whole time.

A room was assigned him, back of Mrs. Washington's sitting room, and all his baggage was stowed in it. The next morning he lay very late, and breakfast was detained for him. When he came out, he looked as dirty as if he had been in the streets all night. Soon after, I discovered that he had brought a miserable, dirty hussy with him from Philadelphia (a British sergeant's wife) and had actually taken her into his room by a back door and she had slept with him that night.

As always, many of the wives of the officers had come to camp to spend the winter. The men of the ranks likewise had their female

*companions. Surgeon Waldo, returned from his furlough, didn't think
too highly of them.*

> What! though there are, in rags, in crape,
> Some beings here in female shape,
> In whom may still be found some traces,
> Of former beauty in their faces,

> Yet now so far from being nice,
> They boast of every barefaced vice.
> Shame to their sex! 'Tis not in these
> One e'er beholds those charms that please.

*An army, no matter how well trained, or how high its morale, is no
better than its health. Washington inoculated his entire army against
smallpox, losing only ten men out of the 4,000 subjected to the sometimes dangerous practice of the day. Private Joseph Martin indulged in
a little folk medicine on his own.*

When I was inoculated with the smallpox, I took that delectable
disease, the itch. It was given us, we supposed, in the infection.
We had no opportunity, or at least we had nothing to cure ourselves
with during the whole season. . . . We often applied to our officers
for assistance to clear ourselves from it, but all we could get was,
"Bear it as patiently as you can, when we get into winter quarters,
you will have leisure and means to rid yourselves of it." I had it to
such a degree that by the time I got into winter quarters I could
scarcely lift my hands to my head. Some of our foraging party had
acquaintances in the artillery, and by their means we procured
sulphur enough to cure all that belonged to our detachment. Accordingly, we made preparations for the general attack upon it.

The first night one-half of the party commenced the action by
mixing a sufficient quantity of brimstone and tallow, which was the
only grease we could get, at the same time not forgetting to mix a
plenty of hot whiskey toddy, making up a hot blazing fire and
laying down an oxhide upon the hearth. Thus prepared with arms and
ammunition, we began the operation by plying each other's outsides
with brimstone and tallow and the inside with hot whiskey sling.
Had the animalcule of the itch been endowed with reason, they would
have quit their entrenchments and taken care of themselves when we
made such a formidable attack upon them; but as it was, we had to
engage, arms in hand, and we obtained a complete victory, though

it like to have cost some of us our lives. Two of the assailants were so overcome, not by the enemy, but by their too great exertions in the action, that they lay all night naked upon the field. The rest of us got to our berths somehow, as well as we could; but we killed the itch and we were satisfied, for it had almost killed us. This was a decisive victory, the only one we had achieved lately. The next night the other half of our men took their turn, but, taking warning by our mishaps, they conducted their part of the battle with comparatively little trouble or danger to what we had experienced on our part.

Many of the firearms with which Washington's soldiers drilled had been furnished by France, the inveterate enemy of Britain. Since the beginning of the rebellion, arms and ammunition had been secretly supplied. American Commissioners in Paris, Silas Deane, Arthur Lee and the redoubtable Benjamin Franklin, had long intrigued to bring France into the conflict as an active ally. But Louis XVI proved stubborn. He preferred a posture of public neutrality, insisting that the Americans should be able to win their independence alone, and then France would be able to step in and reap the benefits. He maintained this attitude despite the constant pressures of Count de Vergennes, French Foreign Minister and leader of those who wished physical intervention, who constantly urged, "The power that will first recognize the independence of the Americans will reap the fruits of this war."

Several considerations brought about a change. First, there was the news that England was making peace overtures to the Americans, and France wished to see England humbled as she herself had been humbled in the Seven Years War. And the victory at Saratoga had implied that the Americans could win battles on their own and now France could come in on the winning side.

On February 6, 1778, a treaty between France and the United States was signed, providing that France would aid the Americans in the winning of independence; and that should France and Great Britain become involved in war, the Americans would come to her assistance; and that neither party would make peace without the consent of the other. On May 1, 1778, Washington received the news, and on May 5 informed the Army. Newspapers reported the celebration which took place the following day:

After the Chaplains had finished their discourses, and the second cannon was fired, the troops began their march to the lines. . . .

Each Major General conducted the first brigade of his company to the ground; the other brigades were conducted to their commanding officers in separate columns. . . . But this arrangement can convey no adequate idea of their movements to their several posts—of the appearance of his Excellency, during his circuit around the lines—of the air of our soldiers—the cleanliness of their dress—the brilliancy and the good order of their arms, and the remarkable animation with which they performed the necessary salutes as the General passed along. Indeed, during the whole of the review the utmost military decorum was present, while at the same time one might observe the hearts of the soldiery struggling to express their feelings in a way more agreeable to nature.

The Commander-in-Chief, his suite; the Marquis de Lafayette, his suite; Lord Stirling, General Greene and the other principal officers, having joined his Excellency, having finished the review, retired to the centre of the encampment, to a kind of amphitheatre, which had been formed to entertain the officers of the army, who were invited to partake of a collation with his Excellency after the *feu de joye*.

On firing the third signal gun, the *feu de joye* commenced. It was conducted with great judgment and regularity. The gradual progession of the sound from the discharge of the cannon and the musketry, swelling and rebounding from the neighboring hills, and gently sweeping along the Schuylkill; with the intermingled huzzas—to "Long live the King of France," "Long live the friendly European powers," and "Long live the American States," composed a military music more agreeable to the soldier's ear than the most finished pieces of your favorite, Handel.

The *feu de joye* being over, and the troops marched back to their different quarters, the officers came forward to the entertainment provided by his Excellency. . . .

About six o'clock in the evening, the company broke up, and his Excellency returned to headquarters. The French gentlemen of rank and distinction seemed peculiarly pleased with this public approbation of our alliance with their nation. The General himself wore a countenance of uncommon delight and complacence. I wish that you who are so adept in preserving the expressions of nature, had been here to have done justice to him and the army. The latter, in particular, never looked so well, not in such good order since the beginning of the war. And here I cannot forbear mentioning a little anecdote that I am told happened during the review. An officer was called to one side in order to know what was to be done with a spy who was making observations on the army. But the officer coolly observed to the gentlemen who gave the information, that he thought it best to take no further notice of the spy, but offer him to return to his employers, as they must feel more pain from his account of the army, than grief on hearing of his detention and death.

Yet to some, including Major Samuel Shaw, the idea of an alliance with France was a little embarrassing.

As an American citizen, I rejoice in the prospect of so speedy and, I hope, an effectual aid. But *as a soldier*, I am dissatisfied. How will it sound in history, that the United States of America could not, or rather would not, make an exertion, when the means were amply in their power, which might at once rid them of their enemies, and put them in possession of that liberty and safety, for which we have been so long contending. By Heavens! if our rulers had any modesty, they would blush at the idea of calling in foreign aid! 'tis really abominable, that we should send to France *for soldiers*, when there are so many sons of America idle. Such a step ought not (had these *great* men any sensibility) to have been taken until the strength of the country had been nearly exhausted, and our freedom tottering on the brink of ruin. Let us be indebted to France, Spain, or even the Devil himself, if he could furnish it, for a navy, because we cannot get one seasonably among ourselves. But do let us, unless we are contented to be transmitted to posterity with disgrace, make an exertion of our own strength by land, and not owe our independence entirely to our allies.

Now the Americans had an ally, a new spirit, and an army that had been hammered into shape by a Prussian drillmaster at the place called Valley Forge. It was time to take the field.

Monmouth

ALTHOUGH roundly cursed by some of the older officers for his inactivity, Howe seemed determined to make his last winter on American soil a pleasant one. Even before the fall of Philadelphia, he had dispatched a letter to Lord George Germain requesting to be relieved from "this very painful service, wherein I have not the good fortune to enjoy the necessary confidence and support of my superiors." As winter of 1777 wore on into spring of 1778, the prophecy of Benjamin Franklin came nearer to fulfillment: "Instead of saying Sir William Howe has taken Philadelphia, it would be more proper to say, Philadelphia has taken Sir William Howe."

It was a gay winter for the younger officers who paid court to the local belles. One rebel lady (who refused to sign her name) reported to a friend:

I will now, my dear, suppose you anxious for an account of our last winter. You have, no doubt, heard that 'twas a gay one, as likewise the censure thrown on many of the poor girls for not scorning the pleasures that courted them. You, my friend, I am certain, have liberality of sentiment, and can make proper allowances for young people in the bloom of life and spirits, after being so long deprived of the gaieties and amusements of life, which their ages and spirits called for. How hard a task it must then be to resist temptation of that nature? Plays, concerts, balls, assemblies in rotation courted their presence.

Politics were never introduced; the known Whig ladies were treated with equal politeness and attention with the Tory ladies. I myself, though a noted one, was at last prevailed on to partake of some of the amusements, though nothing could have made me believe, at the beginning of the winter, that such a thing was possible. I am generally styled, in raillery, with several other ladies, "rebel," but I had always effrontery enough to declare that I gloried in the name, and thought it virtuous to rebel in some cases as in the present. They never failed collecting the Whig news for me, and from them I received the glorious news of Burgoyne's defeat . . . which lengthened faces amazingly.

On May 8, an incoming ship brought news that Howe was relieved of his command, to be replaced as Commander in Chief of British forces in America by the portly, colorless, yet sensitive Henry Clinton. To honor their departing general, the young officers of the Army, under the direction of Captain John André, prepared what was termed a Mischianza, an Italian word indicating a medley. The affair was endowed with all of the trappings and pomp of chivalry. First there was a water parade in ornately decorated barges, boats, and galleys, one of which had a rebel lady aboard.

At length we reached the place of destination (after lying awhile on our oars opposite the *Roebuck*, and the music played "God Save the King"), which was a seat belonging to the Wharton family, about half a mile below the town. . . . Here we landed, and in a lane formed by the grenadiers and guards we proceeded about half way to the house, where we stopped. Here a large triumphant arch in honor of Lord Howe engaged our attention: Neptune with his trident was engraved thereon, and two sisters guarded it with drawn swords; they were placed in little niches formed for that purpose. On each side of this arch were seats for the ladies: steps, one above another, and carpets thrown over the whole.

I am now to tell you that, at the particular request of the managers, fourteen young ladies were dressed alike: white Poland dresses of Mantua with long sleeves, a gauze turban spangled, and sashes around the waists. Seven of them wore pink sashes with silver spangles, and others, white with gold spangles, handkerchiefs of gauze spangled in the same manner. Those of the pink and white were called Ladies of the Blended Rose, and white and gold were of the Burning Mountain. These ladies, with all the others, were seated on these steps, when a herald from the Blended Rose made his appearance (his dress was quite in the Arabian Nights style: a white satin waistcoat, small clothes of the same, monstrously large, in the Spanish fashion, trimmed with broad stripes of pink satin, adorned with silver, thrown in a loose manner down them, and the jacket—

you have no doubt seen such dresses exactly, on the stage, the Spanish dons generally wear them—white leather boots, and round little beavers), with trumpets sounding. This herald declared the Ladies of the Blended Rose to be fairer than those of the Burning Mountain, and dared them in the name of his knights any one to deny it. The herald of the Burning Mountain appeared in the same manner, his dress being [orange] color and black (those of the Rose wore pink sashes spangled, the other orange), and he in the name of his knights denied the assertion, and declared the Ladies of the Burning Mountain to be fairer than any ladies in the world. The knights then made their appearance, attended by their squires, whose dress was fantastical, though in another model, having the short cloak thrown over one shoulder; these preceded their respective knights bearing shield and mace.

Such was the beginning of the tournament in which knights jousted for fair ladies. The Knights of the Blended Rose adopted as their motto "We droop when separated," while those of the Burning Mountain used "I burn for ever." Captain André, a participating knight, sent home an account of the tournament.

After they had rode round the lists, and made their obeisance to the ladies, they drew up fronting the White Knights, and the chief of these having thrown down his gauntlet, the chief of the Black Knights directed his esquire to take it up.

The Knights then received their lances from their esquires, fixed their shields on their left arms, and making a general salute to each other, by a very graceful movement of their lances, turned round to take their career, and, encountering in full gallop, shivered their spears. In the second and third encounter they discharged their pistols. In the fourth they fought with their swords. At length the two chiefs, spurring forward into the center, engaged furiously in single combat, till the Marshal of the Field . . . rushed in between the chiefs, and declared that the fair damsels of the Blended Rose and Burning Mountain were perfectly satisfied with the proofs of love, and the signal feats of valor, given by their respective knights; and commanded them, as they prized the future favors of their mistresses, that they would instantly desist from further combat.

Obedience being paid by the chiefs to this order, they joined their respective bands. The White Knights and their attendants filed off to the left, the Black Knights to the right; and, after passing each other at the lower side of the quadrangle, moved up alternately till they approached the pavilions of the ladies, when they gave a general salute.

The pageantry continued until four in the morning with dancing, dining, gambling and fireworks. The older officers of the Army regarded this fanfaronade as a waste of time, with one veteran artillery officer snorting, "The Knights of the Burning Mountain are tom-fools, and the Knights of the Blended Rose are damned fools!" Ambrose Serle thought any sensible soldier "was ashamed of it."

Shortly afterwards Howe returned to England to meet the criticism of the country. Horace Walpole said, "He returned to England richer in money than in laurels," while his lack of military success was reflected in the observation that "the only bays that he possessed were those who drew his carriage."

The King's government, however, was finding the war in America costly; the rebel alliance with France threatened a two-front war, and France's entry into the war in 1778 gave England an excuse to attempt the seizure of the rich French West Indies, even if it meant the reduction of troops on the Continent. Measures were pushed through Parliament, repealing a number of the obnoxious acts and offering concessions to the rebels, concessions which, had they been offered in 1775, would have been happily accepted by the Americans.

A peace commission headed by the Earl of Carlisle was appointed. Their effort was recognized as a failure almost from the moment the ship dropped anchor off Philadelphia in June. The Carlisle Peace Commission discovered the Army making preparations to evacuate Philadelphia under orders that had been issued before Carlisle had sailed from England, but of which they had not been informed.

On June 13 the Continental Congress passed resolutions declaring that no consideration could be given peace overtures until "the King of Great Britain shall demonstrate a sincere disposition for that purpose. The only solid proof of this disposition will be, an explicit acknowledgment of the independence of these states, or the withdrawing of his fleets and armies." On the following day the Earl of Carlisle wrote his wife that "at present we depend as much upon Fortune as anything else for success. We all look very grave, and perhaps we think we look wise. I fear nobody will think so when we return. As I begin to think our business nearly over, I don't see what we have to do here."

By June 16, the last of the British detachments had marched out of Philadelphia. One unidentified exile returning to Philadelphia noted changes in the city.

The face of the suburbs on the north side of this city is so much altered that people who were born here, and have lived here all their lives, are much at a loss to find the situation of particular houses. The houses themselves are destroyed, and redoubts built in the neighborhood of the spots where some of them formerly stood. The timber has been all cut down and carried off, and the fine fertile fields are all laid waste. In short, the whole is one promiscuous scene of ruin, in which the Tories are interested as well as the Whigs. Advancing near the city, you come to an abatis (chiefly if not entirely made of fruit trees) which extends from Delaware to Schuylkill. Redoubts are built at proper distances in this line; they are so constructed as not to be very easily stormed. . . .

Upon getting into the city, I was surprised to find that it had suffered so little. I question whether it would have fared better had our own troops had possession of it, that is, as to the buildings, but the morals of the inhabitants have suffered vastly. The enemy introduced new fashions and made old vices more common; the former are the most absurd, ridiculous and preposterous you can conceive. I can give no description that will convey an adequate idea of them. So far as they concern the gentlemen, they appear to be principally confined to the hat, which is now amazingly broad-brimmed and cocked very sharp; were they flapped after the manner of the people called Quakers, these brims would be useful in this hot weather, because they would afford an agreeable shade to the face, but in the present mode, they serve only as an encumbrance to the blocks they cover.

The females who stayed in the city while it was in possession of the enemy cut a curious figure. Their hats, which are of the flat round kind, are of the size of a large japanned tea-waiter; their caps exceed any of the fantastic prints you have seen, and their hair is dressed with the assistance of wool, &c., in such a manner as to appear too heavy to be supported by their necks. If the caps would not blow off, a north-wester would certainly throw these belles off their center, as Yorick did the milliner—by accident.

I cannot yet learn whether the *cork rumps* have been introduced here, but some artificial rumps or other are necessary to counterbalance the extraordinary natural weight which some of the ladies carry before them. You will probably be surprised at this, but you may rely upon it as a fact. Indeed, many people do not hesitate in supposing that most of the young ladies who were in the city with the enemy, and wear the present fashionable dresses, have purchased them at the expence of their virtue. It is agreed on all hands, that the British officers played the devil with the girls; the privates, I suppose, were satisfied with the *common* prostitutes.

Last Saturday an imitation of the *mischianza*, with which General Howe was honor'd, was humbly attempted. A noted strumpet was paraded through the streets with her head dressed in the modern British taste, to the no small amusement of a vast crowd of spectators. She acted her part well—to complete the farce, there ought to have been another lady of the same character (as General Howe had two), and somebody to represent a British officer.

The long red column crawled slowly through the Jerseys, the hot July sun often sent the temperature soaring to a hundred degrees. A baggage train of 1,500 vehicles stretched out for twelve miles behind the soldiers. In the first six days only thirty miles were covered.

Washington started his army marching to intercept Clinton's army on the march. Charles Lee, whom Washington had gone to such great lengths to have exchanged, felt that an attack on the British Army would be "criminal." But Lee was beginning to show those characteristics which later led Richard Peters to observe: "He exhibited human nature in whimsical, sarcastical and sombre caricature." During the events prior to the battle of Monmouth, Lee displayed the temperament of a child whose candy has been snatched away. On June 28, young Lieutenant Colonel Alexander Hamilton, Washington's aide, commented on the comic opera.

When we came to Hopewell Township, the General unluckily called a council of war, the result of which would have done honor to the most honorable body of midwives, and to them only. The purport was, that we should keep a comfortable distance from the enemy, and keep up the vain parade of annoying them by detachment. In pursuance of this idea, a detachment of 1500 men was sent off under General [Charles] Scott to join the troops near the enemy's lines. General Lee was *primum mobile* of this sage plan, and was even opposed to sending so considerable a force.

The General, on mature consideration of what had been resolved on, determined to pursue a different line of conduct at all hazards. With this in view, he marched the army next morning towards Kingston, and there made another detachment of 1,000 men under General Wayne, and formed all the detached troops into an advanced corps under the Marquis de Lafayette. The project was, that this advanced corps should take the first opportunity to attack the enemy's rear on their march, to be supported or covered as circumstances should require by the whole army.

General Lee's conduct with respect to the command of this corps was truly childish. According to the incorrect notions of our army, his seniority would entitle him to command of the advanced corps, but he in the first instance declined it in favor of the Marquis.

Some of his friends having blamed him for doing it, and Lord Stirling having shown a disposition to interpose his claim, General Lee very inconsistently reasserted his pretensions. The matter was a second time accommodated; General Lee and Lord Stirling agreed to let the Marquis command. General Lee, a little time after, recanted again, and became very importunate. The General, who all along had observed the greatest candor in this matter, grew tired of such fickle behavior, and ordered the Marquis to proceed.

The enemy, in marching from Allentown had changed their disposition, and thrown all their best troops in the rear. This made it necessary, to strike a blow with propriety, to reinforce the advanced corps. Two brigades were detached for this purpose, and the General, willing to accommodate General Lee, sent him with them to take command of the whole advanced corps, which rendezvoused the forenoon of the 27th at English Town, consisting of at least 5000 rank and file, most of them select troops. General Lee's orders were, the moment he received intelligence of the enemy's march, to pursue them and to attack their rear.

This intelligence was received about five o'clock in the morning of the 28th, and General Lee put his troops in motion accordingly. The main body did the same. The advanced corps came up with the enemy's rear a mile or two beyond the [Monmouth] Courthouse. I saw the enemy drawn up, and am persuaded there were not a thousand men—their front from different accounts was then ten miles off. However favorable this situation may seem for attack, it was not made, but after changing their position two or three times by retrograde movements, our advanced corps got into a confused general retreat, and even rout would hardly be too strong an expression. Not a word of all this was officially communicated to the General; as we approached the supposed place of action, we heard some flying rumors of what had happened, in consequence of which the General rode forward, and found the troops retiring in the greatest disorder, and the enemy pressing upon their rear. I never saw the General to so much advantage.

Shortly afterwards, a Maryland captain was a witness to the face-to-face meeting between Washington and Lee.

He and Colonel Grayson were, therefore, both at the head of the column, when General Washington rode up and upbraided General Lee for his dastardly conduct. General Washington demanded of General Lee the reason for the retreat, to which General Lee replied: "Sir, these troops are not able to meet British grenadiers."

"Sir," said General Washington, much excited, "they are able, and by God they shall do it," and immediately gave orders to countermarch the column.

Major James McHenry continues the story.

It is a circumstance not altogether unworthy of remark, and much to the reputation of our retreating troops, that on the appearance of the General, and under his direction, two regiments immediately formed within about 200 yards of the enemy, who were displayed in front and in full advance. . . . The British grenadiers charged with great spirit and force. We gave way. As a considerable part of General Lee's detachment had retreated to English Town, he retired from the field to collect the stragglers, to which he did not return. . . .

During these contentions the right and left wing unfolded, and the whole order of battle formed on very advantageous ground; the right wing under the command of Major General Greene—the left, of Major General Lord Stirling. The enemy, continuing to press forward, and at the same time inclining to our left, met with a still more serious check from some batteries of cannon, well posted by Lord Stirling on the right of his wing, and seconded by a detachment of infantry . . . of the 1st Virginia Regiment who, penetrating the woods, fell on the enemy's right flank with great spirit and success.

The enemy, repulsed in this quarter, seemed to bend towards our right.

But General Wayne, occupying a barn and an orchard in front, gave them a very warm reception. General Greene at the same critical moment had taken possession of a piece of ground on their left with a brigade . . . where he formed a battery of cannon, which severely enfiladed the enemy, and cooperating with the gallant opposition given the front by General Wayne, obliged them to retire with great loss. . . .

After this we had several contentions, all terminating in our favor, in each of which we forced the enemy. But I cannot close the account without taking notice of an affair much to the honor of our troops. A small party of infantry were ordered to reoccupy a piece of ground from which we had forced the enemy, and to which they were again advancing. In rising the hill, our infantry received an unexpected charge from the grenadiers, which threw them into confusion. But recovering themselves, suddenly formed under the enemy's fire, advanced, and very gallantly made themselves masters of the post. This was in fore of our front line—of the front line of both armies, and had a most beautiful appearance. The rallying and charge were admirably executed.

Night now coming on prevented our pursuing any further the advantages we had gained. The troops that were ordered to gain the enemy's right and left flank did not reach their ground till night came on. The attack was therefore delayed until morning. But the enemy, fearing the event of another day, retreated about midnight, leaving behind them all the marks of disgrace and precipitancy. . . .

I do not think that in any one instance the Commander-in-Chief ever unfolded greater abilities, or any that were attended with happier effects. I am confident by his presence, exertions, and superior conduct, the glory of the day was regained. He, thro' the whole series of actions, at all times appeared in as much danger as any soldier in the field. But it required it, in order to recover what we had lost by our morning's misadventure. . . .

The Marquis De Lafayette was sadly disappointed. He had flattered himself, from his advanced position with General Lee, with the first laurels of the day. The honors of war, you know, have a distinguished place in the heart of a French nobleman. I could see that the Marquis on this occasion felt peculiarly unhappy. He was ordered by General Washington to form in the rear of our army, to support us in case of a retreat. His ambuscades and order on this occasion were very judicious. I am told General Lee claims great praise in what he terms a retrograde maneuver. I confess I am no proper judge of its merit, nor ever heard that it was a preconcerted scheme till after the engagement. But I suppose the measure and matter will be ascertained by the present court-martial.

How General Clinton feels after so inglorious a day, I know not. He thanked General Washington by flag for his humane & generous treatment of the wounded. . . .

Although the victory was not so extensive as we could wish, yet it has every substantial and unequivocal proof of its being one. We gained the field of battle before evening. We encamped on the ground that night. . . .

Anthony Wayne was quick to chide the belles of Philadelphia.

The victory of that day turns out to be much more considerable than at first expected. Colonel Butler, who remained on the ground for two days after the action, says that upwards of three hundred British have been buried by us on the field, and numbers discovered every day in the woods where the action commenced—exclusive of those buried by the enemy, which was not short of a hundred. So that by the most moderate computation, their killed and wounded must be full fifteen hundred men of the flower of their army—among them are numbers of the richest blood in England.

Tell the Philadelphia ladies that the heavenly, sweet, pretty red-coats, the accomplished gentlemen of the Guards & Grenadiers on the plains of Monmouth, "The Knights of the Blended Rose" & "Burning Mount" have resigned their laurels to *Rebel* officers, who will lay them at the feet of those virtuous daughters of America who cheerfully gave up ease and affluence in a city for liberty and peace of mind in a cottage. . . .

Monmouth was the last major battle Washington was to fight in the Northern Department. The real hero was seldom recognized— Baron von Steuben, whose long hours of drill had instilled that discipline which allowed Washington to bring order out of chaos. There was also a scapegoat—Charles Lee. Convicted in a court-martial on three counts, he was suspended from any army command for a period of twelve months. He never returned. It seems only right that his bitter letter of explanation to Robert Morris should follow.

To use the words of my Lord Chatham, have we not a gracious prince on the throne? Is he not still the same? I trust he is, but there is something rotten betwixt him and his people—not content with robbing me and the brave men under my command of the honor due us, a most hellish plot has been formed (and I may say at least not discourag'd by headquarters) to destroy forever my honor and reputation. I have demanded a court-martial, which has fortunately been granted.

If I had been let alone, I should with patience have suffered 'em to pick up the laurels which I had shaken down and lay'd at their feet, but the outrageous attacks made are enough to drive patience itself to madness. I shall not trouble you at present with a detail of the action, but by all that's sacred, General Washington had scarcely any more to do in it than to strip the dead. By want of proper intelligence we were ordered to attack the covering party supposed to consist only of fifteen hundred men. Our intelligence, as usual, was false—it proved to be the whole flower of the British army, grenadiers, light infantry, cavalry and artillery, amounting in the whole to seven thousand men. By the temerity, folly and contempt of orders of General Wayne, we found ourselves engaged in the most extensive plain in America, separated from our main body the distance of eight miles. The force we could bring to action, not more than three thousand men—in danger every moment of having our flanks turn'd by the cavalry. It required the utmost presence of mind and courage to extricate ourselves out of this dangerous situation, and on this occasion it is no crime to do justice to myself.

Upon my soul, I feel I know the whole army saw and must acknowledge that I did exhibit great presence of mind and not less address. Altho' my orders were perpetually counteracted, I maneuvered my antagonists from their advantageous ground into as disadvantageous a one. No confusion was seen, the battalions and artillery supported and were supported by each other through a plain of four miles, without losing a single gun, a single color, or sacrificing a single battalion, until I led 'em, totally exhausted, into the ground where the General was posted who had, as I observ'd before, nothing to do but to strip their dead. It is true they cannonaded each other for some time, but the enemy were so completely worn down that they could never attempt the least impression.

The General has the madness to charge me with making a shameful retreat—I never retreated, in fact (for 'till I joined him, it was not a retreat but a necessary, and I may say in my own defence, masterly maneuver). I say I never retreated but by his positive order who invidiously sent me out of the field when the victory was assur'd. Such is my recompense for having sacrificed my friends, my connections, and perhaps my fortune for having twice extricated this man and his whole army out of perdition, and now having given him the only victory he ever tasted.

The war was to grow a little soft for a while; skirmishes, threats, and blusterings were to lend an impression of combat.

Newport—Experiment in Allied Cooperation

*W*ITH *the proposed reduction in his forces, Sir Henry Clinton could do little more than retain his two posts at Newport, Rhode Island, and New York. His inactivity allowed Washington to take the initiative in little raids and irritants that kept the British off balance and their commander wondering if any of these smaller actions might not suddenly develop into an all-out effort. One that might have become critical for the redcoats was the expedition against Newport. In July, Washington's army had lain around New York, giving Clinton some cause for apprehension. Charles Hector, Comte d'Estaing, Vice-Admiral of the French Fleet, arrived with his vessels off Sandy Hook around the middle of July. When his deep-draft vessels could not successfully negotiate the bar into New York harbor, it was decided that a Franco-American effort should be made against Newport. General John Sullivan was to command the land forces, with Greene and Lafayette acting as subordinates. The New England militia expected to support the expedition did not arrive until ten days after d'Estaing's vessels hove to off Newport. The Chevalier de Pontgibaud chuckled when they came marching in.*

Hardly had the troops disembarked before the militia—to the number, I believe, of about ten thousand men, horse and foot, arrived. I have never seen a more laughable spectacle; all the tailors and apothecaries in the country must have been called out, I should think; one could recognize them by their round wigs. They were mounted on bad nags, and looked like a flock of ducks in cross belts. The infantry was no better than the cavalry, and appeared to be cut after the same pattern. I guessed that these warriors were more anxious to eat up our supplies than to make a close acquaintance with the enemy, and I was not mistaken—they soon disappeared.

After d'Estaing's fleet put to sea to meet the threat of the newly arrived squadron of Admiral Howe, Sullivan reported one misfortune after another.

I issued orders for the army to march the 11th at six in the morning, but fortune, still determined to sport longer with us, brought on a storm so violent that it, last night, blew down, tore & almost ruined all the tents I had. The arms were rendered useless, & almost the whole of the ammunition ruined. The much greater part of the army have no kind of covering, nor would tents, if they had them, prove a sufficient security against the severity of the storm. My men are lying under the fences, half covered with water, without ammunition, and with arms rendered useless. The communication between us and the main cut off by the violence of the wind, which will scarcely permit a whale boat to pass. Should the enemy come out to attack us, our dependence must be upon the superiority of our numbers and the point of the bayonet—how our militia may behave on such an occasion, I am unable to determine. To retreat is impossible; therefore we must conquer or perish. . . .

To combat all these misfortunes, & to surmount all those difficulties requires a degree of temper and persevering fortitude which I could never boast of, & which few possess in so ample a manner. . . .

The same storm that flattened Sullivan's tents also battered the two contending fleets. Howe limped back to New York. D'Estaing sailed back to Narragansett Bay and announced that he was putting into Boston for refitting and repairs. The move did little to improve Franco-American relations. Sullivan complained bitterly to Henry Laurens, President of the Continental Congress.

My letters to General Washington, copies of which he is to convey to Congress from time to time, must have informed you of the return of the French fleet, the loss it sustained in the storm, and their sudden departure for Boston. This movement has raised every voice against the French nation, revived all those ancient prejudices against the faith and sincerity of that people, and inclines them most heartily to curse the new alliance. These are only the first sallies of passion, which will in a few days subside.

I confess that I do most cordially resent the conduct of the Count, or rather the conduct of his officers who have, it seems, compelled him to go to Boston and leave us on an island without any certain means of retreat. And what surprises me exceedingly is that the Count could be persuaded that it was necessary for ten sail of the line to lay in the harbor to attend one which is refitting.

I begged the Count to remain only twenty-four hours, and I would agree to dismiss him, but in vain. He well knew that the original plan was for him to land his own troops with a large detachment of mine within their lines, under fire of some of his ships, while with the rest I made an attack in front. But his departure has reduced me to the necessity of attacking their works in front or doing nothing.

They have double lines across the island in two places, at near quarter of a mile distance. The outer line is covered in front by redoubts within musket shot of each other; the second in the same manner by redoubts thrown up between the lines. Besides this, there is an inaccessible pond which covers more than half the front line. A strong fortress on Tomminy Hill overlooks and commands the whole adjacent country.

The enemy have about six thousand men within these works. I have eight thousand, one hundred and seventy-four. With this force I am to carry their lines or retire with disgrace. Near seven thousand of my men are militia, unaccustomed to the noise of arms. Should I throw my men by stratagem within these lines, it must be my best troops. Should they be defeated, the want of ships will render their retreat impracticable, and most of the army must be sacrificed. You will, therefore, judge of my feelings, and of the situation which my inconstant ally and coadjutor has thrown me into. My feelings as a man press me to make the desperate attempt; my feelings as an officer cause me to hesitate.

Dispatches from Washington reported that Howe had put to sea from New York, possibly carrying reinforcements for Rhode Island. Sullivan began a withdrawal. John Trumbull searched for glory this August 29th of 1778.

The day was spent in skirmishing, and towards evening a body of the enemy (Germans) had pushed our right wing, and advanced so far as to endanger themselves. I was ordered to take General Lovell's brigade of Massachusetts militia and aid in repulsing them. This brigade was very much weakened by the withdrawal of many officers and men, in consequence of the army having been left by the French fleet. For this reason I drew up the brigade in line, and disregarding their original distinctions of regiments and companies, told them off in ten divisions, assigned their officers among them, wheeled them off into column, and advanced towards the scene of action, intending to pass beyond the enemy's flank, and to attack his rear.

As we advanced, the noise of the conflict seemed to retire, until we approached a small wood skirting the open fields, which lay in the direction of our march. This wood was occupied by a party of the enemy, whom it concealed from our view, while the fire which they opened up upon us as we advanced, marked their position. As was common, they fired too high and their shot passed over our heads, doing no harm. In front of the wood, at a distance of thirty or forty yards, ran a strong stone fence, such as are common in Rhode Island. Generally, on such an occasion, this fence would have been made use of as a breastwork to protect us from the enemy's fire. But as my men had hitherto kept their order perfectly, and seemed to be in no degree disconcerted by the sound of the balls, which whistled over their heads (perhaps they did not understand it), I became elated with the hope of doing something uncommon, and therefore determined not to make use of this wall for defence, but to attack. For this purpose it was necessary to remove such an obstacle, for in attempting to climb over it, all order would infallibly be lost. I therefore moved on until the front division of the column was within ten yards of the wall, and then gave the word of command as if on parade: "Column, halt! Leading division, ground your arms! Step forward, comrades, and level this fence, it stands in our way—quick, quick!" The order was obeyed with precision; the fence was levelled in an instant, and we resumed our forward march without having a man hurt. From that moment the firing in the wood ceased, and we could find no enemy; they had already been engaged with, and overmatched by other troops before we approached, and when they saw our cool maneuver, they probably mistook us for veterans coming to the rescue, and prudently withdrew. . . .

I rode forward to reconnoitre and ascertain the position of the enemy. As I rose [over] the crest of the hill, I saw the German troops, who had just been repulsed, in evident disorder, endeavoring to reform their line, but fatigued, disconcerted and vacillating.

I thought it a glorious moment, and hurried back to my brave column with the intention of leading it (under cover of the ground) into the rear of the enemy's flank. Judge of my vexation when I found my men, not in slow motion and good order as I had directed, but halted behind another strong fence, dispersed, without the shadow of order, their arms grounded, or leaning against the fence, exulting in their good conduct and success in having made the enemy run. I was cruelly disappointed, but as the success of the blow which I had meditated depended entirely upon rapidity of movement, and much time must be wasted before we could recover our original order and be prepared to move, I gave up my projected attack, and returned to make my report to my General.

The next day the army kept their ground on Butts' Hill, collected our wounded, buried the dead, and while we made a show of intending to maintain our position, were really busied in preparing for a retreat, which was effected the following night by transporting the whole in boats across Howland's Ferry to Tiverton, without the loss of a man, or of the smallest article.

When the French fleet put into Boston and set up a bakery to supply their vessels, the tantalizing odors of fresh bread set off a riot in which a French officer was killed. This, coupled with the criticism of the Newport withdrawal, jeopardized the alliance. But Nathanael Greene reported to Washington just how John Hancock smoothed troubled waters.

The secret enemies of our cause, and the British officers in the neighborhood of this place, are endeavoring to sow the seeds of discord as much as possible between the inhabitants of this place and the French belonging to the fleet. The French officers are well satisfied this is the state of the case, and it fills them with double resentment against the British. The Admiral and all the French officers are now upon an exceedingly good footing with the gentlemen of the town. General Hancock takes unwearied pains to promote a good understanding with the French officers. His house is full from morning till night.

I had a letter from the Marquis day before yesterday; he writes me that he is endeavoring to represent everything in the most favorable colors to the Court of France, in order to wipe away the prejudices that the letters of some of the more indiscreet may make upon the Court. All the French officers are extravagantly fond of your Excellency, but the Admiral more than the rest. They all speak of you with the highest reverence and respect.

General Hancock made the Admiral a present of your picture. He was going to receive it on board the fleet by firing a royal salute, but General Hancock thought it might furnish a handle for some of the speculative politicians to remark the dangers of characters becoming too important. He therefore dissuaded the Admiral from carrying the matter into execution.

The promises of the French alliance were as yet unrealized.

Skirmishes and Alarums

As the year 1778 came to an end, civilian morale seemed to ebb. Those who had time to review the past and consider the future held some forebodings. For instance there was John White of Salem, Massachusetts.

Dec. 31, 1778. We shall forever have reason (I fear) to lament our gloried Revolution because I have only changed taskmasters; the later the worse because they are poor creatures. Our country is too poor to be a separate nation.

In 1775, April 19th was the first of our battling with the English troops sent here to keep us in subjection to their unreasonable demands in taxation, etc. All, or chiefly, the men of knowledge made no resistance to government, and therefore men of little or no knowledge that took part in the opposition to Britain were preferred to places in our government. Thus came in men, poor, without moral virtue, blockheads, etc., in government. The High Sheriff of this county is a tanner; two magistrates, one a tanner, the other a joiner, neither of them could speak or read English, of this town. . . . Why I describe our conditions in the above manner is because it is impossible such men, without education, should be equal to the business. I bless God it is no worse with me, but I am too proud easily to submit to such things. I am now above 66 years old and am glad and rejoice my trial is almost over.

And then there were the usual trials of life, as indigenous to peace as to war. Consider the case of Jonathan Soule who placed this advertisement in the Connecticut Gazette.

Whereas Mary, my lawful Wife, has behaved in a very indecent Manner, refusing a virtuous Compliance with the Apostle's Injunctions to Wives; but on the contrary has made sundry Attempts to take away my Life, by stabbing me with Knives and Forks, beating me with the Distaff, Tongs and Hammer; scratching me and biting me very inhumanely; and has now eloped from my Bed and Board, and refuses to cohabit with me. I therefore forbid all Persons harbouring or trusting her on my Account, for I will not pay any Debt of her contracting after this Date. And as she has privately conveyed away a Number of Valuable Articles of my Household Furniture, I also forbid any Person whatsoever concealing any such Article on Penalty of the Law.

Not until July, 1779, was there much in the military way that gave any boost to morale. Then came the taking of Stony Point, a British strongpoint on the west side of the Hudson. Anthony Wayne led the attack with unloaded muskets—a lesson learned the hard way at Paoli. Newspapers printed the narrative of one of the participants.

The detachment marched in two divisions, and about one o'clock came up to the enemy's pickets who, by firing their pieces, gave the alarm, and with all possible speed ran to the fort, from every quarter of which, in a short time, they made an incessant fire upon our people. They, with fixed bayonets and uncharged pieces, advanced with quick but silent motion, through a heavy fire of cannon and musketry, till getting over the abatis and scrambling up the precipices, the enemy called out: "Come on, ye damn'd rebels, come on!" Some of our people softly answered, "Don't be in such a hurry, my lads, we will be with you presently."

And accordingly in a little more than twenty minutes from the time the enemy first began to fire, our troops, overcoming all obstructions and resistance, entered the fort. Spurred on by their resentment of the former cruel bayoneting, which many of them and others of our people had experienced, and of the more recent and savage barbarity of plundering and burning unguarded towns, murdering old and unarmed men, abusing and forcing defenceless women, and reducing multitudes of innocent people from comfortable livings to the most distressful want of the means of subsistence; deeply affected by these cruel injuries, our people entered the fort with the resolution of putting every man to the sword. But the cry of "Mercy! Mercy! dear Americans! mercy! quarter! brave Americans! quarter! quarter!" disarmed their resentment in an instant, insomuch that even Colonel Johnson, the commandant, freely and candidly acknowledged that not a drop of blood was spilt unnecessarily. Oh Britain! turn thine eye inward—behold and tremble at thyself! . . .

Among the prisoners are two sons of Beverly Robinson (of New York, now a colonel in the service of the enemy against his country) and a son of the late Dr. Auchmuty, late rector of Trinity Church. It was with great difficulty these three were saved by our officers from being sacrificed to the resentment of the soldiery, who being about to retaliate upon them with bayonets (the usage our people have repeatedly received from the British troops), they begged for mercy, and to excite pity, said they were Americans. This plea, proving them to be traitors as well as enemies, naturally increased the fury of the soldiers, who were upon the point of plunging bayonets into their breasts, when they were restrained by their officers.

Washington could not consolidate his gain. He merely leveled the fort and allowed Clinton to rebuild it. This attack had proved so successful that a month later a similar stroke was planned against Paulus Hook, a redoubt across from New York in what is now Jersey City.

In a bayonet attack led by Henry Lee, himself as flamboyant a character as Anthony Wayne, the post was overrun in what some said "to be the greatest enterprise ever undertaken in America."

Then suddenly it was winter again. Morristown was selected as the site for winter quarters when it became apparent that Sir Henry Clinton was going to winter in New York. The restless, exasperated American Army fretted. Then the weather turned cold, so cold that the Hudson was frozen solid from New York to Paulus Hook, and Simeon DeWitt wrote a friend that "it has been amazing cold to such a Degree that I who never yet flinched to old Boreas, had t'other day one of my Ears froze as hard as a Pine gnot." Inactivity and misery corroded tempers. Surgeon Thacher noted that the men were beginning to grow weary of the continual drilling by Steuben. Then even that stopped—the snows fell.

On the 3rd instant, we experienced one of the most tremendous snow storms ever remembered; no man could endure its violence many minutes without danger of his life. Several marquees were torn asunder and blown down over the officers' heads during the night, and some of the soldiers were actually covered while in their tents, and buried like sheep under the snow. My comrades and I were roused from sleep by the calls of some officers for assistance; their marquee had blown down, and they were almost smothered in the storm before they could reach our marquee, only a few yards, and their blankets and baggage were nearly buried in the snow. We were greatly favored in having a supply of straw for bedding; over this we spread our blankets, and with our clothes and large fires at our feet, while four or five are crowded together, preserve ourselves from freezing. But the sufferings of the poor soldiers can scarcely be described, while on duty they are unavoidably exposed to all the inclemency of storms and severe cold. At night they now have a bed of straw upon the ground, and a single blanket to each man. They are badly clad, and some are destitute of shoes. We have contrived a kind of stone chimney outside, and an opening at one end of our tents gives us the benefit of the fire within.

The snow is now from four to six feet deep, which so obstructs the roads as to prevent our receiving a supply of provisions. For the last ten days we have received but two pounds of meat per man, and we are frequently for six or eight days entirely destitute of meat, and then as long without bread. . . .

As if to make up the full measure of grief and embarrassment to the Commander-in-Chief, repeated complaints have been made to him that some of the soldiers are in the practice of pilfering and plundering the inhabitants of their poultry, sheep, pigs, and even their cattle, from their farms. This marauding practice has often been prohibited in general orders, under the severest penalties, and some exemplary punishments have been inflicted. General Washington possesses an inflexible firmness of purpose, and is determined that discipline and subordination in camp shall be rigidly enforced and maintained. The whole army has been sufficiently warned and cautioned against robbing the inhabitants on any pretence whatsoever, and no soldier is subjected to punishment without a fair trial and conviction by a court-martial.

Death has been inflicted in a few instances of an atrocious nature, but, in general, the punishment consists in a public whipping, and the number of stripes is proportioned to the degree of offence. The Law of Moses prescribes forty stripes save one, but this number has often been exceeded in our camp. In aggravated cases, and with old offenders, the culprit is sentenced to receive one hundred lashes or more. It is always the duty of the drummers and fifers to inflict the chastisement, and the drum-majors must attend and see that the duty is faithfully performed. The culprit being securely tied to a tree, or post, receives on his naked back the number of lashes assigned him, by a whip formed of several small knotted cords, which sometimes cut through the skin at every stroke. However strange it may appear, a soldier will often receive the severest stripes without uttering a groan, or once shrinking from the lash, even while the blood flows freely from his lacerated wounds. This must be ascribed to a stubbornness or pride. They have, however, adopted a method . . . which, they say, mitigates the anguish in some measure; it is by putting between the teeth a leaden bullet, on which they chew while under the lash, till it is made quite flat and jagged. . . .

Another mode of punishment is that of running the *gauntlet*. This is done by a company of soldiers standing in two lines, each one furnished with a switch, and the criminal is made to run between them and receive the scourge from their hands on his naked back. But the delinquent runs so rapidly, and the soldiers are so apt to favor a comrade, that it often happens in this way that the punishment is very trivial, but on some occasions a soldier is ordered to hold a bayonet at his breast to impede his steps.

Death was not an unknown punishment, but upon occasion Washington tempered the sentence with mercy at the last minute. Surgeon Thacher describes one such incident.

The criminals were placed side by side on the scaffold, with halters round their necks, their coffins before their eyes, their graves open to their view, and thousands of spectators bemoaning their awful doom.

The moment approaches when every eye is fixed in expectation of beholding the agonies of death—the eyes of the victims are already closed from the light of this world. At this awful moment, when their fervent prayers are ascending to Heaven, an officer comes forward and reads a reprieve for seven of them, by the Commander-in-Chief. The trembling criminals are now divested of their habiliments of death, and their bleeding hearts leap for joy. How exquisitely rapturous must be the transition when snatched from the agonizing horrors of a cruel death, and mercifully restored to the enjoyment of a life that had been forfeited! No pen can describe the emotions which must have agitated their souls. They were scarcely able to remove from the scaffold without assistance. The chaplain reminded them of the gratitude they owed the Commander-in-Chief for his clemency towards them, and that the only return in their power to make was a life devoted to the faithful discharge of their duty.

The criminal who was executed had been guilty of forging a number of discharges, by which he and more than a hundred soldiers had left the army. He appeared to be penitent, and behaved with uncommon fortitude and resolution. He addressed the soldiers, desired them to be faithful to their country and obedient to their officers, and advised the officers to be punctual in all their engagements to the soldiers, and give them no cause to desert. He examined the halter, and told the hangman that the knot was not made right, and the rope was not strong enough, as he was a heavy man. Having adjusted the knot and fixed it round his neck, he was swung off instantly. The rope broke and he fell to the ground, by which he was very much bruised. He calmly reascended the ladder, and said, "I told you the rope was not strong enough. Do get a stronger one." Another being procured, he was launched into eternity.

It was not until June 6, 1780, that the British made a move. Crossing from Staten Island over to Connecticut Farms in Jersey, the Hessians sacked and burned the village before being driven back to the river, peppered by the New Jersey militia under General William Maxwell. When Knyphausen drove inland again on June 23, he was opposed by a token force under Nathanael Greene. Outnumbered, the Americans fell back to a hill "where we continued spectators to the melancholy, general conflagration of Springfield till they retreated." This skirmish at Springfield was to be the last combat of any consequence in the Northern Department.

"Treason! Treason! Treason! Black as Hell!"

*M*ORE *and more it was becoming evident that victory was dependent upon physical aid from France. The anniversary of the French Alliance was celebrated in a loud and obvious fashion. Any official representative of the Court of France received red-carpet treatment. Private Elisha Fisher recorded one such incident in his own whimsical syntax.*

Sept. 15, 1779—His Excellency Gen. Washington and Gen. Greene with there Addecamps went to New Winsor the honourable Chevelier Le De Luzerne and Embasender from the Court of France and accompened him to Head Quarters at West Point and when they arrived they was Receeved and wellcomed with the salute of Drums and fifes and the gard present there arms. They arrived at three in the afternoon and at five there was thirteen Cannon fired from the fourt on account of his arrival.

And in the spring, when Luzerne visited Morristown, Simeon Dewitt complained, "When the French Ambassador was here My horse got so frightened At the Sound of Gunpowder that he took a Start, and I have not heard of his making a Halt till this Very Hour."

In October, 1779, Clinton had pulled his troops out of Newport. On July 10, 1780, a French fleet had disembarked 6,000 troops under the Comte de Rochambeau and made that town their headquarters. In answer to an address of welcome by the Rhode Island Assembly, the French general proved himself a diplomat.

The King, my master, hath sent me to the assistance of his good and faithful allies, the United States of America. At present, I only

204

bring over the vanguard of a much greater force destined for their aid; and the King has ordered me to assure them, that his whole power shall be exerted for their support.

The French troops are under the strictest discipline, and acting under the orders of General Washington, will live with the Americans as their brethren, and nothing will afford me greater pleasure than contributing to their success.

But the troops promised by Rochambeau remained only a hope. No sooner was his force settled in Newport than the town was blockaded by a British fleet, while a squadron across the Atlantic blockaded Brest.

Not until September 20 did Washington and the French general meet. A young Swede, Count Jean Axel de Fersen, aide to Rochambeau, passionate admirer of Marie Antoinette, and one day to become Grand Marshal of Sweden, described the moment for his father.

An interview was arranged between the generals, Washington and Rochambeau. I was sent on slightly in advance to announce Rochambeau's approach, and thus had had an opportunity of studying this most illustrious man of our century (not to say the *only one*). His majestic, handsome countenance is stamped with an honesty and a gentleness which correspond well with his moral qualities. He looks like a hero; he is very cold, speaks little, but is frank and courteous in manner; a tinge of melancholy affects his whole bearing, which is not unbecoming; on the contrary it renders him, if possible, more interesting. . . .

During our stay in Hartford, the two generals and the Admiral were closeted together all day. The Marquis de Lafayette acted as interpreter, as General Washington does not speak French nor understand it. They separated, quite charmed with one another; at least they said so.

It was after Washington left Hartford, on his way to visit West Point, that the bomb exploded.

The command at West Point had been given to that most controversial of figures, Benedict Arnold. After its evacuation, he had been appointed military commandant of Philadelphia, and there the thirty-eight-year-old general had wooed and won the blond, vivacious, eighteen-year-old Peggy Shippen. There were whispers about his high living and profiteering. After a court-martial found him guilty of misconduct in office, Arnold received a reprimand from Washington, who shortly afterwards granted his request that he be given command of the strategic post at West Point.

Arnold, some said because of the friendship of his wife with British officers, had long been in correspondence with John André, Adjutant-General of the British Army. André came up the Hudson to lay the groundwork for the treason of Benedict Arnold. Lieutenant Joshua King, who first had André under his care, remembered the account the young Britisher gave him of his capture.

He said he came up the North River in the *Vulture* sloop-of-war, for the purpose of seeing a person by flag. That was not, however, accomplished; of course he had to come ashore in a skiff, and after he had done his business, the wind was so high, the Dutchman who took him ashore dare not venture to return him on board. The night following, militia had lined the shore, so that no attempt could be made with safety. Consequently, he was obliged to shift his clothes, and was furnished with a Continental horse, and was to take the route by Peekskill, Crampound Bridge, Sing Sing, Tarrytown, to New York.

Nothing occurred to disturb him in his route until he arrived at the last place, excepting at Crampound. He told me his hair stood erect, and his heart was in his mouth, on meeting Colonel Samuel B. Webb, of our army, plump in the face; an acquaintance of his. He said the Colonel stared at him, and he thought he was gone, but they kept moving and soon passed each other.

He then thought himself past all danger. Whilst ruminating on his good luck, and his hair-breadth escape, he was assailed by three bushmen near Tarrytown, who ordered him to stand. He says to them, "I hope, gentlemen, you belong to the Lower [Tory] Party."

"We do," says one.

"So do I," says he, "and by the token of this ring and key you will let me pass. I am a British officer on business of importance, and must not be detained."

One of them took his watch from him and ordered him to dismount. The moment this was done, he said he found he was mistaken and he must shift his tone. He says, "I am happy, gentlemen, to find that I am mistaken. You belong to the Upper Party, and so do I. A man must make use of any shift to get along, and to convince you of it, here is General Arnold's pass," handing it to them, "and I am at your service."

"Damn Arnold's pass," says they, "You said you was a British officer; where is your money?"

"Gentlemen, I have none about me," he replied.

"You a British officer, and no money," says they, "Let's search him." They did so, but found none. Says one, "He has got his money in his boots," and there they found his papers, but no money. Then they examined his saddle, but found none.

He said he saw they had such a thirst for money, he could put them in a way to get it, if they would be but directed by him. He asked them to name their sum for to deliver him to King's Bridge.

They answered him in this way, "If we deliver you at King's Bridge, we shall be sent to the Sugar House [a local prison] and you will save your money."

He says to them, "If you will not trust my honor, two of you may stay with me, and one shall go with a letter I shall write. Name your sum."

The sum was agreed upon, but I cannot recollect whether it was five hundred or a thousand guineas, the latter, I think, was the sum. They held a consultation a considerable time, and finally they told him, if he wrote, a party would be sent out to take them, and then they would all be prisoners. They said they had concluded to take him to the commanding officer on the lines. They did so, and retained the watch, until General Washington sent for them to Tappan, where the watch was restored to Major André. Thus you see, had money been at the command after the imprudent confession of Major André, or any security given that the patriots could put confidence in, he might have passed on to Sir Henry Clinton's headquarters, with all papers, and Arnold's papers in the bargain.

In the meantime, Washington had sent two of his aides to invite Arnold to have dinner with him. The aides were invited to breakfast. As they ate, one of them saw a servant whispering to Arnold, who excused himself.

A moment before his (Arnold) setting out, he went into Mrs. Arnold's apartment, and informed her that certain transactions had just come to light, which must forever banish him from his country. She fell into a swoon at this declaration, and he left her in it, to consult his own safety, till the servants, alarmed by her cries, came to her relief.

She remained frantic all day, accusing everyone who approached her with an intention of murdering her child (an infant in her arms) and exhibiting every mark of the most agonizing affliction. Exhausted by the fatigue and tumult of her spirits, her frenzy subsided towards evening, and she sunk into all the sadness of distress. It was impossible not to have been touched with her situation, everything affecting in female fears, or in the misfortunes of beauty, everything pathetic in the wounded tendencies of a wife or in the apprehensive fondness of a mother, and every appearance of suffering innocence, conspired to make her an object of pity to all who were present. She experienced the most delicate attentions and every friendly office, till her departure for Philadelphia.

Colonel Benjamin Tallmadge was given the assignment of escorting André to Tappan for trial as a spy.

I soon began to make enquiries about the expected capture of our fortress, and begged him to inform me whether he was to have taken part in the military attack, if Arnold's plan had succeeded. He instantly replied in the affirmative, & pointed to a table of land on the west shore, which he said was the spot where he should have landed at the head of a select corps. He then traversed in idea the course up the mountain into the rear of Fort Putnam, which overlooks the whole parade of West Point, and with greater exactness than I could have done; and as the traitor Arnold had so disposed the garrison that little or no opposition could have been made by our troops, Major André supposed he should have reached that important eminence without difficulty. Thus that important key of our country would have been theirs, and the glory of so splendid an achievement would have been his. The animation which which he gave an account . . . delighted me, for he seemed as if he was entering the fort, sword in hand. To complete the climax, I then enquired what was to have been his reward if he had succeeded. He replied that military glory was all he sought, & that the thanks of his General, and the approbation of his King, was a rich reward for such an undertaking.

I think he further remarked that if he had succeeded (and, with the aid of the opposing general, who would doubt of success) he was to have been promoted to the rank of brigadier general.

As we progressed on our way to Tappan, before we reached the Clove, where we dined, Major André was very inquisitive to know my opinion as to the result of his capture. In other words, he wished me to give my opinion as to the light in which he would be viewed by General Washington, and a military tribunal, if one should be offered. I endeavored to evade this question, unwilling to give him a true answer. When I could no longer evade this importunity, I said to him that I had a much loved classmate in Yale College by the name of Nathan Hale, who entered the army with me in the year 1776. After the British troops had entered New York, General Washington wanted information respecting the strength, position & probable movements of the enemy. Captain Hale tendered his services, went into New York, and was taken just as he was passing the outposts of the enemy. Said I, with emphasis, "Do you remember the sequel to this story?"

"Yes," said André, "He was hanged as a spy, but you surely do not consider his case and mine alike."

I replied, "Precisely similar, and similar will be your fate." He endeavored to answer my remarks, but it was manifest he was more troubled than I had ever seen him before.

In the old Dutch Church at Tappan, John André, Adjutant General of the British Army, heard his fate pronounced by a board of six major generals and eight brigadier generals, presided over by Major General Nathanael Greene—that he "ought to be considered as a spy from the enemy, and that agreeably to the law and usage of nations, it is their opinion that he ought to suffer DEATH." Surgeon Thacher was present to witness the execution, scheduled for October 1, 1780; however, it was postponed because of Sir Henry Clinton's efforts to save his officer. André was a brave soldier, and he wanted to die like a soldier. Even as Clinton's emissaries pleaded for his life, the prisoner was writing to Washington.

SIR:

Buoyed above the terror of death by the consciousness of a life devoted to honorable pursuits, and stained with no action that can give remorse, I trust that the request I make to your Excellency at this serious period, and which is to soften my last moments, will not be rejected.

Sympathy towards a soldier will surely induce your Excellency and a military tribunal to adapt the mode of my death to the feelings of a man of honor.

Let me hope, sir, that if aught in my character impresses you with esteem towards me, if aught in my misfortune marks me as the victim of policy and not of resentment, I shall experience the operations of those feelings in your breast by being informed that I am not to die on the gibbet.

I have the honor to be your Excellency's most obedient and most humble servant,

JOHN ANDRÉ

Washington did not reply. The following day Surgeon Thacher was again on hand for the execution.

Major André is no more among the living. I have just witnessed his exit. It was a tragical scene of the deepest interest. During his confinement and trial, he exhibited those proud and elevated sensibilities which designate greatness and dignity of mind. Not a murmur or a sigh ever escaped him, and the civilities and attentions bestowed on him were politely acknowledged. . . .

The principal guard officer who was constantly in the room with the prisoner, relates that when the hour of his execution was announced to him this morning, he received it without emotion, and while all present were afflicted with silent gloom, he retained a firm countenance, with calmness and composure of mind. Observing his servant enter the room in tears, he exclaimed, "Leave me till you can show yourself more manly!" His breakfast being sent him from the table of General Washington, which had been done every day of his confinement, he partook of it as usual, and having shaved and dressed himself, he placed his hat on the table, and cheerfully said to the guard officers, "I am ready at any moment, gentlemen, to wait on you."

The fatal hour having arrived, a large detachment of troops was paraded, and an immense concourse of people assembled. Almost all our general and field officers, excepting his Excellency and staff, were present on horseback; melancholy and gloom pervaded all ranks, and the scene was affectingly awful. I was so near during the solemn march to the fatal spot, as to observe every movement, and participate in every emotion which the melancholy scene was calculated to produce. Major André walked from the stone house in which he had been confined between two of our subaltern officers, arm in arm. The eyes of the immense multitude were fixed upon him, who, rising superior to the fears of death, appeared as if conscious of the dignified deportment which he displayed. He betrayed no want of fortitude, but retained a complacent smile on his countenance, and politely bowed to several gentlemen whom he knew, which was respectfully returned. It was his earnest desire to be shot, as the mode of death most conformable to the feelings of a military man, and he had indulged the hope that his request would be granted. At the moment, therefore, when suddenly he came in view of the gallows, he involuntarily started backward, and made a pause.

"Why this emotion, Sir?" said an officer by his side.

Instantly recovering his composure, he said, "I am reconciled to my death, but I detest the mode."

While waiting and standing near the gallows, I observed some degree of trepidation; placing one foot on a stone, and rolling it over, and choking in his throat, as if attempting to swallow. So soon, however, as he perceived that things were in readiness, he stepped quickly into the wagon, and at this moment he appeared to shrink, but instantly elevating his head with firmness, he said, "It will be but a momentary pang," and taking from his pocket two white handkerchiefs, the provost marshal with one, loosely pinioned his arms, and with the other, the victim, after taking off his hat and stock, bandaged his own eyes with perfect firmness, which melted the hearts and moistened the cheeks, not only of his servant, but of the throng of spectators.

The rope being appended to the gallows, he slipped the noose over his head and adjusted it to his neck, without the assistance of the awkward executioner. Colonel Scammel now informed him that he had an opportunity to speak, if he desired it. He raised the handkerchief from his eyes and said, "I pray you to bear me witness, that I meet my fate like a brave man." The wagon being now removed from him, he was suspended and instantly expired; it proved indeed "but a momentary pang." He was dressed in his royal regimentals and boots, and interred at the foot of the gallows, and the spot was consecrated by the tears of thousands.

Arnold's past transgressions, even those of a minor nature, were now magnified into major catastrophes. Few remembered his bravery and leadership on the battlefield. Alexander Scammel was bitter in his denunciation of the traitor.

Treason! treason! treason! black as Hell! That a man so high on the lists of fame should be guilty as Arnold, must be attributed not only to original sin, but actual transgressions. Heaven and earth! we are all astonishment—each peeping at his next neighbor to see if any treason was hanging about him; nay, we even descended to a critical examination of ourselves.

This surprise soon settled down into a fixed detestation and abhorrence of Arnold, which can receive no addition. His treason has unmasked him, the eeriest villain of centuries past, and set him in true colors. His conduct and sufferings at the northward has, in the eyes of the army and his country, covered a series of base, grovelling, dirty, scandalous and rascally peculations and fraud, and the army and the country, ever indulgent and partial to an officer who has suffered in the common cause, wished to cover his faults, and we were even afraid to examine too closely, for fear of discovering some of his rascality.

Now, after all these indulgences; the partiality of his countrymen, the trust and confidence the Commander-in-Chief had reposed in him, the prodigious sums he had pilfered from his country, which has been indulgent enough to overlook his malpractices—I say, after all this, it is impossible to paint him in colors sufficiently black. Avarice, cursed avarice, with unbounded ambition, void of every principle of honor, honesty, generosity or gratitude, induced the caitiff to make the first overtures to the enemy.

Thus it was only because three militiamen stopped a traveler on the road to supplement their pay, that a British officer became an American hero, and an American general's name became a synonym for treason.

War on the Frontier

THOSE who dwelled along the eastern seaboard, harassed by the redcoats and Hessians, seldom heard or knew of a sometimes quiet but vicious conflict beyond the mountains. Often it would be a single man plowing a lonesome clearing, a puff of smoke along the edge of the forest, the crack of the musket muffled by the dread war whoop. Too often it would be followed by the screams of a woman, the whimperings of a child, the shouts of savages, or a fusillade of shot fired at some dim figure fleeing through the forest. A thick column of smoke boiling up above the trees suggested that nature would soon reclaim its land. A drying scalp outside an Indian lodge meant that the frontier had been pushed back another notch.

Both sides attempted to enlist the Indians, but the British, with their better organization, and willingness to offer attractive presents, were able to recruit with greater success among the savages. Tory Rangers and Indians under Walter and John Butler sallied out from Fort Niagara to attack lonely settlements. In July, 1778, they swept through Pennsylvania's Wyoming Valley along the Susquehanna. An English Whig publication carried the sequel to the surrender of Fort Kingston to Butler's men.

Colonel Nathan Dennison went, with a flag, to Exeter fort, to know of Colonel John Butler what terms he would grant on surrender. Butler answered, "The hatchet." Colonel Dennison returned to Fort Dennison, which he defended until Sunday morning, when his men being nearly all killed or wounded, he could hold out no longer and was obliged to surrender at discretion. The enemy took away some of the unhappy prisoners, and shutting up the rest in the houses, set fire to them, and they were all consumed together.

These infernals then crossed the river to Fort Wilkesborough, which in a few minutes surrendered at discretion. About seventy of the men, who had enlisted in the Continental service to defend the frontiers, they inhumanly butchered, with every circumstance of horrid cruelty, and then shutting up the rest with the women and children in the houses, they set fire to them, and they all perished together in the flames.

After burning all the buildings in the fort, they proceeded to the destruction of every building and improvement (except what belonged to some Tories) that came within their reach, on all these flourishing settlements, which they have rendered a scene of desolation and horror, almost beyond description, parallel or credulity. . . .

When these miscreants had destroyed the other improvements, they proceeded to destroy the crops on the ground, letting in the cattle and horses to the corn, and cutting up as much as they could of what was left. Great numbers of the cattle they shot and destroyed and, cutting out the tongues of many others, left them to perish in misery.

Cherry Valley, a village some fifty miles west of Albany, also felt the savage storm. Walter Butler led the Tory Rangers, while the 500 Indians were under the command of Thayendanega, a chief also known as Joseph Brant. A Boston newspaper published the story of a survivor.

On Sunday morning, a sergeant and twelve men were sent on the road by Beaver Dam towards the enemy, to continue five days. Another scout with a non-commissioned officer and five men were sent on the road to Springfield, to continue four days. These two roads being the only avenues from the enemy's country to this place, except an old Indian path which had been neglected by us. At the same time we sent by the same roads, scouts in the morning who returned at night.

On Wednesday, the 11th, it rained very hard. The enemy came by the above-mentioned path, past two houses and lodged themselves in a swamp a small distance behind Mr. Well's house, headquarters. Half past eleven A.M., Mr. Hamlin came by and discovered two Indians, who fired upon him and shot him through the arm. He rode to Mr. Well's and acquainted the Colonel, the Lieutenant Colonel, Major and Adjutant being present. The two last (the house at this time being surrounded by Indians) got to the fort through their fire, the Colonel being shot near the fort. The enemy, 800 in number, consisting of some 500 Indians commanded by Brant, fifty regulars under Captain Colvill, and another captain with some of Johnson's Rangers, and about 200 Tories, the whole under Colonel Butler's command, immediately surrounded the fort, excluding several officers who were quartered out of the garrison and had gone to dinner. They commenced a very heavy fire on the fort, which held for three and a half hours, and was as briskly returned. They were so near as to call to the fort and bid the damn'd rebels surrender, which was answered with three cheers and a discharge of cannon and musketry. At four P.M. the enemy withdrew. Captain Ballard sallied out with a party which the enemy endeavored to cut off, but were prevented by a reinforcement. The next day they made it their whole business to collect horses, cattle and sheep, which they effected, and at sunset left the place.

On Friday morning the fort was reinforced by 800 militia. The enemy killed, scalp't, and most barbarously murdered thirty-two women and children . . . burnt twenty-four houses with all the grain, &c., took above sixty inhabitants prisoners, part of whom they released on going off. They committed the most inhuman barbarities on most of the dead: Robert Henderson's head was cut off, his skull bone cut out with his scalp—Mr. Willis's sister was rip't up, a child of Mr. Willis's, two months old, scalp't and arm cut off—the clergyman's wife's leg and arm cut off, and many others as cruelly treated. Many of the inhabitants and soldiers shut out from the fort, lay all night in the rain with children, which suffered very much. The cattle that were not easy to drive, they shot. We were informed by the prisoners they sent back, that the lieutenant colonel, all the officers and Continental soldiers were stript and drove naked before them.

As petitions flowed in from the West, Congress finally decided to send a punitive expedition against the Indians in the summer of 1779. Washington first offered the command to Horatio Gates, who declared himself too old for a wilderness expedition. General John Sullivan was appointed. When Sullivan departed from Wyoming, it was with an imposing column, marching with drums and fifes echoing in the wilderness, and trailed by 1,200 packhorses carrying the baggage of the army. Indian towns, usually deserted, were burned, and their fields laid waste. Not until late August did they meet their first real resistance. Nathan Davis wrote an account of the battle of New Town, August 29, 1779.

Our riflemen discovered at a little distance in front, a sure indication of an ambush. In the direction of our march was a very deep defile, occasioned by a brook of water running through a pine plain; the banks of the brook were very steep and high, and the growth of timber small and very thick. On the opposite bank it was observed to be thicker and in greater regularity than it would have been had dame Nature herself placed it there. The conclusion was that the Indians lay concealed behind it, as finally proved to be the case. They had made a kind of breastwork of small pine timber and had that morning, cut small saplings and stuck them in the ground in front of it. . . .

We had proceeded half a mile when General Sullivan gave orders to Colonel Proctor to open fire with his six or eight brass field guns, from six to three pounders, and also a small howitzer which hove a small bomb upon the enemy's breastwork. The object of this order was to draw the attention of the Indians off from General Poor.

The order was obeyed with promptness, but produced a somewhat different effect from the one anticipated. They immediately ran from their slender works as fast as their legs could carry them, and advanced directly to the hill, where they secreted themselves behind the trees, waiting our approach. When our front had advanced within a short distance of them, they commenced a fire from behind every tree, and at the same time gave a war whoop. Not all the infernals of the Prince of Darkness, could they have been let loose from the bottomless pit, would have borne any comparison to these demons of the forest.

We were expressly ordered not to fire, until we had obtained permission from our officers, but to form a line of battle as soon as possible and march forward. This we did in good order, and at the same time the Indians kept up an incessant fire upon us from behind trees; firing and retreating back to another tree, loading and firing again, still keeping up the war whoop. They continued this mode of warfare till we had driven them halfway up the hill, when we were ordered to charge bayonets and rush on. No sooner said than done. We then, in our turn, gave our war whoop, in the American style, which completely silenced the unearthly voice of their stentorian throats. We drove them, at once, to the opposite side of the hill, when we were ordered to halt, as the Indians were out of sight and hearing.

How many we killed I never could exactly ascertain, but some were killed, and one scalped to my knowledge, and much blood was seen on their track. We also took two prisoners, one Negro and one white man, said to be a Tory. The white man was found painted black, lying on his face, and pretending to be dead. As no blood was seen near him, after a proper discipline he was soon brought to his feelings. He was then stripped and washed, and found to be white. A rope was then tied round his neck, and he was led in front of the troops, whilst every one gave him his sentence, "You shall be hung tomorrow." This, however, was not put into execution.

We remained on the battleground till sunset, when we retreated to the plain and encamped. We had twenty-two killed and a number wounded, some mortally. The next day we buried our dead by the side of the fallen trees near our encampment, not raising their graves higher than the surface of the earth. We then burnt brush over their graves, so that the Indians might not distinguish them from the place where we built our customary fires.

Lieutenant William Barton was among those who were dispatched along the trail to count dead Indians: "Toward noon they found them and skinned two of them from their hips down for boot legs; one pair for the Major and the other for myself."

There was little opposition as Sullivan burned his way through the Indian country. The men grew careless and inattentive to discipline. Major Jeremiah Fogg witnessed one incident as Sullivan attempted to surround the Indian settlement of Seneca Town.

But oh! sad mishap! When our commander advanced to complete his part, to his great mortification, he found the detachments either misled by their guides, or else had mistaken a field of pumpkins for the town. But whatever might have been the cause, the whole party from the monkey to the rat, had armed themselves with almost every species of the vegetable creation, each man with three pumpkins on his bayonet and staggering under the weight of a bosom filled with corn and beans, when he broke out, "You damned unmilitary set of rascals! What, are you going to storm the town with pumpkins! Turn aside, open to the right and left, that men unaccustomed to plundering, and such scandalous conduct, may execute the design! Ye officers, never more show your heads with military characters." In an instant the whole band was disrobed of their vegetable accoutrements and armor, and pumpkins, squashes, melons and mandrakes rolled down the hill like hail stones in a tempest.

Overconfidence was dangerous in that country. Lieutenant Erkuries Beatty told of a scouting party that reconnoitered an Indian town.

Lieutenant Boyd with his party went on without any interruption till he got to the town about daybreak, when he found it evacuated. He then sent two runners back to inform the General, and he retired a little into the woods, in sight of the town, concealed, to try if he could not catch a prisoner. He, soon after, saw four Indians come into town a horseback. He sent five or six men to take them or kill them. The men fired on the Indians, killed and sculped one and wounded another and took a horse, saddle and bridle. He then sent two more runners to the army, but they soon returned to him and informed him they had seen five Indians on the road.

He then thought proper to return with his party to the army which he expected to meet very soon. He had not gone far before he fell in with the same Indians, which he fired on. They run on before him, and he pursued them slowly and every once in a while he would come in sight of them and fire on them. And so they kept on till he came to this hill . . . when he heard our drums and thought himself entirely safe, but to his great disappointment found a large body of Indians behind trees.

He immediately formed his men for action, and began a very heavy fire which lasted for some time, but the Indians, whose number was so far superior to him, surrounded him and made prisoners or killed the whole excepting a few which came in. We found four or five of our men dead and sculped, and it is supposed that Lieutenant Boyd is made prisoner. The enemy had a number killed as the men that was hid in the bushes saw the Indians carry a number off in blankets. . . .

Arrived at Genessee Town which is the largest we have yet seen. It lies in a crook of the river on extraordinary good land, about seventy houses, very compact and very well built, and about the same number of outhouses in cornfields, &c. On entering the town we found the body of Lieutenant Boyd and another rifleman in a most terrible mangled condition. They was both stripped naked, and their heads cut off, and the flesh of Lieutenant Boyd's was entirely taken off and his eyes punched out. The other man's head was not there. They was stabbed, I suppose, in forty different places in the body with a spear and great gashes cut in their flesh with knifes, and Lieutenant Boyd's privates was nearly cut off and hanging down. His finger and toe nails was bruised off, and the dogs had eat part of their shoulders away; likewise a knife was sticking in Lieutenant Boyd's body. They was immediately buried with the honors of war.

In one Seneca town Lieutenant Beatty reported finding white captives.

On the first entrance of our brigade, a young child, I believe about three years old, found running about the houses which one of our officers picked up and found it to be a white child, but it was so much tanned and smoked that we could hardly distinguish it from an Indian child and was exceeding poor, scarcely able to walk. It could talk no English, nothing but Indian, and I believe, but little of that. The officer took great care of it and clothed it, as it was naked when he found it, and could give no account of itself; only said "His Mammy was gone." The men got very little plunder, or anything in the town as the Indians had taken everything with them.

By September 15 the campaign was drawing to a close. It was soon after the burial of Lieutenant Boyd that Major Fogg heard the welcome command.

This day was spent in destroying corn which had become so ripe that we were obliged to burn it in kilns. Some corn stalks were seventeen feet long. The whole army was employed, but at three o'clock we *faced to the right about.* A most joyful day! Marched back to the east end of the great flat and encamped.

By September 30 the army was back at Wyoming, its mission a success. Sullivan on his sweep through the Six Nations had destroyed 41 Indian towns, with a loss of only 41 men, not all of whom had died in combat. He estimated that 1,500 fruit trees belonging to the savages had been destroyed, and over 200 acres of corn, estimated at 160,000 bushels, had been ruined. How effective was it? Indian raids, everyone knew, would continue, for in the words of Jeremiah Fogg, "The nests are destroyed, but the birds are still on the wing."

Probably the best-known operation in the western country, however, was conducted by a young, red-haired, sharp-nosed, blue-eyed, hard-drinking six-footer from Kentucky County, Virginia—George Rogers

Clark. It was his contention that the best way to eliminate Indian forays was to wipe out the fort at Detroit, from whence many of the raids supposedly initiated.

At Detroit, one of the four lieutenant governors of Canada, Henry Hamilton, was in charge of Indian operations. Although the Americans could offer no evidence, it was charged that he was paying for scalps of white settlers, and the epithet of "Hair Buyer" was applied to him. Hamilton himself reported, "The parties sent from hence have been in general successful, tho' the Indians have lost men enough to sharpen their resentment. They have brought in seventy-three prisoners alive, and one hundred and twenty-nine scalps."

This was the man Clark planned to destroy. Traveling eastward to Williamsburg, he confronted Governor Patrick Henry with, "If a Cuntrey was not worth protecting, it was not worth Claiming." Henry persuaded his legislature to appropriate funds for a secret undertaking. Clark's plan was to march first through the Illinois country, and seize the towns of Kaskaskia, Vincennes, and Cohokia, whose inhabitants of French extraction were supposedly friendly to the American cause. Success here would give the Americans control of the Ohio and access to Spanish New Orleans, open up the fur trade, block British operations on the river, and possibly so awe the Indians that they would turn neutral in the struggle for the West.

On June 24, 1778, Clark's 175 men floated down the Ohio in flatboats. To maintain secrecy, he disembarked about ten miles below the mouth of the Tennessee River to begin the 120-mile overland march to Kaskaskia. Clark reported an easy conquest.

On the evening of the 4th of July, we got within three miles of the town, Kaskaskia, having a river of the same name to cross to the town. After making ourselves ready for anything that might happen, we marched after night to a farm that was on the same side of the river, about a mile above the town, took the family prisoners, and found plenty of boats to cross in, and in two hours transported ourselves to the other shore with the greatest silence.

I learned they had some suspicion of being attacked and had made some preparations, keeping out spies, but they, making no discoveries, had got off their guard. I immediately divided my little army into two divisions, ordered one to surround the town. With the other I broke into the fort, secured the Governor, Mr. Rochblave, in fifteen minutes had every street secured, sent runners through the town ordering the people on pain of death to keep close to their houses, which they observed, and before daylight had the whole disarmed. Nothing could excel the confusion these people seemed to be in, being taught to expect nothing but savage treatment from the Americans. Giving all for lost, their lives were all they could dare beg for, which they did with the greatest fervency; they were willing to be slaves to save their families. I told them it did not suit me to give an answer at that time. They repaired to their houses, trembling as if they were led to execution. My principle would not suffer me to distress such a number of people, excepting through polity it was necessary. . . .

I sent for all the principal men of the town, who came in as if to a tribunal that was to determine their fate forever, cursing their fortune that they were not apprised of us to have defended themselves. I told them that I was sorry to find that they had been taught to harbor so base an opinion of the Americans and their cause; explained the nature of the dispute to them in as clear a light as I was capable of, it was certain that they were a conquered people, and by the fate of war was at my mercy, and that our principle was to make those we reduced free instead of enslaving them as they imagined, that if I could only have the surety of their zeal and attachment to the American cause, they should immediately enjoy all the privileges of our government and their property secured to them—that it was only to stop further effusion of blood by the savages under the influence of their Governor, that made them an object of our attention, &c.

No sooner had they heard this than joy sparkled in their eyes, and they fell into transports of joy that really surprised me. As soon as they were a little moderated, they told me that they had always been kept in the dark as to the dispute between America and Britain; that they had never heard anything before but what was prejudicial and tended to incense them against the Americans; that they should be happy of an opportunity to convince me of their zeal, and think themselves among the happiest people in the world if they were united with the Americans, and begged that I would receive what they said were their real sentiments. . . . In order to be more certain of their sincerity, I told them that an oath of fidelity was required from the citizens, and to give them time to reflect on it, I should not administer it for a few days. In the meantime, any of them that chose, was at liberty to leave the country with their families, except two or three particular persons; that they might repair to their families, conduct themselves as usual without any dread.

The priest that had lately come from Canada had made himself a little acquainted with our dispute (contrary to the principle of his brother in Canada) [and] was rather prejudiced in favor of us. He asked if I would give him liberty to perform his duty in his church. I told him that I had nothing to do with churches, more than to defend them from insult; that by the laws of the state, his religion had as great privileges as any other. This seem'd to complete their happiness. They returned to their families, and in a few minutes the scene of mourning and distress was turned to an excess of joy, nothing else seen or heard; adorning the streets with flowers and pavilions of different colors, completing their happiness by singing, &c.

Thirty mounted men under Captain Joseph Bowman were sent to take Cohokia, sixty miles away. The conquest was surprisingly simple. Prairie du Rocher and St. Philippe quickly capitulated to Bowman's detachment. Father Gibault, the priest at Kaskaskia, persuaded the people of Vincennes to offer their allegiance to the Americans.

Many of Clark's men now determined they should go home, "as they were no longer Ingaged surrounded by numerous Nations of Savages, whose minds had been long poisoned by the English."

On August 6, 1778, Francis Maisonville arrived at Detroit from the Illinois country; Henry Hamilton was told of the fall of Kaskaskia. After a journey of 600 miles in 71 days, Hamilton with 34 regulars of the 8th Regiment, 141 volunteers and over 300 Indians, approached Vincennes on December 17, a swirling snowstorm driven by a freezing wind obscuring their approach. The commandant of the local fort, deserted by his garrison except for three of Clark's Virginians, surrendered. Clark himself narrowly escaped capture by a scouting party of 40 Indians.

At Kaskaskia, Clark recruited a force of 170 men, nearly half of whom were French volunteers. On February 5, he marched. Before him lay 240 miles of tortuous terrain, the winter rains spreading streams into the "drowned lands," sometimes four to five miles wide.

I viewed this sheet of water for some time with distrust, but accusing myself of doubting, I immediately set to work without holding any consultation about it, or suffering anybody else to do so in my presence. Ordered a pirogue immediately built, and acted as though crossing the water would only be a piece of diversion, and as but few could work at a time, pains were taken to find diversions for the rest to keep them in high spirits. But the men were well prepared for this attempt, as they frequently waded farther in water, but perhaps seldom above half a leg deep. My anxiety to cross this place continually increased as I saw it would at once fling us into a situation of a forlorn hope, as all ideas of retreat would be in some measure done away with; that if the men began . . . to think seriously of what they had really suffered, that they would prefer risking any seeming difficulty that might turn out favorable, than to attempt a retreat when they would be certain of experiencing what they had already felt, and if the weather should be freezing, altogether impracticable except the ice would bear them. . . .

Fortunately the 15th happened to be a warm, moist day for the season, and the channel of the river where we lay, about thirty yards wide. A scaffold was built on the opposite shore that was under about three foot of water, our baggage ferried across and put on it. Our horses swam across and received their loads at the scaffold, by which time the troops was also brought across, and we began our march, our vessel loaded with those that was sickly, &c.

We moved on cheerfully, every moment expecting to see dry land, which was not discovered. . . . By the evening we found ourselves encamped on a pretty height in high spirits, each laughing at the other in consequence of something that had happened in the course of this ferrying business, as they called it, and the whole at the great exploit as they thought they had accomplished; thus a little antic drummer afforded them great diversion by floating on his drum, &c. All this was greatly encouraged, and they really began to think themselves superior to other men, and that neither the rivers or seasons could stop their progress. Their whole conversation now was what they would do when they got about the enemy, and now began to view the main Wabash as a creek and made no doubt but that such men as they were could find a way across it. They wound themselves up to such a pitch, that they soon took Vincennes, divided the spoil, and before bed time was far advanced on their route to Detroit.

Optimism faded on the banks of the Wabash. Some talked of going home. French guides said that the next high ground was a grove of hard maples, an old sugar camp. Clark resorted to dramatic methods to "spirit up" his men.

I returned slowly to the troops, giving myself time to think. On our arrival all ran to hear what was the report. Every eye was fixed on me. I unfortunately spoke serious to one of the officers. The whole was alarmed without knowing what I said. They ran from one another, bewailing their situation. I viewed their confusion for about one minute, whispered to those near me to do as I did; immediately took some water in my hand, poured on powder, blacked my face, gave the war whoop and marched into the water without saying a word. The party gazed, and fell in one after another without saying a word, like a flock of sheep. I ordered those that was near me to begin a favorite song of theirs. It soon passed through the line, and the whole went on cheerfully. I now intended to have them transported across the deepest part of the water, but when getting about waist deep, one of the men informed me that he felt a path (a path is very easily discovered under water by the feet). We examined and found it so, and concluded that it kept on the highest ground, which it did, and by pains to follow it, we got to the sugar camp without the least difficulty . . . where there was about half an acre of dry ground, at least, not under water where we took up our lodgings.

The following morning the water was rimmed with ice. Captain Bowman described the approach to Vincennes.

Set off to cross a plain called Horse Shoe plain, about four miles long, covered with water breast high. Here we expected some of our brave men must certainly perish, having froze in the night, and so long fasting, and no other recourse but wading this plain, or rather a lake of water. We pushed into it with courage, Colonel Clark being the first, taking care to have the boats close by, to take those that was weak and benumbed (with the cold) into them. . . .

About one o'clock we came in sight of the town. We halted on a small knoll of dry land called Warrior's Island where we took a prisoner that was hunting ducks, who informed us that no person suspected our coming in that season of the year. Colonel Clark wrote a letter to the inhabitants. . . .

In order to publish this letter, we lay still to about sundown, when we began our march, all in order, with colors flying and drums braced. After wading to the edge in water breast high, we mounted the rising ground the town is built on about eight o'clock.

Lieutenant Bailey with fourteen regulars was detached to fire on the town, and ordered to stay until he was relieved by another party which was soon done. Reconnoitered about to find a place to throw up entrenchments; found one and set . . . to work. Soon crossed the main street about 120 yards from the fort gate. . . . Fine sport for the sons of liberty!

Inside the fort, a scout reported seeing fourteen fires. The militia was alerted. Henry Hamilton detailed his own downfall.

About five minutes after candles were lighted, we were alarmed by hearing a musket discharged; presently after, some more. I concluded that some party of Indians was returned or there was some riotous frolic in the village. Going upon the parade to enquire, I heard the balls whistle, ordered the men to the blockhouses, forbidding them to fire till they perceived the shot to be directed against the fort. We were shortly out of suspense, one of the sergeants receiving a shot in the breast. The fire was now returned, but the enemy had a great deal of advantage from their rifles, and the cover of the church, houses, barns, &c. . . .

Tho' the night was dark, we had a sergeant matross and five men wounded. The weather was still so cold we were obliged to bring the wounded into our own quarters. The officers, who had continued in tents all winter, were exposed to the fire of the enemy's riflemen, as the picketing of the fort was so poorly set up that one might pass the hand clenched between the stockades. We dislodged the enemy from the church and nearest houses by a few cannon shot from the blockhouses, but when day appeared, and we saw that the inhabitants of the village had joined the rebels, we despaired of Captain La Mothe's party regaining the fort. But to my great surprise and joy, half an hour before sunrise they appeared and got into the fort over the stockades, which were upright and eleven feet out of the ground, with their arms in their hands. . . .

The firing was but slack after sunrise, and about eight o'clock a flag of truce from the rebels appeared, carried by Nicholas Cardinal, a captain of the militia of St. Vincennes, who delivered me a letter from Colonel Clark, requiring me to surrender with discretion, adding with an oath that if I destroyed any stores or papers I should be treated as a murderer. Having assembled the officers and read this letter, I told them my intention was to undergo any extremity rather than trust to the discretion of such sort of people as we had to deal with. They all approved of this resolution, on which I assembled the men and informed them of our determination. The English assured me that they would defend the King's colors to the last, adding a homely, but hearty, phrase, that they would stick to me as the shirt to my back. They then gave three cheers. The French, on the contrary, hung their heads. I returned for answer to Colonel Clark's note, that threats would not prevent us from doing our duty as British subjects, and the flag having returned, the firing recommenced.

La Mothe's volunteers now began to murmur, saying it was very hard to be obliged to fight against their countrymen and relations, who, they now perceived had joined the Americans. As they made half our number, and after such a declaration were not to be trusted, the Englishmen wounded, six in number, were a sixth of those we could depend on, and duty would fall every hour on the remaining few. Considering we were at a distance of six hundred miles from succor, that if we did not burn the village we left the enemy most advantageous cover against us, and that if we did, we had nothing to expect after rejecting the first terms, but the extremity of revenge, I took up the determination of accepting honorable terms if they were to be procured, else to abide the worst. . . .

About two o'clock a party of Indians with some whites returned from a scout with two Canadians whom they had taken prisoner near the falls of Ohio, probably with information for the rebels at the fort. Colonel Clark sent off a detachment of seventy men against them. The Indian party of fifteen or sixteen men, who seeing the British flag flying at the fort, discharged their pieces (an usual compliment with these people). They were immediately fired upon by the rebels and Canadians, two killed on the spot, one shot in the belly who, however, escaped. The rest were surrounded and taken bound to the village, where being set in the street opposite the fort they were put to death, notwithstanding a truce at the moment existed. . . .

One of them was tomahawk'd immediately. The rest, sitting on the ground in a ring, bound, seeing by the fate of their comrade what they had to expect, the next on his left sung his death song and was in turn tomahawk'd; the rest underwent the same fate, one only was saved at the intercession of a rebel officer who pleaded for him, telling Colonel Clark that the savage's father had formerly spared his life.

The chief of this party, after having had the hatchet stuck in his head, took it out himself and deliver'd it to the inhuman monster who struck him first, who repeated his stroke a second and a third time, after which the miserable spectacle was dragged by the rope about his neck to the river, thrown in, and suffer'd to spend still a few moments of life in fruitless strugglings. Two sergeants who had been volunteers with the Indians escaped death by the intercession of a father and a sister who were on the spot. . . .

Colonel Clark, yet reeking with the blood of these unhappy victims, came to the esplanade before the fort, where I had agreed to meet him and treat of the surrender of the garrison. He spoke with rapture of his late achievement, while he wash'd off the blood from his hand, stained in this inhuman sacrifice. . . .

At ten o'clock of the morning of the 25th, we marched out with fixed bayonets, and the soldiers with their knapsacks. The colors had not been hoisted this morning that we might be spared the mortification of hauling them down. . . .

The evening of the day we capitulated, Colonel Clark ordered neck-irons, fetters, and handcuffs to be made which, in our hearing, he declared were designed for those officers who had been employed as partisans with the Indians. I took him aside and reminded him that these persons were prisoners of war, included in the capitulation which he had so lately put his hand to; he said his resolution was formed, that he had made a vow never to spare woman or child of the Indians, or those who were employed with them. I observed to him that these people having obeyed my orders, were not to be blamed for the execution of them, that I had never known that they had acted contrary to those orders by encouraging the cruelty of the savages . . . and that if he was determined to pass by the considerations of his faith and that of the public, pledged for the performance of the articles of capitulation, I desired that he might throw me into prison, or lay me in irons rather than the others. He smiled contemptuously, turned away, and order'd three of these people to the guard, till the irons should be made. The scalps of the slaughter'd Indians were hung up by our tents, a young man by the name of Raimbault was brought into the fort with a halter about his neck and only for the interposition of the volunteers from the Illinois, some of whom were his relations, would infallibly [have] been hanged without any crime laid to his charge but his having been with a scouting party; he was half-strangled before he was taken from the tree.

Clark did not deny Hamilton's report of his cruelty to the Indians. He justified the slaughter by the reasoning: "I now had a fair opportunity of making an impression on the Indians that I could have wished for; that of convincing them that Governor Hamilton could not give them that protection that he had made them to believe he could, in some measure to incense the Indians against him for not exerting himself to save his friends."

George Rogers Clark became a virtual dictator in the Indian country and, with the exception of two outbreaks in 1780 and 1782 by the Shawnees, kept the Indians of the Illinois country in check. Yet he never realized his ambition of leading an expedition against Detroit to wipe out the seedbed of Indian depredations. His proposed expedition in 1780 was frustrated when Virginia, impoverished and threatened by invasion, could send neither men nor any other aid.

The War Turns South

ENGLISH mercantilists argued that the war had "begun at the wrong end," and from the beginning of the rebellion had insisted that not only would the southern colonies be easier to overcome, but, once subjected, their products of a semitropical nature would be more valuable for the mother country's economy. Josiah Martin, North Carolina's Royal Governor, had long proclaimed his colony to be predominantly loyalist. As a result, before the siege of Boston had been raised, Whitehall had decided there should be an expedition to the southward.

Howe dispatched Sir Henry Clinton from Boston to rendezvous in Cape Fear River with a larger force sailing from Ireland under the command of General Charles Cornwallis and Admiral Sir Peter Parker. There they were to be joined by the North Carolina loyalists. Held up by foul weather, the fleet straggled into the Cape Fear in early spring. By that time the Carolina Tories, in a premature uprising, had been defeated in battle on February 27, 1776, at Moore's Creek Bridge.

Despite this blow, Parker persuaded Clinton to continue the operation against Charleston, the most important port in the South. The Continental Congress succumbed to pressures of southern delegates and Charles Lee was named Commanding General of the newly created Southern Department. By the time that colorful officer arrived in Charleston, the British fleet had already been sighted and the city was in a ferment of preparation. Colonel William Moultrie was in command of the fort on Sullivan's Island.

June 4, [1776.] General Lee arrived from the northward and took the command of the troops. His presence gave us great spirits, as he was known to be an able, brave and experienced officer, though rough and hasty in his manners, which the officers could not reconcile themselves to at first. . . .

When he came to Sullivan's Island, he did not like the post at all; he said there was no way to retreat, that the garrison would be sacrificed; nay, he called it a "slaughter pen," and wished to withdraw the garrison and give up the post, but President Rutledge insisted that it should not be given up. Then General Lee said it was "absolutely necessary to have a bridge of boats for a retreat," but boats enough could not be had, the distance being over at least a mile. Then a bridge was constructed of empty hogsheads buoyed up at certain distances, and two planks from hogshead to hogshead. But this would not answer, because when Colonel Clark was coming over from Haddrell's with a detachment of 200 men, before they were half on, it sunk so low that they were obliged to return.

General Lee's whole thoughts were taken up with the post on Sullivan's Island; all his letters to me show how anxious he was at not having a bridge for a retreat. For my part, I never was uneasy on not having a retreat, because I never imagined that the enemy could force me to that necessity. I always considered myself able to defend that post against the enemy. . . .

General Lee, one day on a visit to the fort, took me aside and said, "Colonel Moultrie, do you think you can maintain this post?"

I answered him, "Yes, I think I can."

That was all that passed on the subject between us.

Another time, Captain Lamperer, a brave and experienced seaman, who had been master of a man-of-war and captain of a very respectable privateer many years ago, visited me at the fort after the British ships came over our bar. While we were walking on the platform looking at the fleet, he said to me: "Well, Colonel, what do you think of it now?"

"Sir," said he, "when those ships" (pointing to the men-of-war) "come to lay aside your fort, they will knock it down in half an hour" (and that was the opinion of all the sailors).

"Then," I said, "we will lay behind the ruins and prevent their men from landing."

The fort on Sullivan's Island became the hinge of victory. Moultrie tells of the attack.

On the morning of the 28th of June, I paid a visit to our advance guard (on horseback three miles to the eastward of our fort). While I was there, I saw a number of the enemy's boats in motion, at the

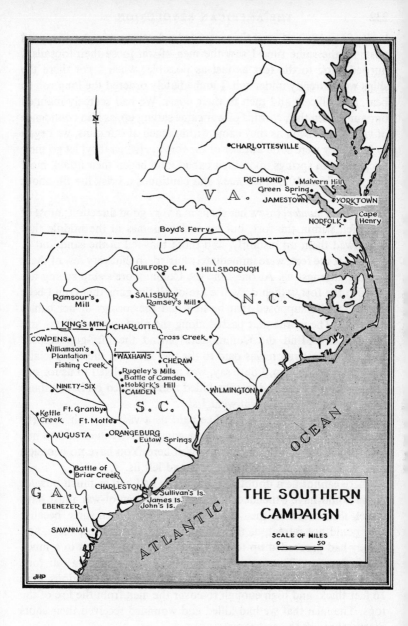

THE SOUTHERN CAMPAIGN

SCALE OF MILES
0   50

back of Long Island, as if they intended a descent upon our advanced post. At the same time I saw the men-of-war loose their topsails. I hurried back to the fort as fast as possible; when I got there the ships were already under sail. I immediately ordered the long roll to beat, and officers and men to their posts. We had scarcely manned our guns when the . . . ships of war came sailing up, as if in confidence of victory. As soon as they came within reach of our guns, we began to fire. They were soon abreast of the fort . . . [when they] let go their anchors, with springs upon their cables, and began their attack most furiously about 10 o'clock A.M., and continued a brisk fire till about 8 o'clock P.M. . . .

She [the *Thunder*] threw her shells in a very good direction; most of them fell within the fort, but we had a morass in the middle that swallowed them up instantly, and those that fell in the sand and in and about the fort, were immediately buried, so that very few of them bursted amongst us. At one time the Commodore's ship swung her stern to the fort, which drew the fire of all the guns that could bear upon her. We supposed that he had had the springs of her cables cut away. The words that passed along the platform by officers and men were: "Mind the Commodore! Mind the fifty-gun ships!" Most all the attention was paid to the two fifty-gun ships, especially the Commodore who, I dare say, was not at all obliged to us for our particular attention to him; the killed and wounded on board those two fifty-gun ships confirm what I say.

During the action, General Lee paid us a visit through a heavy line of fire and pointed two or three guns himself; then said to me, "Colonel, I see you are doing very well here. You have no occasion for me. I will go up to town again," and left us. . . .

There cannot be a doubt but that, if we had had as much powder as we could have expended in the time, the men-of-war must have struck their colors or they would certainly have been sunk, because they could not retreat, as the wind and tide were against them, and if they had proceeded up to town, they would have been in a much worse situation. They could not make any impression on our fort, built of palmetto logs and filled in with earth. Our merlons were 16 feet thick, and high enough to cover the men from the fire of the tops. The men that we had killed and wounded received their shots mostly through the embrasures.

An author, who published in 1779, says, "The guns were at one time so long silenced that it was thought that the fort was abandoned;

it seems extraordinary that a detachment of land forces were not in readiness on board the transports, or boats, to profit of such an occasion."

The guns being so long silent was owing to the scarcity of powder which we had in the fort, and to a report that was brought to me "that the English troops were landed between the advance guard and the fort." It was upon this information that I ordered the guns to cease firing, or to fire very slow upon the shipping, that we should reserve our powder for the musketry to defend ourselves against the land forces, there being a scarcity of powder at this time.

At one time, three or four of the men-of-war's broadsides struck the fort at the same instant, which gave the merlons such a tremor that I was apprehensive that a few more such would tumble them down. During the action three of the men-of-war, in going round to our west curtain, got entangled together, by which the *Acteon* frigate went on shore on the middle ground; the *Sphinx* lost her bowsprit; and the *Syren* cleared herself without any damage. Had these three ships effected their purpose, they would have enfiladed us in such a manner as to have driven us from our guns. It being a very hot day, we were served along the platform with grog in fire buckets, which we partook of very heartily. I never had a more agreeable draught than that which I took out of one of those buckets at the time. It may be very easily conceived what heat and thirst a man must feel in this climate, to be upon a platform on the 28th June, amidst twenty or thirty heavy pieces of cannon in one continual blaze and roar, and clouds of smoke curling over his head for hours together. It was a very honorable situation, but a very unpleasant one.

During the action, thousands of our fellow citizens were looking on with anxious hopes and fears, some of whom had their fathers, brothers and husbands in the battle, whose hearts must have been pierced at every broadside. After some time our flag was shot away; their hopes were then gone, and they gave up all for lost, supposing that we had struck our flag and had given up the fort. Sergeant Jasper, perceiving that the flag was shot away and had fallen without the fort, jumped from one of the embrasures and brought it up through a heavy fire, fixed it upon a sponge staff, and planted it upon the ramparts again. Our flag once more waving in the air revived the drooping spirits of our friends, and they continued looking on till night had closed the scene and hid us from their view;

only the appearance of a heavy storm, with continual flashes and peals like thunder. At night when we came to our slow firing (the ammunition being nearly quite gone) we could hear the shot very distinctly strike the ships.

At length the British gave up the conflict. The ships slipt their cables and dropped down with the tide, and out of the reach of our guns. . . .

Not until 1778 did the British make another attempt to humble the South. In the spring of that year, dispatches from London informed Clinton that the King himself had outlined a grand plan for southern strategy. Savannah was to be an operational base for a second strike at Charleston. Then the South could be rolled up state by state. In November, 1778, Clinton sent 3,500 men under Lieutenant Colonel Archibald Campbell to cooperate with a similar force from St. Augustine under General Augustin Prevost. Defending Savannah was Major General Robert Howe, commanding about 700 Continentals and 150 militia—the only American army in the South. Finding the rebels drawn up in battle array to thwart a drive into the town, Campbell resorted to a maneuver nearly always successful against the Americans—a flanking action. His report contained the details.

Having accidentally fallen in with a Negro [Quamino Dolly] who knew a private path through the wooded swamp upon the enemy's right, I ordered the first battalion of the Seventy-First to form on our right of the road and move to the rear of the light infantry, whilst I drew off that corps to the right as if I meant to extend my front in that quarter, where a happy fall of ground favored the concealment of this maneuver, and increased the jealousy of the enemy with regard to their left. Sir James Baird had directions to convey the light infantry in this hollow ground, quite to the rear, and penetrate the wooded swamp upon our left, with a view to get . . . into the rear of the enemy's right flank. . . .

During the course of this movement, our artillery were formed in a field on our left of the road, concealed from the enemy by a swell of ground in front, to which I meant to run them up for action when the signal was made to engage, and from whence I could either bear advantageously upon the right of the rebel line, as it was then formed, or cannonade any body of troops in flank which they might detach into the wood to retard the progress of the light infantry.

The Regiment of Wellworth was formed upon the left of the artillery, and the enemy continued to amuse themselves with their cannon, without any return upon our part, till it was visible that Sir James Baird and the light infantry had fairly got round upon their rear. On this occasion I commanded the line to move briskly forward. The well-directed artillery of the line, the rapid advance of the Seventy-First Regiment, and the forward countenance of the Hessian Regiment of Wellworth, instantly dispersed the enemy.

A body of the militia of Georgia, posted at the new barracks with some pieces of cannon to cover the road from Great Ogeechee, were at this juncture routed, with the loss of their artillery, by the light infantry under Sir James Baird when the scattered troops of the Carolina and Georgia brigades ran across the plain in his front. This officer, with his usual gallantry, dashed the light infantry on their flank and terminated the fate of the day with brilliant success.

Thirty-eight officers of different distinctions, and four hundred and fifteen non-commissioned officers and privates, one stand of colors, forty-eight pieces of cannon, twenty-three mortars, ninety-four barrels of powder, the fort, with all its stores . . . and in short, the capital of Georgia, the shipping in the harbor, with a large quantity of provisions, fell into our possession before it was dark, without any loss on our side than that of Captain Peter Campbell, a gallant officer of Skinner's light infantry, and two privates killed, one sergeant and nine privates wounded. Eighty-three of the enemy were found dead on the Common, and eleven wounded. By the accounts received from their prisoners, thirty lost their lives in the swamp, endeavoring to make their escape.

Campbell boasted, "I may venture to say, Sir, that I have ripped one star and one stripe from the Rebel flag of America."

Middle-aged, paunchy, balding Major General Benjamin Lincoln, commanding general in the Southern Department, began to send probing detachments southward in March, 1779. Encouraged by successful actions at Beaufort and Kettle Creek, he sent three expeditions into Georgia, one to the east bank of the river opposite Savannah, one to the Black Swamp and another (mostly militia) under General John Ashe to Briar Creek near Augusta. On March 3, 1779, Ashe met smashing defeat as his inexperienced militia broke and ran when attacked from the rear by a detachment under Colonel Mark Prevost.

Prevost, attempting to draw off Lincoln's forces, crossed the

*Savannah and made a feint toward Charleston. Discovering the militia
falling away before him, he marched until, on May 11, he found
himself before the gates of Charleston. The city might well have been
taken had Prevost not been so obstinate in his demands. Governor
John Rutledge offered to surrender Charleston if the rest of the state
and the harbor would be considered neutral for the remainder of the
war. Prevost insisted on nothing less than unconditional surrender.
An intercepted letter revealed that Lincoln was marching swiftly to the
relief of the city. The British pulled back toward Savannah.*

*Soon after the fall of Savannah, Congress dispatched a fast ship to
the Comte d'Estaing in the West Indies, requesting the aid of his fleet
and troops in retaking the town. Lafayette appealed directly to the
French Court. At the moment, d'Estaing was at the height of glory;
he had taken the islands of St. Vincent and Grenada in the West Indies,
and defeated the British fleet under Lord Byron—the greatest French
naval success over the British in a hundred years. The French admiral
agreed to cooperate for two weeks, but no longer, for fear of the
approaching hurricane season. Lincoln hurriedly marched on Savannah
with 2,000 men.*

*Rain postponed operations until September 23, and the first allied
batteries opened on October 4. The royalist Chief Justice of Georgia,
Anthony Stokes, underwent the privations and terrors of bombardment.*

I had some distance to go before I got out of the line of fire,
and did not know the way under Savannah bluff, where I should have
been safe from cannon balls, and therefore, whenever I came to an
opening of a street, I watched the flashes of the mortars and the
guns, and pushed on until I came under cover of a house, and when I
got to the Common and heard the whistlings of a shot or shell, I fell
on my face. . . .

The appearance of the town afforded a melancholy prospect,
for there was hardly a house which had not been shot through, and
some of them were almost destroyed. . . . In the streets and on the
Common there was a number of large holes made in the ground by
the shells. . . . The troops in the lines were much safer from the
bombardment than the people in town. . . . In short, the situation
of Savannah was at one time deplorable. A small garrison in an
extensive country was surrounded on the land by a powerful enemy,
and its seacoast blocked up by one of the strongest fleets that ever
visited America. There was not a single spot where the women and

children could be put in safety, and the numerous desertions daily weakened that force which was at first inadequate to man such extensive lines, but the situation of the ground would not permit the able engineer to narrow them. However, with the assistance of God, British valor surmounted every difficulty.

Comte d'Estaing, finding siege operations too tedious, insisted upon an all-out assault, despite the objections of Lincoln. At four o'clock in the foggy dawn of October 9, three columns of French and American soldiers assembled for the push. Major Thomas Pinckney of the South Carolina militia blamed d'Estaing for the fiasco that followed.

A feint attack by the South Carolina militia and Georgians, under Brigadier General Huger, was ordered to [be] made on the enemy's left. But instead of the French troops being paraded so as to march off at 4 o'clock, it was near four before the head of that column reached our front. The whole army then marched towards the skirt of the wood in one long column and, as they approached the open space, were to break off into the different columns, as ordered for the attack. By the time the French column had arrived at the open space, day had fairly broke, when Count d'Estaing, without waiting until the other columns had arrived at their position, placed himself at the head of his first column and rushed forward to the attack. But this body was so severely galled by the grape shot from the batteries as they advanced, and by both grape shot and musketry when they reached the abatis that, in spite of the efforts of the officers, the column got into confusion and broke away to their left toward the wood in that direction. The second and third French column shared successively the same fate, having the additional discouragement of seeing, as they marched to the attack, the repulse and loss of their comrades who had preceded them.

Count Pulaski who, with the cavalry, preceded the right column of the Americans, proceeded gallantly until stopped by the abatis, and before he could force through it, received his mortal wound. In the meantime, Colonel Laurens at the head of the light infantry, followed by the 2nd South Carolina Regiment and 1st Battalion Charlestown militia, attacked the Spring Hill redoubt, got into the ditch and planted the colors of the 2nd Regiment on the berm, but the parapet was too steep for them to scale it under so heavy a fire, and after much slaughter they were driven out of the ditch. When General Pulaski was about to be removed from the field, Colonel D. Horry, to whom the command of the cavalry devolved, asked what were his directions. He answered, "Follow my lancers to whom I have given my order of attack." But the lancers were so severely galled by the enemy's fire that they also inclined off to the left, and were followed by all the cavalry breaking through the American column, who were attacking the Spring Hill redoubt.

By this time the 2nd American column, headed by General McIntosh, to which I was attached, arrived at the foot of the Spring Hill redoubt, and such a scene of confusion as there appeared is not often equalled. . . . Count d'Estaing was wounded in the arm, and endeavoring to rally his men, a few of whom with a drummer he had collected. General McIntosh did not speak French, but desired me to inform the Commander-in-Chief that his column was fresh, and that he wished his directions, where, under the present circumstances, he should make the attack. The Count ordered that we should move more to the left, and by no means to interfere with the troops he was endeavoring to rally. In pursuing this direction we were thrown too much to the left, and before we could reach Spring Hill redoubt, we had to pass through Yamacraw Swamp, then wet and boggy, with the galley at the mouth annoying our left flank with grape shot.

While struggling through this morass, the firing slacked, and it was reported that the whole army had retired. I was sent by General McIntosh to look out from the Spring Hill, where I found not an assailant standing. On reporting this to the General, he ordered a retreat, which was effected without much loss, notwithstanding the heavy fire of grape shot with which we were followed.

The loss of both armies in killed and wounded amounted to 637 French and 457 Americans. . . . The loss of the British amounted only to fifty-five.

Thus was this fine body of troops sacrificed by the imprudence of the French general who, being of superior grade, commanded the whole. If the French troops had left their encampment in time for the different corps to have reached their positions, and the whole attacked together, the prospect of success would have been infinitely better, though even then it would have been very doubtful on account of the strength of the enemy's line, which was well supplied with artillery. But if Count d'Estaing had reflected a moment, he must have known that attacking with a single column, before the rest of the army could have reached their position, was exposing the army to be beaten in detail. In fact, the enemy, who were to be assailed on a considerable part of their front, finding themselves only attacked at one point, very deliberately concentrated their whole fire on the assailing column, and that was repeated as fast as the different corps were brought up to the attack.

Twice Franco-American cooperation had failed, and Comte d'Estaing had been involved upon each occasion. The way now seemed clear for a British push on Charleston. The British were not unhappy with the bickering among the allies, for, as the loyalist officer John Harris Cruger put it: "They came in so full of confidence of succeeding, that they were at some loss where to lay the blame, each abusing the other for deceiving them. . . . We are all hands sufferers by this unfortunate invasion. The difference is we have acquired glory and our Enemies, Disgrace."

The Fall of Charleston

*S*IR *Henry Clinton made ready to move southward. On December*
26, 1779, his 8,000 troops sailed aboard ninety transports, escorted
by fourteen warships. After a tumultuous voyage from New York,
the troops began to disembark on February 11 on John's Island, near
Charleston. Remembering the failure of an attack from the sea past
Sullivan's Island, the British general now planned to go above the city,
cross the Ashley to throw up a siege line across Charleston Neck
between the Ashley and Cooper rivers to strangle the city gradually.
The fleet, under Admiral Arbuthnot, blockaded the harbor. On March
31, 1780, British soldiers began to dig and scrape away at the sandy
soil, even as the defenders began to lob shells in their direction. The
British ships then sailed majestically past Fort Moultrie on Sullivan's
Island despite a blaze of fire. Clinton and Arbuthnot sent in a summons
to Benjamin Lincoln to surrender the city. It was refused. The siege
began.

A supply route and possible escape route still lay open by way of
Biggin's Bridge near Monck's Corner. Lieutenant Colonel Webster
was given a command of 1,400 men to dislodge General Huger's
detachment and close that gap. Lieutenant Colonel Banastre Tarleton
and his British Legion rode down the American detachment with such
ferocity that henceforth the name "Tarleton" was to become associated
with ruthlessness.

The spade and the pick became as important as siege guns. By
April 19, Clinton's zigzagging saps had worked his parallels to within
250 yards of the American lines. There was little doubt as to the
outcome. Benjamin Smith warned his wife:

This will give a rude shock to the Independence of America,
and a Lincolnade will become as common a term as a Burgoynade....
Nothing prevents Lincoln's surrender but a point of honor of holding

out to the last extremity. This is nearly at hand, as our provisions will soon fail, and my plan is to WALK off as soon as I can obtain permission. . . . A mortifying scene must first be encountered. The thirteen stripes will be leveled in the dust and I owe my life to the clemency of a conqueror.

General Moultrie recorded the death throes.

Tuesday, [April] 25th. Between twelve and one this morning, a heavy fire of cannon and musketry commenced from our advanced redoubt and the right of the lines, occasioned, as it was said, by the enemy's advancing in column. It is certain they gave several huzzas, but whether they were out of their trenches is not clear. They kept up a very heavy and incessant fire with musketry for thirty minutes. The enemy threw several light balls into the town. . . .

Wednesday, 26th. The *Lord George Germain* and a sloop joined the enemy's fleet. The enemy were very quiet all day and last night. We suppose they are bringing cannon into their third parallel. They are strengthening their approaches. Lord Cornwallis took possession of Mount Pleasant yesterday. Brigadier General du Portail arrived from Philadelphia. The garrison ordered to be served with the usual quantity of provisions, a plentiful supply having been received. . . .

On General du Portail declaring that the works were not tenable, a council was again called upon for an evacuation, and to withdraw privately with the Continental troops. When the citizens were informed upon what the council were deliberating, some of them came into council and expressed themselves very warmly, and declared to General Lincoln that if he attempted to withdraw the troops and leave the citizens, they would cut up his boats and open the gates to the enemy. This put a stop to all thoughts of an evacuation of the troops, and nothing was left for us but to make the best terms we could.

With no hope of evacuating his prized Continental troops, Lincoln held out as long as he could. Lincoln determined upon a last show of resistance. Moultrie remembered the night when shells filled the air: "It was a glorious sight to see them like meteors crossing each other and bursting in the air; it appeared as if the stars were tumbling down. The fire was incessant almost the whole night; cannon balls whizzing and shells hissing continually amongst us; ammunition chests blowing

up; great guns bursting, and wounded men groaning along the lines."
But on May 12, as the vanquished marched out of the town, their music
playing the "Turk's March," one onlooker could see "tears coursing
down the cheeks of Gen. Moultrie," whose head was held high in defeat.

About eleven o'clock A.M. on the twelfth of May, we marched
out between 1,500 and 1,600 Continental troops (leaving five or six
hundred sick and wounded in the hospitals) without the hornwork,
on the left and piled our arms. The officers marched the men back
to the barracks, where a British guard was placed over them. The
British then asked where our second division was? They were told
that these were all the Continentals we had, except the sick and
wounded. They were astonished, and said we had made a gallant
defence.

Captain Rochfort had marched in with a detachment of the artillery to receive the returns of our artillery stores. While we were in the
hornwork together in conversation, he said, "Sir, you have made a
gallant defence, but you had a great many rascals among you"
(and mentioned names) "who came out every night and gave us
information of what was passing in your garrison."

The militia marched out the same day and delivered up their
arms at the same place. The Continental officers went into town
to their quarters, where they remained a few days to collect their
baggage and signed their paroles, then were sent over to Haddrell's
Point. The militia remained in Charlestown. The next day the militia
were ordered to parade near Lynch's pasture and to bring all their
arms with them, guns, swords, pistols, etc., and those that did not
strictly comply were threatened with having the Grenadiers turned
in among them. This threat brought out the aged, the timid, the
disaffected and the infirm, many of them who had never appeared
during the whole siege, which swelled the number of militia prisoners
to, at least, three times the number of men we ever had upon duty.

I saw the column march out and was surprised to see it so large,
but many of them we had excused from age and infirmities; however,
they would do to enroll on a conqueror's list. When the British
received their arms, they put them in wagons and carried them to a
store house, where we had deposited our fixed ammunition (about
4,000 pounds) and although they were informed by some of our
officers that the arms were loaded, and several of them went off
before the explosion took place, yet in taking them out of the

wagons they threw them so carelessly into the store that some at last set fire to the powder, which blew up the whole guard of fifty men and many others that were standing by; their carcasses, legs and arms were seen in the air and scattered over several parts of the town. One man was dashed with violence against the steeple of the new independent church, which was at a great distance from the explosion, and left the marks of his body there for several days. The houses in the town received a great shock, and the window sashes rattled as if they would tumble out of the frames.

Most of our militia were still together. After delivering up their arms, they went in a body to assist in extinguishing the fire that had communicated itself to the neighboring houses, and while they were under the dreadful apprehension lest the magazine should take fire . . . at last some timid person called out, that "the magazine was on fire," which gave the alarm. Everyone took fright, both British and Americans, and instantly broke off from work. and ran away as fast as possible through the streets, throwing down, and tumbling over each other, and others coming after tumbling over them, in endeavoring to get as far from the expected explosion as possible. I have heard some of them say, that although they were so confoundedly frightened at the time, they could not keep from laughing, to see the confusion and tumbling over each other. . . . I met a British officer, who asked me how much powder was in the magazine. I told him 10,000 pounds.

"Sir," said he, "if it takes fire, it will blow your town to Hell!"

I replied, "I expected it would give a Hell of a blast!" . . .

After a little time the alarm subsided. They went back and stopped the progress of the fire.

There remained one sizable force at large. Cornwallis, informed that a relief force of 300 Virginians under Colonel Abraham Buford was retreating northward now that Charleston had fallen, dispatched Banastre Tarleton to overtake them. In the subsequent engagement in the Waxhaws, Tarleton earned his epithet of "Bloody Tarleton," and the phrase "Tarleton's Quarters" became a synonym for cruelty. Buford refused Tarleton's demand to surrender. Captain John Stokes was to relate his experiences to William James.

Buford, now perceiving that further resistance was hopeless, ordered a flag to be hoisted and the arms to be grounded, expecting the usual treatment sanctioned by civilized warfare. This, however, made no part of Tarleton's creed. His ostensible pretext for the relentless barbarity that ensued, was, that his horse was killed under him just as the flag was raised. He affected to believe that this was done afterwards, and imputed it to treachery on the part of Buford, but, in reality, a safe opportunity was presented to gratify that thirst for blood which marked his character in every conjecture that promised probable impunity for himself. Ensign Cruit, who advanced with the flag, was instantly shot down. Viewing this as an earnest of what they were to expect, a resumption of their arms was attempted, to sell their lives as dearly as possible; but before this was fully effected, Tarleton with his cruel myrmidons was in the midst of them, when commenced a scene of indiscriminate carnage, never surpassed by the ruthless atrocities of the most barbarous savages.

The demand for quarters, seldom refused to a vanquished foe, was at once found to be in vain; not a man was spared, and it was the concurrent testimony of all the survivors that for fifteen minutes after, every man was prostrate. They went over the ground, plunging their bayonets into everyone that exhibited any signs of life and, in some instances, where several had fallen over the others, these monsters were seen to throw off on the point of the bayonet the uppermost, to come at those underneath. . . .

Captain John Stokes . . . received twenty-three wounds, and . . . never for a moment lost his recollections. . . . Early in the sanguinary conflict he was attacked by a dragoon, who aimed many deadly blows at his head, all of which, by the dextrous use of the small sword, he easily parried; when another, on the right, by one stroke, cut his right hand through to the metacarpal bones. He was then assailed by both, and instinctively attempted to defend his head with his left arm until the forefinger was cut off, and the arm hacked in eight or ten places from the wrist to the shoulder. His head was then laid almost open the whole length of the crown to the eye brows. After he fell he received several cuts on the face and shoulders. A soldier, passing on in the work of death, asked if he expected quarters. Stokes answered, "I have not, nor do I mean to ask quarters. Finish me as soon as possible." He then transfixed him twice with his bayonet. Another asked the same question and received the same answer, and he also thrust his bayonet twice through his body.

Stokes had his eye fixed on a wounded British officer sitting at some distance, when a sergeant came up who addressed him with apparent humanity and offered him protection from further injury at the risk of his life. . . .

Doctor Stapleton, Tarleton's surgeon, whose name ought to be held up to eternal obloquy, was then dressing the wounds of the officer. Stokes, who lay bleeding at every pore, asked him to do something for his wounds, which he scornfully and inhumanely refused until peremptorily ordered by the more humane officer, and even then only filled the wounds with rough tow, the particles of which could not be separated from the brain for several days.

So fell the proud city of Charleston. For many the sun had set, with no promise that it would rise again—when Charleston became an occupied city, Charleston died. Georgia had fallen, and South Carolina was a conquered province. Only eleven colonies remained to carry on the struggle. Perhaps the sun had not set, but the sky had darkened.

"Green Peaches, Green Corn and Molasses"—Camden

A CHAIN of British posts, stretching westward to Ninety-Six, maintained the conqueror's authority in South Carolina. Clinton returned to New York, leaving Charles, Earl Cornwallis, in command. Plundering became common as the Tories, now protected by British regulars, crawled out of the swamps to seek revenge. Eliza Wilkinson, whose plantation was some thirty miles from Charleston, reported one visitation (among many) from the British and Tories.

It was . . . on the 3rd day of June that my father, with an old man who lived a few miles from him, and whose hair was silvered o'er with age (one Mr. Bryant), was sitting on the piazza, when they saw a party of men, some in red, others in green, coming up to the house furiously.

The moment they arrived, they jumped from their horses, and ran into the house with drawn swords and pistols, and began to curse and abuse Father and the other man very much; indeed, took his buckles from his shoes, searched his pockets, and took all they found there. They then went to search Mr. Bryant's pockets; he threw his top jacket aside, and producing his under one, "Here," he said, "I'm a poor old man" (he was so, sure enough). They searched, but I believe found nothing, for by a lucky thought the "poor old man" saved several hundred pounds, by carelessly casting aside his top jacket as if it had no pockets in it.

They then went in the rooms up and down stairs, demolished two sets of drawers, and took all they could conveniently carry off. One came to search Mother's pockets too (audacious fellow!) but she resolutely threw his hand aside. "If you must see what's in my pocket, I'll show you myself," and she took out a thread-case, which had thread, needles, pins, tape, &c., &c. The mean wretch took it from her. They even took her two little children's caps, hats, &c., &c., and when they took Mother's thread, &c., she asked them what they did with such things, which must be useless to them. "Why, Nancy would want them."

They then began to insult Father again in the most abusive manner. "Aye," says one, "I told you yesterday how you'd be used if you did not take a protection! But you would not hear me; you would not do as I told you, now you see what you have got by it."

"Why," said Mother in a jeering way, "is going about plundering women and children, taking the state? I suppose you think you are doing your King a great piece of service by these actions, which are very noble, to be sure. But you are mistaken, 'twill only enrage the people. I think you'd much better go and fight the men, than go about the country, robbing helpless women and children—that would be doing something!"

"O! you are all, every one of you, rebels! and, old fellow" (to Father), "I have a great mind to blow my pistol through your head." Another made a pass at him (inhuman monsters—I have no patience to relate it) with his sword, swearing he had "a great mind" too, to run him through the body. . . .

After drinking all the wine, rum, &c., they could find, and inviting the Negroes they had with them (who were very insolent) to do the same, they went to their horses, and would shake hands with Father and Mother before their departure. Did you ever hear the like! Fine amends, to be sure, a bitter pill covered with gold, and so a shake of the hand was to make them ample satisfaction for all their sufferings. But the "iron hand of Justice" will overtake them sooner or later. Though *slow*, it is *sure*.

After they were gone, poor old Bryant began to bless his stars for saving his money, and to applaud himself for his lucky invention—he was too loud with it. Father admonished him to speak lower, for should any of the servants about the house hear him, and another party come, he might stand a chance to lose it after all. But still the old man kept chatting on, when lo! another company of horsemen appeared in view. The poor soul was panic struck, he looked aghast and became mute. These were M'Girth's men. . . . They did not behave quite so civil to Mother . . . for they took sugar, flour, butter, and such things from her, but not much.

A dispute arose over the selection of Lincoln's successor as command-
ing general in the Southern Department. Washington favored Nathanael
Greene; Congress insisted upon the hero of Saratoga, Horatio Gates.
From Richard Peters, Gates received the optimistic word: "Our
affairs to the Southward look blue. So did they when you took command
before the Burgoynade. I can only say, go and do likewise. God bless
you." But from Charles Lee came the warning, "Take care lest your
Northern laurels turn to Southern willows."

Gates joined his small army, with its nucleus of Maryland and
Delaware Continentals, at Hillsboro in North Carolina. His heart was
gladdened with the report that General Richard Caswell, who had
recently served as first governor of the state of North Carolina, was
coming into the field with "shoals of militia." Gates was a great favorite
with militia, and a great advocate of their use; his victory at Saratoga
bore testimony to his ability with them. To frustrate Lord Cornwallis's
probable expedition into North Carolina and Virginia, Gates planned
a strike at the British post at Camden, South Carolina, at this time
under the command of Lord Rawdon. Marching on July 27, he waved
off protests that there was a scarcity of provisions with the assertion that
"plentiful supplies of rum and rations were on the route, and would
overtake them in a day or two." The army struggled through a barren
and deserted country, with Gates refusing to take a more circuitous
approach even when it was claimed that food and forage were more
plentiful along that route. Extracts from his General Orders illustrate
the problem of a general who made inadequate preparations and who
was too eager to add luster to the glory of Saratoga.

July 30, 1780. . . . The General is much dissatisfied to see almost
every good regulation in the order of march continually violated,
by arms and accoutrements being frequently thrown into the wagons
(and this by some of the baggage guard, and even by the sentinels),
women frequently permitted to ride in the wagons, sometimes
two in a wagon. This, exclusive of the delay it occasions to the line
of march, is an encumbrance to the teams, and much fatigues the
horses. It is positively forbid in the future. None but very sick men
should at any time have this indulgence.

The order and compactness of the line of march is shamefully
broken by the wagoners being sometimes suffered to halt for frivo-
lous seasons. This throws out the weak teams which cannot for a
whole day afterwards recover their distance. The wagon masters

are to be answerable that this does not happen again. Their neglect of duty is the main cause of most of the irregularities and breaches in the line of march; they must reform or be dismissed from the service. . . .

August 4, 1780. . . . The exactest discipline is at all times right, but most essentially so when the enemy think to take advantage of our neglect. The General, therefore, repeats his desire that the troops may upon their march tomorrow, as well as upon all future occasions, conduct themselves as they were every hour to apprehend a surprise. It has never yet been found that Americans were deficient or inferior to Britons, when fairly opposed to them in battle. This army will not, therefore, he is confident, be overreached by military tricks. . . .

August 6, 1780. . . . The General hears with astonishment the shameful irregularity of the troops in straggling from camp, and marauding in a most scandalous manner, even stealing the clothing and furniture of certain inhabitants whom the calamities of war had already rendered but too miserable.

The General expects the commanding officers of regiments and corps will order the rolls to be called four times a day, and confine for disobedience of orders, all such as are not present at roll calling. . . .

These, then, were the troops with which Gates expected to defeat disciplined British soldiers at Camden. His army announced its presence with throbbing drums and squealing fifes. Morning guns boomed the assembly each dawn. Nearing the border of South Carolina, Gates issued a flamboyant proclamation, declaring that by "the exertions of the virtuous citizens of America in the State, and by the approach of a numerous, well appointed and formidable army, [he intended] to compel our late triumphant and insulting foes to retreat from their most advantageous posts with precipitation and dismay."

This "well appointed army," however, was on the verge of collapse. Not only were provisions scant, but rum, considered necessary for an eighteenth-century army, was no longer available. Gates's expedients resulted in a diet that was, to say the least, explosive. Colonel Otho Williams, deputy adjutant general, noted the results.

The distresses of the soldiery daily increased; they were told that the banks of the Pee Dee River were extremely fertile, and so indeed they were. But the preceding crop of corn (the principal article of commerce) was exhausted, and the new grain, although luxuriant and fine, was unfit for use. Many of the soldiery, urged by necessity, plucked the green ears and boiled them with the lean beef which was collected in the woods, made for themselves a repast, not unpalatable to be sure, but which was attended with painful effects. Green peaches were also substituted for bread, and had similar consequences. Some officers, aware of the risk of eating such vegetables, and in such a state, with poor fresh beef, and without salt, restrained themselves from taking anything but the beef itself, boiled or roasted. It occurred to some that the hair powder which remained in their bags, would thicken soup, and it was actually applied. . . .

As there were no spirits yet arrived in camp, and as . . . it was unusual for troops to make a forced march, or prepare to meet an enemy without some extraordinary allowance, it was unluckily conceived that molasses would, for once, be an acceptable substitute. Accordingly the hospital stores were broached, and one gill of molasses per man, and a full ration of corn meal and meat were issued to the army previous to their march, which commenced, according to orders at about ten o'clock at night of the 15th. . . . The troops of General Gates's army had frequently felt the bad provision; but at this time, a hasty meal of quick-baked bread and fresh beef, with a dessert of molasses, mixed with mush, or dumplings, operated so cathartically, as to disorder very many of the men, who were breaking ranks all night, and were certainly much debilitated before the action commenced in the morning.

Gates, informed by a Tory who came out of Camden that the town was his for the taking, marched the night of August 15. Unbeknownst to him, Lord Rawdon had received reinforcements. Lord Cornwallis, upon receipt of intelligence that Gates was marching against Camden, had arrived to assume personal command. Then, "seeing little to lose by a defeat & much to gain by a victory, I resolved to take the first good opportunity to attack the Rebel Army." At 10 P.M., the same time that Gates was beginning his move, Cornwallis filed out of Camden toward the American forces. By coincidence, the route of each army was through Gum Swamp. It was after two o'clock in the morning, at a narrow clearing known locally as "Parker's Old Field," tucked between two branches of the swamp, that the two forces collided in the darkness. Colonel John Senff, chief engineer of the Southern Army, watched the recoil and recovery.

During the march, reconnoitering parties sent out from the advanced corps came back, and nothing seen in the road. Soon after (about half an hour after two in the morning of the 16th August), Colonel Armand's van party got hail'd by an advanc'd party of the enemy. An answer was made directly on our side, on which the enemy's horse immediately charged furiously with a great deal of huzzas. Colonel Armand stood the charge, and Colonel Porterfield's light infantry gave a crossing fire upon the enemy's horse, which made them retreat; immediately upon which the enemy's light infantry advanc'd, and after a fire of about five minutes, drove our advanc'd guard and main body, then likewise retreated. The affair caused a little confusion in the line, but was soon redressed.

Otho Williams, as deputy adjutant general, was deeply involved in subsequent events.

The General's astonishment could not be concealed. He ordered the deputy adjutant general to call another council of war. All the general officers immediately assembled in the rear of the line; the unwelcome news was communicated to them. General Gates said, "Gentlemen, what is best to be done?" All were mute for a few moments, when the gallant Stevens exclaimed, "Gentlemen, is it not too late *now* to do anything but fight?" No other advice was offered, and the General desired the gentlemen would repair to their respective commands. . . .

Frequent skirmishes happened during the night between the two advanced parties, which served to discover the relative situation of the two armies, and as a prelude to what was to take place in the morning.

At dawn of day (on the morning of the 16th of August) the enemy appeared in front, advancing in column. Captain Singleton, who commanded some pieces of artillery, observed to Colonel Williams that he plainly perceived the ground of the British uniforms about two hundred yards in front. The deputy adjutant general immediately ordered Captain Singleton to open his battery, and then rode to the General, who was in rear of the second line, and informed him of the cause of the firing which he heard. He then observed to the General that the enemy seemed to be displaying their column by the right; the nature of the ground favored this conjecture, for yet nothing was clear.

The General seemed disposed to wait events—he gave no orders. The deputy adjutant general observed that if the enemy, in the act of displaying, were briskly attacked by General Stevens' brigade, which was already in line of battle, the effect might be fortunate, and first impressions were important. "Sir," said the General, "that's right—let it be done." This was the last order that the deputy adjutant general received. He hastened to General Stevens, who instantly advanced with his brigade, apparently in fine spirits. The right wing of the enemy was soon discovered *in line*—it was too late to attack them displaying; nevertheless, the business of the day could no longer be deferred.

The deputy adjutant general requested General Stevens to let him have forty or fifty privates, volunteers, who would run forward of the brigade and commence the attack. They were led forward within forty or fifty yards of the enemy, and ordered to take trees and keep up as brisk a fire as possible. The desired effect of this expedient, to extort the enemy's fire at some distance, in order to the rendering it less terrible to the militia, was not gained. General Stevens, observing the enemy to rush on, put his men in mind of their bayonets; but, the impetuosity with which they advanced, firing and huzzaing, threw the whole body of the militia into such a panic, that they generally threw down their *loaded* arms and fled in the utmost consternation. The unworthy example of the Virginians was almost instantly followed by the North Carolinians; only a small part of the brigade, commanded by Brigadier General Gregory, made a short pause. A part of Dixon's regiment, of that brigade, next in line to the second Maryland brigade, fired two or three rounds of cartridge. But a great majority of the militia (at least two-thirds of the army) fled without firing a shot. . . .

The regular troops, who had the keen edge of sensibility rubbed off by strict discipline and hard service, saw the confusion with but little emotion. They engaged seriously in the affair; and, notwithstanding some irregularity, which was created by the militia breaking, pell mell, through the second line, order was restored there—time enough to give the enemy a severe check, which abated the fury of their assault and obliged them to assume a more deliberate manner of acting. The second Maryland brigade, including the battalion of Delawares, on the right, were engaged with the enemy's left, which they opposed with a very great firmness. They even advanced upon them and had taken a number of prisoners, when their companions of the first brigade (which formed the second line) being greatly outflanked, and charged by superior numbers, were obliged to give ground. . . .

The distance between the two brigades did not exceed two hundred yards; their opposite flanks being nearly upon a line perpendicular to their front. At this eventful juncture, the deputy adjutant general, anxious that the communication between them should be preserved, and wishing that, in the almost certain event of a retreat, some order might be sustained by them, hastened from the first to the second brigade, which he found in precisely the same circumstances. He called upon his own regiment (the 6th Maryland) not to fly, and was answered by Lieutenant Colonel Ford, who said, "They have done all that can be expected of them—we are outnumbered and out-flanked—see, the enemy charge with bayonets."

The enemy, having collected their corps, and directing their whole force against these two devoted brigades, a tremendous fire of musketry was, for some time, kept up on both sides with equal perseverance and obstinacy, until Lord Cornwallis, perceiving there was no cavalry opposed to him, pushed forward his dragoons and his infantry charging at the same moment with fixed bayonets, put an end to the contest.

His victory was complete. All the artillery and a great number of prisoners fell into his hands. Many fine fellows lay on the field, and the rout of the remainder was entire (not even a company retired in any order), every one escaped as he could. If, in this affair, the militia fled too soon, the regulars may be thought almost blamable for remaining too long on the field, especially after all hope of victory must have been despaired of. . . .

The torrent of unarmed militia bore away with it Generals Gates, Caswell, and a number of the others, who *soon* saw that all was lost. General Gates, at first, conceived a hope that he might rally at Clermont a sufficient number to cover the retreat of the regulars, but the farther they fled the more they were dispersed, and the generals soon found themselves abandoned by all but their aides. . . .

The militia, the General saw, were in the air, and the regulars, he feared, were no more. The dreadful thunder of artillery and musketry had ceased, and none of his friends appeared. . . .

The North Carolina militia fled different ways, as their hopes led, or their fears drove them. Most of them, preferring the shortest way home, scattered throughout the wilderness which lies between the Wateree and Pee Dee rivers, and thence towards Roanoke. Whatever these might have suffered from the disaffected, they probably were not worse off than those who retired the way they came; wherein, they met many of their insidious friends, armed and advancing to join the American Army, but, learning its fate from the refugees, they acted decidedly in concert with the victors and, captivating some, plundering others, and maltreating all the fugitives they met, returned exultingly home. They even added taunts to perfidy; one of a party who robbed Brigadier General Butler of his sword, consoled him by saying, "You'll have no further use for it." . . .

The general order for moving off the heavy baggage, &c., to Waxhaws, was not put into execution, as directed to be done on the preceding evening. The whole of it, consequently, fell into the hands of the enemy, as well as all that which followed the army except the wagons of Generals Gates and De Kalb which, being furnished with the stoutest horses, fortunately escaped under the protection of a small quarter guard. Other wagons also had got out of danger from the enemy. But the cries of the women and the wounded in the rear, and the consternation of the flying troops, so alarmed some of the wagoners that they cut out their teams and taking each a horse, left the rest for the next that should come. . . .

The only apology that General Gates condescended to make to the army for the loss of the battle was, "A man may pit a cock, but he can't *make* him fight," "The fate of battle is uncontrollable," and such other common maxims as admit of no contradiction. . . .

General Gates perceived no effective succour short of Hillsborough, where the General Assembly of North Carolina were about to convene. Thither he repaired, with all possible expedition, and was followed the next day by General Caswell, who despaired of the meeting of the militia, probably because he thought that their first object, the army, was annihilated.

Gates's flight from Camden to Hillsborough opened the gates of censure. Alexander Hamilton was most outspoken.

What think you of the conduct of this great man? I am his enemy personally, for unjust and unprovoked attacks upon my character, therefore what I say of him ought to be received as from an enemy, and have no more weight than is consistent with fact and common sense. But did ever anyone hear of such a disposition or such a flight? His best troops placed on the side strongest by nature, his worst on that weakest by nature, and his attack made with these. 'Tis impossible to give a more complex picture of military absurdity. It is equally against the maxims of war and common sense. We see the consequences. His left ran away and left his right uncovered. His right wing, turned on the left, has in all probability been cut off. Though, in truth, the General seems to have known very little what became of his army. Had he placed his militia on his right, supported by the morass, and his Continental troops on his left, where it seems he was most vulnerable, his right would have been more secure and his left would have opposed the enemy; and instead of going backward when he ordered the attack, would have gone forward. The reverse of what has happened, might have happened.

But was there ever an instance of a general running away, as Gates has done, from his whole army? And was there ever so precipitate a flight? One hundred and eighty miles in three days and a half! It does admirable credit to the activity of a man at his time of life, but it disgraces the general and the soldier. I always believed him to be very far short of a Hector or a Ulysses. All the world, I think, will begin to agree with me.

But what will be done by Congress? Will he be changed or not? If he is changed, for God's sake overcome prejudice and send Greene. You know my opinion of him. I stake my reputation on the events, give him but fair play.

But, above all things, let us have, without delay, a vigorous government, and a well constituted army for the war.

So faded the laurels of Saratoga, wilted by the military climate of the South.

"The Bull Dog on the Mountain"—King's Mountain

*H*IS only opposition a dispirited army under the command of a
*sulking general, Cornwallis made his move northward from South
Carolina. Major James Craig sailed to occupy Wilmington, North
Carolina, not only to control the Cape Fear River as a supply route
into the interior, but to protect his right. Major Patrick Ferguson was
likewise dispatched to the western back country to keep the mountain
men subdued; there Cornwallis "thought he could do no harm, and
might help to keep alive the spirit of our friends in North Carolina,
which might be dampened by the slowness of our motions." An unidentified, but happy, rebel correspondent recorded British disappointments
as the army moved up to the village of Charlotte in North Carolina.*

The firmness of the people of Mecklenburg and Rowan counties,
when the enemy advanced to Charlotte, evince that they possess the
most genuine principles; they were left to defend themselves against
the whole force of the enemy. His Lordship took post at Charlotte
with amazing pomp. Proclamations were issued, peace and protection
were offered to all returning and penitent rebels, and death, with
all its terrors, threatened to the obstinate and impenitent. Governor
Martin, with great solemnity, assumed the government and conceived himself reinstated.

The people generally abandoned their habitations, some fled with
such of their property as they could carry, others took the field,
determined to dispute every foot of ground, and some assembled
in small parties in their respective neighborhoods, determined to
harass the enemy's foraging parties. His Lordship soon discovered
that he was in enemy's country, without provisions, without forage,
without friends, without intelligence, without a single humble

servant except Peter Johnson and McCaffery, who at last deserted him in the night and came to make peace with us, his communications with Camden cut off, and his dispatches intercepted. . . .

These are stubborn facts, and will do immortal honor to the militia. Lord Cornwallis's aide, in a letter to Colonel Balfour, which was intercepted, says: "Charlotte is an agreeable village, but in a damned rebellious country." Oh! had we a well-appointed, well-disciplined, permanent force, what a delightful back-country dance we should have led his Lordship at Charlotte.

It was Patrick Ferguson, however, who was led through a back-country dance. This Ferguson was quite a soldier. In the army since the age of fifteen, and known as "Bull Dog" among his fellow officers, he had invented a breech-loading "rifle gun" which was so far ahead of the times that its value was not recognized until years later. The military, ever chary of innovations, perhaps lost the war when they decided against using Ferguson's rifle. They had given it a halfhearted test by giving Ferguson permission to arm a special corps with his rifles. Even then, the war might have been won at Brandywine had Ferguson been less the sportsman. He explained in a letter to Scotland:

We had not lain long, when a rebel officer, remarkable by hussar dress, passed towards our army, within a hundred yards of my right flank, not perceiving us. He was followed by another dressed in dark green or blue, mounted on a bay horse, with a remarkably large cocked hat. I ordered three good shots to steal near to them and fire at them, but the idea disgusted me. I recalled the order.

The hussar, in returning, made a circuit, but the other passed again within a hundred yards of us, upon which I advanced from the woods towards him. On my calling, he stopped, but after looking at me, proceeded. I again drew his attention, and made signs to him to stop, but he slowly continued his way. As I was within that distance which, in the quickest firing, I could have lodged a half a dozen balls in or about him before he was out of my reach, I had only to determine; but it was not pleasant to fire at the back of an unoffending individual, who was acquitting himself very coolly of his duty, so I let him alone.

The day after I was telling this story to some wounded officers who lay in the same room with me, when one of our surgeons, who had been dressing some of the wounded rebel officers, came in and told us they had been informing him, that General Washington was all the morning with the light troops, and only attended by a French officer in hussar dress; he himself dressed and mounted in every point as above described. I am not sorry that I did not know at the the time who it was. Farther this deponent sayeth not, as his bones were broke a few moments after.

After his wound at Brandywine, Ferguson's detachment had been disbanded and his breechloaders taken out of action. He was present at the slaughter of Buford's troops in the Waxhaws and, it was said, had become so infuriated by their cruelty that he had to be forcibly restrained from shooting some of Tarleton's men. Since the battle of Camden he had been operating in the foothills, affording protection to Cornwallis's left flank. Learning that a force of "Over-the-Mountain Men" under Colonels John Sevier, Charles McDowell, Isaac Shelby, William Campbell, and Benjamin Cleveland was assembling to march against him, Ferguson fell back toward Charlotte.

Realizing that he could not reach Charlotte, he requested aid of Cornwallis, and stationed himself on King's Mountain, an outlying spur of the Blue Ridge near the North Carolina-South Carolina border. As he waited on this high plateau with the steep slopes, those of his men who did not possess bayonets were instructed to whittle down the handles of their hunting knives that they might be fitted into the muzzles of firearms. It was later reported that Ferguson boasted, on the morning of October 7, that " he was on King's Mountain, and that he was King of that Mountain, and that God Almighty could not drive him from it."

David Vance, youthful rebel volunteer, remembered the histrionics on the march to King's Mountain.

The day and night were occasionally showery. We marched on, crossing Ferguson's trail in the track, and proceeded on to the Cowpens and came to a Tory's house, pulled him out of bed, treated him roughly, and asked him at what time Ferguson had passed that place. He said he had not passed at all; that he had torch pine, that we might light it and search, and if we could find any trace of any army, we might hang him or do what we pleased with him, and if no sign of an army could be found, he would expect more mild treatment. Search was made and no sign of an army found.

We then camped, and began to send persons to find Ferguson's track. Chronicle proposed to send Enoch Gilmer as one; it was objected to because he was not acquainted with the country. Chronicle said that he could find out anything better than those acquainted, for he could act any character he pleased; that he could cry and laugh in the same breath, and those best acquainted would believe that he was in earnest in both; that he could act the fool so that those best acquainted with him would believe him to be deranged; that he was a shrewd, cunning fellow, and a stranger to fear. Hence he was sent, among others.

He went to a Tory's house on Ferguson's trail, and stated to him that he had been waiting on Ferguson's way from Twitty's Ford to Ninety-Six, but missed finding him; that he wished to join the army. The Tory replied that after Ferguson had crossed the river at Twitty's Ford, he had received an express from Lord Cornwallis for him to join the main army at Charlotte, that he had called in Tarleton, and would call in his outposts, and give Gates another defeat, and reduce North Carolina to British rule as he had South Carolina and Georgia, and would enter Virginia with a larger army than ever had been seen in America. Gilmer gave this account to the officers. . . .

They then commenced marching to the Cherokee Ford on Broad River. Night came on, and our pilots missed their way, the night being dark, and occasionally raining, so that when we came to the river it was near daylight. It was agreed that we would send Enoch Gilmer to see whether Ferguson had not been apprised of us and would attack us in the river. Orders were given to keep our guns dry, for it was raining. Gilmer was gone for some time, when his voice was heard in the hollow singing "Barney Linn," a favorite black-guard song. This was notice that all was right. . . . After passing the river it was agreed that Enoch Gilmer should go ahead and make all the discoveries about Ferguson that he could. He went off in a gallop. . . .

After travelling some miles, the officers saw Gilmer's horse at a gate about three-quarters of a mile ahead. They gave whip to their horses, and went at full speed to the gate—alighted, and went into the house. Gilmer was sitting at a table eating. Campbell exclaimed, "We have got you, you damned rascal."

Gilmer replied, "A true King's man, by God."

Campbell, in order to try Gilmer's metamorphosis, had provided himself with a rope with a running noose in it, threw it over Gilmer's neck. Gilmer commenced crying and begging. Campbell swore they would hang him on the bow of the gate—when Chronicle stated that it would be wrong to hang him there, for his ghost would haunt the women, who were now in tears. Campbell observed that was right, that we will hang him on the first stooping limb of a tree that they should pass on the road. Then sending Gilmer along one or two hundred yards, Gilmer crying and begging for his life, the rope was taken from his neck, and he mounted his horse, and was asked what news he had obtained.

He stated as follows. That when he came to the Tory's house, he professed to be a true King's man; that he was wishing to join Colonel Ferguson, and desired to know where he was; and that he had kissed the two Tory women; that the youngest of the two informed him that she had been in Ferguson's camp that morning; that the camp was about three miles distant from that place; that she had carried him some chickens; that he was camped on a ridge between two branches where some deer hunters had a camp the last fall. Major Chronicle and Captain Mattocks stated that the camp referred to was their camp, and that they well knew the ground Ferguson was on. . . .

They immediately began to arrange their men, without stopping, and assigning to each officer the part he was to take in surrounding the hill. By the time this was done, we were close to our enemy. The last whose duty was to be prescribed was Colonel William Graham with his men, who desired a leave of absence, alleging that he had received certain intelligence that his wife was dying with the colic about sixteen miles off, near Armstrong's Ford on the South Fork. Campbell stated to him that should be the greatest inducement for him to stay, that he could carry the news, and if we were successful, it would be to her as good as a dose of medicine.

Graham exclaimed, "Oh my dear, dear wife! Must I never see her again?"

Campbell in an angry tone of voice turned to Major Chronicle and said, "Shall Colonel Graham have leave of absence?"

To which Chronicle replied, "It is woman's business, let him go."

Graham said he must have an escort. Chronicle told him he might have one; Graham chose David Dickey. Dickey said he would rather be shot than go. Chronicle said, "Dave, you must go." Dickey said he would rather be shot on the spot, "But if I must go, I must go, I must." Then Colonel Graham and Dickey immediately took to the woods and disappeared.

Campbell then mentioned to Chronicle that as Graham had gone, you must take his place. . . . Whereupon Chronicle called, "Come on, my South Fork boys," and took the lead. The hill was surrounded in a few minutes and the battle commenced. . . . But we had not a coward to face the hill that day; they all faded off, until within ten minutes of the battle, the last coward left us. Our equals were scarce and superiors hard to find.

Thomas Young, sixteen-year-old private, fought his way up the north slope.

The orders were at the firing of the first gun, for every man to raise a whoop, rush forward, and fight his way as best he could. When our division came up to the northern base of the mountain, Colonel Roebuck drew us a little to the left and commenced the attack. I well remember how I behaved. Ben Hollingworth and myself took right up the side of the mountain, and fought from tree to tree, our way to the summit. I recollect I stood behind one tree and fired until the bark was nearly all knocked off, and my eyes pretty well filled with it. One fellow shaved me pretty close, for his bullet took a piece out of my gun stock. Before I was aware of it, I found myself apparently between my own regiment and the enemy, as I judged, from seeing the paper the Whigs wore in their hats, and the pine knots the Tories wore in theirs, these being the badges of distinction.

On top of the mountain, in the thickest of the fight, I saw Colonel Williams fall, and a braver or better man never died upon the field of battle. I had seen him fall but once before that day; it was in the beginning of the action, as he charged by me at full speed around the mountain. Towards the summit a ball struck his horse just under the jaw, when he commenced stamping as if he were in a nest of yellow jackets. Colonel Williams threw his reins over the animal's neck, sprang to the ground, and dashed onward.

The moment I heard the cry that Colonel Williams was shot, I ran to his assistance, for I loved him as a father; he had been ever so kind to me and almost always carried a cake in his pocket for me and his little son, Joseph. They carried him into a tent, and sprinkled some water in his face. He revived, and his first words were, "For God's sake, boys, don't give up the hill!" . . . I left him in the arms of his son, Daniel, and returned to the field to revenge his fate.

Robert Henry was in Graham's regiment when the command was given to Chronicle.

Then Chronicle, having a military hat but had let it down to shelter the rain from him, and had it not set up, clapped his hand to it in front, raised it up and cried, "Face to the hill!" The words were scarcely uttered when a ball struck him and he dropped, and a second after a ball struck William Rabb, about six feet from Chronicle, and he dropped.

We then advanced up the hill close to the Tory lines. There was a log across a hollow that I took my stand by, and stepping one step back, I was safe from British fire. I there remained firing until the British charged bayonets. . . . The Fork boys fired and did considerable execution. I was preparing to fire when one of the British advancing, I stepped [back] and was in the act of cocking my gun when his bayonet was running along the barrel of my gun, and gave me a thrust through my hand and into my thigh. My antagonist and I both fell. The Fork boys retreated and loaded their guns. I was then lying under the smoke and it appeared that some of them were not more than a gun's length in front of the bayonets, and the farthest could not have been more than twenty feet in front when they discharged their rifles. It was said that every one dropped his man. The British then retreated in great haste, and were pursued by the Fork boys.

William Caldwell saw my condition, and pulled the bayonet out of my thigh, but it hung to my hand; he gave my hand a kick and it went out. The thrust gave me much pain, but the pulling of it was much more severe. With my well hand I picked up my gun and found her discharged. I suppose that when the soldier made the thrust, I gripped the trigger and discharged her; the load must have passed through his bladder and cut a main artery of his back, as he bled profusely. . . .

Being much in pain and drouthy, went down, left my gun, being unable to carry her, and when I got near to the branch, met David Dickey and Colonel William Graham riding his large black horse, wielding his sword round his head, crying at the top of his voice, "Damn the Tories," and ascended the hill. Having seen him get leave of absence at the commencement of the battle to see his wife, I was filled with excitement and a conflict of passion and extreme pain; but this brought on another set of feelings, that may be understood, but I am not possessed of language to describe.

Shelby's column was in the center. In it was the boy James Collins, who fought alongside his father that day.

We were soon in motion, every man throwing four or five balls in his mouth to prevent thirst, also in readiness to reload quick. The shot of the enemy soon began to pass over us like hail. The shock was quickly over, and for my part, I was soon in a profuse sweat. My lot happened to be in the centre, where the severest part of the battle was fought. We soon attempted to climb the hill, but were fiercely charged upon and forced to fall back to our first position. We tried a second time, but we met the same fate. The fight then seemed to become more furious.

Their leader, Ferguson, came in full view, within a rifle shot as if to encourage his men, who by this time were falling very fast; he soon disappeared. We took to the hill a third time; the enemy gave way. When we had gotten near the top, some of our leaders roared out: "Hurrah, my brave fellows! Advance! They are crying for quarter!"

By this time the right and left had gained the top of the cliff; the enemy was completely hemmed in on all sides, and no chance of escaping. Besides, their leader had fallen. They soon threw down their arms and surrendered. After the fight was over, the situation of the poor Tories appeared to be really pitiable; the dead lay in heaps on all sides, while the groans of the wounded were heard in every direction. I could not help turning away from the scene before me, with horror, and though exulting in victory, could not refrain from shedding tears. . . .

On examining the body of their great chief, it appeared that almost fifty rifles must have been leveled at him at the same time. Seven rifle balls had passed through his body, both his arms were broken, and his hat and clothing were literally shot to pieces. Their great elevation above us had proved their ruin; they overshot us altogether, scarce touching a man except those on horseback, while every rifle from below seemed to have the desired effect. In this conflict I had fired my rifle six times, while others perhaps fired nine or ten. . . .

Next morning, which was Sunday, the scene became really distressing. The wives and children of the poor Tories came in, in great numbers. Their husbands, fathers and brothers lay dead in heaps, while others lay wounded or dying, a melancholy sight indeed! . . . Numbers of the survivors were doomed to abide the sentence of a court-martial, and several were actually hanged. . . .

We proceeded to bury the dead, but it was badly done. They were thrown into convenient piles and covered with old logs, the bark of old trees, and rocks, yet not so as to secure them from becoming a prey to the beasts of the forests, or the vultures of the air. And the wolves became so plenty, that it was dangerous for anyone to be out at night, for several miles around. The hogs in the neighborhood gathered into the place to devour the flesh of man, inasmuch as numbers chose to live on little meat rather than eat their hogs, though they were fat. Half the dogs in the country were said to be mad, and were put to death. . . .

Of the troop, or company, to which I belonged, we had two badly wounded; one, a lieutenant by the name of Watson, the other, a private named Caldwell. We carried them to their own homes on the evening, where they both died in a few days. Poor fellows! They were raised together, fought together, died nearly at the same time in the same house, and lie buried together.

In the evening, there was a distribution made of the plunder, and we were dismissed. My father and myself drew two fine horses, two guns, and some articles of clothing, with a share of powder and lead. Every man repaired to his tent, or home. . . .

Cornwallis's "great Western Bugbear," Ferguson, was dead, wrapped in a green oxhide and buried beneath a pile of rocks. Of his force, 157 had been slain, 163 wounded, and 698 made prisoners. The Over-the-Mountain men had lost 28 killed and 62 wounded. Hatred still burned deep, and at Gilbert Town, Campbell was forced to issue orders: "I must request the officers of all ranks in the army to endeavor to restrain the disorderly manner of slaughtering and disturbing the prisoners." At that same place, 36 Tories, brought before a military tribunal, were found guilty of "breaking open houses, killing the men, turning the men and women out of doors and burning the houses. The trial was concluded late at night. The execution of the law was as summary as the trial." David Vance observed that the battle "did not cost the State, or the United States, the worth of a single Continental dollar depreciated down to eight hundred to one."

General William Lee Davidson summed it up in one succinct sentence: "Ferguson, the great partisan, has miscarried."

Cowpens

*T*HE *victory at King's Mountain, no panacea for the shame of Camden, did little for the tarnished reputation of Horatio Gates. With his foes assuming a posture of outraged dignity, many of his friends were embarrassed to the point of assuming the defensive. The choice of his successor seemed to lie between Nathanael Greene of Rhode Island and William Smallwood of Maryland. Greene, however, was not overly popular with some members of the Continental Congress; two months earlier he had resigned in a huff from the post of Quartermaster General and had "thrown Congress into a degree of vexatious distress," so much so that some still-ruffled members of that body were demanding his removal from the Army. But Greene was selected by Washington, and Congress remained silent.*

Greene, who had requested the command at West Point in anticipation of spending a quiet winter with Catherine, his vivacious wife, sought to delay his departure, but the urgings of the Commander in Chief sped him on his way. Washington was sensible of the task before the new southern commander, and after reminding members of the Continental Congress that "the history of this war is a history of false hopes," he urged their support with, "I think I am giving you a General; but what can a General do, without men, without arms, without clothing, without stores, without provisions?"

At Philadelphia Greene pleaded for the support of the Continental Congress; at Annapolis for that of the Maryland Assembly; at Richmond with Virginia's Governor Jefferson. "They all promised fair," he said, "but I fear will do little; ability is wanting with some, and inclination with others."

At Hillsboro he expected to find his new command, but discovered that Gates had marched southward following Cornwallis, who had, after the defeat of Ferguson, fallen back to Winnsboro, South Carolina. Arriving at Charlotte on December 2, 1780, Greene rode into the camp of "but the shadow of an army in the midst of distress."

That same evening Brigadier General Daniel Morgan, accompanied by the cavalry of Colonel William Washington, returned from a foraging expedition, bringing the report of a ludicrous little victory that Otho Williams thought an amusing bit of drollery.

Mr. [John] Rugely, proprietor of a farm called Clermont, had obtained the rank of Lieutenant-Colonel [of militia] in the British Army, and obtained that of Major for his son-in-law. These two officers, with about one hundred British troops and new levies, occupied a large log barn (the old council chamber) which they fortified by a slight entrenchment and a line of abatis, so as to render it impregnable to small arms.

The post was on the left of Morgan's route, as he returned from foraging—but too near to Camden for him to risk anything like a siege or a blockade. It was suggested that the cavalry might go and reconnoitre it. Washington, pleased with the idea, approached so near as to discover that the enemy had discovered him and were intimidated. He humorously ordered his men to plant the trunk of an old pine tree, in the manner of a field piece, pointing towards the garrison. At the same time, dismounting some of his men to appear as infantry, and displaying his cavalry to the best advantage, he sent a corporal of dragoons to summon the commanding officer to an *immediate* surrender. The order was executed in so firm a manner that Colonel Rugely did not hesitate to comply *instantly*, and the whole garrison marched out as prisoners of war. The corporal was made a sergeant of dragoons, the old fort was set on fire, and Washington with his prisoners retired without exchanging a shot. . . .

A manly resignation marked the conduct of General Gates on the arrival of his successor, whom he received at headquarters with that liberal and gentlemanly air which was habitual to him. . . .

General Greene was announced to the army by General Gates; and the same day General Greene addressed the army, in which address, he paid General Gates the compliment of confirming all his standing orders.

Thaddeus Kosciusko, Polish officer serving with the Southern Army, had been ordered by Gates to find an area not depleted by the ravages of two armies. The area along South Carolina's Pee Dee

River, he found, was a promising location for the rebuilding of an army. Even then, the task facing Greene lay beyond the formidable. After his arrival at this new bivouac, he was writing, "This is no Egypt," and complaining to Washington, "This is really making bricks without straw."

Yet before his departure from Charlotte, Nathanael Greene made a bold decision—a decision that was to shape his future. Morgan was placed in command of a detachment to operate between the Pacolet and Broad rivers, its mission to discourage Tory raids and give protection to the Whigs in the country, and "spirit up the people" in general. And should Cornwallis attempt another march into North Carolina, his flanks would be left open to attack by Morgan.

Daniel Morgan, his massive temper boiling because Gates had given him but scant recognition for his role in the victory at Saratoga, and equally humiliated because Congress refused to promote him to brigadier general, had resigned from the Army in 1779. But after the disaster at Camden, Morgan had cast aside his sulks and joined Gates. When Greene arrived, Morgan had but recently received word of his promotion.

As he marched away from Charlotte, small groups of militia straggled in to swell Morgan's manpower. Within five days he had established his camp on the north bank of the Pacolet. There he received a report that a group of about 350 Tories under the leadership of a Colonel Waters had advanced so near as a place called "Fair Forest," and "were plundering and insulting the good people of the neighborhood." Militiaman Thomas Young was one of those sent against Waters.

When we came in sight, we perceived that the Tories had formed a line on the brow of the hill opposite to us. We had a long hill to descend and another to rise. Colonel Washington and his dragoons gave a shout, drew swords, and charged down the hill like madmen. The Tories fled in every distance without firing a gun. We took a great many prisoners and killed a few. Here I must relate an incident which occurred on this occasion. In Washington's corps there was a boy of fourteen or fifteen, a mere lad, who in crossing Tiger River was ducked by a blunder of his horse. The men laughed and jeered at him very much at which he got mad and swore that, boy or no boy, he would kill a man that day or die. He accomplished the former. I remember very well being highly amused at the little fellow charging around a [corn] crib after a Tory, cutting and slashing away with his puny arm, till he brought him down.

Cornwallis lay at Winnsboro awaiting the reinforcements he had requested after King's Mountain. With Morgan in the predominantly Tory area near Ninety-Six, no northward march could begin until this threat was eliminated. On January 1, 1781, Banastre Tarleton, with his British Legion, the first battalion of the 71st Regiment and two light field pieces, was dispatched with orders to flush out Morgan, "push him to the utmost," force a battle and wipe out the rebel detachment. By January 16, the pursuit had so narrowed that at one of Morgan's hastily evacuated camps, Tarleton's men found breakfasts still simmering over the fires. The following morning the word was that Morgan was preparing to make a stand at a place called Hannah's Cowpens, with the Broad River, not too distant in his rear, blocking any retreat. The terrain, said Tarleton, "was disadvantageous for the Americans, and convenient for the British. An open wood was certainly as good a place for action as Lieutenant Colonel Tarleton could desire; America does not produce any more suitable to the nature of the troops under his command."

The one thing that Banastre Tarleton, himself a monument to egotism, overlooked was that his adversary was a soldier's soldier, and a master in handling militia. Thomas Young was won by the burly general's familiarity.

We arrived at the field of the Cowpens about sundown, and were then told that we should meet the enemy. The news was received with great joy by the army. We were anxious for battle, and many a hearty curse had been vented against General Morgan during that day's march for retreating, as we thought, to avoid a fight. Night came upon us, yet much remained to be done. It was all important to strengthen the cavalry; General Morgan well knew the power of Tarleton's Legion, and he was too wily an officer not to prepare himself as well as circumstances would admit. . . .

It was upon this occasion I was more perfectly convinced of General Morgan's qualifications to command militia, than I had ever before been. He went among the volunteers, helped them with their swords, joked with them about their sweethearts, told them to keep in good spirits, and the day would be ours. And long after I laid down, he was going among the soldiers, encouraging them, and telling them that the old wagoner would crack his whip over Ban. in the morning, as sure as they lived.

"Just hold up your heads, boys, three fires," he would say, "and you are free, and then when you return to your homes, how the old folks will bless you, and the girls kiss you for your gallant conduct!" I don't believe he slept a wink that night.

The ground was slightly undulating with a scattering growth of red oak, hickory and pine. Grazing cattle had thinned the underbrush. At the crest of a long, gently rising slope, some 700 yards in length, Morgan placed his prize troops, the Maryland, Delaware, and Virginia Continentals under Colonel John Eager Howard, as the main line of defense. Flank support was by Virginia and Georgia militia. Approximately 150 yards down the slope were stationed the militia of North Carolina, South Carolina, and Georgia, while another 150 yards out were nearly 150 men deployed as skirmishers. Behind the third line was William Washington and his dragoons, out of the line of fire, but still posted in such a manner as to guard the horses of the militia and act in support. Henry "Lighthorse Harry" Lee heard, probably from John Eager Howard, of Morgan's actions just prior to the battle.

On the verge of battle, Morgan availed himself of the short and awful interim to exert his troops. First addressing himself, with his characteristic pith, to the line of militia, he extolled the zeal and bravery so often displayed by them, when unsupported by the bayonet or sword; and declared his confidence that they would not fail in maintaining their reputation, when supported by chosen bodies of horse and foot, and conducted by himself. Nor did he forget to glance at his unvarying fortune and superior experience, or to mention how often, with his corps of riflemen, he had brought British troops, equal to those before him, to submission. He described the deep regret he had already experienced in being obliged, from prudential considerations, to retire before an enemy always in his power; exhorted the line to be firm and steady; to fire with good aim; and if they would pour in but two volleys at killing distance, he would take upon himself to secure victory.

To the Continentals he was very brief. He reminded them of the confidence he had always reposed in their skill and courage; assured them that victory was certain if they acted well their part; and desired them not to be discouraged by the sudden retreat of the militia, *that* being part of his plan and orders. Then taking post with this line, he waited in stern silence for the enemy.

The impetuous Tarleton marched up and immediately deployed his troops. Private Young, with Washington's mounted troops, watched a battle begin.

The morning of the 17th of January, 1781, was bitterly cold. We were formed in the order of battle, and the men were slapping their hands together to keep warm—an exertion not long necessary. . . . About sunrise the British line advanced at a sort of trot, with a loud halloo. It was the most beautiful line I ever saw. When they shouted, I heard Morgan say, "They give us the British halloo, boys, give them the Indian halloo, by God!" and he galloped along the lines, cheering the men and telling them not to fire until we could see the whites of their eyes. Every officer was crying, "Don't fire!" for it was a hard matter for us to keep from it. . . .

The militia fired first. It was for a time, pop-pop-pop—and then a whole volley; but when the regulars fired, it seemed like one sheet of flame from right to left. Oh! it was beautiful! I have heard old Colonel Fair say often that he believed John Savage fired the first gun in this battle. He was riding to and fro along the lines, when he saw Savage fix his eye upon a British officer; he stepped out of the ranks, raised his gun fired, and he saw the officer fall.

The militia fled. Tarleton's cavalry charged them in loose formation and suddenly from out of nowhere came Washington's dragoons. James Collins, who had come into Morgan's camp to escape his Tory neighbors and had been stationed in the first line of militia, experienced his moment of fear.

We gave the enemy one fire; when they charged us with their bayonets, we gave way and retreated for our horses. Tarleton's cavalry pursued us. "Now," thought I, "my hide is in the loft."

Just as we got to our horses, they overtook us and began to make a few hacks at some, however without doing much injury. They, in their haste, had pretty much scattered, perhaps thinking they would have another Fishing Creek frolic, but in a few moments Colonel Washington's cavalry was among them like a whirlwind, and the poor fellows began to keel from their horses without being able to remount. The shock was so sudden and violent they could not stand it, and immediately betook themselves to flight. There was no time to rally, and they appeared to be as hard to stop as a drove of wild Choctaw steers, going to a Pennsylvania market.

In a few moments the clashing of swords was out of hearing and quickly out of sight. By this time both lines of the infantry was warmly engaged, and we being relieved from the pursuit of the enemy began to rally and prepare to redeem our credit, when Morgan rode up in front and waving his sword, cried out, "Form, form, my brave fellows! Give them one more brisk fire and the day is ours! Old Morgan was never beaten!"

The turn in the tide of battle stemmed from one of the little happenstances that so often reverse the course of history. It was still an even fight with the Maryland Continentals warmly engaged when contest suddenly became rout. John Eager Howard, commanding this final line, told how a mistaken order became a signal for victory.

Seeing my right flank was exposed to the enemy, I attempted to change the front of Wallace's company (Virginia regulars). In doing this, some confusion ensued, and first a part and then the whole of the company commenced a retreat. The officers along the line seeing this, and supposing that orders had been given for a retreat, faced their men about and moved off. Morgan, who had mostly been with the militia, quickly rode up to me and expressed apprehension of the event, but I soon removed his fears by pointing to the line, and observing that men were not beaten who retreated in that order. He then ordered me to keep up with the men until we came to the rising ground near Washington's horse, and he rode forward to fix on the most proper place for us to halt and face about.

In a minute we had a perfect line. The enemy were now very near us. Our men commenced a very destructive fire, which they [the British] little expected, and a few rounds occasioned great disorder in their ranks. While [they were] in this confusion I ordered a charge with the bayonet, which order was obeyed with great alacrity. As the line advanced, I observed their artillery a short distance in front, and called to Captain Ewing to take it. Captain Anderson, hearing the order, also pushed for the same object, and both being emulous for the prize, kept pace until near the first piece, when Anderson, by putting the end of his spontoon forward into the ground, made a long leap, which brought him upon the gun and gave him the honor of the prize. My attention was now drawn to an altercation of some of the men with an artillery man, who appeared to make it a point of honor not to surrender his match. The men, provoked at his obstinacy, would have bayoneted him on the spot, had I not interfered and desired them to spare the life of so brave a man. He then surrendered his match.

In the pursuit I was led to the right, in among the Seventy-First, who were broken into squads and, as I called them to surrender, they laid down their arms, and the officers delivered up their swords. Captain Duncanson, of the Seventy-First Grenadiers, gave me his sword and stood by me. Upon getting on my horse, I found him pulling at my saddle and he nearly unhorsed me. I expressed my displeasure, and asked him what he was about. The explanation was that they had orders to give no quarter, and they did not expect any, and as my men were coming up, he was afraid they would use him ill. I admitted his excuse and put him in care of a sergeant.

In material gains, the battle of Cowpens had been rich. Included were two field pieces, two standards, 800 muskets, one traveling forge, 35 wagons, 100 horses and "all their music." There were also 70 runaway Negro slaves used as servants by the British.

The morale factor was even greater. With a motley force of between 900 and 1,000 men (over 600 of whom were militia), Daniel Morgan had defeated a well-disciplined British detachment of 1,037 soldiers. His casualties were amazingly light: only 12 killed and 60 wounded. In contrast, British losses were staggering; 10 British officers were listed among the 100 killed, and 200 enlisted men among the 700 captured had suffered wounds.

Knowing that Lord Cornwallis would never rest until he had attempted to remove some of the tarnish from British glory, Morgan left the local militia to bury the dead and collect the wounded of both commands. Then, on the very day of his victory, he began to retreat northward with his prisoners.

Cowpens meant many things to many people. In London, Horace Walpole saw a resurgence of rebel strength. "America is once more not quite ready to be conquered, although every now and then we fancy it is. Tarleton is defeated, Lord Cornwallis is checked, and Arnold not sure of having betrayed his friends to much purpose."

And in a church meeting over in Rutherford County, North Carolina, John Miller's Scotch burr wrapped itself around his prayer.

Good Lord, our God that art in Heaven, we have great reason to thank thee for the many favors we have received at thine hands, the many battles we have won. There is the great and Glorious Battle of King's Mountain, where we kilt the great Gineral Ferguson, and took his whole army; and the great battle at Ramsour's and at Williamson's; and the ever-memorable and glorious Battle of the Coopens where we made the proud Gineral Tarleton run doon the road helter-skelter, and Good Lord, if ye had na suffered the Cruel Tories to burn Belly Hell's [Billy Hill's] Iron Works, we would na have asked any mair favors at thy hands. Amen.

Even as the country rejoiced, Daniel Morgan, his great body racked by the darting pains of sciatica, struggled through the mud of North Carolina. In South Carolina, Charles, Earl Cornwallis readied his troops for the chase. Before him lay the road to Yorktown.

The War in North Carolina

*A*s *the British Army floundered through swollen streams and along muddy roads in pursuit of Morgan, the electrifying news of Cowpens reached Greene's camp on the Pee Dee. Discarding a first impulse to strike at British posts in South Carolina, Greene started his army of the Pee Dee marching northward under the command of Brigadier General Isaac Huger of South Carolina. Then he sped across the country, accompanied by a sergeant's guard, to join Morgan at the Catawba River.*

Cornwallis, meanwhile, chafed as his army, encumbered with a long baggage train, struggled over soggy terrain. On January 25 camp was pitched on the hill above Ramsour's Mill where, on the preceding June 20, the Whigs and Tories of North Carolina had attempted to settle their political differences with gunpowder. There Cornwallis took a drastic step. To quicken the pursuit, he led his troops in building a great bonfire of all but the most essential baggage and wagons.

Joseph Graham was with Morgan when he arrived at the Catawba on January 29, 1781.

The same evening, General Morgan crossed the river at Sherrill's Ford . . . and the next morning sent on the troops under his command with Colonel Howard directly towards Salisbury. He himself and Colonel Washington came down to Beattie's Ford about two o'clock, and in ten minutes, General Greene and his aide, Major Pierce, arrived. . . . He had come to ascertain the situation of affairs, and gave orders to the officers in this quarter.

General Morgan and Colonel Washington met him at this place by appointment. They and General Davidson retired with him out of camp, and seating themselves on a log, had a conversation of about twenty minutes. They then mounted their horses, General Greene and aide took the road to Salisbury; Morgan and Washington a way that led to the troops marching under Howard. About the time General Greene had arrived, the British vanguard, of about four or five hundred men, appeared on the opposite hill beyond the river. Shortly after their arrival, some principal officer, with a numerous staff, thought to be Lord Cornwallis, passed in front of them at different stations, halting and apparently viewing us with spy-glasses.

In about one hour after General Greene's departure, General Davidson gave orders to the [militia] cavalry and about two hundred and fifty infantry to march down the river to Cowan's Ford, four miles below Beattie's, leaving nearly the same number at that place under the command of Colonel Farmer, of Orange. On the march he stated to the commanding officer of the cavalry "That though General Greene had never seen the Catawba before, he appeared to know more about it than those who were raised on it."

Cornwallis planned his river crossing carefully. Leaving a detachment to make a feint at Beattie's Ford, he directed the main body down to Cowan's Ford, off the chief routes of travel and used only by local people. Brigadier General William Lee Davidson of the North Carolina militia anticipated this possibility when he placed men at Cowan's. Among them was Robert Henry, restless since King's Mountain, but who had decided it was time to begin his formal education.

Robert Beatty, a lame man, had taken up a school near the Tuckaseage Ford, and had taught two days, and was teaching the third, when news came to the schoolhouse that Cornwallis was camped at Forney's, about seven miles from the schoolhouse; that Tarleton was ranging through the country catching Whig boys, to make musicians of them in the British Army. The master instantly dismissed the scholars, directing them to go home and spread the news, and retired himself. I went home, and that night Moses Starret, Alexander Starret, George Gillespie, Robert Gillespie, and Charles Rutledge came to my father's. We lay out that night. . . .

We went up the river to John Nighten's, who treated us well by giving us potatoes to roast, and some whiskey to drink. We became noisy and mischievous. Nighten said we should not have any more whiskey. I proposed to go to the camp at [Cowan's] Ford, if anyone would let me have a gun and ammunition. My brother said he would give me his; Charles Rutledge proposed also to accompany me if he had a gun and ammunition, when Moses Starret gave him his gun. When about to start, I gave Nighten a hundred dollar Continental bill for a half a pint of whiskey. My brother gave another bill of the same size for half a bushel of potatoes. We dispatched the whiskey.

Being thus equipped we went to the ford, which was about a mile and a half. When we arrived, the guard that was there, about thirty in number, made us welcome. The officer of the guard told us that Cornwallis would certainly attempt to cross that night or early in the morning; that each one of the guard had picked their stands to annoy the British as they crossed, so that when the alarm was given they should not be crowded, or be in each other's way, and said we must choose our stands. . . . I went to mine, and was well pleased with it for in shooting, if I would miss my first aim, my lead would range along the British army obliquely and still do damage, and I could stand it until the British would come to a place the water was riffling over a rock, then it would be time to run away. . . .

Shortly after dark a man across the river hooted like an owl, and was answered. A man went to a canoe some distance off and brought word from him that all was silent in the British camp. The guard all lay down with their guns in their arms, and all were sound asleep at daybreak, except Joel Jetton, who discovered the noise of horses in deep water. The British pilot, Dick Beal, being deceived by our fires, had led them into swimming water.

Jetton ran to the ford, the sentry being sound asleep. Jetton kicked him into the river, endeavored to fire his gun, but it was wet, . . . ran to our fires, having a fine voice, cried, "The British! the British!" and fired a gun. Then each man ran to his stand.

When I got to my stand, I saw them red, but thought from loss of sleep my eyes might be mistaken, threw water into them. By the time I was ready to fire, the rest of the guard had fired. I then heard the British splashing and making a noise as if drowning. I fired, and continued firing, until I saw that one on horseback had passed my rock in the river, and saw that it was Dick Beal moving his gun from his shoulder, I expected, to shoot me. I ran with full speed up the bank. . . .

Turning my eye round, designing to run away, I saw my lame schoolmaster, Beatty, loading his gun by a tree. I thought I could stand it as long as he could, and commenced loading. Beatty fired; then I fired, the heads and shoulders of the British being just above the bank. They made no return fire; silence still prevailed. I observed

Beatty loading again—I ran down another load. When he fired, he cried, "It's time to run, Bob!" I looked past my tree and saw their guns lowered, and then straightened myself behind my tree. They fired and knocked off some bark from my tree.

In the meantime Beatty had turned from his tree, and a bullet hit him in the hip, and broke the upper end of his thigh bone. He fell, still hallowing for me to run. I ran at the top of my speed about one hundred yards. . . .

Cornwallis, in his dispatches, made light of his losses at Cowan's Ford, but they were heavier than he admitted. One Tory with his army was to say, "For a while, I saw 'em hollerin and a snortin and a drownin—the river was full of 'em a snortin, a hollerin and a drownin until his Lordship reached the off bank; then the rebels made straight shirt tales, and all was silent . . . and when he rose the bank he was the best dog in the hunt, and not a rebel to be seen."

The Americans had suffered a severe loss in the person of General Davidson, some say shot down by the Tory guide, Dick Beal. Later that same day, while those fleeing from the fords joined refugees from South Carolina in refreshing themselves at Torrence's Tavern, Tarleton's Legion rushed down the lane and rode among them with sabers flashing.

These two engagements, plus the death of General Davidson, were far-reaching in consequence. Greene was forced to dispatch orders to General Huger to change his line of march from Salisbury, the original rendezvous, to Guilford Courthouse. At Guilford, the arthritic Morgan left the army and made his way painfully to his home in Virginia. Greene toyed with the idea of making a stand at Guilford, but was dissuaded by his officers, Then, with Cornwallis's army still hot on their heels, Greene's ragged army played a game of hare and hounds until they were safely across the Dan River into Virginia.

In Hillsborough, North Carolina, Cornwallis raised the King's standard and issued an invitation to all those of loyalist inclinations to repair therewith with their arms. One group of Tories, led by Dr. John Pyle, gathered for the march to Hillsborough. Their request for protection was answered by Cornwallis, who said that Tarleton would be sent out to escort the King's friends into Hillsborough. On February 18, 1781, however, Greene had sent the Legion of "Lighthorse Harry" Lee and the militia under Andrew Pickens to secure information and keep the Tories under control.

No sooner had Tarleton's departure from Hillsborough been reported to Lee and Pickens than they attempted to surprise the "Butcher" in his camp. On their way there was a chance meeting with Pyle's Tories. Lee's Legion, probably the best-dressed unit in the American Army, wore green jackets similar to those of Tarleton's British Legion. Rather than warn Tarleton by skirmishing with Pyle's loyalists, Lee accepted the assumption that he was the British dragoon, and requested Dr. Pyle to stand aside to allow his own men to file past. But the rear of the column had not been notified of the ruse. Joseph Graham, who told his story in the third person, was on the scene when the slaughter began.

Graham, riding alongside of Captain Eggleston, who commanded the rear of Lee's horse, remarked to him, "That is a company of Tories. What is the reason they have their arms?"

Captain Eggleston, addressing a good looking man at the end of the line, supposed to be an officer, inquired, "To whom do you belong?"

The man promptly answered, "A Friend of his Majesty." Thereupon Captain Eggleston struck him over the head. The militia looking on, and waiting for orders, on this example being set, rushed on the Tories like lightning and cut away. The noise in the rear attracted the notice of Lee's men, and they turned their horses short to the right about, and in less than a minute the attack was made along the whole line. . . .

At the time the action commenced, Lee's dragoons, in the open order of march, extended about the same distance as Pyle's men, who were in close order and on horseback. . . . When the alarm was given in the rear, as quickly as their men could turn their horses, they were engaged, and as the Tories were over two to one of our actual cavalry, by pressing forward they went through their line, leaving a number behind them. The continual cry of the Tories was, "You are killing your own men!" "I am a friend to his Majesty!" "Hurrah for King George!"

Finding their professions of loyalty and all they could say were of no avail, and only the signal for their destruction, twelve or fifteen of those whom Lee's men had gone through, and who had thrown down their guns, now determining to sell their lives as dearly as possible, jumped to their arms and began to fire in every direction. Their fierce protection made the cavalry give back a little. But as soon as their guns were empty, they were charged upon on every side by more than could get at them, and cut down in a group together. All the harm done by their fire was that a dragoon's horse was shot down. . . .

Lee's men had so recently come to the South, that they did not understand the usual marks of distinction between Whigs and Tories, and after the first onset, when all became mixed, they inquired of each man before they attacked him, to whom he belonged. The enemy readily answered, "To the King." To many of their own militia they put the same question. Fortunately no mistakes occurred, though in some instances there was great danger of them. . . . Some Catawba Indians, under Captain Oldham . . . did not overtake us until the close of the action with Pyle. To our discredit, it must be stated that when the Indians came up they were suffered to kill seven or eight wounded men with spears before they were made to desist.

At the close of the action, the troops were scattered, mixed and completely disorganized. . . . Lee himself, while they were forming, stayed in the rear of his own corps and in front of Graham's and ordered one of his sergeants to go directly back and get a guide from among the Tories and bring him forward without delay. The sergeant in a short time returned with a middle-aged man, who had received a slight wound on the head and who was bleeding freely. His name was Holt, and he lived near that place. The sergeant apologized because he could find none who were not wounded. Lee asked the prisoner several questions relative to the roads, farms, watercourses, etc., how O'Neal's plantation (where Tarleton then was) was situated, whether open woods, hilly, or level, etc. After answering the several questions, and after an interval of about a minute, while Lee appeared to be meditating, the man addressed him, "Well, God bless your soul, Mr. Tarleton, you have this day killed a parcel of as good subjects as ever his Majesty had." Lee, who at this time was not in the humor for quizzing, interrupted him, saying, "You damned rascal, if you call me Tarleton, I will take off your head. I will undeceive you: we are Americans and not the British. I am Lee of the American Legion, and not Tarleton." The poor fellow appeared thunderstruck.

This massacre, in which ninety of the Tories lost their lives, was most effective in persuading loyalists that perhaps the British Army, unable to protect its own, was not so formidable as first reckoned. Their ardor waned as Cornwallis prepared to move out of Hillsborough.

On February 23, Greene recrossed the Dan into North Carolina and for the next two weeks danced away before Cornwallis as advanced detachments skirmished with each other. Greene camped on the rolling lands above High Rock Ford on Haw River, the rendezvous for the militia hurrying in.

Both armies waited in the tense clamminess that hangs in the air before a storm. British muskets were cleaned and bayonets sharpened. Greene's men treated their cut and bleeding feet and mended their clothes. And in many a home in North Carolina and Virginia, a squirrel rifle was lifted from its hooks over the fireplace, and slung over the shoulder of its owner as he trudged down the path toward the ford on the Haw. It was warmer now, a few buds were beginning to sprout, more often the happy trill of a songbird could be heard about the camp.

To his good friend Joseph Reed, President of the Council of Pennsylvania, Greene detailed his frustrations and disappointments.

North Carolina has been as nearly reduced as ever a state was in the universe, and escape. Our force was small, and Lord Cornwallis's movements were so rapid, that we got no reinforcements of militia, and therefore were obliged to retire out of the state, upon which the spirits of the people sunk, and almost all classes of the inhabitants gave themselves up for lost. They would not believe themselves in danger until they found ruin at their doors.

The foolish prejudice of the formidableness of the militia being a sufficient barrier against any attempts of the enemy, prevented the Legislature from making any exertions equal to their critical and dangerous situation. Experience has convinced them of their false security. It is astonishing to me how these people could place such a confidence in a militia scattered over the face of the whole earth, and generally destitute of everything necessary to their own defence. The militia in the back country are formidable; the others are not, and all are very ungovernable and difficult to keep together. As they generally come out, twelve thousand might be in motion, and not five hundred in the field. . . .

Here has been the field for the exercise of genius, and an opportunity to practice all the great and little arts of war. Fortunately, we have blundered through without meeting with any capital misfortune. On the 11th of this month I formed a junction, at the

High Rock Ford, with a considerable body of Virginia and North Carolina militia, and with a Virginia regiment of eighteen months' men. Our force being now much more considerable than it had been, and upon a more permanent footing, I took the determination of giving the enemy battle without loss of time, and made the necessary disposition accordingly.

On March 11, 1781, Greene marched from High Rock Ford to take a position at Speedwell Iron Works on Troublesome Creek. On the night of March 14, 1781, his army lay encamped at Guilford Court-house. The next morning he deployed his army in battle formation on the long hill that fell westward for half a mile, its toe resting on the banks of a small stream. A fairly dense growth of trees was broken intermittently by the old fields that spotted the slope. The "Great Road" from Salisbury to Hillsborough bisected the area.

Greene stationed his army in a pattern similar to that used by Morgan at the Cowpens. Two brigades of North Carolina militia under Generals Butler and Eaton were stationed near the foot of the slope behind a rail fence that skirted the woods. The second line, 300 yards behind the first, was composed of the Virginia militia of Generals Lawson and Stevens, generally considered above the usual militia groups because of a number of ex-Continental soldiers in their numbers. In the clearing around the courthouse, some 400 yards to the rear of the Virginia militia, Greene stationed his third and final line, composed of the Maryland and Delaware Continentals. The dragoons of Washington and Lee, along with several companies of riflemen, supported the flanks. General Stevens, humiliated by the flight of his Virginians at Camden, was determined not to suffer mortification a second time. He later wrote Henry Lee:

To guard against my men breaking, I informed them they must not be alarmed at seeing the Carolinians retreat, as perhaps, after giving a fire, they would be ordered to do so. I posted in my rear a number of riflemen, behind trees, as you know we were formed in a skirt of a woods. I informed my men they were placed there to shoot the first man that might run, and at the same time they would serve to cover their retreat in case of necessity.

After posting his troops Greene rode along the front line, reminding them they were fighting for liberty and independence, and if they

*would only give the enemy two good volleys they would be allowed
to retire from the field. Hunkered down behind the rail fence was Major
Richard Harrison of Granville County, North Carolina, who had his
mind on other matters—this was the day his wife was to give birth to a
child. Even as he awaited the arrival of the British he scratched out
a hurried letter to his wife, complete with the latest camp rumors.*

It is scarcely possible to paint the agitation of my mind (if it were
worth the while), struggling with two of the greatest events that are
in nature at the same time—the fate of my Nancy and my country.
O my God, I trust them with thee; do with them for the best!

The day seems nearly at hand that will render North Carolina
perfectly happy or completely miserable. Our General is a great and
good man, his army numerous and apparently confident of victory.
The British soldiery, it seems, have mutinied and demanded to be
marched back. Great things have been done in South Carolina by
Marion and Sumter. We daily expect to hear of the surrender of
Arnold. General Greene has published in camp that Count d'Estaing
has taken six British ships of the line, three frigates and forty-five
transports with troops for America.

If we succeed against Lord Cornwallis, we expect to be discharged
instantly, for by that time the Continental troops will eat all the
provisions this country and South Carolina afford. As for myself
and Harry, not much to be feared. Harry is a good soldier and will
be a credit to his family, I don't doubt. It may be that we shall
not fight this two or three days yet, and perhaps not at all, as there
is a way for Cornwallis to get off; but I am sure of this—Greene will
not give ground again. . . .

This is the very day that I hope will be given me a creature capable
of enjoying what its father hopes to deserve and earn—the sweets
of liberty and grace.

*Lee and his Legion, supported by a detachment of riflemen under
Colonel William Campbell, had been sent toward New Garden Meeting
House to gain intelligence of Cornwallis. At daybreak the British
general had marched, with Tarleton ranging out in front. When this
was reported to Lee, he sallied forth, wrapped in the confidence of
his ego.*

The cavalry had not proceeded above two miles, when Lee was

met by Lieutenant Heard and his party, who were retiring, followed leisurely by the enemy's horse. Wishing to approach nearer to Greene, and at all events to gain the proximity of the rifle militia and Legion infantry, lest the British might be up, Lee ordered the column to retire by troops, taking the proper distance for open evolution. The rear troops, under Rudolph, going off in full gallop, and followed in a like manner by the centre troop under Eggleston, the British commandant flattered himself with converting this retrograde movement into a rout, and pressed upon the front under Armstrong, it being necessary, to gain the open order required, that this officer should not change his pace. . . .

At this moment, Lee ordering a charge, the dragoons came instantly to the right about and in close column, rushed upon the foe. This meeting happened in a long lane, with very high curved fences on each side of the road, which admitted but one section in front. The charge was ordered by Lee from conviction that he should trample his enemy under foot, if he dared to meet the shock, and thus gain an easy and complete victory. But only the front section of each corps closed, Tarleton sounding a retreat the moment he discovered the column in charge. The whole of the enemy's section was dismounted, and many of the horses prostrated; some of the dragoons killed, the rest made prisoner, not a single American soldier or horse injured.

Tarleton retired with celerity, and getting out of the lane, took an obscure way leading directly across the Salisbury road toward the British camp; while Lee, well acquainted with the country, followed the common route by the Quaker meeting house, with a view to sever the British Lieutenant Colonel from his army. . . . By endeavoring to take the whole detachment, he permitted the whole to escape; whereas, had he continued to press on the rear, he must have taken many.

As Lee, with his column in full speed, got up to the meeting house, the British Guards had just reached it and, displaying in a moment, gave the American cavalry a close and general fire. The sun had just risen above the trees and, shining bright, the refulgence from the British muskets, as the soldiers presented, frightened Lee's horse so as to compel himself to throw himself off. Instantly remounting another, he ordered a retreat. This maneuver was speedily executed; and while the cavalry were retiring, the Legion infantry came running up with trailed arms and opened a well-aimed fire upon the Guards, which was followed in a few minutes by a volley from the riflemen under Colonel Campbell, who had taken post on the left of the infantry. The action became very sharp, and was bravely maintained on both sides.

The cavalry having formed again in column, and Lee being convinced, from the appearance of the Guards that Cornwallis was not far in the rear, drew off his infantry and, covering them from any attempt of the British horse, retired towards the American Army. General Greene, being immediately advised of what had passed, prepared for battle, not doubting that the long-avoided, now wished-for, hour was at hand.

As the opening guns rumbled and the red line wheeled into formation, Lee, pert as a bantam rooster, "rode along the front line from one end to the other, exhorting them to stand firm, and not be afraid of the British; for he swore that he had whipped them three times that morning, and could do it again." Sir Thomas Saumarez was a lieutenant with the Royal Welsh Fusiliers.

About one o'clock, the action commenced. The Royal Welsh Fusiliers had to attack the enemy in front, under every disadvantage, having to march over a field lately ploughed, which was wet and muddy from the rains which had recently fallen. The enemy, greatly superior in numbers, were most advantageously posted on a rising ground and behind rails. The regiment marched to the attack under a most galling and destructive fire, which it could return only by an occasional volley. No troops could behave better than the regiment and the little army did at this period, as they never returned the enemy's fire but by word of command, and marched on with the most undaunted courage.

When at length they got within a few yards of the Americans' first line, they gave a volley, and charged with such impetuosity as to cause them to retreat, which they did to the right and left flanks, leaving the front of the British troops exposed to the fire of a second line of the enemy, which was formed behind brushwood.

The first line, faced with the cold steel of British bayonets, fled. Henry Lee attempted to rally them.

When the enemy came within long shot, the American line, by order, began to fire. Undismayed, the British continued to advance, and having reached a proper distance, discharged their pieces and rent the air with shouts. To our infinite distress and mortification, the North Carolina militia took to flight, a few only of Eaton's brigade excepted, who clung to the militia under Campbell which, with the Legion, manfully maintained their ground. Every effort was made by Generals Butler and Eaton, assisted by Colonel Davie, Commissary General, with many of the officers of every grade, to stop this unaccountable panic, for not a man of the corps had been killed or wounded. Lieutenant Colonel Lee joined in the attempt to rally the fugitives, threatening to fall upon them with his cavalry. All was in vain; so thoroughly confounded were these unhappy men that, throwing away arms, knapsacks, and even canteens, they rushed like a torrent headlong through the woods.

Although earning Greene's scorn for their flight, the militia had inflicted damage that day prior to their withdrawal. Sergeant Roger Lamb, who tended to lard his narrative with fragmentary verse, was in the vanguard with the Royal Welsh Fusiliers.

Colonel Webster rode forward in front of the 23rd Regiment, and said, with more than his usual commanding voice (which was well known to his brigade), "Come on, my brave Fusiliers." This operated like an inspiring voice; they rushed forward amidst the enemy's fire, dreadful was the havoc on both sides.

> Amazing scene!
> What showers of mortal hail! What flaky fires!

At last, the Americans gave way, and the brigade advanced to the attack of their second line. Here the conflict became still more fierce. Before it was completely routed . . . I observed an American officer attempting to fly. I immediately darted after him, but he, perceiving my intentions to capture him, fled with the utmost speed. I pursued, and was gaining on him when, hearing a confused noise on my left, I observed several bodies of Americans drawn up within the distance of a few yards. . . . Seeing one of the Guards among the slain . . . I stopped and replenished my own pouch with the cartridges that remained in his. During the time I was thus employed, several shots were fired at me, but not one took effect.

Glancing my eye the other way, I saw a company of Guards advancing to attack these parties. . . . It was impossible to join this company, as several American parties lay between me and it. I had no time for deliberation. How to act, I knew not. On the instant, however, I saw Lord Cornwallis riding across the clear ground. His Lordship was riding on a dragoon's horse (his own having been shot), the saddlebags were under the creature's belly, which much retarded his progress, owing to the vast quantity of underwood that was spread over the ground. His Lordship was evidently unconscious of his danger. I immediately laid hold of the bridle of his horse and turned his head. I then mentioned to him, that if His Lordship had pursued the same direction he would, in a few moments have been surrounded by the enemy and perhaps cut to pieces or captured. I continued to run alongside the horse, keeping the bridle in my hand, until His Lordship gained the 23rd Regiment, which at [that] time were drawn up in the skirt of the woods.

St. George Tucker, in the second line, noted: "The Virginia militia had the honor to receive General Greene's thanks for their conduct. Some were undoubtedly entitled to them, while others ought to blush that they were undeservedly included in the number of those who were supposed to have behaved well." A letter to his wife contained the particulars.

When the cannonade ceased, orders were given for Holcombe's regiment and the other regiments on the right of him to advance to and among the enemy's left flank. While we were advancing to execute these orders, the British had advanced and having turned the flank of Colonel Mumford's Regiment . . . we discovered them in our rear. This threw the militia into such confusion that, without attending in the least to their officers who endeavored to halt them and make them face about and engage the enemy, Holcombe's regiment and ours broke off without firing a single gun, and dispersed like a flock of sheep frightened by dogs. With infinite labor, Beverley and myself rallied about sixty or seventy of our men and brought them to the charge. Holcombe was not so successful. He could not rally a man. . . .

With the few men which we had collected, we at several times sustained an irregular kind of skirmishing with the British, and were once successful enough to drive a party for a very small distance. On the ground we passed over, I think I saw about eight or ten men killed and wounded. The greatest satisfaction I had during the battle was in riding over one of the haughty British officers who was lying prostrate at the root of a tree, genteelly dressed. One of our soldiers gave him a dram as he was expiring and bade him die like a brave man. How different this conduct from that of the barbarians he had commanded!

In attempting to rally a party of regular troops, I received a wound in the small of my leg from a soldier, who either from design or accident held his bayonet in such a direction that I could not possibly avoid it as I rode up to stop him from running away. The bayonet penetrated about an inch and a half between the bones of my leg. I felt no inconvenience from it for some hours, but have since been obliged to hobble with the assistance of a stick or of some person to lead me.

In the third line the fighting was fierce. It was during this clash of men and steel that Colonel Stewart of the First Battalion of Guards lost his life, struck down by an officer with the very American name of Captain John Smith. His business partner of a later day repeated the story to William R. Davie.

In the midst of the battle at Guilford, while the Americans and British troops were intermixed with a charge of bayonets, Smith and his men were in a throng, killing the Guards and Grenadiers like so many Furies. Colonel Stewart, seeing the mischief Smith was doing, made up to him through the crowd, dust and smoke, and made a violent lunge at him with his small sword. The first that Smith saw was the shining metal like lightning at his bosom; he only had time to lean a little to his left and lift up his left arm so as to let the polished steel pass under it when the hilt struck his breast. It would have run through his body but for the haste of the Colonel, and happening to set his foot on the arm of a man Smith had just cut down, his unsteady step, his violent lunge, and missing his aim brought him down with one knee on the dead man. The Guards came rushing up very strong. Smith had no alternative but to wheel around and give Stewart a back-handed blow over, or across the head, on which he fell.

His orderly sergeant attacked Smith, but Smith's sergeant dispatched him. A second attacked him; Smith hewed him down. A third behind him threw down a cartridge and shot him in the back of the head. Smith now fell among the slain, but was taken up by his men and brought off. It was found to be only a buck shot lodged against the skull and had only stunned him.

Lee witnessed the desperate measures of Cornwallis when his Guards fell back, after capturing Greene's artillery.

Stewart beginning to give ground, Washington fell upon him, sword in hand, followed by Howard with fixed bayonets, now commanding the regiment in consequence of Gunby being dismounted. This combined operation was irresistible. Stewart fell by the hand of Captain Smith of the first regiment, the two field pieces were restored, his battalion driven back with slaughter, its remains being saved by the British artillery which, to stop the ardent pursuit of Washington and Howard, opened upon friends as well as foes, for Cornwallis, seeing the vigorous advance of these two officers, determined to arrest their progress, though every ball levelled at them must pass through the flying Guards. Checked by this cannonade, and discovering one regiment passing from the woods on the enemy's right, across the road, and another advancing in front, Howard, believing himself to be out of support, retired, followed by Washington.

Although this retreat was "leisurely," Greene, unwilling to risk additional lives with only a slight prospect of victory, withdrew from the field. His draft horses killed, he left his artillery on the field. That night it rained. The darkness pulsated with the groans of the wounded and shrieks of the dying. Lingering memories prompted Sergeant Lamb to include a bit of gory verse in his journal.

> What loads of mangled flesh and limbs
> (A dismal carnage!) bath'd in reeking gore,
> Lay weltering on the ground; while flitting life,
> Convuls'd, the nerves still shivering, nor had lost
> All taste of pain! Here an old vet'ran lies
> Deform'd with years, and scars, and groans aloud
> Torn with fresh wounds; but inward vitals firm
> Forbid the soul's remove, and chain it down
> By the hard laws of nature, to sustain
> Long torment; his wild eye balls roll; his teeth,
> Gnashing with anguish, chide his ling'ring fate.

Cornwallis, on March 18, issued a proclamation pompously claiming a "compleat victory over the rebels." Not even the Tories were deceived by this, and the General complained, "Many of the inhabitants rode into camp, shook me by the hand, said they were glad to see us, and to hear that we had beat Greene, and then rode home again." Greene, to discourage further loyalist operations, had dispatched Lee's Legion to patrol the neighborhood. Alexander Garden, Greene's aide, rode with them.

It was on the second day's march that the Legion was approached by a company of about two hundred men, riding on pacing ponies, in the costume of Quakers, broad-brimmed and short-skirted, and headed by a marauder in full military dress, on their way to congratulate his Lordship on the brilliancy and importance of his victory. The same mistake was again made that led to the defeat of Pyle. Lee and his dragoons were mistaken for Tarleton and his Legion, and these Sons of Peace, supposing that they might speak with impunity, were as free of invective against the supporters of American principles, as if they had been blasphemers from their cradles.

Their leader was pre-eminently distinguished by his abuse and insolence, which he ultimately carried to such extremity, and so highly exasperated the surrounding dragoons with whom he conversed that, yielding to the dominion of passion, one of them drew forth a pistol and fatally discharging it, laid him dead at his feet. The consternation that followed cannot well be conceived of; fear paralyzed exertion. The whole party, stupefied and silent, remained as if awaiting annihilation. Lee, who was ever eloquent, and conspicuously so when called to speak on the spur of the occasion, now advanced, and bidding them dismiss every apprehension for their personal safety, harangued them for a full half hour in such impressive and pathetic language, pointing out the folly and wickedness of their procedure, and representing the vengeance that would inevitably follow the repetition of their offense, that one and all avowed their sense of error, and promised to sin no more. "Retire then," said Lee, "seek your homes, and secure safety by submission."

It was near noon, Sunday, March 18, when the British marched away from Guilford Courthouse, turning eastward toward the coast. Greene followed.

At Ramsey's mill on Deep River, Greene reviewed his situation. Time was running out for the militia—with many leaving, vowed Greene, "to kiss their wives and sweethearts." He suddenly turned southward, hoping to lure Cornwallis into the pine barrens of South Carolina and allowing some respite to North Carolina. The British general refused the bait. Marching toward Wilmington and the promise of supplies, his army no longer bore the martial appearance they so proudly held when they left South Carolina three months earlier. One harassed planter along their route, William Dickson, described their path of destruction for his cousin in Ireland.

The whole country was struck with terror. Almost every man quit his habitation and fled, leaving his family and property to the mercy of merciless enemies. Horses, cattle and sheep and every kind of stock were driven off from every plantation, corn and forage taken for the supply of the army and no compensation given, houses plundered and robbed; chests, trunks, etc., broke, women and children's clothes, etc., as well as men's wearing apparel, and every kind of household furniture taken away.

These outrages were committed mostly by a train of loyal refugees (as they termed themselves) whose business it was to follow the camps and under the protection of the army, enrich themselves on the plunder they took from the distressed inhabitants who were not able to defend it. We were also distressed by another swarm of beings—no better than harpies. These were the women who followed the army in the character of officers' and soldiers' wives. They were generally considered by the inhabitants to be more insolent than the soldiers. They were generally mounted on the best horses and side-saddles, dressed in the finest and best clothes that could be taken from the inhabitants as the army marched through the country. . . .

My sister's husband, William McGowan, was found driving some stock out of their way; he was made a prisoner and after some time under guard, was compelled to pilot them to his own and several of his neighbors' houses where they took all the corn and forage, all the horses and cattle, etc., they could get. The night following, they detained him under guard and went and plundered his house of every thing they found in it worth carrying away, broke every lock, ransacked every chest and trunk, took away all the bedding, etc., all the apparel (even the baby's clothes), stripped the rings off my sister's fingers and the shoes and buckles off her feet, choked the children to make them confess if their father had not hid his money, and to tell them where it was, etc., and many of the neighbors were treated in the same brutish manner.

Guilford Courthouse was another giant step on the road to Yorktown. When the British casualty list, so incompatible with Cornwallis's claims of victory, was published, Charles James Fox was quick to declare, "Another such victory would ruin the British army," while Horace Walpole dipped his pen in sarcasm and wrote, "Lord Cornwallis has conquered his troops out of shoes and provisions and himself out of troops."

The War in South Carolina

*I*T *was near summer in South Carolina, and a burning sun dominated "a Country as hot as the Antichamber of Hell—no pure water for to drink, but sand, mud & water, no bread, but Indian corn chopt fine with a broadax and worked into a kind of bread—this is only the beginning of Sorrows—when will there be an end. I think if I can stand the warmth of this climate, I need not fear Pluto's clime much."*

The state was lacerated by civil war. When the British Army afforded protection, the Tories chased the Whigs. When the Whigs were in power, they had their sport with the loyalists. James Collins was among those who sought back-country recreation in Tory baiting.

There existed at that time at least three classes of Whigs, and three of Tories. The first class of Whigs were those who determined to fight it out to the last, let the consequence be what it might. The second class were those who would fight a little when the wind was favorable, but so soon as it shifted to some unfavorable point, would draw back and give up all for lost. The third class were those who were favorable to the Cause, provided it prospered and they could enjoy the benefit, but would not risk one hair of their heads to obtain it.

There was a class of Tories who, I believe, were Tories from principle. Another class believed it impossible for the cause of liberty to succeed and thought in the end, whatever they got, they would be enabled to hold, and so become rich; they resorted to murdering and plundering and every means to get hold of property. Another class were Tories entirely through fear, and fit for nothing, only to be made tools of by the others, and all cowards, too.

There was another class of men amongst us, who pretended neutrality entirely on both sides; they pretended friendship to all and prayed, "Good God!"; "Good Devil!"; not knowing into whose hands they might fall. . . .

We would meet at a time and place appointed, probably at a church, schoolhouse, or some vacant building, generally in the afternoon, lay off our circuit and divide into two or more companies and set off after dark. Wherever we found any Tories, we would surround the house. One party would force the doors and enter, sword in hand, extinguish all the lights if there were any, and suffer no lights to be made, when we would commence hacking the man or men that were found in the house, threatening them with instant death, and occasionally making a furious stroke as if to dispatch them at once, but taking care to strike the wall or some object that was in the way, they generally being found crouched up in some corner, or about the beds.

Another party would mount the roof of the house and commence pulling it down. Thus, the dwelling house, smoke houses and kitchen, if any, were dismantled and torn down, at least to the joists. The poor fellows, perhaps expecting instant death, would beg hard for life, and make any promise on condition of being spared, while their wives or friends would join in their entreaties. . . . There were none of the poor fellows much hurt, only they were hacked about their heads and arms enough to bleed freely.

William Pierce, of Greene's army, was sickened by man's inhumanity to man.

Such scenes of desolation, bloodshed and deliberate murder, I never was a witness to before! Wherever you turn the weeping widow and fatherless child pour out their melancholy tales to wound the feelings of humanity. The two opposite principles of Whiggism and Toryism have set the people of this country to cutting each other's throats, and scarce a day passes but some poor deluded Tory is put to death at his door. For the want of civil government, the bands of society are totally disunited, and the people, by copying the manners of the British, have become perfectly savage. . . .

I should be ungenerous to pass over in silence the obligations we are under to the ladies of South Carolina, and particularly those of Charleston, who have upon so many occasions given such distinguishing marks of patriotism and firmness. They take every occasion to testify their attachment to our cause, and express their good wishes for our success. When the union rose was established in honor of our alliance with France, the ladies' shoes were ornamented with them as a compliment to the American officers, and they wore them publicly through the streets of Charleston until an impertinent puppy of a British officer ordered a Negro fellow to kiss one of them as she was innocently walking out one morning.

When General Greene arrived, they substituted green ribbons, which still continue to be the fashion. They have uniformly discovered their disgust to the British, and would never visit an assembly or concert given by them during the course of the last winter. . . . Fight on, my dear Colonel; keep up the *gaieté de cœur*, pluck laurels, and deserve the favors of your wife.

British troops were kept off balance by the forays of two colorful and dashing guerrilla bands under the leadership of the cantankerous old "Game Cock," Thomas Sumter, and the swift little Huguenot, Francis Marion, who played the part of the will-o'-the-wisp so well that an exasperated Tarleton dubbed him the "Swamp Fox." Captain Tarleton Brown describes well the scurrying maneuvers of the master partisan.

Marion's route lay then between the Santee and Little Peedee rivers, and being desirous to intercept and defeat Colonel Watts, who was then marching at the head of 400 men between Camden and Georgetown, every arrangement and preparation was made to carry into execution his design. All things being now ready, Watts appeared in sight at the head of his large force, and as they marched down the road with great show and magnificence (hoping, no doubt, to terrify and conquer the country), they spied us; at which time the British horse sallied forth to surround us.

Marion, with his characteristic shrewdness and sagacity, discovered their maneuvers, anticipated their object, and retreated to the woods, some four or five hundred yards, and prepared for them. In a few moments they came dashing up, expecting to find us all in confusion and disorder, but to their astonishment we were ready for the attack and, perceiving this, they called a halt. Colonel Horry stammered badly, and on this occasion he leaned forward, spurred his horse, waved his sword, and ran fifty or sixty yards, endeavoring to utter the word "Charge," and finding he could not, bawled out, "Damn it, boys, you, you know what I mean! Go on!"

We were then doing what we could, pressing with all rapidity to the strife, and before the British could get back to the main body, we slew a goodly number of them. Being eager to do all the damage we could, we pursued the fellows very close to the line of their main body, and as soon as they got in, Watts began to thunder his cannon at us, and to tear down the limbs and branches of the trees, which fell about us like hail, but did no other damage than to wound one of our men, Natt. Hutson, and one horse slightly. Marion, now finding his force, which consisted only of two hundred men (though sterling to a man, brave, fearless, and patriotic), was too small to give Watts open battle, guarded the bridges and swamps in his route, and annoyed and killed his men as they passed.

For prudence's sake, Marion never encamped over two nights in one place, unless at a distance from the enemy. He generally commenced the line of march about sun set, continuing through the greater part of the night. By this policy he was enabled effectually to defeat the plans of the British and to strengthen his languishing cause. For while one army was encamping and resting in calm and listless security, not dreaming of danger, the other, taking advantage of opportunity and advancing through the sable curtains of the night unobserved, often effectually vanquished and routed their forces. It was from the craftiness and ingenuity of Marion, the celerity with which he moved from post to post, that his enemies gave him the significant appellation of the "Swamp Fox." Upon him depended almost solely the success of the provincial army of South Carolina, and the sequel has proven how well he performed the trust reposed in him. . . .

By April 19, Greene had marched through the bright spring sunshine to within four miles of Camden. Preliminary skirmishing revealed that the town was too well fortified to be overrun by direct assault, and he moved around to Hobkirk's Hill, a long, narrow sandy ridge about a mile and a half from Camden. Here he was able to command the approaches, for the road from Charlotte to Charleston ran across the top of the hill in a straight line into the center of town. The thick trees on either side of this unusually wide throughfare provided good cover, while Martin's Spring insured an adequate water supply.

The town itself was surrounded by a square stockade with strong redoubts on each corner, the whole protected by an abatis. In command was a young, energetic, and homely lieutenant colonel, Lord Rawdon, who had fought in America since Bunker Hill. From Rawdon's quarters in Joseph Kershaw's house, Greene could be seen pitching his encampment on the hill. But it was not until a deserter, one Jones, and "a villain of a drummer" came in with the information that Greene had sent back his artillery and wagons while shifting positions around the town, that Rawdon decided to move. Gathering not only his regular troops, but all noncombatants who could shoulder muskets, he sallied out toward Hobkirk's Hill.

Samuel Mathis, paroled when Charleston surrendered, lived near Camden, and it was his observations and the testimony of the officers of both armies that led him to record details of the battle.

Kirkwood's muskets gave the first alarm to the Americans, several of whom were at the spring cooking and washing, and had to run a considerable distance before they got to their arms which were stacked in the very line they had to form. However, the most, if not all of them, did get to their arms and were regularly formed in battle array. The Virginia Brigade with General Huger at its head, having under him Lieutenant Colonels Charles Campbell and Hawes, took the right; the Maryland Brigade led by Colonel Williams, seconded by Colonel Gunby and Lieutenant Colonels Ford and Howard, occupied the left. Thus all the Continentals, consisting of four regiments much reduced in strength, were disposed in one line, with the artillery (which had just come up), under Colonel Harrison in the center. The reserve consisted of the cavalry under Colonel Washington who (being on parade) started at the firing of the first of Kirkwood's muskets, and the North Carolina militia under Colonel Reade also came up at the same time. . . .

The British, when they first attacked near the spring, pressed directly forward and succeeded in turning our left. Their left had displayed towards our right under cover of thick woods, and could scarcely be seen except by our pickets until they began to rise the hill (which is about 150 or 60 yards from bottom to top). Their cavalry had reached the Great Road, and advanced in close order and slow step up the hill directly in front of our cannon which had just arrived and opened on them in the broad road. A well-directed fire with canister and grape did great execution and soon cleared the road so that all their doctors were sent to take care of the wounded. Washington's cavalry, coming up at this moment, completed the rout . . . [and] took all the British doctors or surgeons and a great many others (alas! too many) prisoners—more than one third of Washington's men were encumbered with prisoners, who hindered their acting when necessary. . . .

Our left was somewhat turned or yielding, then our Colonel (Ford) was wounded, but the men were neither killed nor prisoners. The left of the British, at least their cavalry, were routed, many killed and many prisoners. Lord Rawdon, hearing the cannon and seeing his horse dispersed, was stunned and astonished beyond measure, ordered the deserter [Jones] hung and, galloping up to the scene of disaster, was quickly surrounded by Washington's horse and his sword demanded. One of his aides received a severe wound from the sword of a dragoon.

Lord Rawdon is a man of uncommon address. This was a critical moment. Altho' our left was giving way, yet General Huger on our right was gaining ground and was beginning to advance upon the enemy, and Colonel Gunby's regiment of brave soldiers, veterans of the Maryland Line, had all got to their arms, were well formed and in good order, but too impatient waiting the word of command. Some of them had begun to fire in violation of orders and, seeing the British infantry coming up the hill in front of them, Colonel Gunby suffered them to come up within a few paces, and then ordered his men to charge without firing. Those near him, hearing the word first, rushed forward, whereby the regiment was moving forward in the form of a bow. Colonel Gunby ordered a "*Halt*" until the wings should become straight. This turned the fate of the day. Previously being ordered not to fire, and now ordered to *halt* while the British were coming up with charged bayonets, before the Colonel could be understood and repeat the charge, the enemy were among them and made them give way.

Lord Rawdon was surrounded near the head of this regiment, and saw the scene, and also that some of his cavalry had rallied and with infantry was coming to his relief, while he very politely bowed and seemed to acquiesce with the demand of the dragoons around him, pretended that his sword was hard to get out of the scabbard, feigned to endeavor to draw it or unhook it for the surrender required, until the party that took him were attacked and had to fly. Whether it was from that unbounded humanity that generally prevailed in the American Army (and altho' amiable and praiseworthy as it is, yet lost us many a battle), or whether it was from a respect they felt for a person of his appearance; whether he amused them by his manners, or why they did not take him immediately off, is not known. . . .

The scene was quickly changed. Washington's dragoons were now attacked by horse and foot, and the very prisoners they had mounted behind them seized the arms of their captors and overcame them. General Greene now ordered a retreat, and pushed on Washington's cavalry to Saunder's Creek (which lay four miles in rear), to halt the troops and stop the stragglers should there be any either from the militia or regulars attempting to make off. In this he succeeded, carrying off with him all the British surgeons and several officers.

As above mentioned, the artillery had just come up as the battle began. The guns were unhooked from the limbers, or fore-wheels, and let down to fire on the enemy. The horses were not unharnessed, nor had the boys that drove them dismounted, but only removed a short distance from the cannon, and now, seeing a general retreat of the American Army, attempted to get off through the woods without going into, and along the road. They soon got them entangled among the trees, and could not get along, but cut their horses and fled, leaving the limbers of both pieces of cannon in the woods, where they were found by the British and taken.

Under these circumstances, General Greene galloped up to Captain John Smith and ordered him to fall into the rear and save the cannon. Smith instantly came and found the artillery men hauling off the pieces with the drag-ropes. He and his men laid hold, and off they went at a trot, but had not gone far until he discovered that the British cavalry were in pursuit. He formed his men across the road, gave them a full fire at a short distance and fled with the guns as before. This volley checked the horses and threw many of the riders, but they, after some time, remounted and pushed on again. Smith formed his men, gave them another fire with the same effect and proceeded as before. This he repeated several times until they had got two or three miles from the field of action. Here one of Smith's men fired, or his gun went off by accident, before the word was given, which produced a scattering fire, on which the cavalry rushed in among them and cut them all to pieces. They fought like Bull Dogs and were all killed or taken. This took up some time, during which the artillery escaped. Smith had a stout, heavy cut and thrust, and a very strong arm with which he did great execution, both in single and double combats. . . . At length not having a man to support him, being overwhelmed with numbers, he surrendered.

On the next day, Captain Smith was put in close confinement, locked up in jail without being informed what it was for. After lying there twenty-four hours, it was announced to him by the jailer that he should be hung the next morning at 8 o'clock. He desired to know his crime and accuser, but was not gratified. That night a deserter went out and informed General Greene of his situation. General Greene immediately sent in a flag to know the truth of the tale, threatening retaliation. Lord Rawdon informed the officer bearing the flag that two or three women of the British Army had come from Guilford, North Carolina, since the battle there and related that Captain Smith had killed Colonel Stewart of the King's Guards in cold blood two hours after the battle, on his knees begging for mercy. This was found to be false. . . . Upon these facts being stated and proved to the British, they liberated Captain Smith from jail, and soon afterwards on their leaving Camden they left him, and left in his care several of their officers who had been wounded in the late action with General Greene.

Greene, who dreamed of martial glory, could scarce conceal his dejection. "The disgrace," he sighed, "is more vexatious than anything else, though the disappointment in its consequences is a capital misfortune."

Greene's defeat was not without gain. Hobkirk's Hill established a strange pattern of victory. He was not to win a major battle, yet after every engagement the British soon gave up the field and retired toward the coast. So it was on May 10, with the danger of his supply lines being cut by Lee and Marion, that Rawdon evacuated Camden and made his way to Monck's Corner, within thirty miles of Charleston.

"Lighthorse Harry" Lee's Legion, and the partisans of Thomas Sumter and Francis Marion were sent to reduce the chain of British posts stretching across South Carolina and Georgia. First one, then the other, seemed to melt away. Fort Watson on the Santee, Fort Motte and then Fort Granby on the Congaree fell to Lee. Georgetown was evacuated when Marion demonstrated before the town.

South Carolina's militia general, Thomas Sumter, too stubborn to join Greene's army, and carrying on his own private war, took the post at Orangeburg with little trouble. Thomas Young noted the quick surrender: "The Tories were lodged in a brick house, and kept up a monstrous shouting and firing to very little purpose. As soon as the piece of artillery was brought to bear upon the house, a breach was

*made through the gable end, then another, a little lower, then about
the center, and they surrendered."*

Fort Galpin on the Congaree, then the two forts in Augusta fell to
Lee, aided by the militia of South Carolina and Georgia under Andrew
Pickens and Elijah Clarke. Then Lee, proud as a peacock, immediately
marched to join Greene who had laid siege to the westernmost British
post, in the village with the intriguing name Ninety-Six. The town
itself was surrounded by a formidable stockade, on the east side of
which there was a huge yet incomplete "Star" redoubt containing three
three-pounders. On the west side there was a stockade fort, connected
to the town by a covered way. Around the whole ran a dry ditch, the
earth from which was thrown up against the walls to strengthen them.
An abatis bristled outside this dry ditch.

Lieutenant Colonel John Harris Cruger, experienced in repulsing
siege operations at Savannah, commanded nearly 550 men, some 200
of whom were local loyalists.

On May 21, 1781, the vanguard of Greene's army arrived before
the town, and on the following day his army of not quite 1,000 men
began siege operations. Lieutenant Hatton, of the loyalist New Jersey
Volunteers, gave his account of the siege to Roderick Mackenzie,
who later published it in his "Strictures" on Tarleton's history.

Flushed with success from the reduction of a number of British
posts, they with a contemptuousness to the garrison of Ninety-Six,
to this day unexplained, in the night between the 21st and 22nd threw
up two works at no greater distance than seventy paces from the
Star. General Greene did not even condescend to summon the place.
Whether he meant to assault and reduce it by a *coup de main*, or
designed these works for places of arms, is another point as yet
undetermined. It can hardly be conceived that his engineer, Kosciusko, a foreign adventurer whom *they* created a Count of Poland,
would break ground and begin a sap within so small a distance of a
regular fortification, if he had intended its reduction by the common
mode of approaches.

By eleven o'clock in the morning of the 22nd of May, the platform
in the salient angle of the Star, nearest to the Americans, was completed and mounted with guns to fire *en barbet*. These, with incessant
platoons of musketry, played on the works constructed by the enemy
the preceding night, under cover of which, thirty men, marching in
Indian file, entered them and put every man they could reach to the

bayonet. This party was immediately followed by another of the loyal militia who, in an instant levelled these works, and loaded a number of Negroes with the entrenching tools of the Americans. Though General Greene put his whole army in motion to support the advanced corps, they were entirely routed before he could effect his design. The handful of men that performed this service retired into the Star without any loss, excepting that of the officer who led them. . . .

From such a check, the American commander began to entertain a respectable idea of the troops with whom he had to contend. On the night of the 23rd the Americans again broke ground, but at a distance of four hundred paces from the Star, and behind a ravine. They here began two saps, erected block batteries to cover them, and appointed two brigades to their support. Sorties by small parties were made during the night to interrupt the enemy and retard their approaches. These were occasionally continued for the rest of the siege, notwithstanding which, by incessant labor and the numbers employed, the besiegers had completed a second parallel by the 3rd of June, when, for the first time they beat the chamade, and their adjutant general advanced with a flag to speak to the commandant.

Lieutenant Stelle, the officer on duty who met him, observed that it was unusual for commanding officers to receive and answer flags in person, but that if he had anything to communicate, it should be forwarded. The American officer then produced a paper, signed by himself, setting forth with highest eulogiums, the invincible gallantry of their troops, enumerating their recent conquests "upon the Congaree, the Wateree, and the Santee," declaring that the garrison had everything to hope from their generosity, and to fear from their resentment; making the commandant *personally* responsible for a fruitless resistance, and demanding an immediate and unconditional surrender to the Army of the United States of America. He farther protested, that this summons should not be repeated, nor any flag of truce hereafter received, without it conveyed the preliminary proposals for a capitulation.

The commandant directed an officer to inform the person who brought this extraordinary paper, that Ninety-Six was committed to his charge, and that both duty and inclination pointed to the propriety of defending it to the last extremity. He added, that the promises and threats of General Greene were alike indifferent to him.

The truce therefore ceased; the enemy immediately opened four batteries, commenced a heavy cross fire which enfiladed some of the works, and continued this cannonade at intervals for several days, at the same time pushing a sap against the Star and advancing batteries. One of these, constructed of fascines and gabions, at no greater distance than thirty-five feet from the abatis, was elevated forty feet from the earth. Upon it a number of riflemen were stationed who, as they overlooked the British works, did great execution. The garrison crowned their parapet with sand bags, leaving apertures through which the loyal militia fired their rifles with good effect. African arrows were thrown by the besiegers on the roofs of the British barracks to set them on fire, but this design was immediately counteracted by Lieutenant Colonel Cruger, who directed all buildings to be unroofed, an order which, though it exposed both officers and men to the bad effects of the night air, so pernicious in this climate, was obeyed with an alacrity that nothing but their confidence in him could inspire.

With an intention to burn the rifle battery of the assailants, attempts were made to heat shot, but these were frustrated for want of furnaces. The besieged therefore in the Star, being no longer able to continue with the cannon on the platform in the day time, they were dismounted and used only in the night.

Word reached Greene from Sumter that Rawdon had received reinforcements from Charlestown and was now marching fast to the relief of Ninety-Six. Among the militia who drifted in was Thomas Young, who seemed to wander from one engagement to another.

As we every day got our parallels nearer the garrison, we could see them very plain when they went out to a brook or a spring for water. The Americans had constructed a sort of moving battery, but as the cannon of the fort was brought to bear upon it, they were forced to abandon the use of it. It had not been used for some time, when an idea struck old Squire Kennedy (who was an excellent marksman) that he could pick off a man now and then as they went to the spring. He and I took our rifles and went to the woods to practice at 200 yards. We were arrested and taken before an officer, to whom we gave our excuse and design. He laughed and told us to practice no more, but to try our luck from the battery if we wanted to. So we took our position, and as a fellow came down to the spring,

Kennedy fired and he fell. Several ran out and gathered around him, and among them I noticed one man raise his head and look round as if he wondered where that shot could have come from. I touched my trigger and he fell, and we made off, for fear it might be our time to fall next.

Henry Lee, ever the swashbuckler, made his presence known by humiliating the defending forces. Lieutenant Hatton was bitter.

On the 8th of June, the garrison had the mortification to see that of Augusta marched by them prisoners of war. Though the gallantry displayed by Lieutenant Colonel Browne in its defence would have excited admiration in a generous foe, Colonel Lee, by whom they were taken, enjoyed the gratification of a little mind in exhibiting them before Ninety-Six, with a British standard reversed, drums beating and fifes playing, to ridicule their situation. This pitiful recourse had an effect quite contrary to that which it was intended to produce. The soldiers were easily convinced by their officers that death was preferable to captivity with such an enemy. Having enjoyed this triumph, Colonel Lee, with his corps called the Legion, next sat down to reduce the stockade upon the left, which preserved a communication with the water. His approaches, however, commenced at respectable distance, and his advances by sap were conducted with extreme caution, while the operations of General Greene were conducted against the Star.

On the evening of the 9th of June, in the apprehension that something extraordinary was carrying on in the enemy's works, two sallies with strong parties were made. One of these, entering their trenches upon the right, and penetrating to a battery of four guns, was prevented from destroying them for want of spikes and hammers. They here discovered the mouth of a mine, designed to be carried under a curtain to the Star, upon springing of which the breach was to be entered by the American Army, sword in hand. The other division that marched upon the left fell in with the covering party of the besiegers, a number of whom were put to the bayonet and the officer commanding them brought in prisoner. Both parties returned to the garrison with little loss, though it was impossible for that of the enemy not to have been considerable. Never did luckless wight receive a more inglorious wound upon any occasion, than Count Kosciusko did on this—it was in that part which Hudibras has constituted the seat of honor, and was given just as the engineer was examining the mine which he had projected!

Colonel Lee continued his approaches at the stockade upon the left, before which his corps suffered greatly. On the 12th of June, in a paroxysm of temerity and folly, he directed a sergeant and six men to advance with lighted combustibles, and set fire to the abatis of the work which he had invested. Not one of them returned to upbraid him for his rashness, and he was the first to solicit a truce to bury the bodies of the men he had so scandalously sacrificed. Having now redoubled his efforts, and mounted a number of cannon which followed him from Augusta, he completely enfiladed this work by a triangular fire, and by the 17th of June rendered it untenable. It was evacuated in the night without loss and taken possession of by the enemy.

The suffering of the garrison was now extreme. With infinite labor a well was dug in the Star, but water was not to be obtained, and the only means of procuring this necessary element in a torrid climate in the month of June, was to send out naked Negroes, who brought a scanty supply from within pistol shot of the American pickets, their bodies being indistinguishable in the night from the fallen trees, with which that place abounded. . . .

Whilst the commandant was using these endeavors, an American loyalist, in open day, under the fire of the enemy, rode through their pickets and delivered a verbal message from Lord Rawdon: "That he had passed Orangeburg, and was in full march to raise the siege." The name of Rawdon inflamed every breast with additional vigor; they declared they would wait patiently for the assailants, and meet them even in the ditch. How well they kept their word the transactions of the 18th will show.

On the morning of this day, the third parallel of the besiegers was completed; they turned the abatis, drew out the pickets, and brought forward two trenches within six feet of the ditch of the Star. General Greene, well informed of the advance of Lord Rawdon, and knowing that the garrison was equally apprised of it, determined upon a general assault, which he commenced at noon.

Their forlorn hopes, in two divisions, made a lodgement in the ditch and were followed by strong parties with grappling hooks to draw down the sand bags, and tools to reduce the parapet. The riflemen, posted upon their elevated battery, picked off every British soldier that appeared, while the Virginian and Maryland Lines fired by platoons from their trenches. The right flank of the enemy was exposed to the fire of a three-pounder, as well as to that of the block houses in the village, and Major Green, with the troops in the Star, waited with coolness to receive them on the parapet with bayonets and spears. The attack continued, but the main body of the Americans could not be brought forward to the assault; they were contented with supporting the parties in the ditch by an incessant fire from the lines.

At length the garrison became impatient. Two parties, under Captain Campbell of the New Jersey Volunteers, and Captain French of Delancey's, issued from the sally port in the rear of the Star. They entered the ditch, they divided their men and advanced, pushing their bayonets until they met each other. This was an effort of gallantry that the Americans could not have expected. General Greene, from one of the advanced batteries, with astonishment beheld two parties, consisting only of thirty men each, sallying into a ditch, charging and carrying everything before them, though exposed to the fire of the whole army. . . .

The Americans covered their shame in the trenches, nor was it till the next day that they recollected themselves so far as to ask permission to bury their dead. The groans also of their wounded assailed their ears, and called aloud for that relief which ought to have been much earlier administered.

General Greene raised the siege upon the evening of the 19th, and on the morning of the 21st the army under Lord Rawdon made its appearance. . . .

That shy goddess of military men, the lady known as Victory, once again had eluded Nathanael Greene. Yet he managed to maintain his army in the field as a source of concern to the British, taking post in the high hills of the Santee to rest his weary men in a "camp of repose."

Ninety-Six was now an isolated post. Ordering Cruger to destroy the fortifications, Rawdon marched for Orangeburg. There, his health turned delicate by six years' campaigning in a strange environment, Rawdon placed his troops under the command of Lieutenant Colonel Alexander Stuart and returned to England. At sea he was captured by a French 74-gun ship of the line, and taken to Chesapeake Bay where he became a witness to the final humiliation of British arms in America.

On July 23, 1781, Greene's aide wrote: "We are gathering a

*respectable force together, and perhaps before many weeks shall pass
away, we shall be struggling in some bloody conflict. Mischief is
a-brewing by the General, who keeps us in constant hot water, and
never fails to make us fight."*

*Both Greene and Stuart maneuvered for position. The American
Army had now increased to about 2,400, a number of them deserters
from the British. Greene was to say later, "At the close of the war, we
fought the enemy with British soldiers, and they fought us with those of
America."*

*Stuart stationed his nearly 2,000 troops at Eutaw Springs, so named
because of the underground stream that boiled out of the ground to
form Eutaw Creek. In the center of a clearing of almost eight acres
stood an elegant two-story brick mansion. Otho Williams, with the
assistance of several of his colleagues, wrote an account of the battle
that centered on this house, September 8, 1781.*

Colonel Stuart had pushed forward a detachment of infantry to
a mile distant from the Eutaws, with orders to engage and detain
the American troops, while he formed his troops and prepared for
battle. But Greene, persuaded . . . that the enemy was at hand, and
wishing time for his raw troops to form with coolness and recollec-
tion, halted his columns, and after distributing the contents of his
rum casks, ordered his men to form in the order for battle. . . .

The troops moved forward. The whole country on both sides of
the road being in woods, the lines could not move with much expedition consistently with preserving their order. The woods were not
thick, nor the face of the country irregular; it undulated gently,
presenting no obstacles to the march, although producing occasional
derangements in the connection of the lines.

When the first American line reached the ground on which it
encountered Stuart's advanced parties, it was ordered to move on in
order, driving the enemy before it. And in this manner it advanced,
firing while the enemy retreated and fell into their own line.

At about two hundred yards west of the Eutaw Springs, Stuart
had drawn up his troops in one line, extending from the Eutaw Creek
beyond the main Congaree road. The Eutaw Creek effectually
covered his right, and his left which was in the military language, in
air, was supported by Coffin's cavalry, and a respectable detachment
of infantry held in reserve at a considerable distance in the rear of
the left, under cover of the wood. . . .

The superiority of the enemy in cavalry made it necessary that Colonel Stuart should cast his eyes to the Eutaw house for retreat and support. To that, therefore, he directed the attention of Major Sheridan, with orders, upon the first symptoms of misfortune, to throw himself into it and cover the army from the upper windows. On his right also he had made a similar provision against the possibility of his lines being compelled to give ground. In the thickets which border the creek, Major Majoribanks, with three hundred of his best troops, was posted, with instructions to watch the flanks of the enemy, if ever it should be open to attack. This command had assumed a position having some obliquity to the main line, forming with an obtuse angle. The artillery was also posted in the main road.

As soon as the skirmishing parties were cleared away from between the two armies, a steady and desperate conflict ensued. That between the artillery of the first line and that of the enemy, was bloody and obstinate in the extreme. Nor did the American artillery relax for a moment from firing or advancing, until both pieces were dismounted and disabled. One of the enemy's four-pounders had shared the same fate, and the carnage on both sides had been equal and severe.

Nor had the militia been wanting in gallantry and perseverance. It was with equal astonishment that both the second line and the enemy contemplated these men steadily, and without faltering, advance with shouts and exhortations into the hottest of the enemy's fire, unaffected by the continual fall of their comrades around them. General Greene, to express his admiration of the firmness exhibited on this occasion by the militia says of them, in a letter to Steuben, "Such conduct would have graced the veterans of the great King of Prussia." But it was impossible that this could endure long, for these men were, all this time, receiving the fire of double their number; their artillery was demolished, and that of the enemy still vomiting destruction on their ranks. They, at length, began to hesitate. . . .

From the first commencement of the action, the infantry of the American covering parties on the right and left had been steadily engaged . . . But the American left fell far short of the British right, and the consequence was that the state troops were exposed to the oblique fire of a large proportion of the British right, and particularly of the battalion commanded by Majoribanks. Never was the constancy of a party of men more severely tried. Henderson solicited permission to charge them and extricate himself from their galling fire, but his protection could not be spared from the artillery or the militia. At length he received a wound which disabled him from keeping his horse, and a momentary hesitation in his troops was produced by the shock. The exertions of General Wade Hampton, who succeeded to the command ... proved successful in restoring them to confidence and order, and they resumed their station in perfect tranquillity.

In the meantime, things were assuming important changes along the front line. Sumner's brigade, after sustaining for some time a fire superior to their own in the ratio of the greater numbers opposed to them, at length yielded and fell back. The British left, elated at the prospect, sprang forward as to certain conquest, and their line became deranged. This was exactly the incident for which the American commander was anxiously watching, and the next moment produced the movement for availing himself of it. Colonel Williams now remained in command of the second line. "Let Williams advance and sweep the field with his bayonets," was the order delivered to a gentleman of medical staff, who acted the surgeon, aide, and the soldier indifferently, as occasion required.

Never was order obeyed with more alacrity. The two brigades received it with a shout. Emulous to wipe away the recollections of Hobkirk's Hill, they advanced with a spirit expressive of the impatience with which they had hitherto been passive spectators of the action. When approached within forty yards of the enemy, the Virginians delivered a destructive fire, and the whole second line, with trailed arms, and an animated pace, advanced to the charge. Until this period their progress had been in the midst of showers of grape, and under a stream of fire from the line opposed to them. ... The roll of the drum, and the shouts which followed it, drew every eye upon them alone, and a momentary pause in the action, a suspension by mutual consent, appeared to withdraw both armies from a sense of personal danger to fix their eyes upon this impending conflict. ...

The British left wing was thrown into irretrievable disorder. But their center and right still remained, greatly outnumbered the assailing party, and awaiting the impending charge with unshaken constancy. ... They are said to have been so near, that their bayonets clashed and the officers sprang at each other with their swords before the enemy actually broke away. ... In this instance the left of the British center appear to have been pressed upon and forced back by their own fugitives, and began to give way from left to right.

At that moment the Marylanders delivered their fire, and along the whole front the enemy yielded.

The shouts of victory resounded through the American line, affording a gleam of consolation to many a brave man, bleeding and expiring on the ground. . . . The victory was now deemed certain, but many joined in the shouts of victory who were still destined to bleed. The carnage among the Americans had but commenced; it was in the effort to prevent the enemy from rallying, and to cut him off from the brick house, which was all that remained to compel the army to surrender, that their great loss was sustained. . . .

At this stage of the battle, Majoribanks still stood firm in the thickets that covered him, and as the British line extended considerably beyond the American left, their extreme right still manifested a reluctance to retire; and as their left had first given way and yielded now without resistance, the two armies performed together a half wheel, which brought them into the open ground towards the front of the house.

General Greene now saw that Majoribanks must be dislodged, or the Maryland flank would soon be exposed to his fire and the conflict in that quarter renewed under his protection. Therefore, orders were dispatched to Washington to pass the American left and charge the enemy's right. The order was promptly obeyed and, galloping through the woods, Washington was soon in action. . . .

Colonel Hampton, at the same time, received orders to cooperate with Colonel Washington, and the rapid movement which he made to the creek, in order to fall upon Washington's left, probably hastened the forward movement of the latter. On reaching the front of Majoribanks, and before Hampton had joined him, Washington attempted a charge, but it was impossible for his cavalry to penetrate the thicket. He then discovered that there was an interval between the British right and the creek, by which he was in hopes to succeed in gaining their rear. With this in view, he ordered his troops to wheel by sections to the left, and thus, brought nearly all his officers next to the enemy while he attempted to pass their front. A deadly and well-directed fire, delivered at that instant, wounded or brought to the ground many of his men and horses, and every officer except two.

The field of battle was, at this instant, rich in the dreadful scenery which disfigures such a picture. On the left Washington's cavalry, routed and flying, horses plunging as they died, or coursing the field without their riders, while the enemy with poised bayonet issued from the thicket upon the wounded or unhorsed rider. In the foreground, Hampton covering and collecting the scattered cavalry, while Kirkwood, with his bayonets, rushed furiously to revenge their fall, and a road strewed with the bodies of men and horses, and the fragments of dismounted artillery. Beyond these, a scene of indescribable confusion, viewed over the whole American line advancing rapidly and in order. And, on the right, Henderson borne off in the arms of his soldiers, and Campbell sustained in his saddle by a brave son, who had sought glory by his father's side.

Nothing could exceed the consternation spread at this time through the British ground of encampment. Everything was given up for lost; the commissaries destroyed their stores; the numerous retainers of the army, mostly loyalists and deserters who dreaded falling into the hands of the Americans, leaping on the first horse they could command, crowded the roads and spread alarm to the very gates of Charleston. The stores on the road were set fire to, and the road itself obstructed by the felling of trees, for miles, across it. . . .

The survivors of Washington's command being rallied, united themselves to Hampton's, and were again led up to the charge upon Majoribanks, but without success. That officer was then retiring before Kirkwood, still holding to the thickets, and making for a new position, with his rear to the creek and his left resting on the palisadoed garden. By this time, Sheridan had thrown himself into the house, and some of the routed companies from the left had made good their retreat into the picketed garden, from the intervals of which they could direct their fire with security and effect. The whole British line was now flying before the American bayonet. The latter pressed closely upon their heels, made many prisoners, and might have cut off the retreat of the rest, or entered pell-mell with them into the house but for one of those occurrences which have often snatched victory from the grasp of a pursuing enemy.

The retreat of the British army lay directly through their encampment, where the tents were all standing and presented many objects to tempt a thirsty, naked and fatigued soldier to acts of insubordination. Nor was the concealment afforded by the tents at this time a trivial consideration, for the fire from the windows of the house was galling and destructive, and no cover from it was anywhere to be found except among the tents, or behind the building to the left of the front of the house. Here it was that the American line got into irretrievable confusion. When their officers had proceeded beyond the encampment, they found themselves nearly abandoned by their soldiers, and the sole marks for the party who now poured their fire from the windows of the house. . . .

Everything now combined to blast the prospects of the American Commander. The fire from the house showered down destruction upon the American officers, and the men unconscious or unmindful of consequences, perhaps thinking the victory secure and bent on the immediate fruition of its advantages, disposing among the tents, fastened upon the liquors and refreshments they afforded and became utterly unmanageable.

Majoribanks and Coffin, watchful of every advantage, now made simultaneous movements; the former from his thicket on the left, and the latter from the wood on the right of the American line. General Greene soon perceived the evil that threatened him, and not doubting but his infantry, whose disorderly conduct he was not yet made acquainted with, would immediately dispose of Majoribanks, dispatched Captain Pendleton with orders for the Legion cavalry to fall upon Coffin and repulse him. We will give the results in Captain Pendleton's own language: "When Coffin's cavalry came out, General Greene sent me to Colonel Lee with orders to attack him. When I went to the corps, Lee was not there, and the order was delivered to Major Eggleston, the next in command, who made the attack without success." . . .

By this time General Greene, being made acquainted with the extent of his misfortunes, ordered a retreat.

Coffin, who certainly proved himself a brave and active officer on this day, had no sooner repulsed the Legion cavalry than he hastened on to charge the rear of the Americans now dispersed among the tents. Colonel Hampton had been ordered up to the road to cover the retreat at the same time the order was issued to effect it, and now charged upon Coffin with a vigor that could not be resisted. Coffin met him with firmness and a sharp conflict, hand to hand, was for a while maintained. But Coffin was obliged to retire, and in the ardor of pursuit the American cavalry approached so near Majoribanks and the picketed garden as to receive from them a fatally destructive fire. Colonel Polk, who commanded Hampton's left and was, of consequence, directly under its influence, describes it by declaring "that he thought every man killed but himself." Colonel Hampton then rallied his scattered cavalry and resumed his station on the border of the wood. But before this could be effected, Majoribanks had taken advantage of the opening made by his fire to perform another gallant action, which was decisive of the fortune of the day.

The artillery of the second line had followed on as rapidly as it could upon the track of the pursuit and, together with the two six-pounders abandoned by the enemy in their flight, had been brought up to batter the house. Unfortunately, in the ardor to discharge a pressing duty, the pieces had been run into an open field, so near as to be commanded by the fire from the house. The pieces had scarcely opened their fire, when the pressing danger which threatened the party in the house and consequently, the whole army, drew all the fire from the windows upon the artillerists, and it very soon killed or disabled nearly the whole of them. And Majoribanks, who [was] no sooner disembarrassed by Hampton's cavalry than he sallied into the field, seized the pieces, and hurried them under cover of the house. Then, being reinforced by parties from the garden and the house, he charged among the Americans now dispersed among the tents and drove them before him. The American army, however, soon rallied after reaching the cover of the wood, and their enemy was too much crippled to venture beyond the cover of the house.

General Greene halted on the ground only long enough to collect his wounded, all of whom, except those who had fallen under cover of the fire from the house, he brought off. And after having made arrangements for burying the dead, and left a strong picket under Colonel Hampton on the field, he withdrew his army to Burdell's, seven miles distant. At no nearer point could water be found adequate to the comforts of his army.

Eutaw Springs was the last major battle to be fought in the deep South. The Tories and the Whigs still continued despoiling each other in their internecine warfare, but from this time on, Greene's army waited restlessly for the evacuation of Charleston, with one homesick soldier moaning, "The deuce take this country. I would not live in it for a million a year—I am sorry I listed—I wish myself back to the Flesh Pots, the Onions and Garlic of Pennsylvania." Possibly never in the annals of warfare had so much ground been gained without a single decisive victory. After each defeat, Greene had the satisfaction of watching the British remove their troops toward the coast and the safety of Charleston, and the eventual evacuation of that port on December 14, 1782. Watching from New York, Frederick Mackenzie's

British pride was piqued, but he was forced to admit within the privacy of his diary: "Greene is, however, entitled to great praise for his wonderful exertions; the more he is beaten, the farther he advances in the end. He has been indefatigable in collecting troops and leading them to be defeated." And among his own, "Greene is thought to be the Fabius of the age, & the people of this country almost adore him. I fear if he should die, they would deify him." An even more cogent summary of Greene's southern campaign may be found in his own rueful remark: "We Fight, get Beat, Rise, and Fight again."

The Beginning of the End

*L*ORD *Cornwallis had marched from Wilmington into Virginia, with expectations of finding reinforcements for his tattered army. Governor Jefferson had already received a warning from Horatio Gates, whose sarcasm reflected his bitterness.*

If Lord Cornwallis conquers the southern and eastern parts of North Carolina, and extends his posts of communication to Portsmouth, you must expect the weight of the war will penetrate into your bowels and cause such an inflammation there as may (if timely remedies are not applied) consume the life blood of the state. Have you cried aloud to Congress and to the Commander-in-Chief of the Army for succour? Have they listened to your cry? If they have not, are you doing the best thing for yourselves? Military wisdom has ever heretofore been imputed to Virginia. Is there a rottenness in the State of Denmark? Find it out and cut it off. This is a letter of one chess player to another, not a letter of General Gates to Governor Jefferson. I am now at my unhappy house; you are acting in the busy scene of public life, and in a most exalted station, in which I sincerely wish you all the honor and success; happiness, I know, you cannot have.

Even as Gates wrote, Virginia was undergoing the ravages of the detachment under the turncoat Benedict Arnold, now a brigadier general in the British Army as a reward for his treachery. Richmond had been raided, where the smoke of burning supplies had darkened the sky. Arnold had then retired to Portsmouth and there established a base.

Washington had dispatched 1,200 men under the Marquis de Lafayette to the aid of Virginia, and on March 8, 1781, the French fleet sailed from Newport to bottle up the Chesapeake. To counter this move, Sir Henry Clinton embarked 3,000 men under Major General

William Phillips. The two fleets arrived almost simultaneously off the Chesapeake and in a short but indecisive naval action, the French were forced to withdraw and Arnold was reinforced.

Clinton was unhappy with the northward movement of Cornwallis. On May 18 he had written Lord George Germain, "I hope Lord Cornwallis may have gone back to Carolina . . . . If he joins Phillips I shall tremble for every post except Charleston, and even for Georgia." In Virginia, Cornwallis discovered Arnold in the command of the army, Phillips having died of a fever just the week before. With a force of 7,200 men, Cornwallis struck inland, with the "boy," as he termed Lafayette, skipping away before him.

Cornwallis's force was too strong for Lafayette to do more than tease him now and then. Tarleton was sent racing toward Charlottesville, his objective the capture of Governor Jefferson and members of the Virginia Legislature. Jefferson escaped through the woods even as Tarleton's men were ascending the hill to Monticello.

Cornwallis, destroying all tobacco and military supplies in his path, moved into Williamsburg. In deference to a letter from Sir Henry Clinton, calling for 2,000 men for the defense of New York, he moved back to Portsmouth. St. George Tucker marched into Williamsburg with Lafayette after the evacuation by the British.

The traces of British cruelty were but faint as they marched through the country. Here they remained for some days, and with them pestilence and famine took root, and poverty brought up the rear. . . .

Our friend [Bishop James] Madison and his lady (they have lost their son) were turned out of their house to make room for Lord Cornwallis. Happily the college offered them an asylum. They were refused the small privilege of drawing water from their own well. A contemptuous treatment, with the danger of starving, were the only evils which he recounted, as none of his servants left him. The case was otherwise with Mr. McClung. He has no small servant left, and but two girls. He feeds and saddles his own horse, and is philosopher enough to enjoy the good that springs from the absence of the British without repining what he lost by them. Poor Mr. Cocke was deserted by his favorite man, Clem, and Mrs. Cocke, by the loss of her cook, is obliged to have recourse to her neighbors to dress her dinner for her. They have but one small boy left to wait on them within doors. . . .

But this is not all. The smallpox, which the hellish polling of these infamous wretches has spread in every place through which they have passed, has now obtained a crisis throughout the place, so that there is scarcely a person to be found well enough to nurse those who are most afflicted with it. Your old friend, Aunt Betty, is in that situation. . . .

To add to the catalogue of mortifications, they constrained all of the inhabitants of the town to take paroles. After tyrannizing them ten days here, they went to James Town. . . . Among the plagues the British left in Williamsburg, that of flies is inconceivable. It is impossible to eat, drink, sleep, write, sit still, or even walk about in peace on account of their confounded stings. Their numbers exceed all description, unless you look in the eighth chapter of Exodus for it.

Near Jamestown, Cornwallis prepared to cross the James River. It was here, on July 6, that Anthony Wayne found himself engaged in a skirmish with the British pickets that expanded into a full-scale battle. Clearly a defeat, it was reported in so vague a manner as to preserve the cracking varnish of patriotism. The New Jersey Gazette *carried the account of a "Gentleman" in a militia company of light dragoons.*

Lafayette and Wayne are leading the British in Virginia through a very intricate path. The latest operation is that of Wayne, with a handful of Pennsylvanians, frightening the whole of Cornwallis's army of "undaunted Britons." The Tories say it is only "another version of the deceit and unfairness practised by the little Frenchman. . . ."

Cornwallis having encamped near Jamestown in Virginia, the Marquis Lafayette sent General Wayne, with the Pennsylvania Line, to take their station within a small distance of the British army and watch their operations. About three hundred riflemen occupied the ground between General Wayne and Lord Cornwallis, who were directed to scatter themselves in the woods, without order, and annoy the enemy's camp. This they did with such effect, that a small party was sent out against them to dislodge them; each side continuing to reinforce—at length the whole of General Wayne's division were engaged.

They drove the advance detachment back to their lines and, without stopping there, attacked the whole British army, drawn up in order of battle, and charged them with their bayonets. The action was obstinate for the little time it lasted, but the disproportion of numbers was too great. The Marquis arrived, in person, time enough to order a retreat, and to bring off the Pennsylvania troops before they were surrounded, which the enemy were endeavoring to effect, being able greatly to outflank them. Cornwallis did not pursue them more than half a mile in the retreat, apprehending the rest of the Americans were near enough to support them, and not choosing to risk a general engagement. . . .

The British, immediately after the action, which ended about nine o'clock in the evening, crossed James River. The whole army were crossed in the morning, excepting a part of their light horse, for which they had boats ready to bring them over instantly in case of an emergency. Saturday afternoon, or evening, they crossed also.

Wayne's impetuosity in rushing upon the entire British Army in a bayonet charge led many to complain, among them Dr. Robert Wharry: "Madness—Mad Anthony, by God, I never knew such a piece of work heard of—about eight hundred troops opposed to five or six thousand veterans upon their own ground."

When Cornwallis reached Portsmouth there were letters from Clinton directing him to establish a base on the Chesapeake to furnish protection for the British fleet. Neither Portsmouth nor Old Point Comfort suited Cornwallis or his engineers and the decision was to occupy and fortify the little tobacco port of Yorktown, some eleven miles from the mouth of the York River. This village was situated across the river from the spot where Gloucester Point bellied out into the stream to narrow the distance to less than a mile before it widened again. On the river side of the town, 40-foot-high marl banks made access difficult. Two well-nigh impenetrable marshes sprawling on two sides of the town offered natural protection. By August 22, 1781, the army of Cornwallis was throwing up earthworks about the town. Some 2,000 slaves (including some from the plantations of Washington and Jefferson) were formed into labor corps.

Lafayette, his force too small for offensive action, moved about, living off the land. His men enjoyed themselves in paying court and making small talk with the ladies. Dr. Wharry, for instance, reported, "The land is tolerable, the people generally genteel and hospitable, the ladies handsome and witty, and what is still better, they have fortunes— very great loadstones. I have a mind to pay my addresses to eight hundred acres of good land and twenty or thirty black Negroes. . . . Mr. Hovenden is our commander; he is enamoured with a handful of women, about an armful."

Yet young Lieutenant John Bell Tilden found fault with the local belles: "Dined with my friend Feltman, and afterwards walked in the country; chatted awhile with a couple of Virginia girls—one of them as big as a horse (almost), who among a parcel of Negroes could not be distinguished by her speaking, and hardly be known from a mulatto."

In the North, the war had fallen into a listless stalemate. Sir Henry Clinton, in New York, tried to cope with the vague and perplexing directives received from London. His soldiers, as do soldiers of every era, took their fun where they found it. The Hessian sergeant John Charles Philip von Krafft found the antics of the British troops somewhat repulsive.

I met a soldier of the 38th English regiment who asked me where our clergyman [chaplain] lived. He said they had none in their regiment, and the one in Donop's regiment had refused when he desired to be married to a woman whose acquaintance he had made in the street a few hours before. He said he had received permission from the commander of his regiment to marry.

I gave him a short answer, but could not help laughing and proceeded on my way. Such things and a thousand others of like or worse nature were not rare here. A certain sergeant of the above named English regiment, a handsome young fellow, had been married sixteen times to loose women of the town by different English and German chaplains through shrewd contrivances, without the consent of his officers, and he told me he hoped to do so often again, though before making up his mind to take the last one in real earnest.

For the American Army, 1781 had begun in a most dismal fashion. Washington had gone into winter quarters on December 1, 1780, with the Pennsylvania Line at Morristown, the New Jersey Line at Pompton and the New England troops stationed at West Point and other posts along the Hudson. The General maintained his quarters at New Windsor on the Hudson. The grumbling in the ranks was too serious to be considered as customary grousing. The Pennsylvania Line, unpaid, ill-clothed and ill-fed, broke the bonds of discipline when they learned that good hard money was being distributed as a bounty for new recruits.

Lieutenant Enos Reeves welcomed the new year in a pleasant manner on January 1, 1781.

We had an elegant regimental dinner and entertainment. . . . We spent the day very pleasantly and the evening till about ten o'clock as cheerfully as we could wish, when we were disturbed by the huzzas of the soldiers upon the Right Division, answered by those on the Left.

I went on the parade and found numbers in small groups whispering and busily running up and down the line. In a short time a gun was fired upon the right and answered by one on the right of the Second Brigade, and a skyrocket thrown from the center of the first, which was accompanied by a general huzza throughout the line, and the soldiers running out with their arms, accoutrements and knapsacks.

I immediately found it was a mutiny, and that the guns and skyrocket were the signals. The officers in general exerted themselves to keep the men quiet, and keep them from turning out. We each applied himself to his own company, endeavored to keep them in their huts and lay by their arms, which they would do while we were present, but the moment we left one hut to go to another, they would be out again. Their excuse was they thought it was an alarm and the enemy coming on.

Next they began to move in crowds to the parade, . . . which was the place appointed for their rendezvous. Lieutenant White of our regiment, in endeavouring to stop one of those crowds, was shot through the thigh, and Captain Samuel Tolbert, in opposing another party, was shot through the body, of which he is very ill. They continued huzzaing and firing in a riotous manner, so that it soon became dangerous for an officer to oppose them by force. We then left them to go their own way. . . .

About this time General Wayne and several field officers (mounted) arrived. General Wayne and Colonel Butler spoke to them for a considerable time, but it had no effect. Their answer was, they had been wronged and were determined to see themselves righted. He replied that he would right them as far as in his power. They rejoined, it was out of his power; their business was not with the officers but with the Congress and the Governor and Council of the State; 'twas they had wronged and they must right. With that, several platoons fired over the General's head. The General called out, "If you mean to kill me, shoot me at once—here's my breast!" opening his coat. They replied it was not their intention to hurt or disturb an officer of the Line (two or three individuals excepted); that they had nothing against their officers, and they would oppose any person that would attempt anything of the kind.

A part of the Fourth Regiment was paraded and led by Captain Campbell to recapture the cannon; they were ordered to charge and rush on. They charged, but would not advance, then dispersed and left the officer alone. Soon after a soldier from the mob made a charge upon Lieutenant Colonel Butler, who was obliged to retreat between the huts to save his life. He went around one hut and the soldier around another to meet him, met Captain Bettin who was coming down the alley, who seeing a man coming towards him on a charge, charged his espontoon to oppose him, when the fellow fired his piece and shot the captain through the body and he died two hours later.

About twelve o'clock they sent parties to relieve or seize the old camp guard, and posted sentinels all round the camp. At one o'clock they moved off towards the left of the line with the cannon, and when they reached the center they fired a shot. As they came down the line, they turned the soldiers out of every hut, and those who would not go with them were obliged to hide till they were gone. They continued huzzaing and a disorderly firing till they went off about 2 o'clock, with drums and fifes playing, under command of the sergeants, in regular platoons, with a front and rear guard.

General Wayne met them as they were marching off and endeavoured to persuade them back, but to no purpose. He then inquired which way they were going, and they replied either to Trenton or Philadelphia. He begged them not to attempt to go to the enemy. They declared it was not their intention, and that they would hang any man who would attempt it, and for that, if the enemy should come out in consequence of this revolt, they would turn back and fight them. "If that is your sentiments," said the General, "I'll not leave you, and if you won't allow me to march in your front, I'll follow in your rear."

This day January 2 Colonels Stewart and Richard Butler joined General Wayne in hopes they could turn them when they grew cooler, being much agitated with liquor when they went off; it being New Year's Day, they had drawn half a pint per man. The men have continued going off in small parties all day. About one o'clock, one hundred head of cattle came in from the eastward, which they drove off to their main body, which lay in a wood near Vealtown, leaving a few behind for the use of the officers.

When we came to draw provisions and state stores this day, we found that near half the men of our regiment had remained.

The men went off very civilly last night to what might have been expected from such a mob. They did not attempt to plunder our officers' huts or insult them in the least, except those who were obstinate in opposing them. They did not attempt to take with them any part of the state stores, which appears to me a little extraordinary, for men when they get but little, want more.

In an effort to take advantage of the situation, Sir Henry Clinton sent emissaries to the mutineers—they were hanged. The affair was finally settled when a committee of sergeants met with Pennsylvania officials, who agreed to discharge all those soldiers who had enlisted for three years only and had not received a bounty or re-enlisted. Wayne retired to Pennsylvania to rebuild his regiments. When up to fighting strength, they were sent to Virginia where they upheld the reputation of their Line by the valiant bayonet charge at Green Spring.

The malignancy spread. Later in January, at Pompton, the New Jersey Line suddenly exploded in defiance of their officers. Washington acted swiftly. He immediately ordered 500 men under Major General Robert Howe to quell the mutiny. Marching swiftly through a two-foot snow in the early morning chill of January 27, Howe surrounded the camp with men and artillery. Surgeon Thacher watched the collapse of the insurrection.

Finding themselves closely encircled and unable to resist, they quietly submitted to the fate which awaited them. General Howe ordered that three of the ringleaders should be selected as victims for condign punishment. These unfortunate culprits were tried on the spot, Colonel Sprout being president of the court-martial, standing in the snow, and they were sentenced to be immediately shot. Twelve of the most guilty mutineers were next selected to be their executioners. This was a most painful task; being themselves guilty, they were greatly distressed with the duty imposed upon them and, when ordered to load, some of them shed tears.

The wretched victims, overwhelmed by the terrors of death, had neither time nor power to implore the mercy and forgiveness of their God, and such was their agonizing condition that no heart could refrain from emotions of sympathy and compassion. The first that suffered was a sergeant, and an old offender. He was led a few yards distance, and placed on his knees. Six of the executioners, at the signal given by an officer, fired, three aiming at the head and three at the breast, the other six reserving their fire in order to dispatch the victim should the first fire fail; it so happened in this instance, the remaining six then fired, and life was instantly extinguished. The second criminal was, by the first fire, sent into eternity in an instant. The third, being less criminal, by the recommendation of his officers, to his unspeakable joy, received a pardon. This tragical scene produced a dreadful shock and a salutary effect on the minds of the guilty soldiers. Never were men more completely humbled and penitent; tears of sorrow and of joy rushed from their eyes, and each one appeared to congratulate himself that his forfeited life had been spared.

The executions being finished, General Howe ordered the former officers to take their stations and resume their commands. . . .

Not until May did Washington and Rochambeau meet at Wethersfield, Connecticut, to plan a move against Clinton in New York. Word had come that the fleet of the Comte de Grasse planned to operate off the North American coast in July and August, but planned to return to the West Indies no later than October 15 because of previous commitments made to the Spanish.

On June 10, the French Army marched out of Newport, and on July 10, the two armies met at White Plains with Rochambeau reporting: "We have made the most rapid march, without any dissatisfaction, without leaving a man behind us, except ten love-sick soldiers from the regiment of Soissonais who wanted to see their sweethearts at Newport and for whom I am going to send. Our junction was made with great acclamation on the part of the Americans."

The attack against New York faltered when Clinton's defenses were discovered stronger than anticipated, and the New England militia appeared to be taking their time in answering the call to arms. On August 14, dispatches arrived from de Grasse stating that he planned to operate in the Chesapeake, an option secretly given him by Rochambeau, who had never looked with favor upon an assault upon New York. Washington had no choice but agree to march against Cornwallis.

Clinton was kept on tenterhooks by feints at his outposts and the construction of storehouses and bakeries by the enemy. Not until September 5 was he convinced that New York was no longer the objective of the allies. By then the American and French armies had marched through Philadelphia. Surgeon Thacher described the pride and the splendor as the troops swaggered through the city on the afternoon of September 2.

The streets being extremely dirty, and the weather warm and dry, we raised a dust like a smothering snowstorm, blinding our eyes and covering our bodies with it. This was not a little mortifying, as the ladies were viewing us from the open windows of every house we passed through this splendid city. The scene must have been exceedingly interesting to the inhabitants, and contemplating the noble cause in which we were engaged, they must have experienced in their hearts a glow of patriotism, if not emotions of military ardor.

Our line of march, including appendages and attendants, extended nearly two miles. The general officers and their aides, in rich military uniforms, mounted on noble steeds elegantly caparisoned, were followed by their servants and baggage. In the rear of every brigade were several field pieces, accompanied by ammunition carriages. The soldiers marched in slow and solemn step, regulated by the drum and fife. In the rear followed a great number of wagons, loaded with tents, provisions and other baggage, such as a few soldiers' wives and children, though a very small number of these were allowed to encumber us on this occasion.

The day following the French troops marched through the city, dressed in complete uniform of white broadcloth, faced with green, and besides the drum and fife, they were furnished with a complete band of music, which operates like enchantment.

Thomas McKean, President of the Continental Congress, dressed in his best black velvet suit, reviewed the allied troops. One French officer was amused by his ignorance of protocol.

The first division of the army arrived at Philadelphia about eleven o'clock in the morning and in full dress. We went out to meet the M. de Rochambeau, and entered the town among the acclamations of the people, who could not imagine, from the idea that the English had given them, that the French army could be so fine. Passing before the Congress they saluted, and the division went into camp on the commons about a mile from the city.

When the troops deployed before Congress, the general officers at the head of their brigades, the President asked M. de Rochambeau if he should salute or not. The General replied that when the French troops marched past, the King deigned to salute them with kindness. This may give a slight idea of the representative of the American nation.

Joyful news was received September 5 at Chester. Dispatches stated that de Grasse had just dropped anchor in the Chesapeake with twenty-eight ships of the line. Count Deux-Ponts noted the sudden change in Washington, who greeted Rochambeau by excitedly waving his hat around his head.

I have been equally surprised and touched at the true and pure joy of General Washington. Of a natural coldness and of a serious and noble approach, which in him is only true dignity, and which adorns so well the chief of a whole nation, his features, his physiognomy, his deportment—all were changed in an instant. He put aside his character as arbiter of North America and contented himself for the moment with that of a citizen, happy at the good fortune of his country. A child, whose every wish had been gratified, would not have experienced a sensation more lively, and I believe that I am doing honor to the feelings of this rare man, in endeavoring to express all their ardor.

That same day, de Grasse had made contact with the British fleet of Admiral Thomas Graves. Led by the massive Ville de Paris, *the mightiest naval vessel of the day, the French slipped out of the Chesapeake Capes to give battle to the enemy. Outmaneuvered, and outnumbered in heavy ships, twenty-four to nineteen, Graves sparred with de Grasse's squadron, observers noting "many English ships badly damaged which navigated along, some without a main top, some without a bowsprit, some without a fore-topmast. To explain it to one who was not there requires a considerable explanation." By the morning of September 7, the two fleets had drifted far enough southeastward so that the outer banks of North Carolina were clearly visible through the haze. When the French gained the wind, the British "crowded on sail and turned away from us." Other than ships engaged in single combat there was no further action as the British beat back to New York and a hasty refitting. By September 12 the French were again rocking at their anchorage in the Chesapeake.*

In the meantime, French transports had taken on troops at the Head of Elk, Maryland, and transported them down the bay to disembark at Jamestown Island. Washington, placing his troops under William Heath, and accompanied by Rochambeau and the Marquis de Chastellux, rode overland from Baltimore for a brief visit to Mount Vernon—his first in six long years.

Two days were spent savoring nearly forgotten domestic pleasures, then on to Williamsburg where an army was assembling. Lafayette had deployed his troops to block any escape by Cornwallis. Nearly 3,200 Virginia militia had arrived at Williamsburg under the command of General Thomas Nelson, Jr., Jefferson's successor as Governor of Virginia.

The year 1781 had begun with misery, mutiny and waning patriotism; now all of a sudden the entire complexion of the war had changed.

And just twelve miles down the York River, Stephen Popp, Hessian soldier, was wielding a spade: "Day and night we are at work strengthening our lines—have hardly time to eat and little food, but we are getting ready to make a stout defence." From the tops of the marl bluffs, several French ships could be seen at anchor in the mouth of the river. Despite the Teutonic stoicism of the twenty-three-year-old soldier, apprehension was contained in the note in his journal, "There are reports we are in a very bad situation."

Yorktown

GAIETY flowed along Williamsburg's Duke of Gloucester Street like a zephyr in the warm October sun. Hardened veterans laughed like little children in anticipation of a new frolic. Lafayette, by his strategic fading before Cornwallis, had added to his popularity, with Captain Roger Welles noting, "I think we have been exceedingly fortunate. The Marquis has conducted himself more like a Fabius through the campaign than an aspiring boy, as Lord Cornwallis was pleased to call him."

The very presence of the French Army seemed to add martial zest to the proceedings. Joseph Plumb Martin was among those arriving at Williamsburg.

We prepared to move down and pay our old acquaintance, the British at Yorktown, a visit. I doubt not but their wish was not to have so many of us come at once, as their accommodations were rather scanty. They thought, "The fewer the better cheer." We thought, "The more the merrier." We had come a long way to see them and were unwilling to be put off with excuses. We thought the present time as quite convenient, at least for us, as any future time could be, and we accordingly persisted, hoping that, as they pretended to be very courtly people, they would have the politeness to come out and meet us, which would greatly shorten the time to be spent in the visit, and save ourselves much labor and trouble, but they were too impolite at this time to do so.

Cornwallis had continued throwing up earthworks, taking advantage of natural defiles, so that the peaceful little village of Yorktown became a walled fortress with redoubts protecting the approaches. Less formidable fortifications were thrown up across the river on Gloucester Neck.

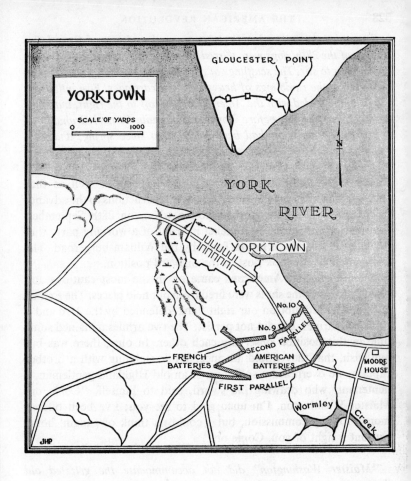

YORKTOWN

SCALE OF YARDS
0   1000

GLOUCESTER POINT

YORK

RIVER

YORKTOWN

No. 10

No. 9

SECOND PARALLEL

FRENCH
BATTERIES

AMERICAN
BATTERIES

MOORE
HOUSE

FIRST PARALLEL

Wormley

Creek

JHP

N

September mornings in Virginia are cool and crisp. Around five o'clock of the 28th, dogs were stirred into barking protests as Williamsburg began to stir. The scufflings of marching men in sandy streets were drowned by the rumblings of heavy artillery carriages. Five miles out, the column divided with the Americans filing off to the right, but came together that evening before Yorktown. Captain Samuel Graham and his Highland regiment had been in Virginia since spring, and were eager to demonstrate their worth in battle.

Our army continued strengthening their posts as well as they could, felling trees and causing such other obstructions to the advance of the enemy as were in their power when, on 28th September, information was given by a picket in front of a working party that the enemy was advancing in force by the Williamsburg road. The army immediately took post in the outward position.

The French and Americans came on in the most cautious and regular order. Some shots were fired from our field pieces. The French also felt the redoubt on our right flank, defended by the 23rd and a party of marines, but did not persist. The two armies remained some time in this position observing each other. In ours, there was but one wish, that they would advance. While standing with a brother captain, we overheard a soliloquy of an old Highland gentleman, a lieutenant, who drawing his sword, said to himself, "Come on, Maister Washington, I'm unco glad to see you; I've been offered money for my commission, but I could na think of gangin' home without a sight of you. Come on."

"Maister Washington" did not accommodate the grizzled old lieutenant. Like a varicolored snake, the marching columns began to wind themselves about the little town. St. George Tucker, filled with a sense of destiny, and who had noted that "the close of the present campaign will probably be more important than any other since the commencement of the American War," determined to fill his obligations to posterity by keeping a detailed journal of the siege. He describes the skirmishing of the first two days.

Sat. 29. This morning about eight o'clock the enemy fired a few shots from their advanced redoubts, our right wing having now passed over Munford's bridge. About nine or ten the riflemen and yagers exchanged a few shot across Moore's mill pond, at different times in the day and about sunset from the enemy's redoubts. We had five or six men wounded; one mortally and two others by the same ball. . . .

Sunday, 30th. This morning it being discovered that the enemy had abandoned all their advanced redoubts on the south and east side of the town, a party of French troops about seven and eight o'clock took possession of two redoubts on Penny's Hill or Pigeon Quarter, an eminence which it is said commands the whole town. About ten a smart firing was heard on the upper end of the town, accompanied by some guns from the ships.

Being at this time in one of the redoubts at Penny's Hill, I saw some of the British retreating, or rather running, very hastily across the sandy beach into the town; soon after which the firing ceas'd and a very considerable smoke (on the upper side of the town across the creek) indicated the destruction of their advanced [Fusiliers] redoubt on that quarter by the French troops. . . . A party under Major Reid, having advanced pretty near to their works on our right, were obliged by a few well-directed shot from them to retire. It is now conjectured by many that it is Lord Cornwallis's intention to attempt a retreat up York River by West Point, there being no ships yet above the town to prevent such a measure.

When Cornwallis abandoned his outer redoubts and pulled in his lines, the allied armies were able to begin siege operations. The first consideration was the construction of batteries to protect those excavating siege lines. James Duncan had been studying for the ministry at Princeton when the rebellion broke out, and had joined the army when "the beating of the damned drums past my window made such a noise I could not study." A captain now, he commanded one of the ten companies designated to construct batteries.

Let me observe here that the enemy, by evacuating their works, had given us an amazing advantage, as the ground they left commanded the whole town. . . . By contrary conduct they must have very much retarded the operations of the siege.

The engineers having fixed on and chained off the ground in two different places to erect their works within point blank shot of the enemy, the parties were called on. . . . We were now conducted to a small hollow way near the ground. Five men were ordered by the engineer to assist him in clearing away the rubbish, staking out and drawing the lines of the work. This was in the face of the open day, and the men went with some reluctance; a little before this we had a shot from the enemy which increased their fears. At dusk of evening we all marched up, and never did I see men exert themselves half so much or work with more eagerness. Indeed, it was their interest, for they could expect nothing else but an incessant roar of cannon the whole night. I must confess I too had my fears, but fortunately for us they did not fire a shot that whole night. I am at a loss to account for it, for the moon shone bright, and by the help of their night glasses they must certainly have discovered us. We were relieved about daybreak, and scarcely had we left the trenches when the enemy began their fire on both works from three pieces. . . .

Oct. 3—Last night four men of our regiment, detached with the first brigade, were unfortunately killed (on covering party) by one cannon ball. . . . A militia man this day, possessed of more bravery than prudence, stood constantly on the parapet and damned his soul if he would dodge for the balls. He had escaped longer than could have been expected, and growing foolhardy, brandished his spade at every ball that was fired till, unfortunately, a ball came that put an end to his capers.

There was activity on the far side of the York. On Gloucester Neck there were no plans for siege operations; the primary objective was to eliminate British foraging expeditions and block that peninsula as a possible avenue of escape. On October 2, Simcoe's Rangers and Tarleton's Legion had been ferried across to Gloucester. Opposing them was the detachment commanded by Brigadier General de Choisy, and composed of militia under General George Weedon, French marines and the mounted Legion under the Duke de Lauzun, whose opinion of his own abilities rivaled the egotism of Banastre Tarleton. With characteristic immodesty, the Duke gave the details of his clash with Tarleton October 3.

I went forward to learn what I could. I saw a very pretty woman at the door of a little farm house on the high road. I went up to her and questioned her. She told me that Colonel Tarleton had left her house a moment before, that he was very anxious to shake hands with the French Duke. I assured her that I had come on purpose to gratify him. She seemed very sorry for me, judging from experience,

I suppose, that Tarleton was irresistible. The American troops seemed to be of the same opinion.

I was not a hundred steps from the house when I heard pistol shots from my advance guard. I hurried forward at full speed to find a piece of ground where I could form a line of battle. As I arrived I saw the English cavalry in force three times my own. I charged it without halting; we met hand to hand. Tarleton saw me and rode towards me with pistol raised. We were about to fight singlehanded between the two troops when his horse was thrown by one of his own dragoons pursued by one of my lancers. I rode up to capture him. A troop of English dragoons rode in between and covered his retreat; he left his horse with me. He charged twice without breaking my line, I charged a third time, overthrew a part of his cavalry and drove him within the entrenchments of Gloucester. He lost an officer, some fifty men, and I took quite a number of prisoners.

This was the last action of any importance in Gloucester, and there was many a snicker in the allied ranks as the story circulated that Tarleton "was rode down by his own men, whose hurry caused them to be very impolite to their commander."

Siege operations in the eighteenth century followed an established and time-honored pattern. First there were parallels, or entrenchments, some 800 to 1,000 yards from the enemy, good range for the artillery of the day. As artillery battered down the defenses, continuous digging carried the lines ever nearer the enemy.

On the night of October 5, Washington was ready to begin the first parallel. Joseph Plumb Martin was among the miners and sappers detailed for the duty.

The next night, which was the sixth of October, the same men were ordered to the lines that had been there the night before. We this night completed laying out the works. The troops of the line were there ready with entrenching tools and began to entrench, after General Washington had struck a few blows with a pickaxe, a mere ceremony, that it might be said "General Washington with his own hands first broke ground at the siege of Yorktown." The ground was sandy and soft, and the men employed that night eat no "idle bread" (and I question if they eat any other), so that by daylight they had covered themselves from danger from the enemy's shot, who, it appeared, never mistrusted that we were so near them the whole night, their attention being directed to another quarter. There was upon the right of their works a marsh. Our people had sent to the western side of this marsh a detachment to make a number of fires, by which, and our men often passing before the fires, the British were led to imagine that we were about some secret mischief there, and consequently directed their whole fire to that quarter, while we were entrenching literally under their noses.

As soon as it was day they perceived their mistake, and began to fire where they ought to have done sooner. They brought out a field-piece or two without their trenches, and discharged several shots at the men who were at work erecting a bomb battery, but their shot had no effect and they soon gave it over. They had a large bulldog and every time they fired he would follow their shots across our trenches. Our officers wished to catch him and oblige him to carry a message from them into the town to his masters, but he looked too formidable for any of us to encounter.

I do not remember, exactly, the number of days we were employed before we got our batteries in readiness to open upon the enemy, but think it was not more than two or three. The French, who were upon our left, had completed their batteries a few hours before us, but were not allowed to discharge their pieces till the American batteries were ready. . . . The whole number, American and French, was ninety-two cannon, mortars and howitzers. Our flagstaff was in the ten-gun battery upon the right of the whole. . . . All were upon tiptoe of expectation and impatience to see the signal given to open the whole line of batteries, which was to be the hoisting of the American flag. . . . About noon the much-wished-for signal went up. . . . A simultaneous discharge of all the guns in the line followed, then French troops accompanying it with "Huzza for the Americans!"

On the 7th, the lines were manned. Captain James Duncan had some uneasy experiences, especially when executing the evolutions prescribed by Colonel Alexander Hamilton.

The trenches were this day to be enlivened with drums beating and colors flying, and this honor was conferred on our division of light infantry. And now I must confess, although I was fond of the honor, I had some fear, as I had no notion of a covered way, and more especially as I was posted in the center with the colors. We, however, did not lose a man in relieving, although the enemy fired much. The covered way was of infinite service. Immediately upon our arrival the colors were planted on the parapet with this motto: *Manus Haec Inimica Tyrannis.*

Our next maneuver was rather extraordinary. We were ordered to mount the bank, front the enemy, and there by word of command go through all the ceremony of soldiery, ordering and grounding our arms, and although the enemy had been firing a little before, they did not now give us a single shot. I suppose their astonishment at our conduct must have prevented them, for I can assign no other reason. Colonel Hamilton gave these orders, and although I esteem him one of the first officers in the American army, must beg leave in this instance to think he wantonly exposed the lives of his men.

It was reported that Cornwallis had established his headquarters in the fine brick house of Governor Nelson. And it is said that the Governor, fat and forty-three, but who moved his bulk with the grace and agility of a big cat, offered a five-guinea reward to the gunner who would rattle the bricks around His Lordship's ears.

On Wednesday, October 10, a flag brought the Governor's uncle, "Secretary" Nelson, formerly secretary of the colony, out of town. No sooner had the gouty old man hobbled across the torn fields than the bombardment was resumed. St. George Tucker questioned the Secretary.

I this day dined in company with the Secretary. He says our bombardment produced great effects in annoying the enemy and destroying their works. Two officers were killed and one wounded by a bomb the evening we opened. Lord Chewton's cane was struck out of his hand by a cannon ball. Lord Cornwallis has built a kind of grotto at the foot of the Secretary's garden, where he lives underground. A Negro of the Secretary's was killed in his house. It seems to be his opinion that the British are a good deal dispirited, altho' he says they affect to say they have no apprehensions of the garrison's falling. An immense number of Negroes have died, in the most miserable manner, in York.

Surgeon Thacher waxed rhapsodic at the grandeur of the scene.

From the 10th to the 15th, a tremendous and incessant firing from the American and French batteries is kept up, and the enemy return the fire, but with little effect. A red-hot shell from the French battery set fire to the *Charon*, a British 44-gun ship, and two or three smaller vessels at anchor in the river, which were consumed in the night. From the banks of the river, I had a fine view of this splendid conflagration. The ships were enwrapped in a torrent of fire, which spread with vivid brightness among the combustible rigging, and running with amazing rapidity to the tops of the several masts, while all around was thunder and lightning from our numerous cannon and mortars, and in the darkness of the night, presented one of the most sublime and magnificent spectacles which can be imagined. Some of our shells, overreaching the town, are seen to fall into the river, and bursting, throw up columns of water like spouting of the monsters of the deep.

We have now made further approaches to the town by throwing up a second parallel line, and batteries within about three hundred yards. This was effected in the night, and at daylight the enemy were roused to the greatest exertions. The engines of war have raged with redoubled fury and destruction on both sides, no cessation day or night. . . .

The siege is daily becoming more and more formidable and alarming, and his Lordship must view his situation as extremely critical, if not desperate. Being in the trenches every other night and day, I have a fine opportunity of witnessing the sublime and stupendous scene which is continually exhibiting. The bomb shells from the besiegers and the besieged are incessantly crossing each other's path in the air. They are clearly visible in the form of a black ball in the day, but in the night they appear like a fiery meteor with a blazing tail, most beautifully brilliant, ascending majestically from the mortar to a certain altitude, and gradually descending to the spot where they are destined to execute their work of destruction. . . .

I have more than once witnessed fragments of the mangled bodies and limbs of the British soldiers thrown into the air by bursting of our shells.

The second parallel opened by the allies could not tie into the river until two strongpoints were overcome. Two British redoubts, numbered nine and ten, squatted like two ugly spiders near the York; bristling with fraise work above a moat, they lay nestled within the tangle of abatis. On Sunday night, October 14, redoubt number nine was to be stormed by Royal Deux-Ponts and Gatenois regiments, under the command of the Baron de Vioménil. Redoubt number ten was to be the objective of a picked detachment of Lafayette's American light infantry, led by Alexander Hamilton who, because he was field officer of the day, demanded that he be given the honor.

Count Deux Ponts was selected to lead the assault of the French.

We then started to go into the trenches. We passed by many troops. . . . Everybody wished me success and glory, and expressed regrets at not being able to go with me. The moment seemed to me very sweet, and was very elevating to the soul and animating to the courage. My brother, especially, my brother—and I shall never forget it—gave me marks of tenderness which penetrated to the bottom of my heart. I reached the place that the Baron de Vioménil had indicated to me. I there awaited nightfall, and shortly after dark, the General ordered me to leave the trenches and to draw up my column in the order of attack. He informed me of the signal of six consecutive shells fired from one of our batteries, at which I was to advance, and in this position I awaited the signal agreed upon. . . .

The six shells were fired at last, and I advanced in the greatest silence. At a hundred and twenty or thirty paces, we were discovered, and the Hessian soldier who was stationed as a sentinel on the parapet, cried out "*Werda?*" (Who comes there?), to which we did not reply, but hastened our steps. The enemy opened fire the instant after the "*Werda.*" We lost not a moment in reaching the abatis, which being strong and well preserved at about twenty-five paces from the redoubt, cost us many men, and stopped us for some minutes, but was cleared away with brave determination. We threw ourselves into the ditch at once, and each one sought to break through the fraises, and to mount the parapet.

We reached there at first in small numbers and I gave the order to fire. The enemy kept up a sharp fire and charged us at the point of the bayonet, but no one was driven back. The carpenters, who had worked hard on their part, had made some breaches in the palisades, which helped the main body of the troops in mounting. The parapet was becoming manned visibly. Our fire was increasing and making terrible havoc among the enemy, who had placed themselves behind a kind of entrenchment of barrels, where they were well massed, and where all our shots told. We succeeded at the moment when I wished to give the order to leap into the redoubt and charge upon the enemy with the bayonet; then they laid down their arms and we leaped in with more tranquillity and less risk. I shouted immediately the cry of "*Vive le Roi*," which was repeated by all the Grenadiers and Chasseurs who were in good condition, by all troops in the trenches, and to which the enemy replied by a general discharge of artillery and musketry. I never saw a sight more beautiful or more majestic. I did not stop to look at it; I had to give attention to the wounded, and directions to be observed toward the prisoners.

Surgeon Thacher visited the redoubt taken by the Americans shortly after its fall.

The one on the left of the British garrison, bordering on the banks of the river, was assigned to our brigade of light infantry under the command of the Marquis de Lafayette. The advanced corps was led on by the intrepid Colonel Hamilton, who had commanded a regiment of light infantry during the campaign, and assisted by Colonel Gimat. The assault commenced at eight o'clock in the evening and the assailants bravely entered the fort with the point of the bayonet without firing a gun. We suffered the loss of eight men killed and about thirty wounded. . . .

During the assault, the British kept up an incessant firing of cannon and musketry from their whole line. His excellency, General Washington, Generals Lincoln and Knox, with their aides, having dismounted, were standing in an exposed situation waiting the result. Colonel Cobb, one of Washington's aides, solicitous for his safety, said to his Excellency, "Sir, you are too much exposed here. Had you not better step a little back?" "Colonel Cobb," replied his Excellency, "if you are afraid, you have liberty to step back." . . .

The cause of the great loss sustained by the French troops in comparison with that of the Americans, in storming their respective redoubts, was that the American troops when they came to the abatis, removed a part of it with their hands and leaped over the remainder. The French troops on coming up to theirs, waited till their pioneers had cut away the abatis *secundum artem*, which exposed them longer to the galling fire of the enemy. To this cause also is to be ascribed the circumstance, that the redoubt assailed by the Americans, was carried before that attacked by the French troops. The Marquis de Lafayette sent his aide, Major Barbour, through the tremendous fire of the whole line of the British, to inform the Baron de Vioménil that "he was in his redoubt, and to ask the Baron where he was." The Major found the Baron waiting to clear away the abatis, but sent this answer: "Tell the Marquis I am not in mine, but will be in five minutes." He instantly advanced, and was, or nearly so, within his time.

Our second parallel was immediately connected with the two redoubts now taken from the enemy, and some new batteries were thrown up in front of our second parallel line, with a covert way, and angling work approaching to less than three hundred yards of their principal forts. These will soon be mantled with cannon and mortars, and when their horrid thundering commences, it must convince his Lordship that his post is not invincible, and that submission must soon be his only alternative. . . .

As the ugly muzzles of allied cannon continued to bark, the British Army began to thrash like a great wounded animal trying to break out of its cage. Colonel Richard Butler recorded one incident of futile bravado the night following the fall of the redoubts.

About 12 o'clock at night, Major Abercrombie of the British, with a party of light infantry and guards, made a sally; and passing between two small redoubts that were unfinished, and where (by the parties being moved in another post to work) the line was weak, got possession of the trench. Thence they pushed rapidly to a French battery and spiked the guns and drove out the people, having killed four or five. Thence to the covert way, or communication, leading from the first to the second parallel, where they halted.

They then discovered a battery commanded by Captain Savage of the Americans and challenged, "What troops?" The answer was, "French," on which the order of the British commandant was, "Push on, my brave boys, and skin the bastards!" This was heard by the Count de Noailles, who had the command of a covering party, which he ordered to advance, and was guided by the "Huzza" of the British. He ordered the grenadiers to "charge bayonet and rush on," which they did with great spirit, crying *"Vive le Roi,"* and to use the British phrase, "Skivered" eight of the Guards and infantry, and took twelve prisoners and drove them quite off. The British spiked Savage's three guns with the points of bayonets, but our smiths and artillerymen soon cleared all the guns, and in six hours chastised the enemy for their temerity with the same pieces. Our loss was very trifling, though the British really executed the sortie with secrecy and spirit.

Despite the heavy and continuing bombardment, Washington was for the second time forced to issue orders clearing the battlefield of spectators. British defenses were crumbling. Banastre Tarleton was involved in Cornwallis's last desperate effort during the blustery darkness of October 16.

A few hours cannonade from the new batteries upon Yorktown, where the fraisings were already destroyed, the guns dismounted, many breaches effected, and the shells nearly expended, would be productive either of a capitulation, or an assault. A retreat by Gloucester was the only expedient that now presented itself to avert the mortification of a surrender, or the destruction of a storm. Though this plan appeared less practicable than when first proposed, and was adopted at this crisis as the last resource, it yet afforded some hopes of success.

In the evening Cornwallis sent Lord Chewton to Gloucester, with explicit directions for Lieutenant Colonel Tarleton to prepare some artillery and other requisites from his garrison to accompany the British troops with which his Lordship designed to attack Brigadier de Choisy before daybreak, and afterwards retreat through the country. . . . A number of sailors and soldiers were dispatched with boats from Gloucester, to assist the troops in passing the river.

Earl Cornwallis sent off the first embarkation before eleven o'clock that night, consisting of light infantry, a great part of the Brigade of Guards, and the 23rd Regiment, and purposed himself to pass with the second, when he had finished a letter to General Washington, calculated to excite the humanity of that officer towards the sick, the wounded, and the detachment that would be left to capitulate. Much of the small craft had been damaged during the siege; yet it was computed that three trips would be sufficient to convey over all the troops that were necessary for the expedition.

The whole of the first division arrived before midnight, and part of the second had embarked, when a squall, attended with rain, scattered the boats and impeded their return to Gloucester. About two o'clock in the morning the weather began to moderate, when orders were brought to the commanding officers of the corps that had passed, to recross the water. As the boats were all on the York side of the river, in order to bring over the troops, it required some time to row them to Gloucester, to carry back the infantry of the first embarkation. But soon after daybreak they returned under the fire of the enemy's batteries to Earl Cornwallis at Yorktown.

Thus expired the last hope of the British army.

The young Hessian soldier Johann Doehla was on the lines on the morning of October 17.

Early at the break of day, the bombardment began again from the enemy side even more horribly than before. They fired from all redoubts without stopping. Our detachment, which stood in the hornwork, could scarcely avoid the enemy's bombs, howitzer shot and cannon balls any more. No one saw nothing but bombs and balls raining on our whole lines.

Early this morning the English light infantry returned from Gloucester and mounted their post in the hornwork again. They said it would be impossible to break through there, because everything was strongly garrisoned and entrenched all the way around by the enemy; also there was a cordon drawn by some squadrons of French Hussars about the whole region, so that nothing at all could pass in and out any more.

Also, this morning right after reveille, General Cornwallis came into the hornwork and observed the enemy and his works. As soon as he had gone back to his quarters, he immediately sent a flag of truce, with a white standard, over to the enemy. The light infantry began to cut their new tents in the hornwork to pieces and many were altogether ruined, so one expected an early surrender.

In response to Cornwallis's proposal that hostilities be suspended for twenty-four hours, Washington answered, "An Ardent Desire to spare the further Effusion of Blood, will readily incline me to listen to such Terms for the Surrender of your Posts and Garrisons at York and Gloucester, as are admissable."

The awesome silence that followed was almost deafening, but Ebenezer Denny declared it "the most delightful music to us all." St. George Tucker lost himself in the silent hush.

Thursday 18th. Lord Cornwallis being allow'd but two hours, sent out another flag to request further time to digest his proposals. It has been granted, and hostilities have been ceased ever since five o'clock.

It was pleasing to contrast the last night with the preceding. A solemn stillness prevailed. The night was remarkably clear, and the sky decorated with ten thousand stars; numberless meteors gleaming thro' the atmosphere afforded a pleasing resemblance to the bombs which had exhibited a noble firework the night before, but happily divested of all their horror.

At dawn of day, the British gave us a serenade with the bagpipe, I believe, and were answered by the French with the band of the Regiment of Deux-Ponts. As soon as the sun rose, one of the most striking pictures of the war was display'd that imagination can paint. From the Point of Rock battery on one side, our lines completely mann'd and our works crowded with soldiers were exhibited to view. Opposite these at the distance of two hundred yards you were presented with a sight of the British works; their parapets crowded with officers looking at those assembled at the top of our works. The Secretary's house, with one of the corners broke off, and many large holes thro' the roof and walls, part of which seem'd tottering with their weight, afforded a striking instance of the destruction occasioned by war. Many other houses in the vicinity contributed to accomplish the scene.

On the beach at York, directly under the eye, hundreds of busy people might be seen moving to and fro. At a small distance from the shore were seen ships sunk down to the water's edge; further out in the channel, the masts and even the topgallant masts of some might be seen, without any vestige of the hulls. On the opposite side of the river the remainder of the shipping drawn off as to a place of security. Even here the *Guadaloupe* sunk to the water's edge show'd how vain the hope of such a place. . . .

This was the scene which ushered in the day when the pride of Britain was to be humbled in a greater degree than it had ever been before, unless at the surrender of Burgoyne. It is remarkable that the proposals for a surrender of Lord Cornwallis's Army were made on the anniversary of that important event. At two o'clock the surrender was agreed upon, and commissioners appointed to draw up the articles of capitulation. They are now employed in that business.

Four commissioners were selected to negotiate the surrender terms.

Washington designated Colonel John Laurens of South Carolina, while Rochambeau selected Viscount de Noailles, brother-in-law of Lafayette. That afternoon, Lieutenant Colonel Thomas Dundas and Major Alexander Ross, aide to Cornwallis, landed at the foot of the high bluffs below the house of Augustine Moore. Moore, a business partner of Governor Nelson, lived in a comfortable, yet unpretentious white frame building, and his home had been selected by Cornwallis as the site in which his fate was to be decided. An American officer repeated a popular account of the negotiations.

Being appointed Commissioner for the capitulation on the part of General Washington, he [Laurens] met Major Ross of the British Army, a.d.c. to Lord Cornwallis, and Commissioner on behalf of the Garrison. Having placed the terms on which the capitulation would be granted before Major Ross, that gentleman observed, "This is a harsh article."

"Which article?" said Colonel Laurens.

"The troops shall march out with colors cased, and drums beating a British or German march."

"Yes sir," replied Colonel Laurens, "it is a harsh article."

"Then, Colonel Laurens, if that is your opinion, why is it here?"

"Your question, Major Ross, compels an observation which I would have gladly suppressed. You seem to forget, sir, that I was a capitulant at Charleston where General Lincoln, after a brave defence of six weeks, in open trenches by a very inconsiderable garrison against the British Army and fleet under Sir Henry Clinton and Admiral Arbuthnot, and when your lines of approach were within pistol shot of our field works, was refused any other terms for his gallant garrison, than marching out with colors cased and drums *not* beating a German or British march."

"But," rejoined Major Ross, "my Lord Cornwallis did not command at Charleston."

"There, sir," said Colonel Laurens, "you extort another declaration. It is not the individual that is here considered; it is the nation. This remains an article, or I cease to be a Commissioner."

The result was, the British army surrendered with colors cased and drums beating a British or German march.

For the first time in Washington's military career, he had been able to dictate surrender terms. He conducted himself with firmness and appeared to use as his guide the terms allowed the Americans by the British at Charleston. He had only to turn to his elbow for expert advice. Major General Benjamin Lincoln, who had since been exchanged, was now second-in-command of the American Army before Yorktown. On October 19, 1781, at nine in the morning, the articles were signed by both parties. The night before, at retreat, the British music had blared out a familiar tune, "Welcome Brother Debtor," and "to their conquerors the tune was by no means disagreeable."

At two o'clock that afternoon, the warm October sunlight played among the trees whose leaves were turning yellow or rusty red. There was Washington on his prancing charger, the youthful Lafayette at the head of his light infantry, while old Papa Rochambeau proudly eyed his colorful troops. From Yorktown, along the Hampton Road, came the colorful tones of "The World Turned Upside Down," a tune with the subtitle "or The Old Woman Taught Wisdom." Ebenezer Denny noted that "drums beat as if they did not care how," while Lieutenant William McDowell observed, "The British prisoners appeared much in liquor."

Surgeon Thacher rode out to witness the final humiliation of British pride.

At about twelve o'clock, the combined army was arranged and drawn up in two lines extending more than a mile in length. The Americans were drawn up in a line on the right side of the road, and the French occupied the left. At the head of the former, the great American commander, mounted on his noble courser, took his station, attended by his aides. At the head of the latter was posted the excellent Count Rochambeau and his suite. The French troops, in complete uniform, displayed a martial and noble appearance. Their band of music, of which the timbrel formed a part, is a delightful novelty, and produced, while marching to the ground, a most enchanting effect. The Americans, though not all in uniform, nor their dress so neat, yet exhibited an erect, soldierly air, and every countenance beamed with satisfaction and joy. The concourse of spectators from the country was prodigious, in point of numbers was probably equal to the military, but universal silence and order prevailed.

It was about two o'clock when the captive army advanced through the line formed for their reception. Every eye was prepared to gaze on Lord Cornwallis, the object of particular interest and solicitude, but he disappointed our anxious expectations. Pretending indisposition, he made General O'Hara his substitute as the leader of his army. The officer was followed by the conquered troops in a slow and solemn step, with shouldered arms, colors cased, and drums beating a British march. . . .

The royal troops, while marching through the line formed by the allied army, exhibited a decent and neat appearance, as respected arms and clothing, for their commander opened his store, and directed every soldier to be furnished with a new suit complete, prior to the capitulation. But in their line of march, we remarked a disorderly and unsoldierly conduct, their step was irregular, and their ranks frequently broken.

But it was in the field, when they came to the last act of the drama, that the spirit and pride of the British soldier was put to the severest test; here their mortification could not be concealed. Some of the platoon officers appeared to be exceedingly chagrined when giving the word, "Ground arms," and I am a witness that they performed this duty in a very unofficer-like manner, and that many of the soldiers manifested a sullen temper, throwing their arms on the pile with violence, as if determined to render them useless. This irregularity, however, was checked by the authority of General Lincoln. After having grounded their arms, and divested themselves of their accoutrements, the captive troops were conducted back to Yorktown and guarded by our troops till they could be removed to the place of their destination.

There was much byplay in the drama of surrender. Count Mathieu Dumas described the initial meeting with O'Hara.

I had orders to go and meet the troops of the garrison, and to direct the columns. I placed myself at General O'Hara's left hand. As we approached the trenches, he asked me where General Rochambeau was. "On our left," I said, "at the head of the French line."

The English general urged his horse forward to present his sword to the French general. Guessing his intention, I galloped on to place myself between him and M. de Rochambeau, who at the moment made me a sign, pointing to General Washington, who was opposite to him, at the head of the American army.

"You are mistaken," said I to General O'Hara, "the Commander-in-Chief of our army is to the right." I accompanied him, and the moment he presented his sword, General Washington, anticipating him, said, "Never from such a good hand."

Rochambeau explained his actions in his Memoirs, reasoning "that the French army being only an auxiliary on this continent, it devolved on the American General to tender him his orders." The next few days were spent in rounding up Negro slaves, burying the dead and sending off the prisoners. One incident left the "Red Raider," Banastre Tarleton, merely red-faced. Many recorded the incident in their journals with a happy smirk.

A Mr. Day came to our tent and said that he was steward to Sir Peyton Skipwith, and that the horse that Colonel Tarleton was riding belonged to his master; that moreover the horse was worth 500 pounds, and he had come all the way from Dan River, determined to get it. Mr. Day went into a marshy place near by and cut him a sweet gumstick as thick as a man's wrist.

It was not long before the mighty Colonel Tarleton with his servant, came riding along in high style. Mr. Day was in the road, and said, "Good morning, Colonel Tarleton, this is my horse, dismount." Holding the horse, he drew his cudgel as if to strike. Colonel Tarleton jumped off quicker than I ever saw a man in my life. . . . Mr. Day went off in a very long trot towards Williamsburg.

Colonel Tarleton went to the tavern, about 100 yards distant, took his servant's horse, and went back to headquarters. Oh! how we did laugh to think how the mighty man who had caused so much terror and alarm in Virginia, had been made to jump off the wrong side of his horse so quickly, with nothing but a sweet gum stick and a chunky little man against him, while he, who was a tall, large, likely man had a fine sword by his side.

Out past the Chesapeake Capes, a rescue fleet sent out by Clinton was slowly tacking about for the return to New York. It had sailed from New York the very day Cornwallis's army was laying down its arms.

From South Carolina Henry Knox received a wistful note from Nathanael Greene. "We have been beating the bush," he said, "and the General has come to catch the bird."

In Yorktown, the young Marquis de Lafayette was jubilant.

The play, sir, is over—and the fifth act has just been closed. I was in a somewhat awkward situation during the first acts; my heart experienced great delight at the final one—and I do not feel less pleasure in congratulating you, at this moment, upon the fortunate issue of our campaign.

Good news travels fast, and on October 22 the word was received in Philadelphia. Newspapers told how the news was spread through the city.

An honest old German, a watchman of Philadelphia, having conducted the express rider from Yorktown to the door of his Excellency, the President of Congress, a few nights ago, continued the duties of his office, calling out: "Basht dree o'—glock, und Gornwal—lis isht da—ken."

"O God! It Is all over!"

THE victory at Yorktown came none too soon. The Continental Congress was nearly bankrupt, not only financially, but in the confidence of the people. France, through her stream of funds and supplies, had been responsible for keeping the Revolution alive.

Shortly after the victory at Yorktown, Joseph Plumb Martin had been paid the astronomical wage of 1,200 paper dollars for his aid in rounding up Negro slaves; he promptly spent the entire amount on a pint of rum!

An even more cogent commentary on the state of finances was that of Elias Boudinot, a member of the Continental Congress.

When the messenger brought the news of this capitulation to Congress, it was necessary to furnish him with hard money for expenses. There was not a sufficiency in the Treasury to do it, and the members of Congress, of which I was one, each paid a dollar to accomplish it.

Frugality was absent as the rebels celebrated their victory.

At Fishkill, New York, the glorious victory was observed with exuberant joy and festivity. A roasted ox and plenty of liquor formed the repast; a number of toasts were drunk on the occasion. French and American colors were displayed, cannon fired, and in the evening, illuminations, bonfires, rockets and squibs gave amusement to the numerous spectators.

At Newburgh the occasion was observed in the same joyous manner, and to enliven the entertainment, they hanged and burnt in effigy the traitor Arnold. In New Windsor, Fredericksburg, and other towns, the same brilliant occasion was observed with demonstrations of gratitude and joy.

The booming of the cannon near Poughkeepsie gave rise to an oft-repeated anecdote.

During the day a scouting party being on their return to camp, heard the firing, and soon after met another party sent out as a relief. A Negro, belonging to the first, calling to one on the latter, said, "Cuffee, whas all dat firing we hear today?" The other replied: "O my dear soul, noffin 'tall only General Burgoyne hab a brodder born today."

There was a different reaction in London. Sir Nathaniel Wraxall recorded the emotional scene.

On Saturday the 25th [November] about noon, official intelligence of the surrender of the British forces at Yorktown arrived from Falmouth at Lord George Germain's house in Pall Mall. . . . Without communicating it to any other person, Lord George, for the purpose of dispatch, immediately got . . . into a hackney coach and drove to Lord Stormont's residence in Portland Place. Having imparted to him the disastrous information, and taken him into the carriage, they instantly proceeded to the Chancellor's house in Great Russell street, Bloomsbury, whom they found at home, when after a short consultation, they determined to lay it themselves in person before Lord North.

He had not received any intimation of the event when they arrived at his door in Downing Street between one and two o'clock. The First Minister's firmness, and even his presence of mind, which had withstood the [Gordon] riots of 1780, gave way for [a] short time under this awful disaster. I asked Lord George afterwards how he took the communication when made to him. "As he would have taken a ball in his breast," replied Lord George. For he opened his arms, exclaiming wildly, as he paced up and down the apartment during a few minutes, "O God! it is all over!"—words which he repeated many times under emotions of the deepest consternation and distress. . . .

After Yorktown, Washington sent the American Army marching northward to winter in New Jersey and the Hudson highlands. Rochambeau and his French troops went into winter quarters at Williamsburg. The French fleet sailed shortly after the guns had stopped firing at

Yorktown, destined to meet an early defeat in the West Indies. Before sailing, one French officer took time to record his pungent observation of the Virginians.

The Americans are phlegmatic, extremely serious, always engaged in their business, and that of state. They are with their wives only to take tea or some other drink. The girls are very free, and can have a lover without their parents finding it amiss; but if they are unfortunate enough to have a child, they must leave the country, unless they get married. But woe to the stranger who in such cases refuses to marry, for he refuses at the risk of his life. The women are as reserved as the girls are unreserved, and I do not think the unfaithful ones can be cited. At all events they behave with the greatest reserve, yet they were very fond of the French officers, whom they preferred even to their own countrymen, but with all possible decency.

This is perhaps the only country where justice is known and rendered. I saw an American, taken in arms among the English, punished with death because he had taken the oath of fidelity to the Congress; and others in the same condition were merely treated as prisoners of war because they had always served the Royalist Party.

The following summer, Rochambeau began a march northward to escape the "fevers" of Virginia. For the officers, it was one gay round of balls in every large town they passed through. Baron Ludwig von Closen reported one accident incurred not in line of duty.

The time we passed in Philadelphia was spent very pleasantly. Everyone renewed his former acquaintance and took advantage of the opportunity to learn all the curious aspects of the city. The ladies of Philadelphia talked a great deal about the effects of love on the French character. They had just had very convincing evidence in the despair of a person named Galvan, who committed suicide when he could not win the heart or hand of a pleasant and rather pretty, but too coquettish lady, who had aroused vain hopes for a rather long time in this poor wretch and then had ended by refusing him abruptly. Many others of his nation had accepted their fate gallantly, but he, whose head had been turned too much by Cupid, could not endure these disasters, and bade adieu to the world with a pistol, despite the care his friends took not to leave him alone. He wrote a tender farewell in a letter. . . . "Love by extinguishing all other passions within me, has rendered me incapable of devoting myself to any pursuit that could turn to the advantage of my country, my friends, or my family. . . . Defend my memory against fortunate lovers. I cannot believe the unfortunate ones will attack it."

In general, however, there was a feeling of good cheer. In New York there was a new British commanding general. Sir Henry Clinton, involved in a bitter wrangle with Lord Cornwallis as to the responsibility for the debacle of Yorktown, had been replaced by Sir Guy Carleton. There were signs of a final settlement in the air. Horatio Gates, once again in good graces, was winding up his military career as senior major general of the American Army. He spoke of his plans for the winter in a letter to Robert Morris.

I am well, and as happy as an old soldier can be in a tent the latter end of October. We move in a day or two to winter quarters, when I hope to get warm for once since I arrived in camp. Upon talking with the General, I have sent for Mrs. Gates to keep me from freezing this winter at, or somewhere in the neighborhood of New Windsor. Mrs. Washington is, I understand, upon the road.

All is secret, and uncertain in regard to the enemy. Sir Guy is so damned close that he must be doing something that he is ashamed of, for everything offensive on his part is at an end, and things must strangely alter before the power of Great Britain can revive. I verily think that is departed, never to rise again in this hemisphere.

All during that summer, Carleton had busied himself in evacuating the southern ports. On July 11, 1782, the British had sailed out of Savannah, and on December 14, 1782, Nathanael Greene had marched triumphantly into Charleston as British vessels slipped over the bar. The French had moved on to Rhode Island, and with peace almost a certainty, had sailed from Newport on Christmas Eve, 1782.

Soldiers, including those of higher rank, drifted off home, and many did not return from furloughs. One general would never return to service. In Philadelphia's Market Street tavern, at the "Sign of the Conestoga Wagon," Charles Lee died October 2, 1782, at the age of fifty-two. Ebenezer Hazard gave the details.

General Lee died in the second story of a tavern, after a few days' illness, in some degree his own physician and but badly attended, except by two faithful dogs, who frequently attempted in vain to awaken their dead master. They laid themselves down by his corpse for a considerable time, so long that it became necessary for new masters to remove them. He lies buried in Christ's Church yard. No stone marks his bed. Indeed, those who saw his open grave can scarcely mark the site, as it is continually trodden by persons going into and coming out of church. Behold the honor of the great!

Lee's will was as bizarre as his life.

I desire most earnestly that I may not be buried in any church, or church yard, or within a mile of any Presbyterian or Anabaptist meeting house; for since I have resided in this country, I have had so much bad company while living, that I do not choose to continue it when dead.

I recommend my soul to the Creator of all worlds and of all creatures, who must, from his visible attributes, be indifferent to their modes of worship or creeds, whether Christian, Mohammedans, or Jews; whether instilled by education, or taken up by reflection; whether more or less absurd; as a weak mortal can no more be answerable for his persuasions, notions, or even skepticism in religion, than for the color of his skin.

By the end of 1782, the prospects of peace were so promising that soldiers were beginning to ponder their future. Congress had done little toward making up arrears in pay other than make recommendations to the states. In December, 1782, a committee of officers had appeared before Congress to demand not only their wages, but, following the European practice, half pay for life for all officers at the disbanding of the Army. Several motions died in Congress. When the officers in winter quarters at Newburgh heard of the failure of their proposals, an undercurrent of anger ran through the camp. Two anonymous and inflammatory statements referred to as the "Newburgh Addresses," and believed to have been written by an aide to General Gates, Major John Armstrong, were circulated freely and called for a mass meeting of officers on March 11. Washington hastened to call a meeting of officers on March 15, ostensibly to hear the report of the committee to the Congress. General Gates was to preside. Washington was not expected to attend. Major Samuel Shaw was among those present.

The meeting of the officers was in itself exceedingly respectable. The matters they were called to deliberate upon were of the most serious nature, and the unexpected attendance of the Commander-in-Chief heightened the solemnity of the scene. Every eye was fixed upon the illustrious man, and attention to their beloved General held the assembly mute. He opened the meeting by apologizing for his appearance there, which was by no means his intention when he published the order which directed them to assemble. But the diligence used in circulating the anonymous pieces rendered it necessary that he should give his sentiments to the army on the nature and tendency of them, and determined to avail himself of the present opportunity; and in order to do it with the greatest perspicuity, he had committed his thoughts to writing, which, with the indulgence of his brother officers, he would take the liberty of reading to them. It is needless for me to say anything of this production; *it speaks for itself. . . .*

His Excellency, after reading the first paragraph, made a short pause, took out his spectacles, and begged the indulgence of his audience while he put them on, observing at the same time that he had grown grey in their service, and now found himself going blind. There was something so natural, so unaffected, in this appeal, as rendered it superior to the most studied oratory. It forced its way into the heart, and you might see sensibility moisten every eye. The General, having finished, took leave of the assembly, and the business of the day was conducted in such a manner which is related in the account of the proceedings. . . .

Washington, with his sentimental appeal, won the day. The officers voted to leave their problems to the General, repudiated the anonymous addresses and adjourned.

Soon after this the General received a letter from Lafayette in France, with an account of the signing of a preliminary peace treaty. The news was soon confirmed in a letter from Sir Guy Carleton. The Continental Congress ratified the treaty on April 15, and on the 17th, issued a proclamation to that effect. On April 19, 1783, the eighth anniversary of the battles of Lexington and Concord, Washington published the news to the Army.

After the first full flush of rejoicing, life assumed a more solemn hue. Now it was spring, and spring was the time for planting crops.

Soldiers clamored for their discharges; many left quietly without the formality of official separation.

Civilians turned to personal problems; soldiers were forgotten in the search for normalcy. One group of Pennsylvania recruits marched on Congress, surrounded the State House; but upon learning that a large force was marching against them, they disbanded with no other damages than the obscenities they fired at members of Congress. Congress immediately picked up and established a new seat of government, although not without escaping the sarcasm of Major John Armstrong: "The grand Sanhedrin of the Nation, with all their solemnity an emptiness, have moved to Princeton, and left a state where their wisdom has long been questioned, their virtue suspected, and their dignity a jest."

With the reality of peace, both Congress and Washington began to tie up the loose ends of the war. On October 18 a Congressional proclamation provided for the discharging of all military men except a small force to be maintained "until the peace establishment should be organized." On November 3, all troops enlisted for the duration of the war were discharged.

The closing scenes were at hand. Washington, his officers and his army were eager to be done with things having to do with war. The felicities of domestic tranquillity beckoned with a seductive finger. Lieutenant Colonel Benjamin Tallmadge, chief of Washington's secret service, could not control the tempest in his bosom as he bade farewell to his General.

The 25th of November, 1783, was appointed for the British troops to evacuate the city. . . . General Knox, at the head of a select corps of American troops, entered the city as the rear of the British troops embarked; soon after which the Commander-in-Chief, accompanied by Governor Clinton and their respective suites, made their public entry into the city on horseback, followed by the Lieutenant Governor and members of the Council. The officers of the army, eight abreast, and accompanied by the Speaker of the Assembly, and citizens on foot, eight abreast, followed after the Commander-in-Chief and Governor Clinton. . . . Every countenance seemed to express the triumph of republican principles over the military despotism which had so long pervaded this happy city. . . . It was indeed a joyful day to the officers and soldiers of our army, and to all friends of American independence, while the troops of the enemy, still in our waters, and the host of Tories and refugees, were sorely mortified. . . .

Governor Clinton gave a public dinner, at which General Washington and the principal officers of the army, citizens, etc., were present. On the Tuesday evening following, there was a most splendid display of fireworks at the lower part of Broadway near Bowling Green. It far exceeded anything I had ever seen in my life.

The time now drew near when the Commander-in-Chief intended to leave this part of the country for his beloved retreat at Mount Vernon. On Tuesday, the 4th of December, it was made known to the officers then in New York, that General Washington intended to commence his journey that day.

At 12 o'clock the officers repaired to Fraunces' Tavern, in Pearl Street, where General Washington had appointed to meet them, and to take his final leave of them. We had been assembled but a few moments, when his Excellency entered the room. His emotion, too strong to be concealed, seemed to be reciprocated by every officer present.

After partaking of a slight refreshment, in almost breathless silence, the General filled his glass with wine, and turning to the officers, he said: "With a heart full of love and gratitude, I now take leave of you. I most devoutly wish that your latter days may be as prosperous and happy as your former ones have been glorious and honorable."

After the officers had taken a glass of wine, General Washington said: "I cannot come to each of you, but shall feel obliged if each of you will come and take me by the hand."

General Knox, being nearest to him, turned to his Commander-in-Chief, who, suffused in tears, was incapable of utterance, but grasped his hand; when they embraced each other in silence. In the same affectionate manner, every officer in the room marched up to, kissed, and parted with his Commander-in-Chief. Such a scene of sorrow and weeping I had never before witnessed, and hope I may never be called upon to witness again. It was indeed too affecting to be of long continuance, for tears of sensibility filled every eye, and the heart seemed so full, that it was ready to burst from its wonted abode. Not a word was uttered to break the solemn silence that prevailed, or to interrupt the tenderness of the interesting scene. The simple thought that we were then about to part from the man who had conducted us through a long and bloody war, and under whose conduct the glory and independence of our country had been achieved . . . seemed to me utterly insupportable.

But the time of separation had come, and waving his hand to his grieving children around him, he left the room and passing through a corps of light infantry who were paraded to receive him, he walked silently to Whitehall, where a barge was awaiting. We all followed in mournful silence to the wharf, where a prodigious crowd had assembled to witness the departure of the man who, under God, had been the great agent in establishing the glory and independence of these United States. As soon as he was seated, the barge put off into the river, and when out in the stream, our great and beloved General waved his hat, and bid us a silent adieu. We paid him the same compliment. . . .

There was still one last duty facing Washington, the business whereby he could "get translated into a private citizen." At Brunswick, Trenton, Philadelphia, and Baltimore he received the plaudits of an adoring citizenry. On December 23 he was in Annapolis "to make his last bow to Congress." James McHenry, in a letter to his betrothed, pictured the scene as General George Washington became George Washington, Esquire.

Today, my Love, the General at a public audience, made a deposit of his commission, and in a very pathetic manner took leave of Congress. It was a solemn and affecting spectacle, such an one as history does not present. The spectators all wept, and there was hardly a member of Congress who did not drop tears.

The General's hand which held the address shook as he read it. When he spoke of the officers who had composed his family, and recommended those who had continued in it to the present moment to the favorable notice of Congress, he was obliged to support the paper with both hands. But when he commended the interests of his dearest country to Almighty God, and those who had the superintendence of them to His holy keeping, his voice faltered and sunk, and the whole body felt his agitations.

After the pause which was necessary for him to recover himself, he proceeded to say in the most penetrating manner:

"Having now finished the work assigned me, I retire from the great theatre of action, and bidding an affectionate farewell to this august body under whose orders I have so long acted, I here offer my commission and take my leave of all the employments of domestic life."

So saying, he drew out from his bosom his commission and delivered it up to the President of Congress. . . .

Then fifty miles across country and Mr. Washington spent his first Christmas at home in eight years.

Benjamin Franklin, writing from Paris to Joseph Banks, expounded on the opportunities of peace.

I join with you most cordially in rejoicing at the return of peace. I hope it will be lasting, and that mankind will at length, as they call themselves reasonable creatures, have reason and sense enough to settle their differences without cutting throats: for in my opinion, *there never was a good war or a bad peace.* What vast additions to the conveniences and comforts of living might mankind have acquired, if the money spent in wars had been employed in works of public utility! What an extension of agriculture, even to the tops of our mountains; what rivers rendered navigable or joined by canals; what bridges, aqueducts, new roads, and other public works, edifices, and improvements rendering England a complete paradise, might have been obtained by spending those millions in doing good, which in the last war have been spent in doing mischief; in bringing misery into thousands of families, and destroying the lives of so many thousands of working people, who might have performed the useful labor!

Glossary of Eighteenth-century Military Terms

Abatis—Trees, felled lengthwise around a strongpoint. Branches in the direction of the enemy were trimmed and sharpened and the trees entangled with each other. Their purpose was to discourage cavalry charges and to slow or hinder infantry assaults, much in the same manner that barbed-wire entanglements are used in modern warfare.

Bateau, or *batteau*—A light, long, and tapering flat-bottomed boat used for navigating shallow and rapid streams.

Berm—A ledge, three to eight feet wide, sometimes left between the moat or ditch and the base of the parapet of a fortification.

Canister—Sometimes called case shot. Canister, along with grape shot, was the shrapnel of the day. The charge was made up of iron balls packed tightly within a metal container fitting the bore of the gun from which it was to be fired.

Cartouche box—A cartridge box to be slung over the shoulder. A cartouche was a measured charge of powder rolled in paper to facilitate loading the musket under battle conditions.

Chasseurs—Soldiers, either of the infantry or cavalry, who have been trained for rapid pursuit, similar to the light infantry of the British Army. In the French Army, the designation was often applied to a group forming the élite of the battalion.

Chevaux-de-frise—A defense or obstruction consisting of spikes projecting from a heavy timber frame. Often used in land operations to protect infantry from cavalry charges. Those used to impede the progress of the British vessels up the Delaware River were said to have been the brain child of Benjamin Franklin.

Continentals—The "regular" soldiers of the American Army. In June, 1775, the Continental Congress adopted the army around Boston and appointed Washington Commander in Chief. Rules and regulations were adopted and the term of enlistment was for one year. In 1776 the Congress attempted to call upon the various colonies to furnish an assigned number of battalions. Eventually the states were called upon to fill their quotas by the utilization of the draft. In late 1776, Congress called for enlistments of "three years or during the war."

Dragoons—Soldiers trained to serve either mounted or on foot. Although originally the term was applied to mounted infantry, armed with a firearm, by the time of the Revolution they usually fought on horseback. The average dragoon was considered "a rough and fierce fellow."

Enfilade—Gunfire that raked from end to end, as along a line of works or a formation of troops.

Esplanade—A sloping or level cleared space outside a fortification where troops were exposed to fire. Sometimes the sloping of a parapet toward the enemy was referred to by this term.

Fascines—Bundles of fagots, or small tree branches bound together at frequent intervals and used as a base for constructing earthworks, filling ditches, etc.

Fleche—Derived from the French *flèche*, meaning arrow, this was a projecting, wedge-shaped earthwork.

Forlorn hope—A body of soldiers detailed for service of great danger, with only a slight chance of returning without injury. Often this was a picked body of men detailed to the front to begin the attack, and sometimes the term was applied to a party storming a strong fortification.

Fraise work, or *fraising*—Sharpened stakes driven into an earthen rampart near the berm, inclining horizontally or upward, designed to prevent an assaulting force from climbing the slope.

Fusilier—Originally a soldier armed with a fusil, or light flintlock musket. By the time of the Revolution several British units bore the name, such as the Royal Welsh Fusiliers.

Gabion—A wicker cylinder or basket, open at both ends, designed to be filled with earth in building earthworks.

Galley—In the American Revolution these were large flat-bottomed boats, propelled with oars, and usually with an artillery piece mounted in the bow.

Grape, or *grape shot*—A number of iron balls, one inch in diameter, fitted into a canvas sack. As the burning powder consumed the sack, the balls sprayed forth from the muzzle of the artillery piece.

Grenadiers—Foot soldiers who threw grenades (the grenade, a small round bomb with a fuse, was developed in 1678), and who were usually selected for their height and strength. Each British regiment or battalion usually contained a company of grenadiers. Although the grenade was out of general use by 1774, the designation "Grenadiers" was retained for a company of the finest and tallest soldiers of each regiment.

Guards—The household troops of the British Army. Formerly a body of picked soldiers for special duty as guards, the name was given to certain regiments such as the Coldstream Guards.

Hornwork—A single-fronted outwork, joined to the primary work by two parallel wings. It was thrown out to occupy advantageous ground that would have been inconvenient to have included in the original fortification.

Hussar—A lightly armed cavalryman originating in Hungary in the fifteenth century. The name was applied to light cavalry units organized in all European countries in imitation. The brilliant uniforms and elaborate equipment of the Hungarians established a pattern for hussars of other nations.

Levies—Soldiers raised by means of a compulsory draft.

Light infantry—Composed of men chosen for physical ability, vigor, and general fighting qualities. They were used in reconnaissance, detached service, skirmishing, and flanking the army on the march.

Match—A slow-burning wick of rope or hemp, tow, cotton, etc., so treated that it was not easily extinguished. Used to touch off artillery.

Matross—A soldier, usually a private, who acted as an assistant to a gunner in the artillery.

Merlons—The solid intervals of a parapet between crenels and embrasures.

Militia—Included potential fighting force of every colony, for every male (unless excused by law) was required to be enrolled. Each man was to furnish his own gun and accouterments, and meet at periodic intervals (perhaps no oftener than four days a year) for training. Company grade officers were usually elected by the rank and file. They were called out for the defense of the colony or state in time of crisis.

Minutemen—A designated group of the militia who were to hold themselves in readiness for instant military service.

Parallel—A siege line, interspersed with batteries, usually parallel to the general face of the works being besieged.

Parapet—A rampart to screen and protect troops, thick enough to resist any shot likely to be discharged against it.

Parole—The practice of setting at liberty a prisoner of war following his pledge of honor that he would not attempt to escape, would return to prison at stated times, and would not again take up arms against his captors.

Picket—Usually a small detached body of troops set out to guard against surprise. The term was sometimes applied to a single sentinel.

Prisoner exchange—Considered "one of the rights of a soldier" in the eighteenth century. This was a mutual agreement for the exchange of prisoners, usually rank for rank. A prisoner so exchanged was free to take up arms again.

Quarter—Mercy, or life, granted to an enemy who surrendered. To cry "Quarter" was to ask for mercy. Apparently its origin was the much earlier practice of providing prisoners with quarters until they could be ransomed.

Redoubt—A small, enclosed, temporary outpost, so located as to defend strategic passes, hilltops, or the approaches to a primary work, and usually situated within musket shot of the main fortification.

Sap—Deep, narrow trench, usually zigzag in shape, or protected by earthen works thrown up in either side, utilized in approaching the enemy's works.

Sappers and *Miners*—Engineer troops employed in building and repairing fortifications and saps. Because they were used to plant mines beneath fortifications, they were seldom granted quarter in the eighteenth century.

Spike—The practice of disabling artillery by using an iron spike to plug or enlarge the touchhole of an artillery piece.

Sponton, or *espontoon*—Short pike or halberd carried by infantry officers from about 1740. It was used not only as an offensive weapon and to parry bayonet thrusts, but also to signal troop movements in the field.

Vidette, or *vedette*—A mounted sentinel stationed in advance of the regular picket of the army.

Yager, or *jaeger,* or *jager*—A Hessian rifleman and sharpshooter. The Yagers were light infantry, recruited from among the foresters of Germany, and armed with rifles and huntsmen's equipment.

Sources

INTRODUCTION

Page

13. "A Chinese History of America," *Historical Magazine*, 2d ser., II (1867), 19–21.

REBELLION IN MASSACHUSETTS

.19. Benjamin Franklin to Lord Kames, April 11, 1767, Abercairny Collection, Scottish Record Office, Edinburgh.

21. Paul Revere to the Corresponding Secretary of the Massachusetts Historical Society, January 1, 1789, *Collections of the Massachusetts Historical Society*, 1st ser., V (Boston, 1898), 106–110.

24. Relation of Lieutenant William Sutherland, 38th Regiment, April 27, 1775, Gage Papers, William L. Clements Library, University of Michigan, Ann Arbor, Michigan.

26. Deposition of Sylvanus Wood, June 17, 1826, Henry B. Dawson, *Battles of the United States by Sea and Land*, 2 vols. (New York, 1858), I, 22–23.

28. Amos Barrett, *The Concord Fight* (Boston, 1924), pp. 12–14.

29. Elizabeth Ellery Dana, ed., *The British in Boston: Being the Diary of Lieutenant John Barker of the King's Own Regiment from November 15, 1774 to May 31, 1776* (Cambridge, 1924), pp. 35–37.

31. Frederick Mackenzie, *Diary of Frederick Mackenzie, Giving a Daily Narrative of his Military Services as an Officer of the Regiment of Royal Welsh Fusiliers During the Years 1775–1781 in Massachusetts, Rhode Island and New York*, 2 vols. (Cambridge, 1930), I, 21–22.

32. William Carter, *A Genuine Detail of the Several Engagements, Positions, and Movements of the Royal and American Armies, During the Years 1775 and 1776. . . .* (London, 1785), p. I.

BOSTON

Page

33. From a Surgeon of one of His Majesty's ships at Boston, May 26, 1775, Willard, *Letters On the American Revolution*, pp. 120–121.

34. Silas Deane to Elizabeth Deane, June 3, 1775, *Silas Deane Papers, 1774–1790*, 5 vols., *New-York Historical Society Collections*. "Publication Fund Series," XIX–XXIII (New York, 1887–1891), XIX, 53–54.

35. Charles Maclean Andrews and Evangeline MacLean Andrews, eds., *Journal of a Lady of Quality; Being the Narrative of a Journey from Scotland to the West Indies, North Carolina, and Portugal in the Years 1774 to 1776* (New Haven, 1923), 189–190.

36. John Trumbull, *Autobiography, Reminiscences and Letters of John Trumbull from 1756 to 1841* (New York, 1841), pp. 18–19.

37. George W. Corner, ed., *The Autobiography of Benjamin Rush* (Princeton, 1948), p. 158.

38. Ethan Allen, *A Narrative of Colonel Ethan Allen's Captivity, Written by Himself*, 3rd edition (Burlington, 1838), pp. 2–22.

40. Charles Henry Lincoln, "Three Documents of 1775 in the Library of the Society," *Proceedings of the American Antiquarian Society*, new series, XIX (April, 1909), 438–442.

42. Thomas Gage to Lord Barrington, June 26, 1775, Clarence Edwin Carter, ed., *The Correspondence of General Thomas Gage with the Secretaries of State, and with the War Office and the Treasury, 1763–1775*, 2 vols. (New Haven, 1831), II, 686.

43. John Adams, "Autobiography," Charles Francis Adams, ed., *The Works of John Adams, Second President of the United States: With a Life of the Author, Notes and Illustrations*, 10 vols. (Boston, 1850–1856), II, 415–418.

45. George Washington to Lund Washington, August 20, 1775, *American Historical Record*, II (Dec., 1873), 552.

46. *New York Journal*, November 23, 1775, quoted in *Historical Magazine*, 2d ser., V (January, 1869), 57.

46. Sir Martin Hunter, *The Journal of Gen. Sir Martin Hunter, G.C.M.G., G.C.H., and some Letters of his Wife, Lady Hunter*. Edited by Miss Anne Hunter and Miss Bell (Edinburgh, 1894), pp. 12–14.

47. Edward Jacob Foster, ed., "A Journal Kept by John Leach, During His Confinement by the British, in Boston Gaol, in 1775," *New England Historical and Genealogical Society*, XIX (June, 1861), 135.

48. "Revolutionary Journal of Aaron Wright, 1775," *Historical Magazine*, VI (July, 1862), 208–212.

Page

50. Harold Murdock, ed., "Letter of Reverend William Gordon, 1776," *Massachusetts Historical Society Proceedings*, LX (1927), 360–366.

CANADA

54. Allen, *Narrative*, pp. 31–37.

56. Isaac Senter, "Journal of Dr. Isaac Senter," Kenneth Roberts, ed., *March to Quebec: Journals of the Members of Arnold's Expedition* (New York, 1947), pp. 199–223.

65. George Morison, "An Account of the Assault on Quebec, 1775," *Pennsylvania Magazine of History and Biography*, XIV (1890), pp. 343–439.

A DECLARATION OF INDEPENDENCE

70. "Orderly Books of Colonel William Henshaw," *Proceedings of the American Antiquarian Society*, new ser., LVII (April, 1947), 131–132, 197–198.

71. John C. Fitzpatrick, ed., *The Writings of George Washington, from the Original Manuscript Sources, 1745–1799*, 39 vols. (Washington, 1931–1944), V, 194–195.

72. John Adams to William Plummer, March 28, 1813, John Adams to Timothy Pickering, August 6, 1922, Adams, *Works*, X, 35–36, II, 513–514n.

73. *Journals of the Continental Congress, 1774–1789*, 34 vols. (Washington, 1904–1937), V, 425.

76. Thomas McKean to Caesar Augustus Rodney, August 22, 1813, *The Magnolia; or, Southern Appalachian*, new ser., I (October, 1842), 263–264.

77. "Extracts from the Journal of Isaac Bangs," *Proceedings of the New Jersey Historical Society*, VIII (1858), 125.

78. Alexander Graydon to John Lardner, July 18, 1776, *American Historical Register*, No. 15 (November, 1895), 413.

79. Edward H. Tatum, Jr., ed., *The American Journal of Ambrose Serle, Secretary to Lord Howe, 1776–1778* (San Marino, 1940), pp. 30–31.

NEW YORK

80. General Orders, July 13, 1776, Fitzpatrick, *Writings of Washington*, V, 268–269.

80. Henry Knox to Lucy Knox, July 15, 1776, Noah Brooks, *Henry Knox, Soldier of the Revolution* (New York, 1900), p. 58.

Page
83. Francis, Lord Rawdon to Francis, tenth Earl of Huntingdon, August 5, 1776, Great Britain Historical Manuscripts Commission, *Report on the Manuscripts of the Late Reginald Rawdon Hastings*, 4 vols. (London, 1930–1947), III, 179–180.

83. Diary of an unidentified Hessian Officer, quoted in Edward J. Lowell, *The Hessians and the Other German Auxiliaries of Great Britain in the Revolutionary War* (New York, 1884), p. 61.

84. Henry Onderdonk, *Revolutionary Incidents of Suffolk and Kings Counties: With an Account of the Battle of Long Island, and the British Prisons and Prison-Ships at New-York* (New York, 1849), pp. 147–148.

85. Joseph Plumb Martin, *Private Yankee Doodle: Being a Narrative of Some of the Adventures, Dangers and Sufferings of a Revolutionary Soldier*, edited by George F. Scheer (Boston, 1962), pp. 23–26.

87. Ezra Lee to David Humphreys, February 20, 1815, *Magazine of American History*, XXIX (March, 1893), 263–265.

89. Lord Rawdon to Earl of Huntingdon, September 23, 1776, *Report on Hastings Manuscripts*, III, 183–184.

91. Joseph Hodgkinson to Sara Hodgkinson, September 30, 1776, *Magazine of American History*, VIII (September, 1882), 627–628.

92. Tatum, ed., *Journal of Ambrose Serle*, pp. 110–111.

92. Extract from a letter from Stephen Hempstead, 1827, Onderdonk, *Revolutionary Incidents of Suffolk and Kings Counties*, pp. 48–50.

94. Lewis Morris, Jr., to Lewis Morris, September 6, 1776, "Letters to General Lewis Morris," *New-York Historical Society Collections*, for 1875 (New York, 1875), 440–443.

94. Frank Moore, ed., *Diary of the American Revolution. From Newspapers and Original Documents*, 2 vols. (New York, 1860), I, 335–337.

97. Robert Auchmuty to Earl of Huntingdon, January 8, 1777, *Report on Hastings Manuscripts*, III, 189–192.

CAMPAIGN IN THE JERSEYS

100. James Thacher, *Military Journal of the American Revolution* (Hartford, 1862), 59–61.

102. "Extract of a letter from an officer of distinction in the American Army," *Pennsylvania Evening Post*, December 28, 1776, quoted in *Archives of the State of New Jersey*, 2d ser., I (Trenton, 1901), 245–247.

103. Moore, *Diary of the American Revolution*, I, 357–358.

Page
103. Samuel B. Webb to Joseph Trumbull, December 16, 1776, Samuel B. Webb, *Correspondence and Journals*, edited by Worthington C. Ford, 3 vols. (New York, 1893), I, 175.

104. James Wilkinson, *Memoirs of My Own Times*, 3 vols. (Philadelphia, 1816), I, 105–106.

105. *The Crisis*, No. 1, Force, *American Archives*, 5, III, 1290.

106. Thomas Jones, *History of New York During the Revolutionary War*, 2 vols. (New York, 1879), I, 716.

106. "Diary of an Officer on Washington's Staff," William S. Stryker, *The Battles of Trenton and Princeton* (Boston, 1898), 360–364.

110. Sergeant R——, "The Battle of Princeton," *Pennsylvania Magazine of History and Biography*, XX (1898), 515–519.

WAR WITHOUT BATTLES

114. Colonel Allen Maclean to Alexander Cummings, March 30, 1777, *New Records of the American Revolution: The Letters, Manuscripts and Documents sent by Lieut.-General Sir Charles Stuart, to His Father, The Earl of Bute, 1775–1779; Also the Letters of General Howe, General Clinton, and other Officers to Sir Charles Stuart, During the Rebellion, 1779* (n.p., n.d.), p. 81.

115. *Continental Journal and Weekly Advertiser*, September 11, 1777.

116. A letter from America to London, n.d., *Magazine of American History*, VI (January, 1888), 56.

116. George F. Scheer, ed., "Some Events of the American Revolution in South Carolina as Recorded by the Rev. James Jenkins," *The Proceedings of the South Carolina Historical Association*, 1945, pp. 25–26.

116. John Adams to Abigail Adams, March 7, 1777, Abigail Adams to John Adams, July 31, 1777, *Familiar Letters*, pp. 249, 286–287.

117. Martha Daingerfield Bland to Frances Bland Randolph, May 12, 1777, *Proceedings of the New Jersey Historical Society*, LI (July, 1933), 151–152.

118. Fitzpatrick, *Writings of Washington*, VIII, 28–29.

119. Moore, *Diary of the American Revolution*, I, 444–445.

120. *The Journal of Nicholas Cresswell, 1774–1777* (New York: The Dial Press, 1924), pp. 251–257.

INVASION FROM THE NORTH

124. Persifor Frazer to his wife, August 6, 1776, "Extracts from the Letters of General Persifor Frazer," *Pennsylvania Magazine of History and Biography*, XXXI (1907), 135.

Page

124. James Phinney Baxter, ed., *The British Invasion from the North* (Albany, 1887), pp. 204–208.

126. Thomas Anburey, *Travels Through the Interior Parts of America; in a Series of Letters. By an Officer*, 2 vols. (Boston, 1923), I, 192–193.

126. Roger Lamb, *An Original and Authentic Journal of Occurrences during the Late American War* (Dublin, 1809), pp. 141–143.

128. William Weeks to Clement Weeks, August 6, 1777, *Five Straws Gathered from Revolutionary Fields by Hiram Bingham, Jun.* (Cambridge, 1901), pp. 14–16.

128. *Continental Journal and Weekly Advertiser*, August 21, 1777.

129. Anburey, *Travels Through the Interior Parts of America*, I, 219–220.

130. Samuel Adams to Roger Sherman, August 11, 1777, *Warren-Adams Letters; Being Chiefly a Correspondence among John Adams, Samuel Adams, and James Warren*, 2 vols. *Collections of the Massachusetts Historical Society*, Vols. LXXII (1917) and LXXIII (1925), I, 353n.

131. *Continental Journal and Weekly Advertiser*, September 4, 1777.

132. Timothy Dwight, *Travels: In New-England and New York*, 4 vols. (New Haven, 1822), III, 196–198.

135. "Account of the Battle of Bennington," *Collections of the Vermont Historical Society*, I (1870), 212–223.

138. Germain to William Knox, October 31, 1777, Great Britain Manuscripts Commission, *Manuscripts in Various Collections*, VI (1909), 140.

139. Anburey, *Travels*, I, 251.

140. Wilkinson, *Memoirs*, I, 237.

140. Baxter, *British Invasion from the North*, pp. 270–274.

141. Anburey, *Travels*, I, 249–251.

143. Thacher, *Military Journal*, pp. 105–106.

143. Wilkinson, *Memoirs*, I, 267–269.

147. Baxter, *British Invasion from the North*, pp. 317–323.

148. Hannah Winthrop to Mercy Warren, November 11, 1777, *Warren-Adams Letters*, II, 451–452.

THE ROAD TO PHILADELPHIA

152. Fitzpatrick, *Writings of Washington*, IX, 17.

152. John Adams to Abigail Adams, August 24, 1777, *Familiar Letters*, p. 298.

153. Jarvis, "An American's Experience in the British Army," *Journal of American History*, I (September, 1907), 448–449.

154. *Bulletin of the Historical Society of Pennsylvania*, I (1848), 58–59.

Page
155. "Extracts from the Journal of Surgeon Ebenezer Elmer of the New Jersey Continental Line," *Pennsylvania Magazine of History and Biography*, XXXV (1911), 104–105.

156. Elisha Stevens, *Fragment of Memoranda Written by Him in the War of the Revolution* (Meriden, Conn., 1922), p. 6.

156. "The Actions at Brandywine and Paoli, Described by a British Officer," *Pennsylvania Magazine of History and Biography*, XXIX (1905), 368–369.

157. "Diary of Lieutenant James McMichael," *Pennsylvania Magazine of History and Biography*, XVI (1892), 152.

158. "Extract from the Diary of General Hunter, originally printed in the *Historical Record of the 52d Regiment*," *Historical Magazine*, IV (November, 1860), 346–347.

159. Battle of Germantown from a British Account," *Pennsylvania Magazine of History and Biography*, XI (1887), 112–113.

160. Timothy Pickering to ——, August 23, 1826, *North American Review*, XXIII (October, 1826), 425–430.

162. John Laurens to Henry Laurens, November, 1777, Frank Moore, *Materials for History, Printed from Original Manuscripts* (New York, 1861), pp. 63–66.

163. "Letters of a French Officer," *Pennsylvania Magazine of History and Biography*, XXXV (1911), 94, 306.

"LORD—LORD—LORD"—VALLEY FORGE

165. "Letters of a French Officer, Written at Easton, Penna. in 1777–1778," *Pennsylvania Magazine of History and Biography*, XXXV (1911), 95–96.

166. Robert B. Douglas, trans. & ed., *A French Volunteer of the War of Independence* (Paris, 1898), pp. 50–51.

166. "Diary kept at Valley Forge by Albigence Waldo, Surgeon in the Continental Army, 1777–1778," *Historical Magazine*, V (1861), 129–134, 169–172. This diary is also printed in the *Pennsylvania Magazine of History and Biography*, XXI (1897), 299–323.

171. *Continental Journal and Weekly Advertiser*, February 19, 1778, March 26, 1778.

173. Tench Tilghman to Cadwalader, January 18, 1787, "Selections from the Military Papers of General John Cadwalader," *Pennsylvania Magazine of History and Biography*, XXXII (1908), 168–170.

174. William Fleury to ——, April 5, 1778, Frederich Kapp, *The Life of Frederick William von Steuben: Major General in the Revolutionary Army* (New York, 1859), pp. 128–129.

Page

175. Elias Boudinot, *Journal or Historical Recollections of American Events During the Revolutionary War* (Philadelphia, 1894), pp. 76–79.

176. Albigence Waldo, "Valley Forge, a poem, April 26, 1778," *Historical Magazine*, VIII (1863), 274.

176. Scheer, ed., *Private Yankee Doodle*, pp. 110–111.

177. *Pennsylvania Packet*, May 13, 1778.

179. Samuel Shaw to John Lamb, July 12, 1780, Isaac Q. Leake, *Memoir of the Life and Times of General John Lamb* (Albany, 1857), p. 243.

MONMOUTH

180. From a Lady in Philadelphia to Mrs. Theodorick Gland, Jr., n.d., *The Bland Papers: Being a Selection from the Manuscripts of Colonel Theodorick Bland, Jr., of Prince George County, Virginia*, 2 vols. (Petersburg, 1840), I, 92, 92–94.

182. *Annual Register, 1778* (London, 1779), pp. 267–269.

184. *Continental Journal and Weekly Advertiser*, July 30, 1778.

185. Alexander Hamilton to Elias Boudinot, July 5, 1778, *Pennsylvania Magazine of History and Biography*, II (1878), 139–145.

187. Thomas W. Balch, *Papers Relating to the Maryland Line* (Philadelphia, 1857), pp. 103–104.

187. James McHenry to John Cox, July 1, 1778, *Magazine of American History*, III (1879), 357-360.

189. Anthony Wayne to Richard Peters, July 12, 1778, Charles J. Stille, *Major-General Anthony Wayne and the Pennsylvania Line in the Continental Army* (Philadelphia, 1893), pp. 153–154.

190. Charles Lee to Robert Morris, July 3, 1778, *The Lee Papers*, 4 vols. (New York, 1873), II, 457–458.

NEWPORT—EXPERIMENT IN ALLIED COOPERATION

192. Pontgibaud, *A French Volunteer of the War of Independence*, pp. 66–67.

193. General Sullivan to Washington, August . 13, 1778, Otis G. Hammond, ed., *Letters and Papers of Major-General John Sullivan, Continental Army*, 3 vols. (Concord, N.H., 1931), II, 205–207, 218–220.

194. Trumbull, *Autobiography*, pp. 54–57.

196. Greene to Washington, September 16, 1778, George Washington Greene, *The Life of Nathanael Greene, Major-General in the Army of the Revolution*, 3 vols. (New York, 1871), II, 143–144.

Page

Skirmishes and Alarums

198. "Extracts from Interleaved Alamanacs Kept by John White of Salem," *The Essex Institute Historical Collections*, XLIX (1913), 93–94.

198. *Connecticut Gazette*, May 8, 1778, quoted in *Magazine of American History*, I (1877), 687.

199. *New York Journal*, August 2, 1779.

200. Thacher, *Journal*, 184–187, 195–197.

"Treason! Treason! Treason! Black as Hell!"

204. Elijah Fisher, *Elijah Fisher's Journal While in the War for Independence and Continued for Two Years After He Came to Maine, 1776-1781* (Augusta, Me., 1880), p. 12.

204. John Russel Bartlett, ed., *Records of the State of Rhode Island and Providence Plantations in New England* (Providence, 1864), IX, 158–159n.

205. "The French Army in the Revolutionary War," *Magazine of American History*, XVI (1891), 62–63.

206. Joshua King to ——, June 9, 1817, *Historical Magazine*, I, 294–295.

207. *Pennsylvania Packet*, October 17, 1780.

208. Benjamin Tallmadge to Jared Sparks, February 17, 1834, *Magazine of American History*, III (1879), 755–756.

209. Benson J. Lossing, *The Two Spies: Nathan Hale and John André* (New York, 1886), pp. 101–102n.

210. Thacher, *Journal*, pp. 226–228.

212. Alexander Scammel to ——, October 3, 1780, *Historical Magazine*, 2d ser., VIII (1880), 145.

War on the Frontier

213. J. Almon, *The Remembrancer: or Impartial Repository of Public Events*, 17 vols. (London, 1775–1784), VIII, 51–54.

214. *Continental Journal and Weekly Advertiser*, December 3, 1778.

216. "Account of Nathan Davis," *Historical Magazine*, 2d ser., III (1868), 200–201.

217. *Journals of the Military Expedition of Major General Sullivan Against the Six Nations of Indians in 1779* (Auburn, N.Y., 1887), pp. 97, 30–32, 99.

220. *Collections of the Illinois State Historical Library*, VIII (1912): (Virginia Series, III, edited by James A. James), 270–274, 159–160.

Page
225. Report by Lieut.-Governor Henry Hamilton on his Proceedings From November, 1776, to June, 1781, Great Britain Manuscripts Commission, *Reports on the Manuscripts of Mr. Stopford Sackville of Drayton House, Northamptonshire*, 2 vols. (London, 1904–1910), 231–241.

THE WAR TURNS SOUTH

229. William Moultrie, *Memoirs of the American Revolution, so far as it is Related to the States of North and South Carolina, and Georgia: Compiled from the most authentic Materials, the Author's Personal Knowledge of the Various Events, and including an Epistolary Correspondence on Public Affairs, with Civil and Military Officers, at that Period*, 2 vols. (New York, 1902), I, 141–144, 174–181.

234. Dawson, *Battles of the United States*, I, 478–479.

236. Moore, *Diary of the American Revolution*, II, 225–228.

237. Franklin B. Hough, *The Siege of Savannah, by the Combined American and French Forces, under the command of Gen. Lincoln, and the Count d'Estaing, in the Autumn of 1779* (Albany, 1866), pp. 164–170.

THE FALL OF CHARLESTON

240. Franklin Benjamin Hough, ed., *The Siege of Charleston, by the British Fleet and Army Under the Command of Admiral Arbuthnot and Sir Henry Which Terminated with the Surrender of that Place on the 12th of May, 1780* (Albany, 1867), pp. 85–86.

241. Moultrie, *Memoirs*, II, 78–80, 96–97, 108–111.

243. William Dobein James, *A Sketch of the Life of Brig. Gen. Francis Marion and a History of His Brigade, from Its Rise in June 1780, until Disbanded in December, 1782, with Descriptions of Characters and Scenes Not Heretofore Published* (Charleston, 1821), Appendix, pp. 3–7.

"GREEN PEACHES, GREEN CORN AND MOLASSES"—CAMDEN

246. Caroline Gilman, *Letters of Eliza Wilkinson, During the Invasion and Possession of Charleston, S.C. by the British During the Revolutionary War* (New York, 1839), pp. 39–43.

248. *Magazine of American History*, V (1880), 310–315.

249. "A Narrative of the Campaign of 1780, by Colonel Otho Williams, Adjutant General," William Johnson, *Sketches of the Life and Correspondence of Nathanael Greene, Major General of the Armies of the United States in the War of the Revolution*, 2 vols. (Charleston, 1822), I, 487, 499.

Page

250. "Plan of the Battle Near Camden, by Colonel Senff," *Magazine of American History*, V (1890), 276.

254. Alexander Hamilton to James Duane, September 6, 1780, Henry Cabot Lodge, ed., *The Works of Alexander Hamilton* (New York, n.d.), IX, 204.

"The Bull Dog on the Mountain"—King's Mountain

256. Moore, *Diary of the Revolution*, II, 352.

257. Ferguson letter quoted in James Ferguson, *Two Scottish Soldiers* (Aberdeen, 1888), pp. 66–67.

258. Robert Henry and David Vance, *Narrative of the Battle of Cowan's Ford, February 1st, 1781, and Narrative of the Battle of Kings Mountain* (Greensboro, N. C., 1891), pp. 21–26.

261. Young, "Memoir," *The Orion*, III (1843), 86-87.

262. Henry and Vance, *Narrative of the Battle of Cowan's Ford*, pp. 34–36.

263. Collins, *Autobiography*, pp. 51–54.

Cowpens

266. Williams, "Narrative," Johnson, *Greene*, I, 509–510.

267. Thomas Young, "Memoir of Major Thomas Young," *The Orion*, III (1843), 87–88.

269. Henry Lee, *Memoirs of the War in the Southern Department of the United States*, edited by Robert E. Lee (New York, 1870), pp. 227–228.

270. Young, "Memoir," *Orion*, III, 100.

270. James P. Collins, *Autobiography of a Revolutionary Soldier* (Clinton, La., 1859), pp. 5–7.

271. John Eager Howard in *Magazine of American History*, VII (1881), 279.

273. Quoted in M. A. Moore, *The Life of Gen. Edward Lacey* (Spartanburg, S.C., 1859), p. 6n.

The War in North Carolina

274. *General Joseph Graham and His Papers on North Carolina Revolutionary History*, edited by William A. Graham (Raleigh, N.C., 1904), pp. 289–290.

275. Henry and Vance, *Narrative of the Battle of Cowan's Ford*, pp. 8–13.

278. Graham, *Papers on North Carolina Revolutionary History*, pp. 318–322.

280. Greene to Joseph Reed, March 18, 1781, Reed, *Reed*, I, 349–350.

Page

281. Stevens to Lee, December, 1809, H. Lee, *The Campaign of 1781 in the Carolinas; with Remarks Historical and Critical on Johnson's Life of Greene* (Philadelphia, 1824), pp. 182–183.

282. Richard Harrison to Anne Harrison, March 15, 1781, *The American Historical Register* (June, 1895), p. 1123.

282. Lee, *Memoirs*, pp. 273–275.

284. Quoted in Rowland Broughton-Mainwaring, *Historical Record of Royal Welch Fusiliers* (London, 1889), pp. 100–101.

284. Lee, *Memoirs*, pp. 277–278.

285. R. Lamb, *An Original and Authentic Journal*, pp. 361–362.

286. St. George Tucker to his wife, March 18, 1781, Coleman-Tucker Collection, Colonial Williamsburg, Inc., Williamsburg, Virginia.

287. Samuel Mathis to William R. Davie, June 26, 1819, *American Historical Record*, II (1873), 109.

288. Lee, *Memoirs*, p. 280.

288. Lamb, *An Original and Authentic Journal*, p. 358.

289. Alexander Garden, *Anecdotes of the American Revolution, Illustrative of the Talents and Virtues of the Heroes of the Revolution, Who Acted the Most Conspicuous Parts Therein*, 3 vols. (Brooklyn, 1885), II, 342–343.

290. William Dickson to Rev. Robert Dickson, November 30, 1784, James O. Carr, ed., *The Dickson Letters* (Raleigh, N.C., 1901), pp. 15–16.

THE WAR IN SOUTH CAROLINA

292. Collins, *Autobiography*, pp. 23–24.

293. William Pierce to St. George Tucker, July 20, 1781, *Magazine of American History*, VII (1881), 434–435.

294. Tarleton Brown, *Memoirs, Written by Himself*, edited by Charles I. Bushnell (New York, 1862), pp. 34–38.

296. Samuel Mathis to William R. Davie, June 26, 1819, *American Historical Record*, II (1873), 103–110.

300. Roderick Mackenzie, *Strictures on Lt. Col. Tarleton's History "Of The Campaigns of 1780 and 1781, in the Southern Provinces of North America"* (London, 1787), pp. 144–153.

302. Young, "Memoir," *The Orion*, III (1843), 103–104.

303. Mackenzie, *Strictures*, pp. 153–164.

306. "Battle of Eutaw—Account furnished by Col. Otho Williams, with additions by Cols. Hampton, Polk, Howard, and Watt," Gibbes, *Documentary History of the American Revolution*, III, p. 144–158.

Page

The Beginning of the End

314. Gates to Jefferson, Boyd, ed., *Jefferson Papers*, IV, 501.
315. St. George Tucker to his wife, July 11, 1781, *Magazine of American History*, VII (1881), 207–208.
316. Moore, *Diary of the Revolution*, II, 450–453.
318. *Collection of the New-York Historical Society for 1882* (New York, 1883), pp. 139–140.
319. Enos Reeves, "Extracts from the Letter-Books of Lieutenant Enos Reeves, of the Pennsylvania Line," *Pennsylvania Magazine of History and Biography*, XXI (1891), 72–75.
321. Thacher, *Journal*, pp. 252–253, 271–272.
323. "Diary of a French officer," *Magazine of American History*, IV (1880), 444.
324. Samuel Abbott Green, trans., *My Campaigns in America: A Journal Kept by Count William de Deux-Ponts, 1780–1781* (Boston, 1868), pp. 126–127n.

Yorktown

326. Scheer, ed., *Private Yankee Doodle*, p. 228.
328. James J. Graham, ed., *Memoir of General Graham, with Notices of the Campaigns in which he was Engaged from 1779 to 1801* (Edinburgh, 1862), pp. 58–59.
328. Edward M. Riley, ed., "St. George Tucker's Journal of the Siege of Yorktown, 1781," *William and Mary Quarterly*, 3d ser., V (1948), 381.
329. "Captain James Duncan's Diary of the Siege of Yorktown," *Magazine of American History*, XXV (1905), 410–411.
330. "Narrative of the Duke de Lauzun," *Magazine of American History*, VI (1881), 52–53.
331. Scheer, ed., *Private Yankee Doodle*, pp. 230–233.
332. Duncan, "Diary," *Magazine of American History*, XXV (1905), 412.
333. Riley, ed., "St. George Tucker's Journal . . .," *William and Mary Quarterly*, 3d ser., V (1948), 386–387.
333. Thacher, *Journal*, pp. 283–284.
335. Deux-Ponts, *My Campaigns in America*, pp. 144–147.
336. Thacher, *Journal*, pp. 284–286, 285–286n.
337. "General Richard Butler's Journal of the Siege of Yorktown," *Historical Magazine*, VII (1864), 110.
338. Tarleton, *Campaigns*, pp. 387–388.
339. *The Journal of a Bayreuth Soldier, Johann Conrad Doehla, During the North American War for Independence* (Bayreuth, 1913), p. 148.

Page

339. Riley, ed., "St. George Tucker's Journal. . . .," *William and Mary Quarterly*, V (1948), 391–392.

341. "Major Jackson's Mss.," Thomas Balch, ed., *Letters and Papers Relating Chiefly to the Provincial History of Pennsylvania, with some Notice of the Writers* (Philadelphia, 1855), pp. 284–285.

342. Thacher, *Journal*, pp. 288–290.

343. Mathieu Dumas, *Memoirs of His Own Time*, 2 vols. (Philadelphia, 1839), I, 52–53n.

344. Lillie Du Puy Harper, ed., *Colonial Men and Times, Containing the Journal of Colonel Daniel Trabue* (Philadelphia, 1916), p. 115.

345. Lafayette to M. de Maurepas, October 20, 1781, *Memoirs, Correspondence and Manuscripts of General Lafayette, Published by His Family* (New York, 1837), p. 444.

345. Moore, *Diary of the Revolution*, II, 518.

"O God! It Is All Over!"

346. Elias Boudinot, *Journal or Historical Recollections of American Events During the Revolutionary War*, pp. 38–39.

347. Moore, *Diary of the Revolution*, II, 527, 527n.

347. Sir Nathaniel William Wraxall, *The Historical and Posthumous Memoirs of Sir Nathaniel William Wraxall, 1772–1784*, edited by Henry B. Wheatley, 5 vols. (New York, 1884), II, 137-142.

348. John D. Gilmary Shea, ed., *Operations of the French Fleet Under Comte de Grasse in 1781–1782, as Described in Two Contemporary Journals* (New York, 1864), pp. 86–88.

348. Evelyn M. Acomb, trans. and ed., *The Revolutionary Journal of Baron Ludwig Von Closen, 1780–1783* (Chapel Hill, 1958), pp. 230, 230n.

349. Gates to Robert Morris, October 25, 1782, Stanislaus V. Henkels, *The Confidential Correspondence of Robert Morris* (auction catalogue; Philadelphia, 1917), pp. 108–109.

349. Ebenezer Hazard to Jeremy Belknap, January 29, 1783, *Mass. Hist. Soc. Colls.*, 5th ser., II, 184.

350. "Lee Papers," *New-York Historical Collections for 1874* (New York, 1875), pp. 31–32.

351. Samuel Shaw to Rev. Eliot, February 23, 1783, Josiah Quincy, ed., *The Journals of Major Samuel Shaw, the First American Consul at Canton* (Boston, 1847), pp. 103–105.

352. Henry Phelps Johnston, ed., *Memoir of Colonel Benjamin Tallmadge* (New York, 1904), pp. 96–98.

Page

354. James McHenry to Margaret Caldwell, December 23, 1783, Bernard
     C. Steiner, *The Life and Correspondence of James McHenry*
     (Cleveland, 1907), pp. 69–70.

355. Benjamin Franklin to Joseph Banks, July 27, 1783, John Bigelow,
     Benjamin Franklin, Complete Works, 10 vols. (New York, 1887–
     1889), X, 147–148.

Acknowledgments

The author wishes to thank the following publishers for permission to reprint material published by them:

The American Antiquarian Society, for passages from the *Proceedings of the American Antiquarian Society*, new series, volumes XIX and LVII, copyright 1909 and 1947.

The Dial Press, Inc., for passages from *The Journal of Nicholas Cresswell, 1774-1777*, copyright 1924, 1928, 1956.

Doubleday & Company, Inc., for passages from *March to Quebec*, edited by Kenneth Roberts, copyright 1938, 1940 by Kenneth Roberts.

Harvard University Press, for passages from *The British in Boston: Being the Diary of Lieutenant John Barker of the King's Own Regiment from November 15, 1774 to May 31, 1776*, edited by Elizabeth Ellery Dana, copyright 1924; *Diary of Frederick Mackenzie, Giving a Daily Narrative of His Military Services as an Officer of the Regiment of Royal Welsh Fusiliers During the Years 1775-1781 . . .*, copyright 1924, 1928, 1930.

Houghton Mifflin Company, for passages from Thomas Anburey, *Travels through the Interior Parts of North America*, copyright 1923; *Letters on the American Revolution, 1774-1776*, edited by Margaret W. Willard, copyright 1925.

Henry E. Huntington Library and Art Gallery, for passages from *The American Journal of Ambrose Serle, 1776-1778*, edited by Edward H. Tatum, Jr., copyright 1940.

Illinois State Historical Society Library, for passages from *George Rogers Clark Papers, 1771-1781*, edited by James Alton James (Illinois State Historical Library *Collections*, Volume VIII), copyright 1912.

Institute of Early American History and Culture, for passages from

"St. George Tucker's Journal of the Siege of Yorktown, 1781," edited by Edward M. Riley, *William and Mary Quarterly*, 3rd Series, Volume V.

Little, Brown and Company, for passages from *Private Yankee Doodle*, by Joseph Plumb Martin, edited by George F. Scheer, copyright 1962 by George F. Scheer.

Massachusetts Historical Society, for passages from Massachusetts Historical Society *Proceedings*, copyright 1927; *Warren-Adams Letters . . . 1743-1814*, copyright 1917, 1925.

New Hampshire Historical Society, for passages from *Letters and Papers of Major-General John Sullivan*, edited by Otis G. Hammond, copyright 1931.

New Jersey Historical Society, for passages from *Proceedings of the New Jersey Historical Society*, Volume LI, copyright, 1933.

University of North Carolina Press, for passages from *The Revolutionary Journal of Baron Ludwig Von Closen, 1780-1783*, edited and translated by Evelyn M. Acomb, copyright 1958.

Princeton University Press, for passages from *The Papers of Thomas Jefferson*, Volume IV, edited by Julian P. Boyd, copyright 1952; *The Autobiography of Benjamin Rush*, edited by George W. Corner, copyright 1948.

Yale University Press, for passages from *Journal of a Lady of Quality*, edited by Charles M. and Evangeline Andrews, copyright 1923; *The Correspondence of General Thomas Gage*, edited by Edwin Carter, copyright 1931.

And certainly every one who writes in the period of the American Revolution should offer up frequent thanks to the Essex Institute, the New-York Historical Society, the Pennsylvania Historical Society, and all similar organizations, whose publications are so rich in documentary materials.

For permission to quote from their manuscript collections, the author is beholden to Colonial Williamsburg, Inc., for materials from the Coleman-Tucker Collection; to the Scottish Record Office for the Franklin letter at the beginning of the first chapter, from the Abercairny Collection; and to the William L. Clements Library of the University of Michigan for the Relation of Lieutenant William Sutherland from the Thomas Gage Papers.

Index